V. DANDRÉ

ANNA PAVLOVA

CASSELL
AND COMPANY LIMITED
LONDON, TORONTO, MELBOURNE
AND SYDNEY

First published in 1932

This edition published in 2020 by

The Noverre Press
Southwold House
Isington Road
Binsted
Hampshire
GU34 4PH

© 2020 The Noverre Press

ISBN 978-1-906830-91-5

Anna Pavlova

in

Art & Life

1932

ANNA PAVLOVA
(from a Painting by Stemberg St. Petersburg, 1909)

AUTHOR'S FOREWORD.

I have had the temerity to undertake a book about Anna Pavlova for two reasons. The first is that in the whole course of her theatrical life I was her closest associate. As her husband I had her unbounded confidence, managed all her affairs — theatrical and private — carried on all her correspondence, received those who came to see her (Pavlova herself could only very rarely receive anyone), was present at and assisted her in all her interviews for the press — and she was obliged to grant interviews to press representatives all over the world — spent with her her hours of leisure, made the necessary plans for new tours and discussed with her details of our vast and complicated enterprise. I stood nearer to her than anybody, and I knew and understood her thoughts and aspirations, her disappointments and chagrins better than anyone else.

In addition to my personal nearness to Pavlova, I met the thousands of people in all the corners of the earth who came to voice their enthusiasm and love. Through talking with them and receiving letters from them, during Pavlova's life as well as after her death, I am in a position to judge better than any other to what a remarkable degree she shone forth a beacon of beauty and love. All human testimony from whatever sources only goes to confirm my judgment of her exceptional personality.

The second and chief reason for the appearance of this book is the wish of Anna Pavlova herself. Many and many a time in the course of her life she told me that I ought to write a book about her, as nobody knew her so well as I did. This was of course impossible while she was alive, but now it is my duty. I shall be happy beyond measure if I succeed in this book in giving an image of Pavlova full of that spiritual beauty, for which as a woman and as an artist she was so beloved. And I do not think this will be difficult, for in order to render unto her that which is justly hers, one has only to speak the truth.

V. DANDRÉ.

Little Niura 6 years old.

CHAPTER I.

EARLY DAYS.

On the 31st of January 1882, in St. Petersburg, two months before the full time, a little girl was born. She was so weak and puny that her parents decided to baptise her without delay and on the 3rd of February she was christened Anna, in honour of the saint whose feast was held on that day.

For several months the child was kept in cotton-wool, the spark of life in her burning only very faintly. As Anna grew a little older, she was destined to battle with many a childish ailment — measles, scarlatina, diphtheria.

At the age of four, playing near the tea-table, she pulled the cloth, brought down the samovar and scalded her left hand. The marks of this remained with her all her life.

In order to improve the health of the little girl, it was decided to place her in the care of her grandmother in Ligovo (a summer resort twenty-five versts from St. Petersburg). A warm affection grew up between little Anna — or Niura, as she was called — and her grandmother, who devoted herself entirely to the care of her small granddaughter, and the child in her turn attached herself with the whole of her heart to her grandmother. This love lasted until the death of the old lady. Life in the country proved very beneficial. In the open air, the little girl grew stronger. Ligovo, which has since become a small town, was at that time a village surrounded by the fields and woods of wealthy landowners. This direct touch with the severe and melancholy nature of Northern Russia produced on the child an impression that was never to be effaced. There were no amusements. The family of Niura was poor. The child took particular pleasure in finding snowdrops in early spring. All her life Anna had a special tenderness for this flower. All the phases of spring were lived through joyously. The first flowers appeared. The woods were made to yield their rich store of lilies of the valley, which grew freely in these rather damp parts of the country. Then came the summer and the happy games in the flower-covered meadows, the picking of berries, and, later, in the autumn, the gathering of mushrooms — that favourite occupation of Russian children.

But the winters were also beautiful, with their deep snow-drifts and the magic of the woods powdered over with snow. The soul of the child was deeply touched by the charm of the simple landscape, and ever after she retained a feeling for nature and an understanding of it. I have never seen a person to whom the beauties of nature everywhere made such an irresistible appeal — from the mountains of Norway and Italy to the tropical forests of Java. The sighing of the trees, the sight of flowering fields, the setting sun — all equally spoke to her of something mysterious, that is not heard or felt by others.

Pavlova always retained the tenderness of a first love for Ligovo; possibly because it was there that she first understood and learnt to love nature. Even after she had visited the whole of Europe, and seen the beauties of Norway and Italy, on her return to Russia she hastened home to Ligovo, and although she saw that the woods were being cut down, that the surrounding country was being built over, she never failed to find some spot that linked her to the past. Sometimes I used to laugh at her weakness for this place, until I saw that she was really deeply hurt, surprised at my lack of understanding of the bonds that attached her to her beloved Ligovo. As the years passed, her feeling for nature only grew stronger. After she had travelled all over the world, visiting the most beautiful spots on earth — Ceylon, Java, the Malay Peninsula — where we gazed with awe at the riot of flowers and foliage, at the beauty of tropical forests, Pavlova always said that, however marvellous it was, such exotic beauty frightened her by its power and its wildness. It was her own landscapes that drew her, so dear to her and so understandable in all their moods.

Pavlova loved the play of sunbeams, verdure in all its varied hues, the falling of autumn leaves, the outlines of trees in misty gloom, she loved even rain: all these gave her happiness. On returning home sometimes as late as one o'clock in the morning after her performances during her London season, she never entered the house before first making a tour of the garden to admire the dark masses of the trees against the background of the sky. She loved her swans, moving in vague white forms on the black waters of the lake. Her favourite tree was the birch — of all trees the most Russian.

It was Ligovo that saw the beginning of her education. A local teacher, of whom she ever kept a grateful and affectionate memory, taught her Russian and Scripture.

On one occasion, wishing to give pleasure to the little girl, her mother took her to a holiday matinée of "Sleeping Beauty". This proved a decisive day in the future life of Anna Pavlova. The ballet made a deep and vivid impression on the child, who, though obedient and docile by nature, now for the first time expressed a very firm resolve, namely, to choose the career of a ballet-dancer.

In obedience to the girl's insistent requests, her mother took her to the Imperial Ballet School, but to her bitter disappointment, they found that children under ten were not eligible. She had two years more to wait. The mother expected her daughter to forget her wish in these two years, but actually it grew only stronger, for the child thought and spoke of nothing else.

At last, the longed-for, and at the same time the awful, moment arrived and she was taken to the school tests.

I should explain why I say "awful". The number annually chosen was seven or eight girls, whereas generally a hundred and sometimes more desired to enter the school. The jury which elected the suitable candidates was composed of the management, the teachers, and former and present ballet-dancers. It was first necessary to pass a medical examination, that being indispensable in order to show how far the child's physique promised good health for the future — a necessity in the profession of dancing.

Under these circumstances, the chances of a thin and frail little girl among a hundred or more competitors were not very great.

Pavlova used to say that on the memorable day many girls of richer families arrived specially well-dressed for the occasion, and she thought that the chosen ones would inevitably be selected from these, that she in her modest dress would not be even noticed. And then, after much discussion, the names of the candidates selected were read out and she heard her own name.

Before speaking however of Pavlova's years of study, I must say a few words of the ballet-school itself; it is first necessary to correct some erroneous impressions. I read quite lately in an article dedicated to Pavlova, that in the former Imperial Theatrical School the discipline was of an unheard-of severity, that the girls were half-starved, that they were over-worked and that in fact their life was a very painful one. Where such information could have

At the age of 9.

been obtained is absolutely incomprehensible as they are absolutely incorect.

The school, like the theatres, was an Imperial institution, maintained by the Imperial Court. It was housed in a magnificent building, which was also the headquarters of the administration of the Imperial Theatres, and in which the director of the theatres lived himself. In years gone by, the Emperor and members of the Imperial family paid frequent visits to the school, were nearly always present at the school performances and spent whole evenings in the company of the pupils. All the artists who went through the school

House at Ligovo where little Niura spent her early childhood.

unanimously agree that the food was excellent, that the hygiene, cleanliness, personal care and supervision left nothing to be desired. It must also be added that both the maintenance of the pupils and their education were entirely free.

I have heard that those who were brought up there have retained the most pleasant memories of their school days. And Pavlova herself invariably confirmed this. Those in the school received a general education as well as a training in dancing and great attention was paid to the religious side. The school had a chapel of its own, and the pupils were expected to be present at the services. The boys and girls sang in the choir and the scripture master was the officiating priest. It is a fact worth recording that this solid religious foundation laid in early years at school, has remained with all ballet-dancers. Many of them, years after having finished the school and some even after the end of their Government service, continued to attend the Theatre Chapel. And the majority of ballet-dancers, both great and small, have remained faithful to the custom of crossing themselves before making their appearance on the stage.

"Every morning", Pavlova used to say, recounting her memories, "the solemn tolling of the great bell used to wake us at 8 o'clock, and we dressed hastily under the eye of an inspectress, who saw that we washed and cleaned our teeth and nails properly. The dressing finished, we went to prayers, read in a sing-song voice by one of the pupils before an icon having a little red light flickering like a star before it. Then, at nine, we had breakfast consisting of tea and bread and butter, after which came the dancing lesson.

For this, we were all collected in one big, lofty, light room. The furniture consisted of several small sofas, a piano and some immense looking-glasses reaching to the floor. Portraits of Russian emperors hung on the walls. Our favourite was that of the Empress Catherine II; her proud, and at the same time laughing, eyes seemed to look straight at us, as if following each p a s, criticising and encouraging us.

The younger pupils danced first and then came the older ones. At midday the bell rang and we had lunch. Then we were taken for a walk, followed by more lessons until four o'clock, and then came dinner. After dinner we had a little free time and then lessons began again — fencing, music, and sometimes rehearsals of the dances in which we had to appear on the stage of the Marinsky Theatre. Supper was usually at eight o'clock and by nine we were in bed.

On passing to the question of teaching in the school, I am again obliged to make a slight digression.

In her book, "My Life", Isadora Duncan tells of how she was invited to visit the Imperial Ballet School where, she says, she saw the small pupils going through tortures of exercises. "They stood on the tips of their toes for hours, like so many victims of a cruel and unnecessary inquisition. The great, bare dancing-rooms, devoid of any beauty or inspiration, with a large picture of the Tsar as the only relief on the walls, were like a torture-chamber. I was more than ever convinced that the Imperial Ballet School is an enemy to nature and to art." It is true, Duncan, was an enemy of the ballet, she says so herself. She looked upon it as a false and absurd art. But one might, at least, have expected a true exposition of the facts from her. On the same page she recalls a visit when she was present at Pavlova's lesson and for three hours witnessed how she was tortured by the famous professor Petipa, who played his violin all the time, and then she says: "The whole tendency of this training seems to be to separate the gymnastic movements of the body completely from the mind. The mind, on the contrary, can only suffer in aloofness from this vigorous muscular discipline."

Everything in this story is wrong. Pavlova never had any tuition from Petipa, who was a ballet master and not a teacher. Duncan saw Pavlova at her lesson with Maestro Cecchetti, who never handled a violin in his life. And the lesson did not last three hours but an hour and a half.

Why classical dancing, which develops grace and the beauty of line, should make for the separation of bodily movements from the thinking faculties is not very clear. One can only find an explanation for the impression carried away by Duncan from her visit to the Imperial Ballet School by remembering her general antipathy to the ballet. Not only were the children there not tortured, nor was the schooling too severe and intensive, but Pavlova with others, always said that the teaching of dancing at the school was too slow and protracted. What was accomplished at the Imperial Ballet School in seven years could easily have been done in five. A proof that Pavlova was right in this view can be found in the fact that in private schools the full course is comfortably passed in five years. In the Imperial Ballet School, where the teaching of dancing went on side by side with ordinary education, there was no hurrying and to talk of this teaching as torture, can only point to some preconceived idea.

But I will let Pavlova speak again:

"One of the first problems to be faced by the future dancer is that of learning to keep the equilibrium when standing on the tips of the toes. At first a child in unable to stand in that position for even a minute, but gradually sufficient strength is developed in the muscles of the toes to enable a few steps to be taken, uncertainly at first, as in skating, then with more and more assurance, and finally without any difficulty at all."

At the age of 15 in her school dress.

"When this first difficulty is conquered, one is taught various steps. The mistress performs them and a small group of five or six repeats them after her for about ten minutes. Then they rest and another group takes the place of the first one."

"Besides the various complicated pas of the classical ballet, we had to learn in our school a great number of historical and national dances — the minuet, the mazurka, Hungarian, Spanish and Italian dances."

"The older pupils practised a great deal by themselves. I knew one man-dancer who practised for six hours a day. As in any other art, success is chiefly dependent upon personal initiative and perseverance. Even a ballerina who has attained success cannot allow herself to become idle. She is obliged to practise daily in order to keep up her technique, like a pianist, who is daily obliged to play scales and exercises. She must have an absolute command over her technique, so that on the stage she need think and trouble about nothing but expressing herself."

Pavlova working with Maestro Cecchetti in her studio in St. Petersburg.

CHAPTER II.
TEACHERS.

Pavlova's first teacher of dancing was a former dancer, A. Oblakov, but already in her second year she passed into the class of the one-time famous ballerina Ekaterina Vasem, a pupil of the well-known choreographer Huguet. Vasem was a dancer of the severely classical school. Her dancing was crisp, tireless, sure and unusually firm of toe. The double tours, which at that time were considered a particularly bold innovation, she executed without the least difficulty. From Vasem Pavlova passed into the class of the celebrated dancer and remarkably fine actor, Paul Gerdt, of whom she cherished the kindest and most grateful recollections. Gerdt was a pupil of Johannsen and Petipa and he was noted for the extreme artistry of whatever he did. He thought out every role in detail. His make-up was marvellous and he possessed a wonderful talent for wearing costume. In addition, he had a remarkable nobility of gesture and elegance of manner and was an excellent and graceful partner. He belonged to the classical dancers of the purest style.

In spite of the fact that in 1905 he celebrated his forty years' jubilee[*], he continued not only to act leading parts, but also danced in an important five-act ballet "Pharaoh's Daughter", with Pavlova in the title role.

Very early he noticed Pavlova's unusual gifts, but at the same time he was afraid that her frail physique would not stand the strain of strenuous work. He therefore did everything in his power to save her from overfatigue. He succeeded in transmitting to her his elegance of movement and pose, his powers of mime and his distinctive trait — the incarnation of beauty in every scenic figure.

Pavlova finished the Imperial School at the age of seventeen with the grade of "first dancer". Her début is described as follows by the well-known connoisseur of ballet, V. Svetlov, in his book "Terpsichore":

"On one of the evenings of our pale and sickly northern spring, when periodically at intervals of five minutes it rains and clears, when the cold and the mud overcome the inhabitant of St. Petersburg, I found myself in a cosy little corner, in the lighted, warm green realm of the dryads. This little corner was the Mikhailovsky Theatre and the dryads proved to be

---

[*] This means that he was not less than 58 years old.

unreal, for they were represented by ordinary pupils of the Theatrical School. But no matter. On the other side of the thick stone walls of the theatre an unpleasant, soaking rain was drizzling, whereas on the stage young life was bubbling like a spring. And all this was agreeable and cheering, as well as aesthetically pleasing."

"On the stage there was a young count and his student friend; then there was the old steward with his young and pretty daughter; there was a baroness, her friends and her governess, the villagers and village maidens, who used to be known as 'paysans' and 'paysannes' in the ballets of former days. In fact, quite the usual pupils' performance."

"The jury sat in the front row, putting down marks to the dryads. This alone somewhat destroyed the illusion of a hot southern summer on this cold northern spring evening."

"It was on this evening that for the first time the public saw the pupil Pavlova, and it was on this evening that for the first time she attracted the attention of everybody. Slender and graceful as a reed, and as supple, with the ingenuous face of a girl of southern Spain, ethereal and light, she seemed like a fragile and elegant Sèvres statuette. But every now and then she struck up attitudes and poses in which something classical could be felt. If at that moment she had been dressed in an antique peplum, there would have been a striking resemblance to a Tanagra figurine. With childish ingenuous-ness she acted a scène de coquetterie with a young peasant and with playful wantonness danced with the imaginary dryads. All this was youthfully gay and pretty and nothing more need be said, except that the play of this child's features in the scene with the peasant was already full of expression, and one had the feeling that here was something individual, something that was not learnt by rote at school. But in the solo variation from "The Vestal Virgin" (music by Drigo and here inserted) one already felt something more, something that made it possible for one, without posing as a prophet, to foresee in the youthful dancer a future great artist."

When already on the stage, Pavlova worked for some time in a special class arranged by the management of the Imperial Theatres in connection with the Ballet School for the further perfection of the dancers. This class was under the guidance of Christian Johannsen, who in his day was a very fine dancer and a pupil of the Copenhagen choreographist Gustav Bournonville, in his turn a pupil of the celebrated Vestris.

In no other form of art do the human links extend over so long a period. For instance in the course of a whole century there is only one generation between Johannsen and Vestris. The explanation lies in the extraordinary longevity of ballet dancers: Petipa composed ballets at the age of eighty,

Pavlova with Maestro Cecchetti in her garden at Ivy House.

Johannsen was nearly ninety when he taught in a dancing class; and Kshessinsky was still dancing on the Imperial stage when he was seventy-five.

Pavlova began very rapidly to make a career for herself from her first year on the stage. In the second year of her service she was given the chief part in a small ballet called "The Awakening of Flora". A year later she had to dance one act from the ballet „La Bayadère" at a performance in the Imperial Hermitage*. It must be explained that the Winter Palace (in St. Petersburg) is connected by a passage to the Hermitage, which had a small theatre especially reserved for gala Court performances. These performances were only attended by members of the Imperial family, the diplomatic corps and distinguished guests.

After this the very difficult ballet "Giselle" was added to Pavlova's repertoire. This might be called her touchstone for it demanded great acting powers from the dancer in the first act, and an ethereal lightness in the second. Pavlova came out of this trial brilliantly and after that was given one ballet after another, including "La Bayadère", "Paquita", "The Corsair", "King Candaulus", "Pharaoh's Daughter", etc.

* The Picture Gallery.

Pavlova with Maestro Cecchetti in Milan
(Their last meeting).

Pavlova possessed one very unusual quality, one that is very rare in scenic artists as a whole, namely, that no success ever turned her head. She never lost her natural modesty or her wish for continual improvement, nor did she take offence at unfavourable criticisms, but on the contrary set great store by them. When already a recognised ballerina, enjoying great popularity and admiration, she gratefully and attentively listened to the criticisms of her older comrades of the corps de ballet, who, being very greatly attached to her, considered it their duty to point out mistakes and shortcomings. She understood very early that, all success notwithstanding, she must continue serious work. At that time the fame of the Italian ballerina Beretta stood very high. Pavlova went to her in Milan to do some serious work instead of taking a summer holiday. On her return she went to a Russian ballerina very well known in her time, Eugenie Sokolova, who had the reputation of being one of the best dancers of the classical school, and at the same time was known for her exceptional gracefulness and elegance. For two years Pavlova worked with her daily and most assiduously. She felt that there were certain defects in herself which she failed to remedy, but did not know what was the best thing to do.

Eventually, in 1905, having gone to Moscow to dance there in the summer, she met the Maestro Enrico Cecchetti. After a performance she invited him to her house and asked him to give his frank opinion about her dancing. Cecchetti praised her gifts very highly, but pointed out certain faults of a purely technical order caused by the weakness of the back. Pavlova was well aware of this, but unfortunately her teachers could not help her. The meeting with Cecchetti resulted in her asking him to come to St. Petersburg to work solely with her. Her two years' work with him did her an immense amount of good, her back grew stronger, her confidence increased and technical difficulties that used to frighten her before, were now gradually mastered without apparent effort.

When it became known that Pavlova was working under Cecchetti, it was feared that the purely Italian school, with its accepted emphasis, more particularly in the manner of the carriage of the arms, would have an ill effect on her, for her dancing was associated with the elegance and refinement of the strictly French school. But Pavlova was already a finished artist, and while learning from Cecchetti what she needed, she kept to the purity of style learned at school.

Cecchetti is so great a personality and he played so important a part in the career of Pavlova, that I consider it necessary to devote a few words to him.

Enrico Cecchetti, the son of a famous maitre de ballet and dancer, was born in Rome in 1850. He was taught by Giovanni Lepri, a pupil of the celebrated Blasis. At the age of twenty he first danced on the stage of the Milan "Scala" with considerable success. In '82 he came to Russia and danced in the Moscow Imperial Ballet, but only for a short while. Five years later, together with the famous dancer Limido, who was considered a phenomenon of technique and the essence of choreographic classicism, he appeared on the stage of the St. Petersburg "Arcadia" Theatre during the summer season, gaining an immediate success by the unequalled lightness and virtuosity of his dancing, proving himself to be a fine classical dancer and at the same time an excellent grotesque. He was so generally admired, that he was at once invited to join the St. Petersburg ballet. He danced there for the first time in the same year, '87, and soon became one of its chief ornaments.

After fifteen years' service on the Imperial stage, he gave up dancing, confining himself to purely acting parts and later opened a private school of his own, where many of the best dancers came for finishing touches to their education.

A whole series of distinguished Russian ballerinas owe a great deal to him. Kshessinskaya, Preobrajenskaya, Egorova, Sedova, Njinsky and many more completed their studies under his tuition. After his departure from St. Petersburg, Cecchetti accepted the post of maitre de ballet and teacher at the Warsaw Theatre and, later still, went to Italy.

As his service as a young man had commenced at the "Scala" in Milan, Cecchetti always dreamed of going back there as the head of the school, considered the first in Italy, and responsible for a whole series of world-famous dancers. On his merits and by his knowledge, he had certainly every right to fill the post, but a number of obstacles presented themselves. During the War "La Scala" was temporarily closed, and the school connected with it, having lost all importance within the last few years, closed also. When the celebrated Toscanini was invited to regenerate the Milan opera, taking the management into his own hands, he decided that the once glorious ballet must also be restored and asked Cecchetti to undertake the task. The latter gladly agreed, but stipulated as conditions that the schooling must be entirely free, that pupils of all nationalities should be accepted, and that during lesson-time there should be no question of taking pupils away for rehearsals. These conditions having been accepted, Cecchetti took up the beloved work with enthusiasm.

In the summer of 1926 Pavlova was resting in Italy. When Cecchetti heard of this, he begged her to visit Milan, as he wanted to show her his school. We went there on our way back from Salzo-Maggiore and the very

Pavlova with Ivan Clustine in her garden at Ivy House.

Pavlova in "Chopiniana"
St. Petersburg.
(Photograph by Bransburg)

next day paid a visit to "La Scala". I was destined that morning to be present at a very touching reception which Cecchetti had arranged for his divina Anna, as he always called Pavlova. In the main room of the school all the pupils, (about 60) were assembled, the dancers, Cecchetti's assistants, he himself and his wife. All the pupils carried flowers, while Cecchetti himself went forward to meet Pavlova on the stairs and led her into the room. Here he made a speech in which he said that this was one of the happiest days of his life, for he had the joy of seeing his pride, Pavlova in the school of the "Scala" which he had brought to life again and which he regarded as the last beloved child of his old age. The old man wept, Pavlova wept, all wept. Then one of the children, a little Russian girl, spoke a greeting from the school to Pavlova, after which the lessons began. Cecchetti wanted to show what he had accomplished in his three years of management.

We were again in Salzo-Maggiore the following year, and Cecchetti asked to be informed of the date of Pavlova's passage through Milan as he wanted to fix the finishing examinations of his school for that day.

The examinations took place on the stage and the "Scala" Theatre was almost filled with the relatives and friends of the pupils. When we entered, Cecchetti led Pavlova up to two ladies, in one of whom we recognised with some difficulty a former favourite of the St. Petersburg public, Pierina Legnani, and in the other also a one-time celebrity, Virginia Zucchi. The latter, in spite of her years, was so active, elegant and upright, that she did not at all give the impression of an old woman. In answer to my question as to her age, Cecchetti said, in her presence and not in the least abashed, that she was four years older than himself — and he was seventy-six.

A dais had been erected on the stage for the jury who were to judge which of the pupils merited rewards. Each class was to receive one gold medal as well as two silver ones and other marks of distinction. In spite of all Cecchetti's entreaties, Pavlova refused to be a member of the jury, of which Zucchi, Legnani and Cecchetti's wife formed part, and we looked on at the examination from a box. It was very interesting and did great credit to the teacher. Some of the girls appeared completely finished dancers. Owing to the national temperament, the results of the examination were accompanied by loud expressions of joy on the part of the fortunate ones and storms of tears from those who were disappointed.

In the winter of that same year, quite unexpectedly, Cecchetti's wife died. She had been an excellent dancer in her time and later a very fine actress with great nobility of carriage. She was also a teacher. Josephine Cecchetti was adored by all for her exceptional kindness of heart and to her husband she was a veritable guardian angel. In his letter to us at the time of her death, he wrote that his life was over and that he would not long outlive her. But one more great happiness was in store for the great maestro — the arrival in Italy of Pavlova with her company in the spring of 1928 and the series of performances she gave in Milan. The old man was very proud of Pavlova and seemed to share in all the applause she received in Italy. Also, he would bring his pupils in turns, every day, into the two boxes that were kept for him during the whole series of these performances. There he sat with them and would look on and explain Pavlova's dancing. That was the last joy of the old maestro, for he died in the autumn of that year.

A few years ago a book of memoirs written from the words of Cecchetti himself appeared in London. Pavlova wrote a preface at his request. I think it right to quote it here as showing Pavlova's profound gratitude and esteem for this extraordinarily single minded personality. With Cecchetti there has departed the last great teacher of his era — independent, sincere and firm as a rock in his convictions.

Here are Pavlova's words:

"My dear Maestro,

How happy I am to write a few words of preface to this book about you. The feeling of deep gratitude I have for what you have taught me, is blended with my love and respect for your personality. In an age when people no longer understand that to teach others it is necessary first to work hard and long oneself and to have an actual experience of the stage, when by the aid of self — advertisement anyone can take the name of "professor", when schools are opened at random where pupils are taught anything except the art of dancing, — you with infinite patience and loving care have honestly and modestly pursued the great work of inculcating your pupils with the covenants of true art.

When you finished your brilliant career as the first dancer of your day, you devoted your life to the difficult art of teaching others, with what proud satisfaction you can now look round, for in every part of the world nearly all who have made a name for themselves in choreography at the present time, have passed through your hands. If our goddess, Terpsichore is still in our midst, you, by right are her favoured High Priest.

Guard, my dear Maestro, for many long years to come the sacred flame burning on the altar of our goddess and teach your pupils to treasure the divine sparks, carrying them to the further-most corners of the earth as they speed on their way."

Pavlova at the beginning of her career in St. Petersburg.
1. As the Spanish Doll in the Ballet "Fairy Doll".
2. Representing Rime in the Ballet "The Four Seasons".
3. In Magic Flute.
4. In Don Quixote.

Pavlova in Giselle.

CHAPTER III.

MAITRES DE BALLET AND HOW PAVLOVA WORKED.

When Pavlova had finished at the Ballet School and entered upon her stage career at the Marinsky Theatre, the principal maitre de ballet was Marius Petipa. I feel it my duty to say a few words about this great artist-choreographer who, first as a dancer and then as ballet-master, was for a period of nearly sixty years in the service of the Imperial theatres, and there created an epoch of his own. I quote the particulars referring to him from A. Plescheev's book "Our Ballet".

Marius Petipa was born on March 11th, 1822, in Marseilles, and began his career on the stage at the age of sixteen in Paris, where for the benefit night of Rachel at the 'Comedie Francaise' he danced a pas de deux with Carlotta Grisi, and at the Grand Opera for the benefit night of Fanny Elsser. Then he went on to Nantes, being invited there in the capacity of dancer and maitre de ballet. Shortly after, young Petipa went as first dancer for three years to Bordeaux, and then on to Spain for about three years. He came to St. Petersburg on May 24th, 1847, starting as first dancer and becoming ballet-master in 1858, when he staged his first small ballet "Marriage during the Regency", for his own benefit night. After the departure of the famous maitre de ballet, Perrault, Petipa continued for some years to share the work of ballet-master with the well-known choreographist, St. Leon, who had been invited to St. Petersburg. After the departure of the latter and having composed a series of very successful ballets and strengthened his reputation as a talented and indefatigable maitre-de-ballet, Petipa became the undisputed dictator of the St. Petersburg ballet. Before his arrival in St. Petersburg, Petipa had composed seven ballets. In the years he was there, however, he was responsible for no less than forty-four independent ballets (mostly of four or five acts), the revival of sixteen old ones, and a large number of separate classical and character dances, without including the thirty-five operas for which he also composed the ballets. Nearly everything produced by Petipa is remarkable for its taste, style and artistic merit, while a large number of his works are master-pieces.

I have seen how Petipa worked. Notwithstanding his inexhaustible imagination and his fifty years of experience, he always worked out the plan of his production carefully and prepared for each rehearsal separately, taking down notes and making sketches of figures for the groups. The old ballet-masters had the enormous advantage of not having to think of the music. It was at their service, in the persons of conductors who were at the same time composers to order. A maitre-de-ballet thought out a subject or made use of one offered him by someone else, and worked it out in detail. This required great knowledge and ability, for the ballets of the Imperial theatre had to occupy a whole evening and could never be shorter than three acts, and very often contained four or five, with seven or eight scenes. Ballets of this kind gave the maitre-de-ballet an opportunity of showing his gifts for comic and dramatic scenes, as well as his imagination in various character, national and purely classical dances. On receiving the detailed libretto of the maitre-de-ballet, the composer would begin to write the music, keeping strictly to the directions given him, and the maitre-de-ballet, having heard the score, would cut it down or amplify it in accordance with the exigencies of the dance or the scene. The quality of this music was naturally not very high and it would not be easy to listen to it nowadays. One must not forget, however, that this was between the fifties and eighties of last century and that the music answered admirably the purpose it had to fulfil, which was worked out in every detail conjointly between the composer and the ballet-master.

Our best Russian composers began to take an interest in the ballet a long while ago, allotting a very considerable place to it in their operas, as witness Glinka, Serov, Rubinstein, then Rimsky-Korsakov, and Borodin. But the first great musician to apply his talents to the ballet was Tchaikovsky. He also started with opera ("Eugene Oneguin", "The Queen of Spades", etc.) in which ballet had a place. Making friends with Petipa, he decided to write an entire ballet in three acts and four scenes — "The Swan Lake". At first this ballet did not meet with much success; the public, accustomed to composers like Pugni and Minkus, found the beautiful, poetic music of Tchaikovsky beyond its powers of appreciation. To them it seemed too complicated and not sufficiently "dansante". Then Tchaikovsky wrote two more ballets, "The Nutcracker" and "The Sleeping Beauty", which became favourites at the end of the nineteenth and the beginning of the twentieth centuries. They were written by Tchaikovsky in close collaboration with Petipa. Having complete confidence in Petipa's experience, taste and knowledge of style, Tchaikovsky willingly took his advice. And as for Petipa, he had long felt the obsolete character of the music of Pugni and Minkus, and was glad

Pavlova in Rondino.
(*Photograph by Becker & Mass, Berlin*).

of the interest Tchaikovsky was taking in the ballet. After Tchaikovsky, several remarkable ballets were written by Glazounov — "The Seasons", "The Trial of Damis", "Raimonda" — all composed in collaboration with Petipa. After Glazounov, ballet music was written by one of Rimsky-Korsakov's most talented pupils — N. Tcherepnin.

Fokine, with whom the new epoch in the Russian ballet began, found it more difficult to obtain the right music for his works. For his first ballet "Eunice", the score was written by Scherbachov. The music of "Pavillon d'Armide" is Tcherepnin's. For his other ballets he was obliged to turn to music already existing and was fortunate enough to find in Chopin

Pavlova in The Dragon Fly.
(Photograph by Mishkin, New York).

the ideal setting for one of his best works, namely the ballet "Sylphides". Then he took Schumann's "Carnival" and also composed a ballet to Rimsky-Korsakov's "Cheherazade".

At a later period Stravinsky wrote regularly for the Russian ballet, first for Fokine ("The Fire-bird", "Petroushka") and then for other choreographists of Diaghilev's second period, ("Sacre du Printemps", "Noces", "Mavra", "The Fox", etc.).

To revert to the question of how Petipa and Fokine composed their ballets, it is necessary to state that I was personally present during Fokine's composition of two of his ballets for Pavlova in Berlin. "The Seven Daughters" to the music of Spendiarov and Liszt's "Preludes". Speaking of this, I cannot help recalling how, after the first performance of Liszt's "Preludes", both Richard Strauss and Nikisch came behind the scenes to give Pavlova and Fokine their opinions. Here the difference in the temperaments of these two great musicians showed itself in a remarkable manner. Strauss expressed his great pleasure to Pavlova and paid a few compliments to Fokine, whereas Nikisch was genuinely enthusiastic, declaring that the could not imagine a better interpretation of Liszt's music and Lamantine's poem.

These, to be sure, were among Fokine's first compositions. He has since been responsible for dozens of others, gaining much experience and greater maturity. But I think that the fundamental qualities of his work differed essentially from Petipa's. When Fokine composed a ballet he was all aflame, suffered positive tortures, lost heart, then bounded up very high again, recovered confidence in himself, sometimes working very quickly, sometimes very slowly, and reshaping what he had already done. Petipa's work (I must admit that he was seventy when I saw him at work) was methodical, well-thought-out and prepared beforehand. One might say that whereas Fokine created, Petipa built up. Both obtained marvellous results, giving the world masterpieces, although they followed different paths. The one worked like the painters of old — with perfect technique and knowledge of colours; whereas the other, bringing modern nervosity and sensitiveness into his work, led the art of the ballet from old forms into new, in which much beauty can be expected from his exceptional gifts.

The Romans, with whom the art of dancing stood on a high level, required a great deal from the maitre-de-ballet. Lucian says that he should know prosody, music, geometry and philosophy. It is possible that these requirements are exaggerated, but a modern ballet-master must undoubtedly be a talented artist and musician. In my opinion, to these gifts must also be added intelligence and education. The two maitres-de-ballet whom I knew, Petipa and Fokine, possessed all these qualifications.

Petipa, being, as one may say, the undisputed sovereign of the Imperial, ballet for fifty years, having unlimited authority, being absolute master in the choice of the repertoire, of his collaborators and artist, and working calmly in that wonderfully dignified atmosphere, which alone could be provided by the Imperial theatres, had every opportunity of showing each side of his talent.

Fokine's career opened with the brilliant successes of his first ballets, but at the same time he had to suffer the pinpricks of the opposition, many of which came from the partisans of old traditions in his own company. After his departure abroad with Diaghilev, his talent developed quickly and the series of masterpieces which he composed, placed him in an exceptional, one might almost say unequalled, position, as maitre-de-ballet. The Grand Opera in Paris, the Scala in Milan and a whole list of other important theatres, asked him to take up the direction of their ballet. But Fokine, having already an excellent, well-trained company of artists who had worked with him, and having also the advice in matters of art of such counsellors as Bakst, Benois, Serov and others, now his close friends, was unwilling to give up the work that was largely the outcome of his talents.

Soon, however, owing to his rupture with Diaghilev, he was forced to do so, and then the outbreak of the war changed the circumstances finally. At first he went to St. Petersburg, and later was invited to Stockholm and Copenhagen, where he staged some ballets. Finally he settled in America, but America could not give him very much. The only theatre that had a permanent ballet and unlimited means for productions — the Metropolitan — staged two of his ballets "Petroushka" and "Coq d'Or", before ever he arrived in America. And then, like every opera house with a large company of singers, conductors, stage-managers etc., the Metropolitan does not want an independent ballet. This has often more success than anything else in an opera, but at the same time its separate orchestra rehearsals complicate the work, in addition to which the orchestra is usually already overloaded with rehearsals, costing, by the way, a great deal of money in America. Whatever the reason, the Metropolitan did not invite Fokine to join, and at first he gave separate performances with his wife, and later opened a school in New York, occasionally giving performances with his pupils and putting on, it is said, some very interesting productions. Now and again he was asked to stage separate dances and scenes in long spectacular plays, and eventually devoted himself entirely to teaching. He is not fifty, and yet he, the greatest living choreographer, in the prime of life is doomed to inactivity. Owing to the war, the Russian revolution and the general decline of interest in art, there is now no field for Fokine's labours, strange as it may seem. There are only two or three theatres in the whole of Europe that could invite his collaboration. But to secure him for any length of time would only be a wise policy if the theatre in question made a permanent repertoire of ballets as independent performances, allowing him to stage several a year,

Pavlova in The Dragon Fly.
(Photograph by Hill's Studio, New York).

Pavlova in The Dragon Fly.
(Photograph by Hill's Studio, New York).

and this does not enter into the programmes of theatres. In any case it would cost too much in these days of universal economy, and for Fokine to leave America in order to stage one or two ballets is hardly worth while.

How Pavlova used to dream of working with Fokine! Not only did she regard him as a ballet-master of genius, one before whom she was ready to bow her head, but he was also infinitely dear to her, as a great Russian of lofty ideals, who had uttered a new word, a living and beautiful word, in her beloved art. Pavlova was always haunted by the thought that interest in ballet might grow less, perhaps be lost altogether, and in Fokine she saw the man who could and should carry on the work. Firmly believing that in his hands it would be capable of strong vitality, she was ready to enter any enterprise which had him at its head. Our own organisation, owing to its size and its peculiar conditions, made it impossible to invite him to collaborate. In order to unite the work of Pavlova and Fokine and give them the right atmosphere, either the old Imperial theatres would have been necessary or some lavishly subsidised theatre like the Metropolitan in New York. Often enough did Pavlova bitterly complain to English interviewers of the lack of interest in art in official circles in England, pointing out that England was the only country that had no royal theatre and had never subsidised a single theatre, which was quite incomprehensible considering the Englishman's love for the theatre and for music, and the wealth of the country. She used to cite Denmark as an example, of a country which had supported a national theatre of opera, drama, and ballet for two hundred years. Other examples were Sweden, Belgium, and Serbia, quite small countries which nevertheless spend considerable sums on the theatre and support their own national art.

When speaking of Pavlova's maitres-de-ballet, one must not omit the name of I. Clustine, who was with her for seven years, and composed many ballets and separate dances for her. Pavlova looked upon Clustine as a very talented man. I must admit that never have I elsewhere met such an ability for handling crowds and such rapidity in composition. I have seen him at rehearsals in the Bolshoi Theatre in Moscow and at the Grand Opera in Paris, where he had a very large corps de ballet at his command; more particularly in Moscow where three hundred people took part in his ballet "The Stars". During one of our seasons at the Hippodrome in New York, where Pavlova and her company had been engaged for the duration of the season, "Sleeping Beauty" was produced on Pavlova's advice. To those who do not know the New York Hippodrome, it is necessary to explain that it is a huge theatre seating five thousand persons and possessing an enormous stage. "Sleeping Beauty" cost the management over 150,000 dollars, which is not surprising, for more than five hundred persons dressed in gorgeous Bakst costumes took part in the performance. I have never seen a more brilliant picture than the second act representing the arrival of foreign notabilities at the Court of King Florestan. This scene contains Tchaikovsky's famous valse, for which Clustine made use of the entire Hippodrome corps de ballet (of 120) as well as our ballet of thirty. In its groupings and beauty of line, this was one of the most remarkable ballet productions. It was Clustine's misfortune that the Moscow of those days, always behind St. Petersburg in matters of art, did not give the maitre-de-ballet any material for the development of this own powers. What Clustine did was entirely his own. His debut as ballet-master began with the very successful ballet " The Stars", then he began to work on "Don Quixote", but he fell seriously ill after completing only the first act, and had to make a year's break in his stage career. Later, leaving the service of the Imperial theatres altogether to go abroad, he became the maitre-de-ballet of the Paris Grand Opera for five years. Arriving in Paris the day after war was declared and hearing that the French Government was intending to close down the Grand Opera, Pavlova suggested to Clustine that he should come with us to America. From that moment he was never parted from us for seven years. I cannot compare Clustine to either Petipa or Fokine, and being a very modest man he would be the last to aspire to any such distinction. I must say, however, that he understood Pavlova better than anybody else, worshipped her and put his whole soul into everything he did for her. In his day he had himself been an excellent classical dancer of the old school and therefore in every ballet kept up the tradition of adagios, pas d'action, and so on, but this he did so skilfully - presenting Pavlova to the public just in the way it wanted to see her, that is, giving it the chance of admiring her every appearance, her every dance whether solo or with a partner, moving aside her entourage in order that its movements should not draw attention from her, or screen her from view. This principle is often incompatible with the action of the modern ballet and in these newer productions the ballet masters do not care about providing a special place for the prima ballerina.

Of the ballets staged by Clustine, the greatest success fell to "Snowflakes", "Amarilla", "The Fairy Doll", "Chopiniana", "Dionysius", and among the separate dances to "Gavotte", "Scene Dansante", which Pavlova later gave to other dancers in her company, "Syrian Dance", "Valse Triste", "The Dance of the Hours", and many others.

In later years, her dancing partner, Novikov, composed ballets for her, having already done much of this work in Moscow. Among his compositions, "Russian Fairy Tale" with décor by Bilibin and music by Tcherepnin is quite interesting. The first act of "Don Quixote" was staged by Novikov almost in the same way as it was given on the Imperial stage, but the second (Dulcinea's garden) was entirely new and extremely clever.

HOW PAVLOVA WORKED.

Pavlova in The Butterfly.
(Photogr. Schneider, Berlin).

How often have I heard and read that Pavlova spent a long time practising her dances, endlessly repeating the same one before a mirror, and even that she kept swans in order to study their movements, before the dance "The Dying Swan" was composed for her.

I must destroy this legend. "The Dying Swan" was composed by Fokine in 1907 or 1908, that is, some years before she bought Ivy House her London home, and her English admirers presented her with the swans for the little lake, which was then much narrower and which was widened for the birds. The dance of "The Dying Swan" was the work of a moment of inspiration, like so many works of genius.

It happened that a big charity performance was being organized in St. Petersburg and Pavlova had promised to take part in it. M. Fokine, whom she approached with a request to stage something for her for that evening, suggested taking the music of Saint-Saens from "La vie des animaux".

The idea appealed to Pavlova and in about an hour Fokine composed the dance poem, which has become one with Pavlova forever, and the figure of that regal, snow-white bird, will be her eternal symbol. How many times have others danced the "Swan" since the night when Pavlova first danced it! In the theatres and concert halls of the whole world the poor swan has been made to die by dancers of all nationalities (I once saw a dusky mulatto in that role!). Even amateurs have attempted it, taking advantage of the fact that it is not technically difficult, and the mystical figure and touching music generally succeed in appealing to the public.

From the stage the "Swan" passed into dancing schools. At one time every pupil who had learned to walk on her toes danced the "Swan". I remember the late Maestro Cecchetti telling me that he had been invited to be the guest of honour and to act as judge at an examination of the best pupils of several London schools. In all there were twenty-eight debutantes

Pavlova in The Butterfly.
(Photograph by Schneider, Berlin.)

and it was decided to divide them into two groups. When, out of the fourteen in the first group, twelve had danced the "Swan", Cecchetti declared that he could stand no more, and that if it were desired that he should remain to see the second group also, they would have to choose something else.

We have often seen advertisements of ballet schools and teachers of dancing in America saying that modern and classical dancing were taught, "as well as a special course of tuition in Pavlova's 'The Dying Swan'".

It is worth noting that Pavlova's death has made the dancing of the "Swan" impossible. Whether the dancers themselves feel the tactlessness of doing it, or realise that the public would look upon it as a profanation, the fact remains that this dance is no longer seen.

Those dances of Pavlova's which she composed herself — "The Dragonfly", "The Californian Poppy", "Rondino", etc. she created very quickly. Hearing "Schön Rosmarin" at a concert of Kreisler's, she immediately invented a dance with the movements of a dragon-fly. The dance itself was thought out almost on the spur of the moment, but as the tempo was quick and the movements were difficult for the breathing, it required training. Later, Pavlova designed a costume for it as well.

One of the favourites with the public was "The Californian Poppy" and the following circumstances inspired it.

We were journeying from the north of America to California in the winter and, after being nearly snowbound in the pass over the mountains, we came down into a delightful valley, flooded with sunshine and covered with flowers. On stepping out of the carriage, Pavlova caught sight of a mass of golden-yellow flowers, called Californian poppies, whose charm is that they open with the rising of the sun and close again at its setting.

She felt a desire to picture this flower in a dance, and chose for this a melody of Tchaikovsky, the delicacy and simple charm of which blended admirably with the subject. It was not easy to think out the right costume, one that would give the impression of the flower and make it possible to draw in the petals and close them with the last rays of the setting sun. The Californians were very grateful to Pavlova for having chosen their modest poppy for, as California is the native land of this flower, they regard it as their state emblem. This dance was particularly well received and its performance was invariably followed by a presentation of a huge bouquet of these poppies.

When we were in Valparaiso, in Chile, some time afterwards, we went by motor car for a run into the mountains and were amazed to see a quantity of these Californian poppies, evidently feeling perfectly happy there, at least 6000 miles from home. Probably the whole of the Pacific coast of both Americas is favourable to the growth of this flower. The Chileans knew nothing about it and were not interested, but when Pavlova dug up several plants by the roots and brought them to Santiago, where they were planted in the garden of some friends and flourished exceedingly, everybody took notice of them and later we had letters saying that A m a p o l a P a v l o v a was now to be seen in many gardens.

When we arrived in South Africa, among the huge crowd which came to meet Pavlova at the steamer in Cape Town, was a group of women, who explained that they were the representatives of an association of men and women teachers of dancing. Pavlova, at once interested, asked:

"How many are there, then, of such teachers in Cape Town?"

To her surprise she heard that they numbered 108. The association gave a reception in her honour, at which she was presented with a lovely fan of ostrich feathers. Pavlova expressed her thanks, and promised that before her departure she would dance something with this fan, and using for the purpose the beautiful music of Beethoven-Kreisler, she composed her "Rondino".

All the elements of the dance were so completely at Pavlova's command for the expression of her most fugitive emotions, that no effort was necessary on her part to give them form. The dance shaped itself spontaneously and simply as the most natural way of expressing her ideas.

I have known and seen many famous dancers to whom a mirror was a necessity. They worked before it, correcting and studying their movements and poses, and when composing a dance of their own, watched all the time the results of their attempts.

I have never seen Pavlova at work before a mirror. A dance formed itself in her soul, if I may say so; and when she felt it, after hearing the music played through several times as if gradually merging it into the figures formed in her mind, she would endeavour to express it, first by the movements of her arms which were remarkably eloquent, and then, as if listening to the song in her soul, she would slowly translate the movements into dance.

It was quite another matter when Pavlova composed something for herself surrounded by other dancers, or put on something for her company. This was much more difficult and complicated. Pavlova wanted to imbue everyone with her own understanding of the piece and her mood in regard to it, and required her dancers to assimilate and interpret her ideas — one might say to live through her ideas.

On the other hand, to achieve this, she was ready to rehearse endlessly, allowing herself to be carried away by what she felt, repeating the dance over and over again, as if it were already on the stage, and not sparing her strength, if she could only thereby make it plain and comprehensible to others.

Her best work was her ballet "Autumn Leaves". She had had it long in mind, but realising that it would require many rehearsals, she put off the production of it to a time of greater leisure. At last in Buenos Aires, where we had a two months' season, and performances did not take place every day, she took the opportunity of completing it.

In Paris "Autumn Leaves" became a favourite ballet at once. The French thought so much of this delicately poetical work, that they readily forgave the orchestration of Chopin, against which they usually protest.

Pavlova herself did not place a very high value on her choreographic experiments. She was very fond of "Autumn Leaves" because this ballet responded to her moods and was danced to her favourite music. She chose the music with great care, playing and re-playing Chopin several times. The execution of "Autumn Leaves" is not very difficult, but there must be complete unity between dance and music. Pavlova used to insist that, before beginning the ballet, the part where the leaves, blown by the wind, run swiftly across the stage, be rehearsed by the company. The dancers would find it difficult to enter into their parts all at once, but after having done the run two or three times, would grow more confident and more used to the disposition of the scenery, which was constantly being changed according to the dimensions of the stage. Having perhaps a deeper feeling for this ballet than for any other, Pavlova, its author, required the whold company to give particular attention to it. She was always present at rehearsals and insisted that everything must go as smoothly and perfectly as on the night of the performance.

View of the lower part of the garden of Ivy House.

Ivy House as it appeared till 1929.

CHAPTER IV.
ABROAD AND IVY HOUSE.

After having been abroad several times, and seen the unsatisfactory position of the art of ballet in such large centres as Paris and Milan, Pavlova decided to show Russian ballet at all costs. Her first journey from St. Petersburg was to Riga, where she gave several performances. The following year she undertook a more extensive tour, beginning at Helsingfors and including Stockholm, Copenhagen, Berlin, Leipzig and Prague. This journey confirmed the opinion regarding the Russian ballet already expressed by foreigners. The troupe brought by Pavlova, although small, contained such fine dancers as Mmes. Egorova, Wiell, Mms. Bolm, Shiriaev, Obuchoff and others, and met with quite remarkable success. But the most enviable laurels awaited Pavlova and her troupe in Berlin.

The performances beginning successfully, finished triumphantly. At the farewell performance the German public exhibited a quite unwonted enthusiasm, breaking the barrier in order to get nearer the stage to throw flowers.

View of the lawns in front of the house.

The success of this first large tour gave rise to so much interest, that Pavlova and her company started on another one the following year, this time visiting a number of towns in Germany, as well as Vienna. From Vienna she went to Paris to take part in the Diaghilev season. Her brilliant success there brought an invitation to London, King Edward VII having expressed a wish to see her. The performance given in honour of the King and Queen and their kindness to her, for they expressed themselves as perfectly charmed, resulted in all the impresarios in London offering her contracts.

Simultaneously with this, Americans, who had seen her in Paris, invited her to give performances at the biggest American theatre, the Metropolitan in New York. The success of her first appearance there was even greater than her triumphs in Europe. After each one of her journeys abroad, Pavlova would come back to St. Petersburg and dance at the Marinksy Theatre, keeping thereby in touch with her native stage and her teachers.

In spite of constant work and regular training, Pavlova was always afraid that the abnormal conditions of work inseparable from continual

Pavlova's favourite spot in the garden.

Pavlova with her Mother feeding the pigeons.

View from Balcony at Ivy House.

change of place and of stage, the constant repetition of one and the same repertoire, the too-easy successes, might have an effect on her dancing detrimental to the requirements and traditions of the Imperial school. Every time she came back from abroad therefore, she went diffidently to her first lesson with Sokolova or Cecchetti, fearing that they might find in her some falling-off from the nobility of style of the strictly classical school. These examinations however invariably ended in her teachers not only finding nothing to criticise, but expressing their astonishment at finding her dances better than ever.

The declaration of war found her in Berlin. She managed to get to England via Belgium, and after a short time there, she collected a company and went to North America, spending all the years of the War between North and South America. She came back to Europe nearly five years

The Lake

Ivy House and the Conservatory.

Pavlova with her Mother.

Pavlova and her Husband.

Pavlova at Ivy House.

later. The first towns in which she danced were Lisbon, Madrid and then Paris. She was a prey to agitation and doubts on again appearing before a Paris audience. Much had changed, a new class of spectator had appeared, taste had become quite different, but with great joy she saw her art still meeting with the same success and the critics unanimously agreed, that even in our age the romanticism of the old ballet was neither dead nor grown old, that it had lost neither its freshness nor its charm. One of the critics said "When we leave the noise and tumult of the modern world and go into a theatre in which Pavlova is dancing, we feel as though we had left a miserable hovel and entered a temple".

Pavlova made her home in London, continuing meanwhile her foreign tours, which always embraced more and more distant lands.

Here I should like to say a few words about Ivy House, Pavlova's favourite place of rest for many years.

Commencing with the year 1910 for five consecutive years Pavlova had "seasons" in the London "Palace Theatre". These seasons began in May and went on for sixteen or twenty weeks. When we came to London in 1910 we stayed at the Hyde Park Hotel, because it faced Hyde Park. But Pavlova felt so much the necessity of having in the summer a small garden of her own, where she could spend a few hours in privacy in the open air, that a week later we went to Golders Green, and rented there a small house with a garden. The next season we went direct to Golders Green to another house and began to look round for something more suitable. We did not have to look for long, for nearly opposite to where we were living, was a house with a large, neglected garden to be let or sold. The stone wall round the house and a part of one of the walls of the house itself were overgrown with ancient ivy, whence the name of the house — Ivy House.

The chief attraction of the house was its situation on the highest part of London. Each time on our return home from town in the heat of summer we felt the freshness and the difference of the air. Owing to its high situation the view from the balconies extended for many miles. A plot of land of about two acres, narrow in its upper part near the house and then widening, sloped to a small lake. The boundary on one side was the road and on two of its other sides the house adjoins a large public park, so that from the windows on the park side no buildings were to be seen, only a mass of trees.

Within the last years this part of London has been very much built over, but some fifty years ago the owners of Ivy House possessed large tracts of land. A friend of ours, a doctor, an old inhabitant of the neighbourhood, used to tell us, that being delicate in his youth and ordered fresh

The Hall — Ivy House.
(Pavlova's Practice Room.)

The Dining Room — Ivy House.

46

The Lounge — Ivy House.

Ivy House after reconstruction in 1929.

milk by the doctors, his parents, who were acquainted with the owners of Ivy House, placed him with them and several times a day the boy drank fresh milk from a herd of cows grazing on what is now the most populous part of Golders Green and where the Underground station lies.

According to the former owners of Ivy House it was for a long time tenanted by the famous painter Turner.

Pavlova was immediately attracted to Ivy House. At first we rented it

Pavlova with her Swans.

Pavlova with Jack, her favourite Swan.
(Photograph by Lafayette, London.)

and then, after having lived there one summer, she resolved to buy it and began to settle into it, bringing over her furniture from St. Petersburg.

We lived in Ivy House during the season of 1913—1914 and left for America on the outbreak of war, not returning from there until 1919, since when Pavlova passed each year her short period of rest at Ivy House, becoming more and more attached to it and especially to the garden. And indeed, for her Ivy House had considerations difficult to overvalue. Although only fifteen minutes from the centre of London, thanks to its situation, its roominess and its big garden, it gave her all the conveniences of a country life. In character the building was a typical old English mansion, containing in the middle a large hall which extended up through two storeys. This hall served Pavlova for her exercises and partly for rehearsals, thus saving her from the necessity of going for these purposes into town.

Pavlova with Jack. (Photograph by Lafayette, London.)

Pavlova with Jack.
(Photograph by Lafayette, London.)

We also had a very large quantity of theatrical properties. The scenery and some of the properties could be stored, but the costumes demanded constant attention, as also the wigs and the music, of which we had an enormous amount and which had always to be at hand. All this could be very conveniently stored in the magnificent stone cellars which ran under the whole extent of the house.

As all our big tours started from London, it was extremely convenient for us to have Ivy House as a jumping-off place.

Pavlova with Jack.
(*Photograph by Lafayette, London.*)

Above all things Pavlova was fondest of birds and flowers. The garden of Ivy House made it possible for her to keep swans, flamingoes and pigeons, while the big greenhouse, turned into a huge cage, made an excellent home for a number of small birds, brought from various lands. The garden gave her a great deal of trouble, but also not a little joy. She spent the greater part of her day in it, going into every detail. Her favourite spot was the terrace where a little pool and a fountain had been made. Here, lying in a hammock, she would watch the birds taking their bath. Here, also, was the tent in which she liked to have tea with her friends.

Pavlova had long been interested in the East and in 1922 undertook a journey round the world with her company. She travelled from London via Canada and began her tour in Japan, continuing it through the towns of China, Manilla, Singapore, India and Egypt.

She was invited more than once to Australia, but so long a journey, requiring a five weeks' sea voyage, frightened her.

In 1925 she was again asked to dance in Australia and New Zealand. In order to make the journey shorter and less fatiguing, we decided to break it by giving some performances in South Africa. We left London at the beginning of December and remained in South Africa until the middle of February, and then toured Australia and New Zealand for nearly five months.

In 1928 she accomplished her second extensive tour in the East, beginning it in Egypt, then through India, Burma, Singapore, on to Java and Australia. This tour lasted about nine months. In the intervals of these long journeys she made annual tours in Europe and invariably gave a short season in London.

Pavlova in The Dying Swan.
(Photograph by Strelezki, New York.)

Pavlova in The Dying Swan.
(Photograph by van Riel, Buenos Aires.)

Pavlova in The Dying Swan.

Pavlova in The Dying Swan.

Pavlova in The Dying Swan.
(Photograph by van Riel, Buenos Aires.)

Pavlova in The Dying Swan.
(Photograph by van Riel, Buenos Aires.)

Pavlova in The Dying Swan.

Pavlova in The Dying Swan.
(*Photograph by van Riel, Buenos Aires.*)

Pavlova in The Dying Swan.
(Photograph by van Riel, Buenos Aires.)

Pavlova in "The Dying Swan". (Photograph by van Riel, Buenos Aires.)

CHAPTER V.

THE COMPANY.

The first time Pavlova had a small company of her own was for her first engagement at the London Palace Theatre. She was not then dancing whole ballets, but only short numbers and it was necessary for her to fill in the time between her dances while she changed. She brought over eight dancers from the Imperial Theatres. The success achieved was so great that the management arranged a series of ballet matinees for the following season, at which fragments from various ballets were to be performed. This necessitated a certain increase in the size of the company, which she then took first for a tour in England before starting the new season at the Palace Theatre. In 1913 Pavlova signed a contract for a tour in America, and undertook to bring a full company, together with costumes, scenery, etc. and from that moment onwards she had a permanent organization.

At first we used to engage, as far as possible, Russian and Polish dancers, but as those of the Imperial theatres were busy during the winter, one had to take what one could get. Even before the Russian Ballet made its appearance in London, some good dancing schools existed there, whose best pupils were excellent material for any company. Pavlova became interested in the aptitude of English girls for dancing.

She chose a few promising girls and began working hard with them. Of the eight selected three made such rapid progress that she took two of them into her company and engaged the third a year later. One of them married and soon left the theatre, while another fell to the temptation of a music hall career in America. Only the third — Muriel Stuart — remained with Pavlova, dancing in her company for ten years. Eventually she also got married and forsook us, going to America. This dancer was entirely trained by Pavlova, having passed through the whole course with her and never having had any other teacher. Muriel Stuart was very handsome, had a very elegant carriage and was indebted for much to Pavlova. Her grace and her beautiful carriage of head and arms made her much noticed and only the shyness and lack of self-assurance peculiar to English girls prevented her from reaching the top of her profession.

After the appearance of Pavlova in London and later of the Diaghilev Russian Ballet, interest in dancing increased considerably and many ballet schools were opened, including several Russian ones. In a short time so many good and properly trained dancers were available that one could have assembled a company without any difficulty. At the request of the schools Pavlova held an annual audition to which they sent their pupils. She used to subject them to an examination, make a special note of the more finished and promising dancers, and these she would take into her company whenever vacancies occurred.

I feel it necessary to say a few words about English dancers, our most faithful and devoted collaborators for so many years. But first I must compare their training with that of their Russian and Polish colleagues.

During the years of our journeyings, in the course of which we covered the whole world several times, we had dancers of various nationalities — Russians, Poles, Americans, English.

There are two magnificently organised schools in Russia with centuries of tradition behind them, and which have a first-class staff of instructors. These schools, moreover, were attached to the Imperial theatres and the children in them took part in the performances from the very beginning, seeing the best contemporary dancers on the stage and taking them for their models.

In Poland also there was a well-organised school attached to the Warsaw State Theatre. Polish dancers therefore had every opportunity for serious training.

The Russians and Poles had one great advantage. On graduating from the school they had no need to think of the morrow. Immediately, one might say automatically, they passed into the service of the Imperial or the State theatre, where they continued under the supervision of their teachers, themselves in most cases dancers, maitres de ballet, stage managers or people holding similar appointments.

The position of English and American dancers is totally different. The private schools of which they were pupils gave them a more or less thorough grounding, occasionally turning out dancers of fine quality. But they lacked what every Russian and Polish dancer who has been through the schools possessed, namely, experience of the stage, the ability to make up, to wear costume and so forth. Apart from these external causes, there is also the

Pavlova with N. Legat in "Lac du Cygne".

temperamental difference between the two races. The soul of the Slav has in it a native gentleness, a sort of freshness, a naturalness and simplicity in the expression of moods and emotions. In life, this is not always possible or even desirable; on the stage it is indispensable.

In English dancers one often notices a lack of individuality and naturalness in giving expression to their sentiments on the stage. Pavlova often spoke about this, finding the explanation in the English system of education which tends to discourage self-expression, inculcating self-control and to a marked degree the repression of the spontaneous manifestations of emotion.

Pavlova would often become quite angry and say to her dancers:

"Why do you always go about with your lips tucked in expressing nothing? Cry when you want to cry and laugh when you want to laugh."

Pavlova with Mordkin in "Pas de Deux".

This native reserve prevented English dancers from attaining the success their technical powers and the elegance of their dancing deserved and they were unfortunately the first to suffer. On the other hand, there was much about them that was very attractive as members of the company — their extreme conscientiousness, diligence, sense of duty, their breeding and tact. In this they were beyond reproach, and working with them was a real pleasure. Pavlova was well aware of this and deeply appreciated them.

In England the career of a dancer is considered quite suitable for a young girl. The artistic professions in general enjoy considerable respect in that country. The parents, even in families of good standing, do not protest as a rule against a daughter's wish to go on the stage. But the outlook in these matters is quite different in the case of men. The wish of a boy to become a dancer is regarded as an attempt to avoid serious work. And yet, some excellent male dancers have sprung up among the English, especially within the last few years, dancers capable of taking a responsible position in any company. Among these young men are some who have gifts above the ordinary, and a feeling for and excellent taste in ballet production.

During the War, Pavlova was travelling between North and South America. She was asked several times to come to Europe, but in view of the danger from submarines she did not care to take upon herself the responsibility of bringing the company over. Under these difficult circumstances it was not easy to keep the organization intact during the whole of those five years, but we succeeded in keeping our artists with us all the time and only brought the company back to London after the end of the War.

In the course of these five years of joint work, the members of the company made such enormous progress, some of the dancers had so improved, that Pavlova was very proud of her enterprise and wanted on her return to London to show what could be done with English dancers. She was, however, doomed to disappointment. At her very first interview with representatives of the English press, she was full of enthusiasm saying how happy she was to be able to show the English public their own English dancers. To her surprise and dismay her hearers did not exhibit any corresponding enthusiasm. Some even said that they would not advise her to lay too much stress on the fact that most of her dancers were English, as that would only lessen interest in the ballet.

There are an enormous number of schools in America. Unfortunately, the good ones are the exception and not the rule. The majority are not only of very poor quality, but some positively endanger the future career of the children entrusted to them. Anybody can call himself a professor of any subject in America, and advertise himself in the most blatant manner. I have often had to go to a certain big building on Broadway, New York, where a friend of mine has his office. This building was the favoured residence of a large number of professors of singing, each one advertising his own particular system of voice-production with guarantees of success. When chancing to walk along the corridors, I have heard such extraordinary noises and shrieks coming from the "studies" of these so-called professors that one might have imagined oneself surrounded by dentists' parlours. Similar "professors" of dancing, mostly female, can be counted in thousands, nay even tens of thousands. When and where they themselves learnt, nobody knows. In our lengthy tours in America, we have often had convincing proof of the appalling ignorance of these instructors. I will give two or three of the more characteristic instances.

In every town that Pavlova visited, she was invariably approached by a number of people wanting her to see their children and give her opinion of their abilities. When it was a case of parents wishing to choose the career of dancing for a child, Pavlova would refuse outright to give any advice, saying that she could only judge after the child had worked for two or three years under a teacher. Only then and according to the progress made, could one say anything definite regarding a child's aptitude and ability as a future dancer.

If, on the other hand, little girls having already had some tuition were brought to her, she generally agreed to see them, fixing some free hour for this, occasionally at night after the performance.

I was often rebuked for not dissuading Pavlova from these examinations, which in any case led to nothing and only deprived her of some minutes of necessary rest. But she looked upon this as her duty and steadfastly performed it. She would not refuse it, if only because many of those who came to her for her advice and opinion were poor. There were cases of mothers bringing an only daughter who wanted to become a dancer and whose teacher regarded her as very promising. The mother found it very difficult to pay for the lessons, but if her daughter were really gifted, she — the mother — would make any sacrifice for the girl's training, and she had therefore come for Pavlova's advice, knowing that she could trust it implicitly.

At first Pavlova was rather embarrassed to speak the truth in such cases, especially as nearly all the girls came with their teachers. But later, having seen so many cases of disgraceful exploitation and ignorance, she began to tell them the truth, sometimes very sharply. She had seen children of seven or eight crippled for life, because their "professors" began teaching them to walk on the tips of their toes at the age of four or five, and knowing

Pavlova with Volinine in "Autumn Leaves".

Pavlova with Novikoff in "The dance of Hours".

nothing themselves, had made the child do p a s that led to irreparable damage to the knees. On one occasion she had promised to look at two or three little girls, but feeling tired, had asked maestro Cecchetti to examine them for her. And as the maestro did not speak English, I went with him. A teacher with her pupils was waiting for us on the stage. As is usual in such cases, the children were dressed in their best, their hair down the back and large bows on their heads. The class began and the ignorance of the teacher became instantly evident — the children were made to walk on their toes, their knees bent, to kick their legs above their heads, etc.

After all this had been gone through, the teacher asked the maestro's opinion of the children. Hardly able to contain himself with fury, Cecchetti said that the children, like all children, were very sweet.

"And what do you think of their instructress?" said the teacher coyly, with an ingratiating smile.

"I would hang her", said the maestro, and I confess that I translated it.

On another occasion, when we were in Chicago, the porter of the hotel announced that there was a lady to see Pavlova. We were on our way to the theatre at the time. In the lounge a woman of enormous size, aged about fifty, came forward to meet us. Approaching Pavlova she said she wanted to take dancing lessons from her. This was so extraordinary that for a moment Pavlova was dumbfounded and then said she did not give any lessons. The woman, however, insisted.

"Name your own price".

When Pavlova repeated her refusal rather more sharply, the woman entreated her to give her at any rate one lesson, at any price she liked. Then I, thrusting myself into the conversation and confirming Pavlova's statement that she never gave lessons, tried to explain how senseless it would be to take one lesson only, but the woman replied in tones of vexation:

"Don't you understand how important it is for me being a teacher myself be able to say that I am a pupil of Madame Pavlova's?"

Here is another case.

We arrived in a large town in the Middle West and found awaiting us in the hotel an invitation to be present at a lesson arranged in honour of Pavlova at some dancing school. The surname of the mistress did not convey anything to us, and Pavlova decided not to go, asking me, however, to attend, for the whole company had been invited. Arriving at the school, I saw in a very large hall a number of little girls waiting for the class to begin. Going up to the mistress — an elderly woman — I told her how sorry

Pavlova was not to be able to be present. After talking to me for a little time, the teacher said:

"You don't recognise me?" And she reminded me of having once met us in Europe and asking Pavlova to recommend a professor for her daughter in St. Petersburg, where she was then shortly going. Pavlova gave her a letter to E. P. Sokolova, who later told us that some American girl and her mother had been and taken lessons from her for about a month.

"Now you see", continued the woman, "my daughter has married and gone away with her husband, so I decided to open a school of dancing, making use of what I had seen Madame Sokolova do when I visited the lessons"

To my ironical question as to how the business was getting on, in her expert hands she replied with great assurance:

"Splendidly. Americans think a great deal of the genuine Russian school."

During the last few years American dancing instruction has undergone a considerable change for the better. Schools have been opened by Fokine, Bolm, Novikov, Kobelov and a number of other Russian teachers, former dancers of the Imperial theatres, with a wide experience of the stage. Moreover, they have special annual classes for teachers, and in this way hundreds of them get at any rate an elementary knowledge of the system of correct instruction in classical dancing.

Now and then we also had American dancers in our company. Some of them were very capable and had great success. But they have one grave fault: the majority lack patience and wish to arrive at striking results in the shortest possible time.

*

Pavlova was very strict in the matter of the conduct of her company. It is only natural that during long sea voyages friendships are made, dances and games arranged, and ballet-dancers, being graceful and often good-looking, find themselves much in demand. But gossip also circulates very easily. Pavlova made it a rule that whether travelling by sea or land, dancers should travel not as private individuals, but as members of the Pavlova company, and must therefore keep up the good reputation everywhere enjoyed by the company. In England, France or Germany a young girl can return home alone after the evening performance, but there are countries even in Europe where this is far from perfectly safe, and it is even less so in South America. They still associate every theatrical company from Europe — with the possible exception of opera companies — with a life of great freedom.

Pavlova, Novikoff and Zaylich in the "Invitation à la Danse".

Pavlova with Novikoff and Company in the "Invitation à la Danse".

It was therefore necessary to exercise a great deal of care in order to avoid being involved in unpleasant incidents. Pavlova's strict views were also shared by her dancers, girls who had been well brought up, were very friendly among themselves and were proud of the company's good name. A side-light was thrown on this by two pictures that appeared side by side in a South American paper. The first representing the arrival of the company, depicted the menfolk highly elated at the prospect, and smiling, while their wives were weeping and sad; the second, showing the situation a month after the arrival of the company, told a different tale — all the men were dejected and the wives beaming and laughing.

A highly pleasing little incident occurred in a small town in Chile. When we arrived we were met at the station by an English clergyman and his wife. He came up to Pavlova and said that as there were so few hotels in this town and rooms were not easily found, they invited two of our girls to be their guests during the whole of our stay, as they had a room free and knew the excellent reputation of Madame Pavlova's dancers.

Some of our English girls, being catholics, used to go to the cathedral at Buenos Aires and became acquainted with the bishop. We left Buenos Aires on board an English steamer, and the captain, a typical old sea-dog, told us that before sailing from Buenos Aires he had received a letter from the catholic bishop, asking him to take great care of our dancers, whom he "highly recommended" to him.

The captain added laughingly that this was probably the first occasion upon which a bishop had committed ballet-dancers to the special care of a sea-captain.

Wherever we went, the English and American consuls arranged receptions in honour of the whole company.

I have spoken elsewhere of our arrival at Panama, on our way from South America to Europe, on the day of the armistice. We were obliged to remain in Panama for three weeks before we succeeded in leaving on board a French cargo boat carrying nitrate. While we were in Panama a large ocean steamer arrived with Australian officers returning from Europe to their own country. A ball was given to celebrate the occasion and the most interesting ladies present were our dancers. At the end of the evening the senior officers came up to Pavlova to express their pleasure at having met again real English ladies, for, they said, there had been terrible changes in manners in England, as elsewhere in Europe, during the War and this type had nearly disappeared. It was true for our girls left England in 1914 and all had pre war manners.

The following incident will show how widespread was the good reputation of our company.

Before our departure for the Far East one of the dancers fell ill and a substitute had to be found. One of the schools sent us a charming and very capable young girl, but so young did she appear that I asked her her age. She answered, fifteen. I thereupon told the mother that to my great regret, we could not think of taking anyone so young on a long trip like ours, and expressed my surprise that a mother could let her child go for a journey round the world with strangers. To this the mother replied with conviction that with Pavlova, she knew her girl would be in trustworthy hands. We decided to take her and she was a very loyal member of the company for six years. On their side the dancers also highly valued the respect and attention which they received and did all in their power to uphold this enviable reputation.

The only time that Pavlova was called upon to protect the dignity of her company, occurred in Guayaquil (Republic of Ecuador). There were also other incidents in connection with our stay there, which will help to give a graphic picture of local conditions. It should be explained that on our way to Peru and Chile we were supposed to give some performances in the capital of the country, Quito. On our arrival at Guayaquil, from whence we were to go by train to Quito which is high up in the mountains, we learnt that there had been a serious landslide and that railway communication was in consequence interrupted for two or three weeks, and possibly even longer. The impresario at Guayaquil suggested our giving several performances in that town. To go further would have been useless, for the theatres in Lima and Valparaiso were booked up and to give our performances elsewhere in those towns was an impossibility. We had therefore to remain in Guayaquil, though we knew nothing about the place. Only a day or two later, having become acquainted with the local consuls, we learnt that from a sanitary point of view, this town had the worst reputation of any in the two Americas, possibly even in the world. In consequence of the constant floods of the huge river that flows near the town, the surrounding country is all bog land, and malaria, yellow fever and bubonic plague are always rampant.

The Europeans living there expressed their surprise at our courage and told us that the few companies that had ever visited the place generally left a member or two in the cemetery.

Pavlova's state of mind can be imagined. Every morning we anxiously cross-examined the company to know whether everybody was well and to our untold relief, during the ten days that we were obliged to remain there, nobody fell ill. The day when we boarded an English steamer was one of gladness indeed.

The Republic of Ecuador covers a very large area and owing to particular political conditions is considered very backward in the matter of civilization, but the inhabitants are known for their piety. In the large cathedral in the centre of Guayaquil there seemed always to be a service proceeding and it was invariably filled with the devout. All the women go about in black dresses and long trains. Their heads are hidden under black shawls. The impression they produce is that of nuns. The streets are in an impossible state, frightful dust at the sides and puddles of mould-covered water in the middle.

The whole of our company found accommodation in the American hotel, built on hygienic principles, with mosquito nets over the windows and so on, while we lived in the old hotel, which had the reputation of being the best. In the evenings when the insects crawled out of the countless cracks, the immense rooms inspired fear. Before going to bed, we used to examine it and the sheets very carefully in case some dangerous animal had managed to creep in, and tucked in the curtains to avoid any such visitation.

How far the local inhabitants get used to these things can be judged from the following incident.

During dinner on one occasion I was waving aside a mosquito, the carriers, as one knows, of malaria and yellow fever germs. The landlord of the hotel, who was present, locked carefully at the mosquito in question and said:

"That's not a dangerous one, you see his tail is pointing upwards. The dangerous ones are those that have a tail pointing downward."

Pavlova's dancing partner, who also stayed at the same hotel, said that on entering his bathroom one evening, he saw several scorpions come to drink the water. As they showed no wish to vacate the place for him, he was obliged to put them to flight with shots out of a revolver.

So this was the sort of place where we found ourselves unexpectedly detained, and where Pavlova and her company gave several performances. The day after our arrival an article appeared in the local paper informing the public of the event and adding that nobody could tell what the nature of the performance was going to be, but that at first sight the company did not produce a very decent impression. Pavlova was greatly upset and asked me to go to the editorial offices and find out what was meant. I took our manager, a Spaniard, with me and we went off. The editor explained that his paper, the chief one in Guayaquil, was Catholic and considered it its duty to look after public morals. He could not, therefore, have written otherwise.

Pavlova "Invitation à la Dance".

When I asked him what it was that had produced this bad impression upon him, he replied indignantly:

"But all your women are in short skirts, with bare necks and arms, and all your men are without hats!"

We did our best to explain that it was the present day fashion, that short skirts were seen everywhere and the Spanish manager assured him that even the Queen of Spain wore skirts only to her knees. But the editor could not be convinced. To my remark that on the equator it was quite natural to go about with bare necks and arms, he replied:

"You have seen how all respectable women go about here?"

Curiously enough, after the first performance, this editor became the most fervent admirer of Pavlova and the ballet, and used to write enthusiastic articles about the performances, saying at the end of his last one that to his great regret his countrymen were not yet able to appreciate such beauty.

We had to contend with increasing difficulties when some of the South American States joined in the War. There was trouble with passports and as among the members of our company some were not certain of their documents being in order, they had to be left behind in one of the neutral republics. We had in the company a male dancer who had married an American, also a dancer of ours. On our arrival in Brazil we learnt that this republic had also declared War and that all foreigners who arrived there were subject to very strict control. When our passports were examined, the Brazilian officials discovered that this man was a Czech, consequently belonged to a country at war with Brazil and therefore had to be interned. We protested and he explained in detail that he had left his native land fifteen years ago and that the Czechs should not be looked upon as enemies, for they had formed legions of their own and were fighting the Germans. But it was all of no avail. He was not allowed to continue the tour with us. Thereupon his wife decided to go back to her parents in New York, where her child was. To her horror she learnt from the American consul there, that having married a Czech, she had become an Austrian subject and could not be allowed to enter America. Neither her prayers nor her assurances that she had never been to her husband's country, that she was married in America, that her parents were native Americans and that she herself as well as her child were born in America, helped her in any way. After the war this Czech rejoined our company and suddenly everything was changed! He was a full-blown citizen of the Czecho-Slovakian Republic and the road was open to him everywhere, while Pavlova and all of us who were Russians, had in the meantime become a suspect and undesirable element, and our arrival in any country was hedged around with countless and tiring formalities. Thanks, however, to the name of Pavlova, we managed successfully, but how many unfortunate Russians did we meet whose movements were hampered at every turn by insuperable obstacles!

*

It is only natural that Pavlova, always very exacting with herself, working harder than anybody, carrying on her shoulders all the responsibility for the artistic as well as the financial success of the undertaking, should also expect much from her dancers.

With her great love for the art to which she had given herself up entirely, deeply reverencing it as something sacred, she would not allow even the shadow of disrespect towards it or any carelessness in work which might spoil the harmony and unity of the whole. When tired out or upset by a bad stage or a bad orchestra and seeing the violation of the approved order or lack of attention on the stage, Pavlova would fall upon the guilty one with a sharp reproof; but those who knew her well would never take it in ill part. In their essence these rebukes were always deserved, and the form they were clothed in can be excused by the nervous strain inseparable from the performance. As a rule, when the performance was over, the culprit would go into Pavlova's dressing-room, explanations would follow, frequently to the accompaniment of tears on both sides, and peace would be restored.

When issuing any instructions to the company Pavlova was careful to explain exactly what she wanted. She advised the dancers first to visualise what was required of them, to take in a mental picture of what they had to do, and she would make this very clear, repeat it, and lay it down almost as a commandment. Then only were they to translate it into action and movements and if they performed these at all mechanically, Pavlova would be very annoyed.

Her knowledge gave her boundless authority to demand anything which she was convinced was right and necessary. She was not given to whims and if she did give a reproof, sometimes even rather peremptorily, it was only because she felt herself to be in the right. And knowing this, appreciating her sincerity and uprightness and her complete lack of malice, one could not take offence. As likely as not, a few minutes later she would forget all that she had said and would be talking to the culprit in the most kindly tones.

She had the great merit that she had no favourites and treated everybody alike. She advanced those who worked and showed some individuality, and did not value very highly those who exhibited only technical ability. No influence or personal solicitations on behalf of anyone had any effect on her.

This trait in her character, added to the great talent that placed her beyond the reach of the other dancers, made her greatly beloved.

This can be understood for Pavlova was also exceptionally kind and sympathetic. Her simplicity, her frankness, her sincere readiness to help, made it perfectly easy for any member of the company to approach her at any time. She was quickly touched by another's sorrow and was wholeheartedly responsive to all the family troubles of her dancers, never refusing her help or support.

If any members of the company fell ill, they received gratuitous medical treatment and were paid their salaries, even when such illnesses lasted for months.

Here I must touch upon a question which I should not otherwise have mentioned, had I not been constrained to do so by a statement made by the author of a book "The Genius of the Dance" written about Pavlova. In his book Mr. Hyden says that Pavlova "by no means paid lavish salaries".

Meanness is not a pleasing trait, but how can one associate it with Pavlova! One's mind involuntarily conjures up the touching and poetic figures which she created, figures that brought tears to the eyes of many. One thinks of her as the ideal of a whole generation of young dancers — and then to imagine for a moment that she could suffer from so degrading, so soul destroying a fault as meanness!

The author of the book claims to have been closely connected with Pavlova for twenty years. This is not so, Mr. Hyden was only a pianist for rehearsals — and even that not continuously, but with an interval of several years in between — and he was conductor by chance during a short tour in England and in the Far East, pending the arrival of the chief musical director, Mr. E. Kurtz. The reader of his book might easily gain the misleading impression that there had been some twenty years' colloboration between its author and Pavlova. One is left amazed, wondering what reasons the author could have had to cast a shadow on the memory of a great artist. As the husband of one of our dancers he must have known perfectly well what salaries were paid to the company. It would have been more honest, and certainly more convincing, if, in proof of his contention of Pavlova's lack of generous treatment towards her artists, he had brought forward instances of the exact salaries paid. I must therefore do so.

The minimum salary paid to dancers in Pavlova's company was ten pounds per week, and this increased progressively until it reached thirty pounds and more for leading dancers. And the author must know quite well that corps de ballet dancers in England get three-pounds ten, four, and sometimes, but rarely five pounds, but never more than five pounds, and that only on condition that they dance twice a day. In Europe

Pavlova with Hitchins in "Autumn Leaves".

the salaries are still less. It is only in North America that artists are better paid.

On what grounds, then, does he reproach Pavlova with meanness?

I have received letters from our dancers, even from those who left the company long ago, asking me what is the meaning of all this, as Pavlova was known to have paid artists more highly than anyone else.

In a further attempt to prove his contention that Pavlova was mean, Mr. Hyden cites the fact that her company travelled second class and not first class. In all my extensive experience and knowledge of the theatrical business I have never yet heard of any theatrical company travelling first class, and in England, Germany and practically all other countries it is well-known that they travel third.

And then, later, he declares that only those who left Pavlova have ever got on in their careers. He does not however mention a single name of these successful ones — where are they? They do not exist.

Whenever our dancers received advantageous offers, far from placing any obstacles in the way of their accepting them, we did whatever was possible to help them by giving testimonials and letters of recommendation.

I might add here that many years ago I introduced the system, approved by Pavlova, of having no written contracts with members of the company. I found them quite useless, for Pavlova's principles prevented her from breaking them and when a contract was broken by a dancer, we would not in any case have hindered or sued her. And I proved to be right, for none of the dancers ever left us except for reasons connected with their private lives, and some remained with us for ten years and longer.

Anyone desiring to leave, however, could do so at any moment. As I have already said, those who did leave us, did not, unfortunately, succeed in making a career. Possibly this was because they did not possess the necessary gifts to become distinguished classical dancers, or perhaps they lacked the self confidence to clear a path for themselves in the music-halls. And often even those who left our employ begged to be taken back again a few months or a year later, and though Pavlova was against doing this in principle, she would finally consent. And it was these dancers who re-joined the company who particularly appreciated service with Pavlova and were among its most faithful members.

Mr. Hyden's inaccuracy is most vividly proven by the fact, for instance, that two of Pavlova's leading English dancers, Hilda Butsova and Ruth French, could not get any engagements at all in England. Hilda Butsova came to us first at the age of sixteen, beginning in the corps de ballet, later dancing solo and finally being entrusted with entire ballets. She was very capable, had an excellent technique and a good deal of charm, and easily managed such ballets as "Coppelia" and "The Flute" as well as many separate numbers. She left the company when she married and went to America, but a year later she returned to England, tried vainly to find engagements there and had to go back.

The other, Ruth French, is undoubtedly the best English dancer of our day. Well-made and possessing natural stage gifts, she attained great proficiency under the tuition of her teacher Morozov; and continuing to work hard, she became a very strong technical dancer, retaining at the same time all the elegance of style and the purity of classicism. Pavlova could never understand how a dancer, having every right to the first place in any ballet troupe, should be unable to find any use for her talent in England.

Ruth French was with us for two seasons and danced a series of important ballets — "Visions", "The Romance of a Mummy", etc. — to the complete satisfaction of Pavlova. She is now twenty seven years of age, but owing to the absence of suitable engagements, has opened a school in London. To her honour it must be said that she has a great respect for her art and when offered work unworthy of the dignity of classical ballet, always refused it.

The extent to which all those who were employed in our company preserved a kindly recollection of Pavlova and a sentiment of deep respect, love and loyalty to her, is shown by the letters she was always receiving from former dancers, even from those who had left us many years ago, had married and become mothers, or had opened dancing schools of their own.

When telling her of this or that family event or the progress of their schools, they would invariably add that, however well life had treated them, they always looked back on the years they passed with Pavlova as their happiest, and only now realised how much they owed to her for instilling into them a sense of duty, respect and love for art.

What then does the author mentioned mean when he says that Pavlova's dancers could never make a career while with her, but only after leaving her? Does he think perhaps that Pavlova stood purposely in their way and prevented their gifts from showing? He does not know the number of times that Pavlova insisted upon the dancers being given more to do and appearing more frequently, dancing whole ballets and even arranging whole performances without her. She had a naive belief that the public was interested in young dancers, would come to look at them and would support their initiative. Of course I hotly argued the impossibility of such experiments, but she would not believe me and continued to insist upon them and only the emphatic protests of the impresarios and the theatre management would cause her to abandon the idea.

Pavlova with Vladimiroff.
(*Photograph by Bocanegra, Buenos Aires.*)

But can Pavlova be seriously suspected of envy or jealousy of the success of any of the dancers? The truth of the matter is that the public wanted to see Pavlova and only Pavlova. It is true that, knowing the impossibility of her dancing the whole evening, it was also ready to look at the first part of the programme without her, but that was in the expectation of her appearing in the second. If one were to announce that she would not be dancing at all, it is doubtful whether one quarter of the audience would have come to look at the dancers taking her place.

I must admit that in the last year or two interest in the ballet has considerably declined, and it is only the name of Pavlova that kept it at its rightful level. Where she did not show herself for a long time the attraction of the ballet dwindled and consequently the number of pupils to enter the schools diminished.

Letters of thanks came from various schools and teachers, who wrote in this strain: "Madame, you do not know what we owe you. Your arrival has revived the interest in dancing; our schools, which were rapidly losing ground, have now taken on a new lease of life. Your art shows

Pavlova and Vladimiroff.
(Photograph by Yarovoff, Montevideo.)

what heights can be reached and that attracts the pupils, and the parents, who before were sceptical of the ballet as a possible career for their children, have now quite changed their views."

One of the reasons that made Pavlova agree to another American tour, which was to have begun in October 1931, was that she received so many letters from various parts of America begging her to come and save the position of the ballet. In America her prestige was unequalled. She was the first to show that country what dancing was, and for the Americans has always remained "the incomparable Pavlova". In many papers, in speeches made in her honour, Americans have declared that they do not look upon her as a famous artist, but as a "national institution".

Pavlova's visit to America was important and necessary, for without her there was a gradual weakening of interest in the Ballet.

Americans love all novelties and throw themselves into them like children with new toys. The fashion, lately blown in, of "tap-dancing" — the beating of the rhythm with the heels as in negro dances — and other similar crazes completely absorb the American public, which has for the moment taken up very hotly this latest idea. Everyone wants to learn ,,tap-dancing" and therefore schools, if they hope to exist, must bring it into their curriculum. Woe to those teachers who should in the name of art decline to teach it! Such schools will have to close their doors, for classical dancing is not learnt any more, in any case not until a fresh change in taste is manifest, until the wind veers. Last year Wigman came to America with her school, and the Americans threw themselves on this novelty also.

A visit by the all-adored Pavlova had the effect of putting everything in proper perspective. Crammed theatres, immense success, enthusiastic press articles, silenced those who dared to raise a voice against the ballet. Pavlova's dances in themselves revived the belief in art, and the schools would begin to fill again with those who wanted seriously to study. Tap-dancing and other novelties would be thrust aside — it is true, only until the appearance of the next new craze.

Pavlova was often asked why she kept a company, costing a great deal of money and necessitating a heavy outlay; why she assigned such large sums for production and the maintaining of a large staff; for all this, it was said, hampered her freedom. Having a company, her time was not her own, for she had always to see that her dancers and employees were not left without work.

This question was put to Pavlova a long time ago by American impresarios, who tried to persuade her to give up her company and the enormous accessories it entailed, promising to pay her and her dancing partner the same sums as she was being paid for bringing the whole company. In this way she would be making very much more money. It was also more profitable for them, as they would be economising on the transport of so many people and of the baggage.

Much in this proposal was very tempting, for it did away with the worry and anxiety inseparable from a large and complicated enterprise. Every year new scenery and costumes, costing large sums of money, had to be ordered, music had to be found, new ballets staged, without knowing whether they would be a success, though certain in advance that a portion of the public and press would find them in any case old-fashioned and not like those to which one had lately become accustomed.

To throw all this aside, to become free of all responsibilities entailed by having a company was, I repeat, tempting, but in spite of the attractiveness of such offers, Pavlova did not decide to accept them for two reasons.

First of all, without a company of her own Pavlova could not have given her own ballets, and could not, therefore, have appeared before the public in her favourite parts, such as those in "Giselle", "Chopiniana", "Autumn Leaves". It would have meant limiting herself to concert programmes made up of separate dancing numbers, or dancing in the already-existing ballets like those of the Grand Opera in Paris or the Metropolitan in New York, or other theatres with a repertoire of their own, repertoires in the majority of cases quite unsuited to her. Whereas, by having a company, she could choose her repertoire, developing her business in the direction she considered best.

Secondly, having her own organization with a permanent troupe of dancers and a number of employees around her, she could not have given them up after so many years of devoted work together.

With the advent of the world crisis of the last few years and the consequent decline in theatrical business, parting with the company would have been perfectly justified. But then came the question — how could one discharge the company in these difficult times, knowing that the dancers had practically no chance of finding other employment?

Taking all this into account, therefore, we continued our tours, Pavlova dancing five or six times a week, often under conditions of great difficulty, only doing this so that the dancers and the staff should continue to receive their salaries. Pavlova herself made nothing and I was glad if I could meet expenses.

In bringing this chapter to an end, I consider it my duty to draw attention to a little-known fact, namely that in all the years of her career and work, Pavlova never received any subsidies. No one gave her money to finance the business, never did she approach any art-patrons, but carried on the concern solely with her own money and at her own risk.

Several times, it is true, she had been offered sums of money to finance her undertaking, to make it into a corporation or syndicate in her name, and put a large capital into it. From a business point of view, I advised her to accept these suggestions, which took the risk off her shoulders and gave more lavish means for staging new ballets, but each time she firmly refused to consider them.

"How can I agree", she would say, "that people should risk their money by putting it into a business that depends wholly on my success and on the success of my productions? The consciousness of accepting such a responsibility would be torture to me and when anything was not successful, I should feel miserable as one having failed in a trust."

Pavlova with few members of her Company in "Sleeping Beauty".

Pavlova with Volinine in "Gavote".
(Photograph by Times Photo, London.)

CHAPTER VI.

DANCING PARTNERS AND CONDUCTORS.

The first partner with whom Pavlova danced was M. Fokine in the ballet "Harlequinade" in St. Petersburg. She also danced quite often with him later, when she was a ballerina. He danced the chief role with her in the important ballet "Paquita" and it was with him that she appeared in practically all the early ballets of his composition — "Pavillon d'Armide", "Nights of Egypt", "Sylphides".

Fokine was a magnificent dancer, very graceful and very strong. Unfortunately, his activity as a maitre de ballet prevented him from keeping up his dancing, and after leaving Russia he practically gave it up.

I found Fokine an ideal partner for Pavlova in height as well as in figure and there can be no doubt that his ballets were never better performed than by Pavlova and himself. This is quite natural, for in all his first works he gave the chief parts to Pavlova, working out all the details and discussing his ideas with her. She liked working with him and, as I have already said, always faithfully and disinterestedly acted as material for his productions. When they took the chief parts in his ballets, the result could not bettered. I found, for instance, that when Fokine danced the famous valse in "Sylphides" with Pavlova, the impression was finer even than when Nijinsky was her partner.

Pavlova also danced a great deal with her former teacher, P. Gerdt. In spite of being nearly sixty years of age at the time, he looked a handsome young man on the stage, so fine was his carriage. In the first ballet that Pavlova danced with him, "The Awakening of Flora", she was Flora and he was Phoebus. Later she danced with him the long and important ballet "La Bayadère", in which there are many classical dances requiring much "supporting". After "La Bayadère" she danced "Paquita" with him and "The Corsair", and then the huge ballet "The Daughter of Pharaoh", in which Gerdt not only "supported" her, but danced with her.

Then, when Gerdt gave up dancing and confined himself to acting parts only, Pavlova's partner in "Paquita" and "La Bayadère" was the young and capable Andrianov. She danced "Giselle" with the well-known dancer of the St. Petersburg ballet, N. Legat, (later a maitre de ballet). N. Legat and his brother Sergei were the favourite pupils of the eminent choreographist Ch. Johannsen. They were both fine dancers of a strictly classical style and excellent partners.

On her first tour abroad Pavlova was partnered by A. Bolm. He was also a dancer of the St. Petersburg ballet, and was the organiser of the tour. He too was an excellent dancer. Eventually he joined the Diaghilev company when it went to America, where he remained and worked a good deal, dancing separately and then becoming the maitre de ballet of the "Metropolitan" and of the Chicago Opera. He also opened a school of his own. Being greatly attached to his art and deeply interested in it, he always searched for something new in all the countries he visited and with this in view frequented all the museums. He successfully composed several ballets.

On her second tour abroad Pavlova had two dancing partners — N. Legat and A. Bolm. When this tour ended in Vienna, she immediately proceeded to Paris in order to take part in Diaghilev's season. There she had to dance with Nijinsky, Fokine and Kozlov. It so happened that once she had to appear with Nijinsky at a charity performance at the Grand Opera. On the eve of the performance he was suddenly taken ill and she had to dance impromptu with M. Mordkin. She took a great liking to him as a dancing partner and invited him to dance with her in London, where she was to appear before King Edward VII. At her wish, a contract was also made with Mordkin by the Palace Theatre.

On her first American tour, where she was booked for a whole month for the „Metropolitan", she also danced with Mordkin, as well as during her extensive tour in North America. M. Mordkin graduated in the Moscow Theatrical School, remained in the service of the Bolshoi Theatre and soon made a name for himself as one of the foremost dancers. His dances were not remarkable for their virtuosity, but he could show them off to great advantage, as he had a fine, powerful figure, an expressive face, and was an excellent actor and mime.

Pavlova, frail and slender, and Mordkin, in complete contrast, strong and manly, suited each other remarkably well; many of their dances together will remain forever in the memory. When Pavlova was first seen in America with Mordkin, the combination was considered ideal and her dancing partners who later replaced Mordkin found some difficulty in making the audience forget their predecessor.

Her next partner was L. Novikov, whose acquaintance Pavlova had made during his stay in London, where he danced on the stage of the Alhambra Theatre with Geltzer, Tikhomirov and a large company of Russian dancers.

Like Mordkin, Novikov was a pupil of V. Tikhomirov and graduated from the Moscow Ballet School. He came to the fore swiftly, being very soon given responsible parts and dancing the principal roles with the ballerinas. Novikov belonged to the severely classical dancers, had a great mastery of technique and a very fine 'leap'. Pavlova engaged him for her last weeks at the Palace Theatre and discovering that he "supported" her very well, suggested that the should join her in her forthcoming tour in America.

Novikov danced with her for three years, during which he took his place in the repertoire and accompanied Pavlova in the ballets "Giselle", "Preludes", "Chopiniana", "The Fairy Doll" and others. He then went back to Moscow, where he remained all through the War.

In the summer of 1914 V. Tikhomirov danced with Pavlova. He was a fine artist and teacher. All the best Moscow male dancers were his pupils — Mordkin, Volinin, Novikov, Zjukov, Svoboda and many others. In spite of his great height and big build, Tikhomirov was noted for his remarkable lightness. For their correctness, crispness and finish, his dances can be considered models of the classical school.

In the autumn of 1914, just before the war, Pavlova took as dancing

Uda Shankar as Krishna in the ballet "Oriental Impressions".

Pavlova as Rhada in "Oriental Impressions".

partner A. Volinin, who remained in that capacity for the following seven years. In my opinion, as a dancer, Volinin can be considered the finest after Nijinsky. He possesses all the necessary qualities — he is ideally made, his spare, slender figure does not show up his muscular development, and only at the moment when, without the slightest effort, he lifts the ballerina, can one judge of his strength. His technique leaves nothing to be desired, he is very light and can 'leap' magnificently. Considering his natural gifts and the fine results which he has achieved, one can confidently assert that had he been as assiduous in his work as many of the others he would have attained remarkable heights.

Pavlova was very fond of him as a partner who worked conscientiously and one who was moreover a very agreeable and charming man. An excellent comrade and a kind, thoughtful friend. Volinin was a general favourite with the whole company.

For a period of five years after 1922 Pavlova was again partnered by L. Novikov and during our last tour in America she had two partners simultaneously — Volinin and Novikov.

When their dancing careers were over, Volinin opened a school in Paris and Novikov became the maitre de ballet of the Chicago opera and the director of its school.

Pavlova's last dancing partner was P. Vladimirov. As she was a pupil of the St. Petersburg Theatrical School, it is strange that during the whole of her stage career abroad her partners invariably came from Moscow, Vladimirov being the only one from the same school as herself.

I recollect the first years of Vladimirov's career. He was considered to be of great promise, promise which he has since fulfilled, being a first-class dancer. Unfortunately the revolution, escape from Russia, absence of theatres in which he could continue working seriously, only gave him opportunities of a casual nature for dancing. He did work in Diaghilev's company, but the atmosphere there proved unsuitable to him, as he was a classical dancer. He was a splendid partner, very attentive, careful and thoughtful.

For a comparatively short time Pavlova also danced with Nijinsky, chiefly in "Sylphides" and "Giselle". Of course Pavlova placed him very high as a dancer and liked dancing "Sylphides" with him; his acting in "Giselle" however did not satisfy her, which is not surprising as acting was never his strong point.

I cannot pass without mention another collaborator of Pavlova's, one who was with her for eleven years, M. Pianovsky. A graduate of the Warsaw ballet school, he remained on the stage of the State theatre after finishing; later, he joined Diaghilev's company and was in it for some years. After leaving Diaghilev, he received an engagement as maitre de ballet in South America, where he met us and joined our company in the capacity of Clustine's assistant.

Pianovsky is a very capable dancer. He used to dance in ballets — in "Polish Wedding" for instance, a ballet of his own composition — and also in separate numbers. Possessing a wonderful memory and being musical, Pianovsky used to rehearse all the ballets that were given by us and when any new ones were added, he would be present while they were being staged assisting the maitre de ballet, and in the end always knew the ballet as well as the author himself. His knowledge of the business and his capacity for work made him very useful in the company; he always carried through with complete success the very responsible and difficult task of keeping in order our large repertoire and having everything in readiness.

When Pavlova left the school and went on the stage, her first conductor was R. Drigo. He was originally the musical director of the opera in St. Petersburg and on its abolition was made the leader of the Imperial Ballet. In spite of the fact that this field of activity was only known to him in operas, he very quickly familiarized himself with it and became quite an outstanding ballet conductor.

Being present at all the rehearsals, for which he often played the piano himself, he could conduct almost the entire repertoire without the score, and could thus devote his whole attention to the stage and the dancers. He knew everybody in the company from the time they were on school benches and could tell infallibly when a certain dancer was not feeling very strong and required a slower tempo, and when another, on the contrary, required it quickened. All the dancers knew that with him they could feel at ease — maestro Drigo could always be relied upon to come to the rescue. At the same time he was an excellent musician and wrote a number of tuneful ballets, which were never removed from the repertoire. If he noticed that some variation did not suit the dancer who had to perform it, he would write a new one and present it to the executant. In this way he wrote two very fine variations for Pavlova.

One was a harp solo for the ballet "Paquita" and the other in "Pharaoh's Daughter". Drigo loved his work and was so beloved and esteemed by all around him — not only by the company, but also by the orchestra — that in spite of his advanced years he did not want to relinquish his post.

During our stay in Italy we went to visit him in Padua, where he was born and where he always stayed when he went to his own country for a holiday. The little house standing in the shade of a huge fig-tree, bearing several hundred pounds of fruit each year, was filled with photographs, presentation

Pavlova with Novikoff and Domoslavski in "Christmas".

pieces and all kinds of souvenirs of his beloved St. Petersburg, where nearly the whole of his life had been spent.

Another musical director with whom Pavlova had much to do in St. Petersburg was the famous musician and opera conductor Napravnik, who was much respected and whose prestige was quite exceptional. Pavlova had to dance in several operas in which there are important ballets — "Russlan and Ludmilla", "Carmen", "The Demon", etc. She used to say that Napravnik gave proof of rare sensitiveness and understanding of the dance, watching carefully and helping the dancer in every possible way.

Abroad, in Diaghilev's ballet season, the conductor was N. Tcherepnin, a professor of the St. Petersburg conservatoire and the composer of many

Pavlova with Volinine and Company in the Ballet "The Awakening of the Flora".
(Times Photo. London.)

ballets. In later times he wrote three ballets for Pavlova and came to London for their rehearsal and to conduct them on the opening nights.

At the Palace Theatre in London, where Pavlova danced for five summer seasons, the conductor was a talented Englishman, Mr. Finck, himself the composer of much melodious popular music. He was very quick to grasp what Pavlova needed, and in all those years there was never the slightest friction between them.

A conductor was required for her first tour in America and fate brought her and Theodore Stier together. He later became her faithful musical director and friend for fourteen years. By nationality an Austrian who had finished the violin course of the Vienna conservatoire, Stier was quite a young man when he came to England and settled there. He first played the violin in one of the symphony orchestras and then in the small private orchestra of the Prince of Wales (later King Edward VII), who was very fond of music. Afterwards Stier became a conductor and for some years was at the head of the concerts of classical music in London.

Stier was a good and serious musician, perhaps too conservative, but a conscientious and hard worker. For her first American season Pavlova only stood in need of two programmes, which were therefore repeated all the time. Stier, of course, grew to know them perfectly. For the next tour two other programmes were wanted, and so on. In this way he gradually learnt the whole repertoire; having worked through every ballet dozens of times from beginning to end, he grew to know all Pavlova's requirements and every one of her dances by heart. I do no think that he had much understanding of the dance, but he was so conscientious in his close study of every ballet, that Pavlova could be perfectly at ease with him, and he spared her the trouble of being personally present at the orchestral rehearsal in every new town.

In private life Stier was an exceedingly pleasant, tactful man; he was fond of company, spoke French as well as English, was an excellent conversationalist and Pavlova's devoted friend. Sudden heart trouble, however, put an end to his career. After having conducted the orchestra during the Covent Garden season and the short tour through England in 1925, he had to leave Pavlova. In the spring of 1927 he died.

When America joined in the War, Stier, in New York at the time, was interned as an Austrian, and therefore could not accompany us to South America. His place was temporarily taken by Alexander Smolens, a very capable musician working with the Boston opera. Smolens, being Russian by origin was very much in sympathy with Russian music and consequently conducted Tchaikovsky and Glazounov ballets excellently.

It fell to his lot to work very hard during our South American tour.

Orchestras in such countries as Costa Rica, Ecuador, Venezuela proved to be beneath all criticism. To have endless and constant rehearsals with them in the tropical heat was a torment and it was only by his wonderful tirelessness and energy that he managed to keep it up, often sitting down to the piano himself when he noticed the orchestra going astray and humming when some instrument failed.

One would imagine that in such countries audiences would not be such sticklers for etiquette. Smolens, suffering from the terrible heat, which was increased by the amount of energy necessary to conduct the orchestra, had a dress coat made of a thin black material. But the very next day after he first wore it, the critics, while praising the performance, mentioned also the conductor, but referred to him in every instance as "the gentleman in the alpaca dress coat". Much to his distress, he had, consequently, to return to his legitimate evening clothes.

When we finished our English season of 1925, we had tours in South Africa and Australia before us. A few years earlier we had made the acquaintance of L. Wurmser, who conducted the orchestra for Pavlova during the whole of her season at the Champs Elysées in Paris, and we decided to engage him as our conductor, knowing him to be an excellent musician and a very pleasant man. He accompanied us on the whole of our 1925/26 tour and in the autumn of 1926 went with us on a tour in Germany. During this journey we made the acquaintance in Stuttgart of the young conductor of the local symphony orchestra, E. Kurtz. This young man had finished the St. Petersburg conservatoire in Glazounov's class of composition, then worked for some time under Nikisch and gave concerts of his own, which drew attention to him, and was finally engaged by the town of Stuttgart. He was only busy for about half the year and could therefore accept our offer to conduct for us during our short seasons. His first appearance in England was in Covent Garden in 1927, then in Paris in the spring of 1928, in Barcelona and finally he accompanied us on a long tour in Australia.

Taking advantage of the fact that the conductor of the Zagreb opera house, Baranovitch, was free during the season of 1927/28, we asked him to come to us, taking E. Schicketanz as second-conductor.

Baranovitch proved to be a splendid musician and conductor, and we were very sorry when we were obliged to part with him on his resuming his appointment at Zagreb.

We also had as conductor W. Hyden, who was with us for a short time in 1927 and also took part in our oriental tour in 1929. Mr. W. Hyden was a good pianist, but there was often trouble between him and Pavlova when he conducted. He made the mistake, common to young and at the same time self-assured conductors, of thinking music to be the chief part of a ballet, forgetting that though music is a very important element in dancing, it is nevertheless only a component part, as an accompaniment. Of all the conductors who worked with Pavlova, W. Hyden was the only one to consider that her art should subordinate itself to his baton, and not the orchestra's part to follow her and help her to express what she was interpreting in her dance. Eventually we parted with him.

From that time and until Pavlova's death, our conductor for the last two seasons was E. Schicketanz. After so many changes and the constant rehearsals they entailed — for with each new conductor it was necessary to go through the whole repertoire — Pavlova could breathe freely.

E. Schicketanz, an extremely modest, hard-working man and an excellent musician, understood Pavlova's requirements and by watching her very attentively, did his utmost to help her. He remembered every detail and his memory never played him false. It was customary after every performance for the conductor to come round to Pavlova and have pointed out to him either any shortcomings or the necessity for some alteration for the next performance. Schicketanz, like all the others, used to appear every evening. Halfway through the first season, however, Pavlova told him, with a smile of satisfaction, that he need not come again as everything was going so well.

A very fine conductor was the young and gifted Frenchman, A. Goldschmann. He conducted the orchestra for Pavlova's brilliant performance in the park of the Bagatelle and the performances in the Trocadero.

Goldschmann belongs to a very rare type of conductor. He is extremely sensitive to dance and is instantly able to grasp what is required. Owing to the continual change of programme, he had frequently to conduct a large symphony orchestra after only one rehearsal.

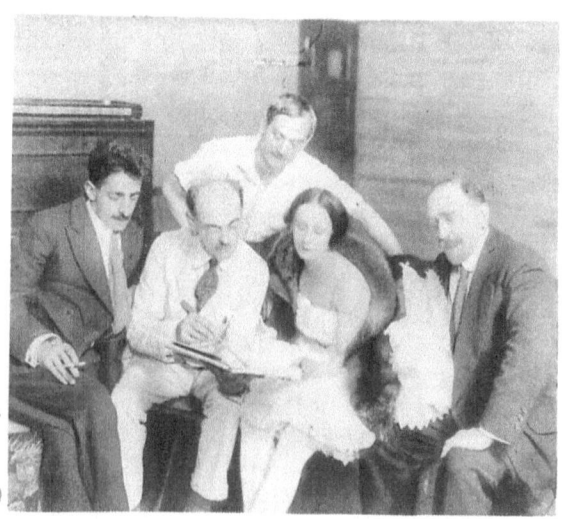

Pavlova at Rehearsal with Stier (in the centre) Clustine (on the right) Volinine (at back) and Smollens. (Photograph by White, New York.)

Pavlova with Vladimiroff, Varzinski, Hitchins and Sergieff in the "Invitation to the Dance".

CHAPTER VII.

BEHIND THE SCENES.

Probably not many of those who saw Pavlova on the stage creating those visions of beauty and smothered in flowers, have stopped to ask themselves what the life of this "spoilt child of Fortune", as many considered her, was really like, how she lived during those constant tours, and under what conditions she had to work.

Before going on with my story, however, I must give a description, though only a short one, of the present position of the theatrical business. When I speak of the theatre, I mean serious theatre — drama, comedy, opera and ballet — performances in other words, of an artistic nature.

During the War it became noticeable that those who were passing through its horrors preferred to seek oblivion and look for relaxation in spectacles of a light and cheerful order. For those arriving from the Front, as well as those remaining at home, the serious theatre held no attraction, the productions it had to offer lost all appeal.

By the end of the War, the public's taste for frivolous shows had taken firm root, and to this was added a phenomenon of another nature, namely, the loss of the more cultured public, those habituated to and liking the serious theatre, who were now obliged to cut down expenses owing to the increased cost of living and the growth of taxation, and had, consequently, almost entirely to give up going to the theatre. The new type of public, however, the people enriched by the war, take no interest whatever in art, frequenting only the cinema or the music-hall.

This phenomenon has repeated itself everywhere, and even Germany, which has always supported the theatre and music, has not been able to escape it. On our arrival in Berlin in 1925, for the first time after the War, we were amazed at the decadence of the German theatre. Whereas in earlier times one heard of the great success achieved by new plays of note, or of the appearance of new artists of distinction, now we came to the conclusion that there was nothing new or notable and that the public was not interested in serious productions. The magnificent state opera and drama, despite the facilities granted to the poor by the socialist government, were only filled to sixty per cent of their capacity, while nine theatres, giving revues with naked women, were doing splendid business.

At the same time the improved cinematograph and the advent of talkies, owing to their cheapness, began more and more to draw the public away from the serious theatre. Then came the world trade crisis, which, affecting in varying degrees every branch of commerce and industry, was naturally bound to have an enormous effect on the theatre. While on this subject I cannot refrain from mentioning one very peculiar aspect: in the general rise of prices for all commodities of primary necessity, the public is very often obliged to pay as much as twice and even three times the pre-war prices. Labour has also gone up very considerably. And at the same time prices went on rising for several years after the war had come to an end. And yet, all this frantic rise has not touched one thing-the salaries of artists (other than those connected with revue and variety). It would seem only natural, that if the prices of rents, food and their clothes have gone up, salaries, the price of their work, should go up also. But this did not take place. There are two reasons for this in my opinion. Firstly the prices of theatre seats have increased very little. They have, of course, not quintupled in price in Paris in proportion to the fall of the franc. Secondly, there is the absence of a strong actors' union. They are not united even up to the present and cannot fight for their own interests as, for instance, the united musicians, who have succeeded in getting their salaries doubled, or the scene-shifters.

Of late years, the crisis has become still more acute and in certain countries (Germany, for instance) it has brought the theatrical business almost to the point of catastrophe. Germany more than any other country seriously supported theatrical and musical art, the Germans seeing in music and the drama a necessity rather than an amusement. Neither the inflation nor the parlous state of the treasury deprived state theatres of their considerable subsidies. Apart from state theatres, the German government also helped municipalities to maintain their symphonic orchestras and their theatres. Even as late as 1929 there were 55 opera theatres in Germany, maintaining excellent orchestras and operatic and dramatic companies. Naturally, paying only modest salaries, these theatres could not have any out-of-the-way performers, but in the matter of artistic unity and musical execution their performances were excellent.

Some of these theatres gave what were certainly model productions. They had well defined budgets, which were calculated over a season of eight to nine months. The crisis affected the receipts of the box-office, thereby upsetting calculations, and the theatres, unable to pay the salaries of their actors and employees, were forced to curtail their seasons and finish earlier.

The growing poverty of the public made the lowering of prices for tickets a necessity and the resultant position became quite untenable. Whereas scenery, costumes, labour, musicians, railways, advertisements, everything in fact connected with theatrical production had gone up very considerably in price, the theatres were forced to give performances at cheap rates.

This matter of lowering the prices was regarded so seriously, that when German municipalities leased us their theatres, we were obliged to accept their schedule of prices for the seats.

So expensive an organisation as ours could not give performances at cheap prices and we had sometimes long arguments with the municipalities before agreeing on what we considered a possible minimum. It was very difficult to economise in our business, and to cover the outlay there was only one way, namely, to give as many performances in the week as possible, for whether four or six performances are given, the weekly expenses remain the same.

It is a recognised practice in England and America that the number of performances in the week be eight (six evening performances and two matinees). In other countries the number is generally six or seven.

The most profitable tours are the American ones, as a definite sum is paid there per week. On knowing beforehand the number of weeks a tour will last, an exact calculation can be made of all the monies to be allotted.

Pavlova with Novikoff in "Bacchanale".
(Photograph by Schneider, Berlin.)

Pavlova in the ballet from the opera "Orpheus and Euredice".
(Photograph by Strauss-Peyton, Kansas City.)

But Pavlova found these tours very fatiguing, for they used to last for twenty to twenty-five weeks without a break and eight performances had to be given every week, with constant travelling in between.

According to the custom in America, companies like ours could not stay more than three days even in large towns of a million inhabitants, like St. Louis or Pittsburg. A very large number of towns could not support more than one performance with the result that for some weeks we would have to give a performance in a different town every evening. One of the greatest difficulties from which Pavlova suffered was the prolonged journeys by train. Two or three hours were bearable, but it was very difficult to dance after five or six hours passed in a railway carriage. Pavlova found that from the shaking the muscles lost their elasticity and to regain it much work was necessary before the performance.

Another thing which upset Pavlova and all the members of the company was the early departures, for often it was necessary to leave one town in the early morning in order to be in time for the performance at the next. In such cases the train frequently left at 8 or even 7 a. m. and as dancers do not go to bed directly after a performance they all used to come to the station insufficiently rested and depressed.

In all other countries we arranged our tours independently and at our own risk, thus having the possibility of deciding in advance the length of the tour, any breaks between the performances (even short ones), or the longer stays in certain towns. Pavlova preferred touring Europe, as, having a liking for old towns, paintings and more particularly for sculpture, she had the opportunity of either taking a drive through the town, visiting a museum or examining the statues.

But of all the tours, two — in the Far East and Australia, and her tours in South America, gave her most pleasure. The East had a strong attraction for her, more particularly India. She adored that country, having quite a special feeling for it. She liked the scenery, was interested in the various types of people, was full of admiration for the brightly-coloured costumes, the grace of the women, the simplicity of the people, their holy poverty. She felt very well there and was so bright and happy, she vowed that she could spend her whole life in that country. And the tours in the East, Australia and South America were far less tiring, for one was able to stay in one place for several weeks and the long voyages from one place to another also acted as a rest.

But no matter in what part of the world the tour might be, the manner of life and the character of the work remained much the same.

Preparations began a long time in advance. New scenery had to be ordered, new costumes made and old ones renovated and boxes and trunks repaired — a considerable item in itself. The transport and delivery of baggage is always a great problem for any company with an extensive repertoire. On our long tours our luggage would frequently amount to 400 pieces, consisting of about 40 cases of scenery each weighing from 400 to 700 lbs., many boxes of stage properties, about 120 baskets and trunks with costumes and ballet skirts, several cases with electrical appliances, music, wigs, shoes, etc. and also the private luggage of the dancers.

On a journey by boat the transport of the luggage is considerably simplified.

In the case of train journeys, however, a very important consideration is the arranging for the transport at the most economical scale of charges, which is of course transport by goods train.

Then comes the problem of delivery from the station to the theatre. Here it was also necessary to economise, for transport by lorries is an expensive business. It had therefore to be arranged that on the arrival of the goods train in some town the luggage vans should be opened and what was required for the first performance taken out.

All this was arranged and as a rule worked very well, but if there was a sudden change just before the performance, it entailed the hurried dispatch of people to the station, the finding of the van and the search in the darkness with only the help of pocket lamps, for some necessary trunk or basket.

When organising long tours in Europe, we decided to have motor lorries of our own in order to simplify all these matters, and bought a large powerful car to which a trailer of the same size could be attached.

This system was excellent when the distance to be covered was not very great but in the case of long journeys mishaps were not infrequent. Our heavily loaded car could do a maximum of 20 kilometres an hour, and thus if the journey was one of 150/200 kilometres the car would have to start immediately after the performance and travel all night and more than once it was delayed en route by snow or rain and turned up only at the last moment. After trying this mode of transport for two seasons we gave it up and went back to railways.

We made up a company of 45 to 47 persons, sometimes more; the ballet itself consisted of 32—33 performers; 4 to look after the wardrobe, a hairdresser, a mechanic, an electrician, the conductor (sometimes two), 3 soloist musicians, myself and my secretary.

The tour was, of course, arranged a long time in advance, every town booked in dates up to the date of leaving, so that the dancers were given a printed list with the dates, towns, the number of performances in each place, the names of the theatres and the addresses of the hotels.

Pavlova with Novikoff in "Chopiniana".
(*Photograph by Spencer Stier, Melbourne.*)

Pavlova with Novikoff and the Company in "Chopiniana".
(Photograph by Spencer Stier, Melbourne.)

As a rule we arrived in the first town two or three days before time, in order to rehearse and make final arrangements. For Pavlova the arrival in every town began with an invariable welcome at the station. When the distance from one place to the next was considerable, the journey was usually made at night and we used to arrive in the early morning, and frequently Pavlova, tired and sleepy, would have to leave the carriage and receive representatives of the town, of local societies, deputations from schools and other bodies and finally to pose to a dozen or more photographers, to say nothing of two or three cinematograph operators. And all this accompanied by an immense concourse of curious people.

Invariably one would notice one and the same scene; at the moment of taking the picture those near Pavlova, artists or her representatives were pushed aside and perfectly unknown persons surrounded her, evidently people suffering from an unconquerable desire to appear in the papers next to the great dancer. The welcome at the station over, we would go to our hotel, where interviewers were already awaiting Pavlova and a conversation on general topics lasting about an hour would take place. The more important newspapers would also ask for a separate interview for their representative.

Pavlova disliked interviews; the majority of the questions put to her were banal and uninteresting. I had always to be present, for left to herself Pavlova was always afraid of saying more than was necessary and the answers given had very often to be extremely diplomatic, so as not to find oneself in an awkward position later. Being by nature very sincere and straightforward, Pavlova always detested what she called "shuffling". Occasionally, however, the interviewer would prove to be a man with a love for and an understanding of art, one who had prepared himself for the conversation and would ask Pavlova interesting questions, and then she would eagerly give expression to her thoughts, talk about her plans, about modern tendencies in art, etc. Unfortunately this did not happen very often; in the majority of cases the interviewers confined themselves to such questions as how she liked the town, where had she come from, was it true that she used up ten thousand pairs of shoes a year and so on, invariably ending with:

"What does Madame Pavlova think of modern dances?"

Interviewers, especially in America, at the end of the conversation, would very often ask her to relate some humourous episode. This was most distasteful to her and she always answered a request of this nature by saying coldly that her art, for which she had a profound respect, did not lend itself to funny stories or anecdotes.

After the interviews were over, Pavlova would go to her room to unpack and to rest, and I to the theatre, where the local administration, the conductor, the maitre de ballet and our employees were awaiting me. The rehearsals had to be fixed for the orchestra and for the ballet, dressing rooms had to be allotted, etc.

The most important question of all was the quality of the floor on the stage, and also the powers of the local orchestra. Where dancing is concerned, the floor, of course, is of the utmost importance. For the opera and the drama, where the actors only walk, the floor is a secondary matter. And as the arrival of a ballet is always an exception, whereas operas and dramas run all the year round, it stands to reason that nobody worries very much about the state of the floor and it was frequently found to be in a truly awful condition — warped with age, showing enormous cracks, made of uneven planks, bumps here, holes there, etc.

On our arrival in Milan, we found the floor in such a state that dancing on it was obviously impossible. A linoleum factory had immediately to be visited and a thick linoleum of a suitable colour chosen wherewith the whole stage had to be covered. All possibility of catching the foot in a crack or tripping over an unevenness was thus eliminated, but Pavlova complained that the linoleum robs dancing of its crispness. However, the covering of the stage with linoleum, the planing of the planks, etc. are only possible expedients when there are two, or at least one free day before the performance. When we arrived on the day itself only very minor repairs could be effected, such as filling in the cracks with strips, covering the holes with tin plates and stretching over all the large linen carpet we carried with us. Frequently, however, one had to content oneself with marking off the dangerous places with chalk, in order that Pavlova should as far as possible avoid them.

I made the experiment once in America of having a portable floor made. It consisted of fitted boards firmly nailed to a cloth, which could be rolled up when being removed and when laid out on the stage gave an ideally smooth surface. But Pavlova was unable to dance on it; the feeling of a floor was lost. For her the floor was necessarily of vital importance, and it was quite painful to see how she suffered, at times undergoing sheer physical pain, forced to think where to step and always having to be on her guard, at a time when her whole heart and soul should have been given to the creation of such artistic images as her spectators should carry away and treasure ever after. For, after all, some of them had come distances of nearly three hundred miles, as was frequently the case in South Africa, New Zealand and even North America.

In spite of our caution however, it did happen in India once that a plank on which Pavlova stepped broke under her. Fortunately, the tightly stretched linen carpet saved her from falling through.

The Company in "Chopiniana".

The size of the stage, as well as the condition of the floor is of great importance. Australia possesses magnificent large theatres but with the exception of the comparatively good theatres in Egypt and Singapore and a fine new theatre in Calcutta those in the East are small, inconvenient and badly equipped. Our scenery was made for large theatres and it was very difficult to get it into small ones. It had to be folded at the sides and at the top, creased and spoiled, with the result that its effect was lost, a matter though that did not appear to upset the unsophisticated audiences. All these artifices, however, tended to reduce the size of an already small stage, leaving practically no

The Company in "Chopiniana".

room for dancing, especially in the case of ballets like "Chopiniana" and "Invitation" to the Dance, where the costumes were very full.

Also we often had trouble when we gave the ballet "Don Quixote". The large number of additional artists and supers made it very difficult to stage the ballet on a small scale. Another difficulty was that this ballet required a house and a donkey. When we gave it for the first time in London the donkey brought to the theatre was a beautiful little animal, but the coffee coloured horse appeared far too smart and wellfed for the part. The matter was put right by an artist-decorator, who happened to be working in the theatre. What he did was very simple; he painted such prominent ribs and gave the horse such a wretched look, that on the day after the performance an inspector of the R.S.P.C.A.* came to the theatre. He showed us a letter received by the Society from some tender-hearted old lady, saing that she had been indignant to see at our performance in what a terrible condition we kept our horse. But when he saw the horse without the make-up, the inspector was completely satisfied. It was only very tiresome that this make-up had to be put on anew at every performance for the horse's owner refused to ride it home in that state.

During our tour in America we had many amusing incidents with our horse and donkey. In spite of the fact that the local manager had been warned a long while before our arrival that these animals would be required for certain of our performances, it often happened on the day itself that the manager would come to explain that the town did not possess a single donkey and that the only hope was in the local Zoo. Sometimes the authorities at the Zoo would sympathise with our predicament and lend us a donkey in exchange for a few tickets for the performance. But such donkeys, unaccustomed to riders, would buck, refuse to go on the stage and cause endless trouble. It has actually happened that Sancho Panza has been obliged to make his entrance on foot. In one town, where a donkey was unobtainable, the local property-man suggested its place being taken by a pony.

"But what about the ears?" we asked him.

"I'll dress his ears up in covers shaped like the ears of a donkey," he replied.

"And what about the tail?"

But his inventive powers did not carry him so far, and Sancho Panza had to come on without a donkey.

The horse was also the cause of trouble. Horses used to be brought that in the majority of cases in no way fitted one's idea of Rosinante. The white horse obtained for us in Cleveland might be cited as an example. It was enormous and so broad that poor Don Quixote could hardly get his legs round it. When I was curious enough to enquire what the horse did in private life, its owner told me with great pride that it had been taking milk round the town for twenty-two years. It is most surprising that we never had any really serious trouble, for, excepting in London and New York, both the horse and the donkey were after all only débutantes, who had never before been on the stage, and it showed great good sense and self-control on their part not to be frightened by the unusual, bright lights, the lime-lights, the orchestra, the crowd of strangely dressed people and, last of all,

* Royal Society for the Prevention of Cruelty to Animals.

the dark cavern of the hall, from which came a thunder of applause. Once or twice, however, the horse under Don Quixote did get restive and the knight was obliged to climb down as quickly as possible and send Rosinante into the wings.

Apparently not all American critics are acquainted with the story of Don Quixote, for in one town the local critic, while praising the performance, expressed his surprise that the management could not provide Don Quixote with a better mount. "A knight like Don Quixote", explained the critic, "must naturally have had an excellent horse and not the wretched creature provided by the management."

We were once witnesses of the following incident. During that season Pavlova was touring in North America in conjunction with the Boston Opera Company, the performances combining separate ballets as well as operas. In Dallas (Texas) the opera "I Pagliacci" was given first with the ballet to follow. As is well-known, this opera requires a donkey harnessed to a cart in which the hero of the play drives into the market square of the little town where the action takes place. A donkey had been obtained. The stage of the huge "auditorium", where the performance takes place, was only some ten or twelve steps above the level of the street, but though planks had been laid down for it, the donkey refused to mount. Finally it was tied about with ropes, dragged on to the stage and harnessed. But when the moment came to drive out in front of the footlights, and Zenatello, who played the clown, got into the cart, the donkey turned obstinate. It was jerked, pushed, pummelled, but nothing did any good. The moment for beginning the aria could not be lost, and the members of the chorus pushed on the donkey and the cart. But even then, instead of drawing the cart, the donkey stuck his four legs into the ground and would not budge. The effect produced by this "entry" was most amusing. Eventually the opera came to an end, the donkey was unharnessed and its owner, a huge cowboy, had to take it away. But on approaching the stairs, the animal refused to descend. Neither beating nor coaxing had any effect, and as the stage-manager insisted upon it leaving before the ballet started the cow-boy, cursing, decided to employ, desperate measures — he squatted down, took the forelegs of the donkey upon his shoulders, heaved it upon his back and with a mighty effort descended the stairs. The donkey was of considerable size and must have been terribly heavy.

It is remarkable that always and everywhere the first appearance of Don Quixote and Sancho-Panza creates an impression. They seem to bring with them an atmosphere of humour and kindly good nature, and from that moment the admiring public takes them under its protection.

*

Pavlova in "Christmas".
(Photograph by d'Ora, Paris.)

Pavlova in "Christmas".
(Photograph by d'Ora, Paris.)

It is hardly necessary to explain that a good orchestra is essential to dancing. If in Europe or in America the quality of an orchestra depends on the cost, in a country like Egypt, and more especially in India or Java, there is no choice — one has to take such musicians as are available. And the musicians in these places are usually unable to play classical music. Fortunately, we always had three first-class soloists with us, a pianist, a violinist and a cellist, who not only played all Pavlova's solo parts, but at times even entire ballets, as for instance "Chopiniana" and "Autumn Leaves". I must say that the playing of "Autumn Leaves" by this well-disciplined trio was better and far more effective than that of a big and excellent orchestra.

The lighting is also of enormous importance to a ballet. Knowing how unsatisfactorily equipped are the majority of theatres, even European theatres, in this respect, we always carried lime-lights and about twenty hanging reflectors, with lamps of 2,000 watts each, in addition, of course, to a large number of spare lamps, some of which were smashed at every move. These lamps were our saving in cases when we could utilise them. But very often there was not enough current, or the local administration feared to do harm to the wiring and would not give us permission to use them. Performances in such cases had to take place in semi-darkness, and we could only follow Pavlova with the lime-lights in order that the audience should see her dancing and acting. Another difficulty was that the Arabs in Egypt, the Hindoos in India and the Malays in Java do not speak any European tongue. As a rule the foreman alone knows a few words; as for the rest, one has to explain oneself by signs.

And when one thinks that under such conditions the scenery was hung up, the stage repaired, the lighting seen to, the luggage distributed among the various dressing-rooms, it is a matter of wonder that the curtain rose at the time fixed, the performance was given, Pavlova danced and the public was satisfied.

Pavlova at all times was a model of energy and firmness, and was an example to everybody. But her creative work demanded a certain atmosphere, and if the floor was bad, the orchestra impossible, the dressing-rooms inconvenient, with no place even for exercises, Pavlova would be upset to the point of tears. Yet when the moment of facing the footlights drew near, everything would be forgotten: once more before us was a being exalted by inspiration, bountifully squandering the riches of her art before the astonished and conquered public.

But when the atmosphere was of the right kind, Pavlova would be happy and gay, and the performance would pass for her without conscious effort. When in this mood she would often say to me after it was over.

"Do you know, I'd dance the whole programme over again with pleasure."

If the tour was in America or in Europe and there were performances every day except Sunday, the whole of Pavlova's life was regulated by the clock and nothing was allowed to interfere with the routine. She rose at about 9 o'clock and by ten was already at the theatre starting her "work", i. e. going through all those exercises — first at the bar and then in the centre of the stage — which she considered necessary in order to have full control over her muscles and sinews.

This work went on for an hour-and-a-half or two hours, after which she took part in the rehearsal with the company. At about one o'clock the rehearsal would be over and everyone would go home to lunch. After lunch, if the weather were good and there was a park or anything of interest in the town, Pavlova would go out for half-an-hour. On returning, she would rest for an hour-and-a-half and at about six o'clock go to the theatre for the evening performance.

Putting on her rehearsing costume, she would start making-up (this she always did very artistically) and then go again on the stage to practise; after that she would put the finishing touches to her make-up, put on her wig and costume and be ready for her appearance on the stage.

She was always in a state of great agitation before the actual entry before the footlights. During an opera once she noticed behind the scenes that Chaliapin was also in a state of agitation before his appearance, and said laughingly to him:

"You are as excited before going on as I am."

To which he replied:

"I would not be Chaliapin, nor you Pavlova, if we were not excited."

During the interval she changed, putting on another wig, make-up and costume if necessary, invariably changing her shoes, in which she never danced more than one act, and drank a cup of weak tea. Under no circumstances would she allow any strangers on the stage during the performance and never received anybody in her dressing-room between the acts. At the end of the evening's performance, on the contrary, she liked people to come and see her. The nervous strain disappeared, she became gay and lively, exchanged impressions and willingly answered questions about the evening's performance. Nearly always some ten to fifteen local society people would come to make her acquaintance and to give utterance to their admiration. On her return home after the theatre, she would make a light supper and drink tea, but as the excitement after the performance did not calm down at once, she would spend an hour or so in conversation or reading before going to bed.

Pavlova in the Ballet "Dionysus".
(Photograph by Claude Harris, London.)

Newspaper interviewers and especially the representatives of fashion journals endeavoured to worm out her secret: How did Pavlova manage to retain her marvellously girlish figure?

They were convinced that she kept to some particular diet and would not believe her when she said that she ate everything, only avoiding, of course, dishes that were very rich; and that the whole of her secret lay in eating moderately and taking a great deal of physical exercise — that is, dancing.

Another "secret" that intrigued everybody was her wonderful complexion. And, indeed, she had made up for the stage for so many years that it was remarkable how she succeeded in keeping her skin so smooth and fresh. Everyone tried to find out what creams or lotions she used, and people were very disappointed when she told them that all her life she had used nothing but pure white vaseline.

Large sums were offered repeatedly to induce her to give her name to some cream and to certify that she used it, and each time she replied that she would willingly do so and give the money to her charities, but unfortunately could not, as she really could only recommend vaseline.

Pavlova in the ballet from the opera "Orpheus and Euredice".
(Photograph by Strauss-Peyton, Kansas City.)

During our tours in the East I always arranged for some free days between the performances, and such days were veritable holidays for Pavlova. Excursions to the Pyramids or in the desert on camels could be planned in Egypt; in India we went to see the glorious palaces in Delhi and Agra, and during our last Eastern tour (1929) we went to look at Benares, which had long had an attraction for Pavlova as the holy city of India.

We spent a day there, most of the time in a big boat floating slowly past the shores of the Ganges, admiring the beauty of the countless temples and palaces on the steep banks, and watching the hundreds of thousands of pilgrims gathered on the shores of the sacred river from all the corners of India for ablution and prayer. The expressions on the faces of these pilgrims, standing for hours in the water in an ecstasy of prayer, made a profound impression on Pavlova. Here, on the banks of the Ganges also smoked the pyres erected for the burning of corpses. The dream of every orthodox Hindoo is to be burnt after death on the banks of the Ganges and to have his ashes cast upon the waters.

We also made excursions in Java and in the Malay Peninsula, and were amazed at the luxuriant beauty of the tropical scenery. Pavlova was indefatigable in trips of this kind. Being well able to stand the heat, she could remain for hours under a blazing sun, and each such journey refreshed her and gave a new impetus to her work.

She grew very weary of hotel-life and liked to escape from it by arranging, even temporarily, something resembling real home-life. When we were in any town for several weeks, we used to rent a house and settle ourselves in it as at home — with our servants, Pavlova's birds and our personal belongings. On our last journey to Australia, we spent six weeks like this in Melbourne and another six in Sydney. We managed very well, especially in Sydney, where we had a house and a small garden in a lovely spot on the shores of the harbour. The house lay outside the town and it took twenty minutes by motorcar to reach the theatre. On some days the theatre had to be visited twice, but in spite of all such discomforts, Pavlova liked this "home-life" so much that she never even felt the fatigue.

As I have already mentioned, Pavlova was very fond of South America. There is a wonderful theatre in Buenos Aires, the Colon, which can be considered the finest opera theatre in the world. Its magnificent auditorium can seat 4,000, it has a beautiful foyer, is wonderfully equipped with all kinds of mechanical appliances, is excellently lighted and has all the necessary conveniences for the artists. There are also fine municipal theatres in Rio de Janeiro and San Paulo. The South American public is very fond of the ballet and Pavlova, immediately recognised as "La reina de la danza", was greatly admired and her performances were enormously successful.

Twice we crossed the Andes on our journeys between the Argentine and the Pacific Ocean. This often involves the risk of being held up for several weeks owing to the snow, and when this happens the pass has to be negotiated on mules.

Pavlova's success in Chile and Peru was even greater than in Brazil and the Argentine. The municipal council of Lima arranged a solemn banquet in her honour and presented her with a gold tablet on which a greeting was engraved.

Our first tour in Brazil began from the north. Prior to that we were in Porto Rico. Owing to war conditions the usual steamship lines were discontinued and I had to go hurriedly to New York to arrange for some steamer to agree to change its route and put into Porto Rico for our company.

The first town of Brazil that we came to was Para — a town lying on the Amazon, near its mouth, and formerly the centre of the world trade in rubber. Although the days of the town's glory are over, Para has nevertheless kept its excellent order and we found there to our surprise an admirable municipal theatre and a good hotel. As Para was the first Brazilian town in which Pavlova danced, the local scientific societies arranged a reception in her honour, at which were present the town dignitaries, representatives of the schools and a crowd of people. The president of the local geographical society welcomed Pavlova in the name of Brazil. At the end of her performances several other local organizations together with the press and the municipality decided also to give a reception in her honour and the town council resolved that a marble plaque should be put into the wall of the theatre, bearing the words "Anna Pavlova danced in this theatre". This made a very unpleasant impression on Pavlova, for it was her opinion that such things should not be done during the life of an artist. In spite of all my inducements, she refused to be present at the reception, and excused herself on the score of illness. The reception was very succesful, a great concourse of people was present, representatives of the municipality and the press made speeches pointing out the significance to the country of the arrival in it of an artist like Pavlova.

When musing on these distant countries, the lovely scenery and the magnificent towns, Pavlova would often ask herself where she would like to settle, and would invariably answer after some moments of reflection:

"Somewhere in Russia."

Having left the country sixteen years ago, knowing that everything there was no longer the same, she was nevertheless irresistibly drawn to it.

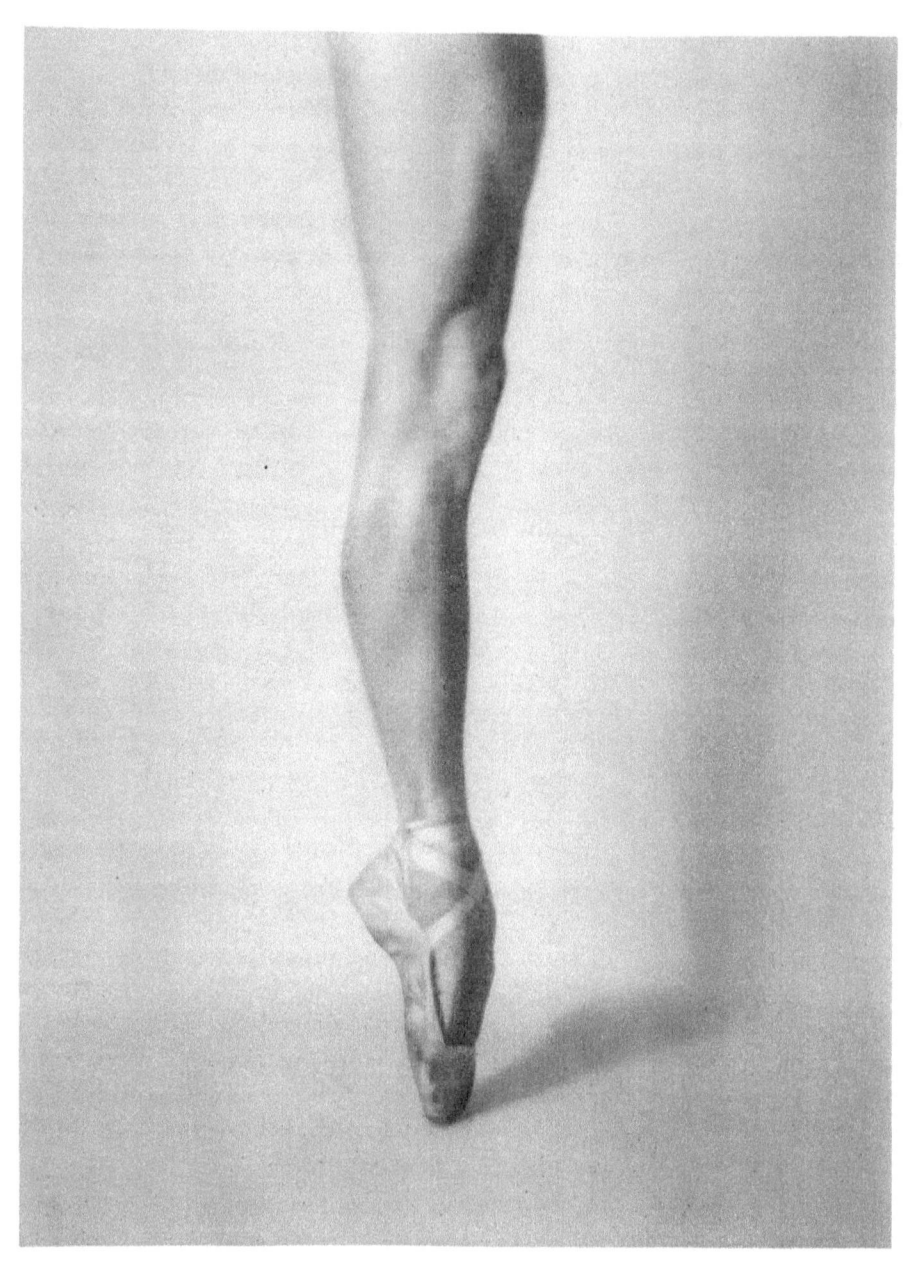

Pavlova's Foot.

Pavlova in "Chopiniana".
(Photograph by Andrew Studio, New Zealand.)

CHAPTER VIII.
IDEAS AND VIEWS.

As I had long and frequent discussions with Pavlova on many subjects, and was present at her interviews with the representatives of the press and during her conversations with friends, I have naturally, voluntarily and involuntarily, stored up in my mind her ideas and opinions on matters of art. I should like to give them here as nearly as possible in her own words:

"Every time before going on the stage, I feel that peculiar nervousness that is so well-known to novices and stage performers. As far as I myself am concerned, this nervousness, instead of diminishing as the years go by, has only increased. I am ever more conscious of the fact that with the growth of my reputation, my responsibility grows also. These feelings of anxiety, uneasiness and strain are always with me, I have them wherever I happen to be.

"I have never stopped learning and I continue to do so, always devoting the greatest care to perfecting my dancing. And I can therefore say with perfect sincerity that for my triumphs I am chiefly indebted to my ceaseless work. But much also is due to my teachers. My first steps after leaving the school were guided by Marius Petipa with whom I studied my first roles.

"In that I was particularly fortunate.

"Regarding the new tendencies and changes in the ballet, my views are very simple: I value Fokine very highly and am certain that of all the reformers of the dance he is the most gifted.

"He made use of me as material for his works. Our opinions have always agreed, we both sought new revelations in an art to which we were equally devoted and about the aims and problems of which we both think alike.

"It is my opinion that we must accept all that is beautiful in new artistic achievements, and at the same time not lose the courage to hold on to what is beautiful in the older forms as well. Looked at from that standpoint, much of what was left by Marius Petipa is remarkable. Art must not, and cannot remain static. Evolution is its law. We must be immeasurably grateful to Fokine for the innovations which he introduced into the frozen forms of our choreography. But it was Marius Petipa who cleared the path for Fokine and made his advent possible by placing our ballet on so high a pinnacle. In order to dance the new ballets successfully, it is indispensible to have passed through a school of classical dancing.

"Repeated praises have been sung to my talent. There is nothing secret about its evolution. This evolution has taken place before the eyes of all. From a timid and painstaking pupil, I became a dancer. But I felt that there were still imperfections in my art, which I tried to correct, tenaciously developing my abilities.

"And when I felt myself sufficiently strong, I gave myself up entirely to the creative impulse that was working in me. That would have been impossible without a good schooling and without practice. Abroad in various directions, it was said that my dancing contained something 'new'. But all that has been done by me is to make the physical elements of the dance subservient to the psychological conception. I have always attempted to throw an aetherial veil of poetry over my dance, the charm of it screening the purely mechanical elements. It often happens that I improvise in dancing, particularly if the part inspires me and carries me away. From the palette of choreography I take the colour that best suits my mood of the moment. I always try to give the greatest possible value to the smallest detail. That is the way in which probably, I have given the effect of 'novelty'. As far as I can judge myself, that is the main 'secret' of my art."

She was often asked:

"How do you understand the problems of your art?"

Pavlova replied:

"I try to express by dancing what the composer puts into his music, what the painter expresses with his colours and brushes, the actor with the spoken word. I try to express this with my body and my spirit, that most universal of all languages. An artist always attempts to express life in its most hidden depths. And my dance is also life stripped of its accidental and irrelevant coverings."

An American journalist once asked her wherein lay the secret of her success. Being present at the time, I thought to myself, 'That is a question that will not be easy to answer, and answer in a few words'.

But to my astonishment Pavlova answered without hesitation:

"I presume in the sincerity of my art."

And the more I think of it the more convinced I become that she was right. She never tried to astonish her public, or to show a dance in a way that would amaze the spectator by its technique. She danced as she felt, doing all in her power to express to the public what she was living through herself. And it invariably reached the public, whatever the mood or emotion.

At the time of her last appearance in Australia, just before leaving, she gave an interview to some Australian journalists.

"Dancing" she said "is my life". It is easy to understand that one can give oneself up entirely to this art, which in itself comprises so many others. In a ballet you have before you the music, design, colour and movement, welded into one beautiful, harmonious whole by a master-hand. You express surprise that so many of the celebrated dancers come from Russia and ask why it is that the art of the ballet should have flourished so wonderfully in my country. The fact is that dancing is in the character of the Russians. The Slavs are dancers by nature, just as the Italians are singers by nature.

"Every country, of course, has its admirable born dancers. Some of the best performers of my company are English. But it is only in Russia, owing to the spirit and the customs of the people, that the atmosphere exists in which dancing flourishes best of all. An explanation as to why a particular race is successful in a given art and another not, must be sought for in the character and temperament of the races.

"You, English, are always afraid to give free rein to your emotions. Your calmness, reserve and self-control are splendid qualities for everyday life, but they are a hindrance to the scenic artist, whether he be actor, musician or singer. A talented person on the stage should always share his individuality with his public fully, generously and expressively. You must allow yourself

Pavlova in "Gavotte".
(Photograph by Tornquist, New-Zealand.)

Pavlova with Novikoff in "Giselle".
(The Times Photograph.)

to weep when you are sad, and be expansive in your joy when you are happy, and not make a secret of your emotions.

"A true artist should have no secrets. On the stage you must be able to manage your personality in such a way as to transmit every emotion to the spectator. It is quite clear isn't it? — that we can only do this successfully if off the stage we give perfect freedom to our feelings — weep when we are sad, laugh when we are happy. We ought to live in order to feel our art and to make our spectators feel it with us."

Asked as to the steps taken when a new ballet is first conceived and staged, namely, whether the subject is thought of first, i. e. the various scenes and movements, and the music found to suit a theme already worked out, Pavlova said that in former times the music was completely subservient to the subject. Later came the collaboration of the composer and the ballet-master. And finally, the making of a ballet nowadays starts with the music; that at any rate being the way the majority of contemporary ballets are written.

"The possibilities of the ballet are boundless", she used to say. "There is no emotion that cannot be expressed by the dancer. A ballet can be tragic or comic or fantastic; only a dance should never be vulgar or ugly. The art of dancing is often degraded. It is dreadful: what is called dancing is often only a series of clumsy, meaningless movements without the least approach to grace or beauty. I have seen some like that, — so-called dances — on the stage and in the ball-rooms of England and America, and I feel sad when I think how much a nation loses when an art that might give so much of beauty and joy is deprived of its meaning and charm. We want all the happiness that we can give ourselves. Life would probably have far more meaning and light if, side by side with the teaching of reading and writing, people were also taught to dance beautifully."

It has been said that Pavlova obtained her swans with a view to copying their movements for her dance "The Dying Swan", but to say that is to understand her very little. She could not copy; that was entirely contrary to her nature. Her "Swan" was a mystical being. The graceful motions of its imaginary wings gave the impression of immortality. It is not death, it is the freeing of the soul from bondage. The dance, originally set by a ballet master of genius, she transformed in her soul into a symbol of a swan-song, and it has become forever a symbol of her own spirit and her own life.

Pavlova hated all imitation and could not bear copying, seeing in them a vivid proof of the artist's lack of talent. She used to relate how, when she was still a pupil of the Imperial School, several little girls — she and her friends, captivated by the dancing of some famous ballerina, would choose her as a model, trying to copy her in every particular. It happened in our company more than once, that some dancer, influenced involuntarily by the constant contemplation of Pavlova, would begin to imitate her movements and gestures. Pavlova invariably stopped this, explaining that the tendency to copy another deprived a person of his own individuality.

Pavlova never paid any heed to the size of an audience. The importance of the town, or the number of spectators present at her performances, made no difference to her dancing: she cherished her beloved art and gave herself up to it completely. Also she never spoke of her triumphs: quite often she did not even notice them.

It has happened that after some particularly triumphant performance, when repeated calls before the curtain and ovations seemed to have no end, while they were drinking tea on her return home, one of her fellow artists would draw attention to the fact, and Pavlova would ask in astonishment:

"But was the success so great to-night?"

Those present would laugh and say:

"What sort of greater success do you want?"

And Pavlova would answer in confusion:

"I really did not notice."

Sometimes her thoughts and spirit would wander far away and then, with a start, she would come back to reality. She herself was hardly ever satisfied with her performances, often saying:

"I know that I could have danced better."

On entering her dressing-room after the performance, I have sometimes found her in tears. It seemed to her — perhaps owing to over-strained nerves that on that particular evening she had danced badly. On my showing perfectly sincere surprise (for in actual fact on that particular evening she had danced beyond all compare) she would explain that nothing had seemed to go quite as usual. I would succeed in comforting her, for she knew me to be a severe critic and one who never paid empty compliments; she knew that from me she would never hear anything but the truth.

Pavlova often gave expression to the thought: "Where there is no heart there is no art".

This was not a mere phrase. For, indeed she put her heart into every dance, that heart so full of charity and human kindness. It always seemed as if by dancing she was giving herself happiness, that the particular dance she was at that moment executing was her favourite. And for that reason everything that she did became perfect. One became oblivious to her perfect technique and it seemed quite natural that this wonderful being should remain unaffected by the law of gravitation. She was so light in her dances, so ethereal, so spiritualized, so chaste, that one felt like going on one's knees before her. The feeling of ethereality that emanated from her, reached the spectators as if wafted across from the land of dreams.

One of Pavlova's distinguishing traits was the exceptional variety of her moods; they all seemed to live in her, coming to the surface at the required moment without any strain or effort. From the vivid tempestuous colours of the "Bacchanal" or the "Syrian Dance" she could pass to the most delicate of pastel shades, and this passage was not attained by the character of the dance, by the costume or the music, not by any external means but by an inner feeling, which came into expression quite unnoticed by herself and gave to the figures created with such verisimilitude, a touching simplicity and an inexpressible charm. Each one of her dances was imbued with a special "touch" peculiar to herself, such as I have never seen in another dancer. This "touch" was a distinguishing feature of her incomparable technique. Pavlova never "worked" on the stage and even in moments of the greatest technical difficulty no effort or strain was ever visible. She danced in a whisper, if one may use the expression, gliding imperceptibly along the stage.

It was my good fortune to watch the dances of Pavlova at closer range and more often than anybody else, and always they gave me the same unaltered happiness. They were, indeed, of inexpressible charm, ever fresh, harmonious and full of subtle spirituality.

But possibly I only think so because Pavlova was very near and dear to me, and I am not an unprejudiced judge? Perhaps the effect on others was different? Yet, no. I can assert with absolute impartiality that others felt the same. Here is an example. Our performances always consisted of three parts, — the first two made up of ballets and the last of a number of short dances or divertisements. According to the programme of the divertisements, some of the dancers were engaged and others not. Those who were not dancing that night in the divertisements could leave the theatre after the second part of the performance. One would have thought that the dancers, tired out after a lesson, a rehearsal and an evening performance, would be glad to hurry home. But invariably, I saw dancers who were free, having already changed into their street clothes, standing behind the scenes awaiting Pavlova's turn and only going home after it. Others, engaged in the divertissements, would hasten to change for their next dance, so as not to miss seeing Pavlova. It is particularly remarkable when one remembers that these dancers had been doing this every night for many years. It was interesting to watch the expressions on the faces of the workmen on the stage watching her dancing. One electrician, whom I had to upbraid for lights turned on at the wrong moment, said apologetically:

Pavlova in "Fairy Doll".
(Photograph by S. Bransburg.)

"It's the first time that I have seen Madame dance the 'Swan' and I forgot everything."

A big charity performance was arranged in the New York theatre Hippodrome; the chief attraction of this performance was the participation of Anna Pavlova with her partner Volinin and of the very popular American conductor and composer John Philip Souza with his enormous orchestra. When the programme was being discussed it was found that the number of artists taking part was so great that Pavlova would be able to dance one dance only, and the management, in order to avoid the expense of a separate orchestra, asked Souza and his orchestra to play what was necessary for her. During the later discussions Souza asked Pavlova to dance something to one of his valses. She agreed and chose the one she considered the most suitable, but as it was very long, when she went through it with Souza, she explained what "cuts" would be necessary in order to shorten the valse by about a half. Then she rehearsed it with Volinin and the result was a very attractive number.

The performance was brilliant. At last Pavlova's turn came. At first everything went off very well and then to her horror she saw that Souza did not stop where a large "cut" had been necessary but went right on. To stop dancing was impossible and Pavlova and Volinin had to go on, partly repeating, partly improvising. At the end both dancers were completely exhausted, so that when the valse was finished they could hardly walk off the stage.

When Pavlova saw Souza at the end of the performance and expressed her just anger at his having forgotten the "cut" he replied very amiably: "Madame, I did not forget it, but I was so happy that Pavlova was dancing my favourite valse, that it was quite beyond my power to end it so quickly."

As I have already said, Pavlova did not like anecdotes or funny stories about the stage or connected with the performances. Her art was too sacred to her. But once she had to exercise all her self-control in order not to laugh during a performance of the 'Swan'. It was at a charity matinée given at one of the large English seaside resorts and many children were present. Suddenly during the dance, in the absolute stillness of a breathless audience, a thin childish voice was heard in the hall:

"Mummy, mummy, look, what a dear little white duck!"

Pavlova treated the artistic creations of others with extraordinary respect and delicacy. When dancing any dance she kept rigorously to the composition of the author, never permitting herself the smallest changes, to say nothing of additions. The work of a ballet-master — whether it was great or small — she considered inviolable. She felt that any intrusion into the work of another was inadmissible without the author's permission. In the whole of her repertoire, consequently, nothing was ever included that did not belong to her, contrary to what is now done practically by everybody.

She often used to say to her artists:

"Master technique, and then forget all about it and be natural."

I read somewhere that Pavlova was very ambitious. That is totally untrue. She was possessed of an unusual natural modesty, which was quite incompatible with ambition. She never expected and never sought any outward marks of success, never strove to play a part in society, never wished to be surrounded by expressions of adulation. Her constant desire was to spend her hours of leisure in the circle of her friends in her garden and to be as little noticed as possible. I fail to see what part worldly ambition plays in this. Her own words confirm it:

"In order to preserve unspoilt the pictures created by him the artist should show himself to the public only on the stage, never in private life."

Exceptionally tolerant and easy-going in her private life, Pavlova became completely changed as soon as it was a question of her art. The stage was not only her life, but her Holy of Holies, and like a high priestess she sternly guarded the sacred fire. She carefully kept away from her art anything coarse or showy, any attempt on its dignity. The slightest disrespect shown to the stage, any negligence towards one's work, always wounded her deeply and immediately raised in her a spirit of determined resistance. Always she was modesty itself, never demanding any praise or unwonted deference, nor wishing to be the cause of constraint to anyone, yet Pavlova could be very firm in her demands when necessary, especially in cases when the management of a theatre or the local impresario failed to do what she considered necessary.

In this connection an incident in Rio de Janeiro is significant. Our performances were given in the municipal theatre. After the Colon in Buenos Aires, this is the best theatre in all South America. But its excellent arrangements and equipment, the work of well-known foreign firms, began to decline under the municipal management. During her first performance there, Pavlova noticed that the curtain did not draw back to the width of the stage, but approximately only to half and this precluded the possibility of any of her fellow-artists being led out by her to answer the calls of the audience. After the performance this deficiency was pointed out to the manager, who explained that the curtain was worked by electricity and that the electrician would put the matter right the very next day. At the next performance, however, the curtain was still out of order, and this again raised Pavlova's displeasure. I spoke to the management once more and this time received a

Pavlova in "La Fille mal Gardée".
(Photograph by Mishkin, New York.)

definite promise that it would be attended to at once. There was a matinée the next day. All the seats were taken and the performance started off very well. But at the end of the first act, the curtain drew back even less than before. Pavlova declared that she would dance no more, demanding that the money be refunded and an explanation of why she refused to dance given to the audience. Those around tried to talk her over and pacify her, but seeing in this incident a lack of respect towards herself and her perfectly reasonable wishes, she firmly refused to alter her decision. The matter would probably have been arranged, however, had not a municipal official, who had thrust

Pavlova in "Russian Dance".

himself into the argument, spoiled everything. He demanded a personal interview with Pavlova at which he informed her that if she did not dance she would be arrested. This, of course, only added fuel to the fire. Pavlova told him that she would be glad of it — let the public of Rio de Janeiro see how negligent the municipality was, and the whole world learn of the bad manners of Brazil! Putting on her hat and coat she was on the point of leaving, when near the door of her dressing-room she saw a lady she knew — an Englishwoman with a charming little girl of about seven. When this lady expressed her astonishment at seeing her leaving Pavlova explained that she was not going to dance any more and was going home. Seizing her mother by the hand, the little girl exclaimed through her tears:

"But you did promise me that Pavlova was going to dance the 'Swan' to-day!"

The mother then explained that she had brought her small daughter to see the 'Swan' as a birthday treat. Pavlova was immediately mollified. She kissed the little girl and comforted her by promising that she should see the 'Swan'. Ten minutes later she was on the stage again.

The next day the curtain was in perfect order.

Pavlova hardly ever read the theatrical criticism of herself. They were, I should say, of no interest to her except in the rare cases where the articles were written by well-informed and competent people. To compliments also she remained quite indifferent. In fact she was rather irritated by them, regarding them as superficial and unnecessary. On the other hand serious ideas or pertinent remarks by understanding people she valued very highly.

If everything that was written about Pavlova in the *) forty-four countries in which she danced were to be gathered together, the articles, criticisms, notices, interviews, etc. would in themselves represent an immense amount of material, but apart from this and the number of separate articles devoted to her that appeared in Russia and elsewhere, she was also the subject of several books. The first to appear was a small collection of articles about her by German writers. Then came the great work of Valerian Svetlov. This was a sumptuous volume that appeared simultaneously in French and English. In it Svetlov gives a detailed analysis of all the various aspects of her art, portrays

---

* The following is the chronological order of the countries which Pavlova visited: Russia — Poland — Finland — Norway — Sweden — Denmark — Germany — Austria — France — England — United States — Canada — Cuba — Costa Rica — Panama — Equador — Peru — Chile — Argentine — Uruguay — Porte Rico — Brazil — Venezuela — Mexico — Portugal — Spain — Belgium — Japan — China — Phillipine Ils. — Malay States — Burma — India — Egypt — Holland — Switzerland — Hungaria — Yugo-Slavia — Italy — Czecho-Slovakia — South Africa — Australia — New Zealand — Java.

her in the different parts she created and cites the opinion of the more distinguished French and English critics. In 1928 came Theodore Stier's book "Round the World with Anna Pavlova". Its author was Pavlova's conductor and for fourteen years her faithful friend. This book, however, is of a narrative order and confines itself to the relation of various episodes that took place during the author's long service with Pavlova. After her death a book appeared about her in Dutch. Its author was Ernst Krauss, a poet and writer, who was closely connected with the arrangements of Pavlova's tours in Holland and Germany, and it is the result of his study of various material connected with her art and her life. A few further works are in preparation in America. One is a book containing material for her biography and another — to appear in California — a magnificent publication containing artistically reproduced sketches of Pavlova, in pencil and in colour, by the author. There was also published a book by Walford Hyden, entitled "The Genius of the Dance".

Keeping in touch with the press, receiving cuttings from the papers of the whole world and reading all that was written about her after her death, I am forced to the conclusion that the best contributions were those made by Russian critics and writers, possibly because it was only in Russia that the real connoisseurs of the ballet existed; not casual amateurs but men who constantly followed the art, knew its literature and treated it, not condescendingly as a spectacle of a lower order, but as an art having the right to stand side by side with opera and drama.

The majority of these men, besides being professional critics are also gifted writers. I have on another page mentioned the names of the poet Andreievsky, Skalkovsky, the writers Belaiev, Plescheev, Svetlov, André Levinson, also the philosopher Volynsky, whose remarkable work on Leonardo da Vinci has made him known everywhere. These literary men, analysing the ballet, did not confine themselves to a repetition of the same epithets and a summary of the technical feats of the dancers, but have known how to say something more profound and interesting, of value to the dancers themselves. Criticisms, often far from flattering, but true, have made many a dancer aware of her shortcomings and helped her to overcome them.

Next to the Russians I think one has to place the French critics. Although yielding to the Russians in their knowledge of the subject, they have many interesting ideas brilliantly and elegantly expressed.

With a few exceptions English critics never took much interest in the ballet, only writing about it because it was necessary to say something about a performance that had taken place. After a perusal of hundreds upon hundreds of articles and reviews, one arrives at the conclusion that in the main they consist of a repetition of various adjectives, giving one rather the measure of the pleasure received by the spectator than a critical analysis of what was seen on the stage. The same can be said of the articles written about Pavlova after her death. Some were good and intelligent but in the majority of cases the authors limit themselves to a repetition or a re-printing of certain well-known episodes of her career — and that in a country where she was so well-known and such a favourite. It is a noteworthy fact that many of those who saw her, even without knowing her personally, wrote me letters after her death, — letters so full of correct estimation and understanding of her work, so full of love and gratitude and so beautifully expressed, that I feel it my duty to give extracts from them in this book.

I have still to speak of German and American critics. In Germany the art of the ballet had long been a thing of the past. The Royal Theatre in Berlin used to keep up a ballet troupe, at the head of which stood the once-time famous dancer Antoinette Del Era, a woman of such advanced years that there could be no question of her dancing herself. From time to time ballets were given, but of an archaic character and poorly executed. It is consequently not surprising that German critics considered this art as dead and buried. Pavlova's arrival with a company of dancers from the Imperial theatres created, therefore, quite a sensation. It was seen that this art, far from being dead, was flourishing and had attained perfection. A Russian critic, who happened to be in Berlin at the time, wrote as follows of the first performance:

"...... It was a real triumph, a triumph which Berlin, always reserved in the manifestation of its feelings, does not accord to many. The customary mask of German staidness, it would seem, had been dropped. Berlin opened its heart to the Russian artist, welcoming her with an overflowing hall that shook with applause. Applause interrupted the dances, drowned the orchestra and after the 'Dying Swan', grew to such a roar, that the artist, finding no possibility of satisfying the public by bows alone, was obliged to repeat the dance — and this was the only possible expedient, for otherwise the old building of the Royal Opera stood in danger of complete collapse. I was reminded of Pavlova's visit to Moscow: Berlin differed little in its reception. But in order to turn Berliners into Moscovites, it required Pavlova. What precious treasure did that fragile vessel contain — a slender, elegant, sensitive woman, with sharp swiftly changing features, difficult for the portrait painter to seize, with a noble and high forehead framed in smoothly dressed hair, the black brilliancy of which seemed so well suited to the large burning eyes..."

German critics welcomed Pavlova as a vision from heaven and from that first day invariably received her every visit with enthusiasm. To do them justice German critics are very conscientious and some of them possess immense erudition.

Pavlova in "Christmas".
(Photograph by d'Ora, Paris.)

The Americans were not acquainted with the classical ballet at all before the arrival of Pavlova. They certainly had a ballet in connection with the Metropolitan Theatre, but only as an addition to the opera, and if ever small ballets were given it was only to fill up the programme. To the Americans Pavlova came as a revelation.

Among American reviewers there were two or three who made a serious study of the ballet, and one Boston critic, the most competent of all, used to write very fine articles, showing great understanding and even analysing the technical side of the performance. In a very large majority of cases, however, they gave merely very flattering notices, with a paraphrase of the plot, descriptions of the executants, costumes, etc.

The critics of the Latin republics of South America, having no knowledge of the art of the ballet, never attempted to analyse the technique of dancing, but wrote enthusiastic, and often beautiful articles about the art of Pavlova and the impression produced by it.

We were often surprised at the conscientiousness shown by the critics of such far away countries as Australia and South Africa. They had practically never seen a ballet and had obviously read up the subject in preparation for Pavlova's arrival. In their articles they showed considerable acquaintance with the subject and with the views expressed by Pavlova years previously. Speaking of the critics I must say that I could never understand how it was possible for any of them to look at the dances of Pavlova and criticise her art without feeling that they were confronted with something unique, beyond analysis and criticism. To say this is not to extol her beyond measure, but merely to place on record the fact that Pavlova was a unique phenomenon, which it was the good fortune of the people of her generation to enjoy. During the twenty years that she tirelessly danced in all parts of the world, everyone became used to the idea that she was imprescriptibly "ours" and no one ever dreamed that a moment would come when she would be no more.

And when this moment came so unexpectedly, the whole world — one can say it without exaggeration — received a shock and suddenly became sensible to the full of its loss.

When we think of Pavlova there is one question which rises involuntarily. Was her genius fully estimated during her lifetime? I find the answer in the following words of A. Plescheev:

"A great deal of literature about Pavlova already exists, but more will be written by those historians of the theatre of the future generation, who had the happiness of seeing her.

It is difficult to say it, and yet none the less true that the realisation of this artist's genius had grown daily since her death, and her absence, which has formed an irreparable breach, shows us more and more convincingly the nature of the artist we have lost.

Pavlova's artistic personality now seems to us limitless."

In all her press interviews abroad, in England, America, Australia, on every convenient occasion Pavlova pointed out the necessity for a state or subsidised theatre or conservatoire. Of all the great nations England alone has never had either a state or subsidised theatre and this is difficult to understand as firstly, the fondness of the English for the theatre is well known and secondly, England is a wealthy country which spends huge sums on its amusements and sports. The explanation, perhaps, lies in the fact that England does not like serious theatres. How else is one to explain that in the native land of Shakespeare, it is very rarely that one sees his plays? The last actors to support serious dramatic art were Henry Irving, Herbert Tree and Ellen Terry. After their deaths, the theatre fell a prey to revue, and revue is still flourishing there.

Is it not strange that in London, with its eight million population, the need for a permanent opera is not felt? The summer season generally lasts from eight to ten weeks, and when it is over Covent Garden Theatre with its age-long traditions, is turned into a dance hall. There are some magnificent actors in England, but they find practically no demand for their services, as serious plays do not attract the public. In revue and musical comedy the fashion now is for American performers. Managers declare that American artists are more individual, gayer and funnier than the English. Be that as it may, the English theatre is now passing through a serious crisis and actors are having a very hard time.

As Pavlova very correctly pointed out, a government mindful of the education of its people should also have in view its cultural development, in which the theatre plays an important part. But it is also necessary that the people should learn to consider the theatre not as an amusement only, but as something more serious — a medium of education. The Russians and the Germans are an illustration and can set an example in this matter. Why should an interest in serious comedy be taken in Russia and not in England? In all probability because there have always been state and subsidised theatres in the above countries, and not being dependent on box office returns, the theatres are not obliged to pander to the tastes of the public, and, moreover being managed by educated and well-versed people, they can produce plays which by their subject matter and artistic merit are of advantage to the educational development of the masses. Having the necessary financial means, a theatre of this kind can afford the services of first-class artists for the designing of scenery and costumes, of famous musicians and of the best

Pavlova in "Sleeping Beauty".
(Photograph by Mishkin, New York.)

actors. A unity of all the chief branches of art is thus obtained and the resultant performances are eagerly sought after by the public. When a theatre of this nature has existed for many years, it undoubtedly moulds public taste and raises it to a standard of serious repertoire.

The same can also be said of opera. Although theatres giving drama, which requires far less expenditure, can exist — not without difficulty — as a commercial undertaking, it has long been an established fact that opera

Pavlova practising on the stage before the Performance.
(Photograph by Abbe.)

cannot without a considerable subsidy. Of course I am not here speaking of popular managements, who give opera at cheap prices and have a public of their own. In the Russian Imperial Opera the system of visiting performers did not exist. There were permanent casts composed of good artists. Foreign celebrities were not engaged, but there was a model chorus, a very fine orchestra, an artistic setting, and the theatre was always full. This, of course, is possible when the season lasts eight or nine months instead of as in England, ten weeks — a totally inadequate period in which to form a good chorus and orchestra — while the overhead expenses spread over only two and a half months, threaten a heavy deficit.

The state does not subsidise any theatre in America either. But there private persons contribute generously to the support of the two opera houses in New York and Chicago, as well as some symphonic orchestras. Having obtained a thorough knowledge of the working of these two theatres and of several symphonic orchestras during our frequent tours in that country, Pavlova expressed her astonishment more than once at the enormous sums expended and the poor results achieved. The secret lies in the fact that in forming and subsidising these theatres the main object was not to create something useful for the musical education of the people or something to aid youthful talent in its development, but the desire of certain persons to play the part of Maecenas, or the pride of a certain town in being considered highly cultured and musical. I know that for one such orchestra the best soloists of various European towns were engaged. Some of them were professors in conservatoires, who had to be paid high fees, for they were throwing up their posts to go to America. The demand for symphonic music is, nevertheless, very limited. The annual number of concerts is small and the deficit is therefore enormous. I have been told by the manager of an orchestra (and this is no secret, it being known to all) that the local Maecenas, a man of fabulous wealth, had to add yearly a sum of three hundred thousand dollars for the upkeep of the orchestra. This amount translated into francs, equals seven and a half millions, whereas the Grand Opera of Paris only receives an annual subsidy of a million and a half!

I do not know how the matter stands with the Chicago* opera at the present time, but when we were in that town some years ago, the deficit was equal to five hundred thousand dollars. It may be argued: why should rich people not be patrons of art and, at any rate, spend their money with profit to the country? Yes, such an argument would have a solid basis, if there were several state conservatoires in America and those seeking a serious musical

---

* After these lines were written the Chicago opera was closed, owing to their inability to obtain the enormous sums needed for its support.

education did not have to come to Europe to get it; if the Americans stood so high in music as not to be satisfied merely by good orchestras, such as existed in Russia, and such as exist in Germany — in that case, certainly such expenditure might be justified. But at the present moment, when for the whole of America with its 120 million people, there are only two opera houses and some ten symphonic orchestras, costing their patrons enormous sums, I think it would be much more reasonable if this money were put together to form some big and, for the country, really useful enterprise. America possesses all the necessary means to arrange a large, and in the educational sense, really useful theatrical organisation. Quite apart from the fact that she has the required financial resources and hundreds of rich people who would gladly subscribe to such an object, there are also in nearly all the big towns magnificent auditoriums, in most cases belonging to the municipality, seating from six to twelve thousand people. These exist for various congresses and in America there are very many of them — exhibitions, concerts and performances. Owing to the technical arrangements, these halls can be very quickly turned into real theatres, with stage and all necessary equipment.

We often had to give our performances in these halls. If performances for the people at cheap prices were arranged here, they would undoubtedly produce excellent results, as was the case in Russia, where, with the monopolising of the sale of vodka, the government was able to give large sums for the promotion of cheap educational performances for the people. A large theatre was built in St. Petersburg, called the People's Palace, where plays, chiefly of a patriotic or historical nature, were given, as well as operas by Russian composers. The immense success of this theatre encouraged the government to create another such enterprise in the workmen's quarter of St. Petersburg (Steklianny Zavod). Theatres of a like nature were also opened in Moscow and a number of other towns and everywhere they met with the same success.

In addition to these halls, there are a number of big Greek theatres in America, where open-air performances are periodically given. With all these resources at hand experienced and energetic people could easily form something really serious and useful.

With the small subsidy that the French Government gave to the actor Gimier, he succeeded in putting on some excellent performances for the people in the Paris Trocadero. In my opinion it is only a question of initiative; in the matter of money and sympathy there is never any lack in America. Pavlova gave it more than once as her opinion, that if all the money annually spent in these directions in America, were expended rationally and with foresight, both musical education and cheap theatres for the people could undoubtedly be better arranged there than in any country in Europe.

Pavlova in her Garden at Ivy House.

CHAPTER IX.

PAVLOVA IN EVERY-DAY LIFE.

Those who have known or seen Pavlova will not require any description to supplement or refresh the impression she made on them, but for the sake of those who did not know her and for future generations, I will endeavour to give some idea of her personal appearance. For this I shall make use of the pen portrait of the English critic, C. Beaumont. In his obituary article on her, he wrote:

"Her body was ideally formed for dancing. She had lovely arms with tapering fingers, and her legs and feet, particularly the insteps, were superb. Her face was pale and oval, her forehead high, her hair dark and drawn close to the head; her nose was slightly aquiline, her cheek bones high, her eyes large and the colour of "ripe, dark brown cherries." Her head was beautifully poised on a swan-like neck, her expression was part elfin, part malicious, part imperious, and it could be as changeable as the very face of

Pavlova.
(Photograph by B. Hori, New York.)

nature. Her body was a perfect instrument of expression, it would instantly respond to the mood of a dance, just as a tuning-fork vibrates to a blow."

At the first glance, dressed in her ordinary clothes, Pavlova did not produce an impression out of the ordinary. Many journalists and people from the audience confessed that they could hardly believe that this frail, and to all appearances delicate little woman, with a pale face and smooth hair, dressed so modestly, could be the Anna Pavlova, the creator of such charming, graceful figures on the stage and the possessor of such magic power, and of such marvellous dancing virtuosity. But as soon as she spoke and her eyes rested on her companion, the impression received changed immediately and once again the miracle of her all-conquering magnetism was overwhelmingly felt.

Pavlova's remarkable grace did not leave her in her private life either. All her movements were so gentle, so harmonious, so full of an irresistible charm, that those who came to see her could not help feeling the deepest admiration when they chanced to see her walking, or pouring out tea, or relating some incident. The London "Radio Times" in its article about Pavlova quotes these words:

"A famous poet once revealed to us that the most exquisite moment of vision ever granted to him was when, walking in the early morning on the terrace of an hotel at Amalfi, he saw Pavlova step onto a balcony and, unconscious of being watched, stretch out her hands in greeting to the beauty of an Italian day. There must have been many such moments of loveliness for those who knew her...."

Many people have told me that at the very first meeting with Pavlova, they felt that before them was a remarkable personality. The spiritual force emanating from her produced so great an effect that people lost all wish to analyse or even to speak on the subjects about which they had come. This is all the more extraordinary as simplicity and accessibility were her distinctive traits. Practically all the impresarios, theatrical managers and artists who came to see her, were surprised to see how little she resembled a celebrity, a diva, spoiled by the worship of the whole world. "How kind and human she is!" they would exclaim, after having spent perhaps only a few minutes in her company.

She possessed remarkably eloquent hands. They were always taking part in the conversation and she used them so expressively to illustrate her words and ideas, that even those who did not understand the language in which she spoke, could guess at the subject under discussion, however trivial, by the movements of her hands.

Her neck gave a marvellously beautiful line to the poise of the head and the slope to the shoulders. She was extraordinarily well-proportioned. To the end of her life she had the figure of a young girl, a matter of astonishment to all dressmakers. Her feet, with unusually high insteps, were very strong and hardy. In all the years of dancing, with the constant moving from place to place, with the changes of climate and theatres, she only twice had any trouble with her feet.

The first time was many years ago in St. Louis in the U.S.A. Dancing a valse-caprice in sandals perfectly calmly, and without the least effort making the necessary movements to get on tip-toe, she suddenly felt that something had happened to one foot, for she could not step on it. It was the last item of the programme and the last bars of the valse had been reached.

The curtain was lowered and Pavlova was carried to her dressing-room. A doctor was summoned, but could discover nothing amiss and advised her to drive immediately to a hospital and have the foot X-rayed. The X-ray photograph also did not establish very clearly whether there had been a fracture or not. As, in any case, we were due in Chicago in a few days, we decided to go directly there, cancelling our engagements in the other towns. At a consultation in Chicago, the doctors could not agree. An American surgeon and one other doctor diagnosed a broken bone at the back of the instep and declared that she would not be able to dance for two months. A professor of the Chicago University, however, considered it to be nothing but a strained sinew, and thought that in ten days she could again appear before the public.

And so it turned out to be. The foot was wrapped in an adhesive bandage, which held it very firmly. Gradually it grew stronger and three weeks after the breakdown everything was well and in order again.

Pavlova explained this mishap by the fact that in the preceding dance her shoes had heels, and the change-over to sandals caused some awkward movement which damaged the sinew. After this, Pavlova was always afraid to dance the valse-caprice in sandals and invariably performed it in ballet-shoes, claiming that they held the feet more firmly.

The second time frightened her a great deal more.

In the adagio of the ballet "Amarilla" she so forgot herself in her part that she dropped on her knees very abruptly, the impact with the floor being heard even in the hall. At the moment she did not notice anything and it was only some time after the performance that she felt any inconvenience. The doctor who was called in found nothing serious in the matter. Another doctor suggested bandaging the knee, though at the time it was difficult to bend it even without the bandage. And finally a third, a well-known New York physician, having made an examination, decided that Pavlova would have to drop her tour and undergo an operation, the result of which would show if she could ever dance again or not.

Pavlova and all of us were, of course, considerably perturbed, but, for some reason, the doctor did not inspire great confidence, and she continued to dance, though with difficulty.

On arriving at the town of Springfield, we learnt that it contained a famous special hospital for professionals of all kinds — athletes, footballplayers, etc. at the head of which was an excellent and experienced doctor.

Pavlova consulted him and, applying diathermia, which was then coming into usage, he comforted her immediately, advising its use on every possible occasion, with daily massage.

Pavlova in Mexico among the Cactee.

A few weeks later, the knee was better and when the season was over, Pavlova went to Salzo-Maggiore, where the mud-baths completed the cure. It must be kept in mind that Pavlova danced on an average 220 times a year, in the worst possible conditions, often on impossible stages, and she must therefore be considered very fortunate that in all her career she only had these two mishaps.

Once a very weak child, Pavlova gradually grew into a strong and hardy woman, surprising one by her indefatigable energy and her indomitable will. She never allowed herself to be defeated by unfavourable conditions, always putting heart into others, even when herself suffering from ill-health or overstrung nerves, and considered it inadmissible to let the public notice anything wrong.

In the days when she was on the stage of the Marinsky Theatre she used to complain of a pain in her side. A well-known surgeon diagnosed it as appendicitis and advised an operation. That very same summer in Switzerland, I took the opportunity of taking her to the celebrated Professor Kocher, who confirmed the diagnosis of the St. Petersburg doctor

Pavlova in St. Petersburg 1908.

and said that, although an immediate operation was not necessary, it would be better if it were done. Shortly after, the pains ceased and never recurred.

It is only natural that under such strenuous conditions of work there should occasionally be slight indispositions. She was examined at various times by the best doctors of Europe and America and they all agreed that her heart, lungs and main organs were in perfect order.

In the course of time, Pavlova developed a system of cures of her own. When feeling that she had a cold, she would force herself to go to the theatre and there went through a lengthy exercise, considering that perspiration was the very best cure. She never gave way or laid up on account of any of her indispositions and never cancelled a performance on account of them.

While on a journey between Salt Lake City and Los Angeles, we found ourselves in a place surrounded by floods and were obliged to remain there for three days and three nights while the damaged bridges were being repaired. On arrival at Los Angeles several members of the company became ill. Pavlova herself had a bad throat and the doctor forbade her to dance. But she insisted, and every evening the doctor came to the theatre to give her an injection to enable her to finish the performance. To persuade her or force her to cancel a performance in such cases was impossible. She was endowed with a quite extraordinary energy and one often wondered how so frail a woman could possess such wonderful strength.

On the front of the General Post Office building in New York is the following inscription: "Neither rain nor snow, nor storm ever stops the American post from performing its duty." Pavlova had equal right to take the motto for herself, for no difficulties nor private afflictions could prevent her from doing what she considered her duty.

In the chapter entitled "Behind the Scenes" I have already mentioned under what difficult conditions she was sometimes obliged to dance. To these, of course, should also be added physical indispositions, and, frequently, vexations in connection with the business or trouble caused by news from Russia. It has therefore happened that Pavlova would leave her dressing room very much upset and with tears in her eyes, though taking care that they should not spoil her make—up. If this took place before a dramatic ballet, such as "Amarilla" or "Giselle" where such a frame of mind was explicable, it passed without exciting notice, but when she had to appear in the "Fairy Doll" a great effort was required to gain control over herself and to come onto the stage with a face full of gaiety and happiness. But Pavlova firmly believed in the principle that she had set herself, namely, that the indispositions and the moods of the dancer are no concern of the public: that the public has come to the theatre to see those figures which the dancer is there to create, and if she is unable to do this the performance had better be put off; if however the dancer undertakes to appear, she must try and get the better of her indispositions and forget her griefs for the time. Her invariable reply was that she had no right to disappoint the audience, many of whom had possibly come long distances to see her. And, indeed, at the moment when she had to appear her tears would dry and she would dance out happy and joyful, and the public would think how fortunate she was, this Pavlova, always gay and able to achieve everything so easily!

Eventually after a long tour of 7—8 months, Pavlova would return to her home in London, worn out by work, by constant travelling and by life in hotels. One would expect the short period which she spent at home to be really given up to rest. As a matter of fact such rest would only last two or three days, and then her tireless energy would again assert itself in everything connected with her house and garden. She was very fond of her garden and spent most of her time in it.

Although, perhaps, the preceeding year it had been replanned by a famous London firm of landscape gardeners, Pavlova would invariably decide that some path or other spoiled the view and should therefore be turfed. Workmen bringing turf would arrive the very next day and the work would be carried our under Pavlova's personal supervision. Then it would appear that certain bushes in another part of the garden obstructed the view and they would have to be transplanted. Or again the flowers planted round the lake would prove to be unsuccessful and others would have to replace them. After that would come the turn of the house, which consisted of two stories with large cellars stretching under the whole of it. These cellars served for housing the library of music and the theatrical wardrobe. Pavlova would decide that it was necessary to relay the floors, to add to the number of cupboards, to alter the door of one of the rooms, to widen the veranda — her schemes were endless. When she saw that our pigeon family had again increased and was suffering from want of space she went onto the roof herself and gave directions for the building of the new pigeon house, so that the birds should be comfortable. And in doing all this it was not only the interest which she took in everything, but also her care, determination and thoroughness which were remarkable.

She would be highly pleased if among the workmen she found one interested in her plans ready to help her with advice. She was so fond of anything to do with building operations about the house and so interested

Pavlova in practice Dress.
(Photograph by W. Albee, Seattle.)

Pavlova.
(by Yarovoff, Montevideo.)

in every detail, that she used laughingly to agree with me when I told her that instead of being a dancer she should have been an architect.

She had the ability of concentrating her will-power at any given moment and so producing the maximum of energy. I have witnessed this on several occasions and in various circumstances. As this is a book about Pavlova, there is no reason why even trivial episodes should not be described, and I remember one such. A bottle had to be opened. No corkscrew was handy and the cork was so deeply embedded that only a small part of it projected above the neck of the bottle. It was impossible to get a grip on it and not one of the young and strong dancers present was able to do anything. Pavlova asked for the bottle to be handed to her, and everyone watched her with a smile. Suddenly her face expressed a great concentration of will-power and this, being transmitted to the muscles of her hands, without any visible effort, she pulled out the cork with her small, thin fingers to the amazement of those present.

In her tastes, Pavlova was not very exacting, but she had a fondness for Russian cooking. Consequently, on arriving to rest in London between the tours, after many months of hotel life, we always had Russian food. Black bread, buckwheat, mushrooms, rissoles in sour cream, sturgeon, were the dishes that were most often on our menu. But when working or travelling, she cut down her menu and it then mostly consisted of chops, chicken and stewed fruit.

She was also very fond of tea with honey or jam. When not dancing, she used to enjoy a glass of claret with her dinner. While working she took no wine, but very occasionally, and when not feeling very well, she would swallow a few drops of brandy before the performance.

With her great love for architecture, sculpture and painting, Pavlova was most attracted to Italy, and of all the towns of Italy, to Florence.

We had to go three times to a certain well-known watering place called Montecatini, an hour's journey from Florence where we would go every Saturday and Sunday. An old St. Petersburg friend, N. Ottokar, now a professor of history in the University of Florence, would act as our guide, showing us round all the museums and the sights of the town.

The air of Florence had a particularly beneficial effect on Pavlova. She could remain for hours on the Piazzale Michelangelo enjoying the view of this incomparable town by moonlight.

Of the other Italian towns she was fondest of Venice and Sienna.

She regularly and dutifully visited all picture-galleries. She was specially fond of the Uffizzi, the Louvre, the National Gallery in London and the Pinacothek in Munich, Thorwaldsen's Museum in Copenhagen and Rodin's in Paris. Her favourite sculptors were Michelangelo and Donatello, and of the painters, Leonardo da Vinci, Botticelli and Sodoma.

Pavlova loved warmth and sunshine and would have liked to spend all her times of rest in Italy or in the South of France. She could stand tropical heat without the least inconvenience and could easily walk about under a blazing sun. Heat, in her opinion, had a good effect on the sinews and fewer preparatory exercises were necessary in tropical climates. In a cold climate, on the other hand, it took a long time to "warm up".

When we were in New Zealand the weather was wintry and very severe. The evenings and nights were very cold and the theatre was not heated. Hours of exercises had to be done in order to "warm up" before the performance. In one of the towns the local mayor had several gas-stoves placed in the wings, and round these the dancers in costume and make-up would "warm-up" before appearing on the stage.

Pavlova preserved her childhood's love of Christmas, and wherever we happened to be, she would invariably have a tree on Christmas Eve, to which all our artists and employees were invited. She took tremendous pleasure in choosing all the presents herself. At times, however, a Christmas-tree had to be procured in places where it was no easy matter.

I remember our tree in Rangoon where, with the greatest difficulty, we managed to get a tiny fir-tree; then the tree in Bombay, and the one in mid-ocean, on the way from England to South Africa. In this latter case we had to bring a tree from England and prepared all the presents beforehand. It was a strange and touching sight to see this tree decked with artificial snow on a moonlight night on the Equator.

The first and only time Pavlova had a Christmas-tree in her own house was in 1929. We had just completed a short tour in England and chanced to have a fortnight's interval before going off on a Continental tour. The last days of '29 and the first days of '30 we spent in London and Pavlova was happy at the idea of spending Christmas and New Year at her own home, Ivy House.

She also kept to the Russian customs for Easter. In whatever place fate found us, the table had to be adorned with pascha*, koulitch** and red painted eggs, and all the Russian members of our company were invited. At the time of our last Eastern tour, Easter found us in Sydney, where it was not easy to obtain pascha and koulitch. Chance, however, came to our aid in the person of an educated Russian woman who, with

---

* A sweet dish made of curds.

** A sort of large, sweet bun. Both Easter dishes.

Pavlova in practice Dress.
(Photograph by W. Albee, Seattle.)

Pavlova in a classic Attitude.

her husband and children, had escaped from Siberia, and who proved to be an excellent housewife. She helped us and our Easter feast left nothing to be desired.

On these occasions Pavlova was a charming hostess, cordial and considerate to everyone. She had a kind word for everybody and made a thoughtful reference to the distant families of her guests. Her own feelings were mixed — she was happy to see our large theatrical family gathered around her, the happy, animated company and to share in this happiness herself, but at the same time, she could not help remembering the Christmas-tree parties of former days, the winter in Russia, far-away Ligovo and Christmas holidays in her own native land, which seemed to be always drawing her back.

No matter in what place we were destined to find ourselves in these latter years, we invariably met some Russians, living under the most diverse conditions, often very difficult ones. But somehow they managed to settle down, to live and educate their children, and even dreamt of returning to Russia.

It is not surprising that most of them found some sort of work in America — an immense and wealthy country — but it was most unexpected to learn that a Cossack settlement is to be found near Brisbane, in North Australia, with an ataman of their own — Russians, who found no difficulty in acclimatizing themselves to the tropical climate. And even under these conditions the Cossacks carried on farming very successfully.

There was a Russian club in Sydney, consisting of about 150 members, and having a small cheap restaurant and a library. In another Australian town the Russians formed themselves into a close community comprising a doctor, an architect, a captain of cuirassiers, a naval officer and one or two others. Their wives kept dress-shops and the men did work of all kinds. When the time for cutting sugar-cane came round, they all enrolled to do this hard, but well-paid work. There was also a well organised Russian club and a library in Cairo.

Everywhere Pavlova was gladly and enthusiastically welcomed by the Russians as the pride of their country. The majority remembered her from the days of the Marinsky Theatre. It gave her sincere pleasure to meet Russians, and it was the cause of much satisfaction to her to see how, in spite of hard conditions and ignorance of the language, they managed to settle down, to bring up their children and to develop in these latter the consciousness that they were Russians and the love of their distant mother-country.

Everywhere the Russians seem to have managed to get on — with the exception perhaps of Japan and Mexico.

In Japan the wage is so small and the Japanese themselves so hardworking and so modest in their requirements, that no European can make a living there by manual labour.

And in Mexico the local communistic tendencies make life for the European workman quite impossible.

Pavlova always received a great number of letters from the Russians after our tours in these far-distant lands. They wrote that her arrival raised the prestige of the Russian nationality, that in consequence they were being treated with more consideration and that help was extended more willingly.

It is worthy of note that Pavlova had no enemies. One would expect her rapid career to have engendered envy and malice. Her progress had indeed been very swift. She was already dancing responsible ballets two years after leaving school and she received the rank of ballerina after three years of service, whereas others had to wait for ten years. But her great gifts, her unassuming modesty and her kindly thoughtfulness for others, made her a general favourite. If she ever had ill-wishers, they could not, or dared not, raise their voices. The defenders of new tendencies in the dance saw in her a formidable foe, but in criticising and attacking the classical school, they never touched her personally, knowing full well that her prestige was unshakable.

There are natures — very rare, to be sure — so lavishly endowed that genius in them is combined with a noble, lofty character, a wide charity and pure open-hearted simplicity. Such personalities become symbols of sublime beauty for mankind and even in these days when ideals find scant reverence, are lifted to a place above common humanity. Those who undertake to examine, analyse and judge such characters must do so with exceptional care and only on two express conditions: that they exercise scrupulous conscientiousness and study only authoritative material.

The never-to-be-forgotten image of Pavlova who in her travels all over the world inspired everywhere a feeling of deeply touching gratitude, received unsurpassed adoration as a great artist and was beloved as a human being, is such a symbol. People venerated her during her lifetime: after her death she became even dearer. Criticism of her, whose whole life was a sacrifice to her art and to the world, must be made if not with reverence as great writers and critics do, at least with respect. This should be felt more particularly by those who had been her collaborators. It is a mistake to take as an example the servant of the philosopher Kant, who after being in his employ for thirty years, when people came from all over Germany to greet him on his jubilee, was surprised to learn that her master was a great man.

In a recently published book "The Genius of the Dance", the author, W. Hyden, portrays Pavlova, the woman, in a far from kindly spirit.

With the most profound conviction and a sense of justice I must bear witness that Pavlova was a rare combination of an artist of genius and a woman of kind, understanding spirit, and a large heart, to whom all evil was alien. One can only speak of her faults if absolutely determined to find them. She was, of course, human, and so had certain weaknesses, but they were the small unavoidable weaknesses to be found in every sensitive and impressionable woman. One must, however, always remember who Pavlova was, the responsibility that weighed upon her and the hard, self-sacrificing life which she led, and then, all the momentary outbursts of irritation, which were due to the strain of the business side of her art, will become intelligble and pardonable. Naturally those who surrounded her, her nearest collaborators were the first to feel such outbursts, and naturally too they were also directed at me (I was responsible for the administrative side) as well as at the maitre de ballet and the conductor. If a rebuke, even a sharp one, were received with the idea that in making it Pavlova did not wish to hurt, that it was fully justified, and that any kind of disorder was bound to upset her, making concentration on her own work difficult, the one rebuked would try to explain, and in a moment she would be perfectly calm again. But if any one of us, without considering the essence of the matter, made it a personal question, Pavlova would become seriously upset, for it showed that her collaborator, instead of trying to help her and make her task easier, was not really anxious to rectify the fault to which his attention had been drawn. But even these rare, more serious misunderstandings were cleared up very quickly. I have already mentioned that Pavlova's pliability of temper was truly extraordinary. In all sincerity she would forget what had happened and if I reminded her later that in the heat of the moment she had made such and such a remark. She would be very distressed and would say:

"Did I really say that?"

One should not forget that, firstly, such incidents were by no means frequent, and, secondly, that they only touched her regular collaborators, who had worked with her for a number of years. Those who knew her understood that these were not mere whims and fancies, but real worries relating to the enterprise. She had a right to expect her assistants to understand her — why should one aggravate such frictions, such very understandable flashes of temper? I must say in perfect good faith, that she was nearly always in the right. She had an unusually quick eye, taking in everything at a glance. On coming into a room, she would instantly see that a picture did not hang quite straight or that a bracket or a shelf was dusty. And it was the same

Pavlova's Arabesque.

on the stage. Giving a last glance before the performance, she would see in a second that so-and-so's make-up was not in order, that someone else's costume was creased, or that the shoe-ribbon of a third was not tied with due care; and Pavlova would be angry — why should she worry herself about these details, have her attention distracted, her mood spoiled, because the wardrobe supervisor had not noticed the crumpled dress or the stage-manager the faulty make-up? Similarly in the dances, she would instantly notice that one of the girls in the pas de quatre bent her head rather more than the others, or that in such-and-such a place she raised her arm sooner than she should have done. It was not the girl that in such cases became the object of her anger, but the maitre de ballet or the stage manager for not having rehearsed the ballet sufficiently. Naturally, now and again some fault is bound to occur and Pavlova was perfectly well aware of this. But she also knew that only by strict discipline, and a systematic insistence on a high standard from the artists, added to their own sense of responsibility on the stage, could the enterprise be kept in that atmosphere of art, which she had created by putting her whole soul into her work. She could not tolerate untidiness or carelessness in work. And yet, in spite of her being so strict and exacting, during all the years that I was with her, I can remember only two occasions when an artist was fined for some neglect. As a rule it went no further than a reproof.

What other faults, then, had she? She gave the greater part of her life to her art and the rest almost entirely to her home, charities, flowers, birds, sculpture, etc. She went nowhere, she had only a few friends, she was herself without the least sign of vanity or love of display, a model of modesty, sincerity and simplicity. Her life was so lived that one does not even know in what province of her heart or soul to look for faults.

After some outburst of Pavlova's, distressed by her tears, which invariably accompanied such moments, Clustine, our ballet-master, would come to me with his troubles and always ended with:

"Ah well, there's nothing to be done. She would not be Pavlova if she were like everybody else."

Speaking of Pavlova as an individual, I must say that she was very intelligent, and this must not be taken in the ordinary sense of the word. Not the intelligence that is a frequent attribute among people and is the result of education and experience, but in her there was a wisdom which showed itself frequently in her remarks, profound and pertinent. How often she regretted that she had never had a wider education, for the curriculum of the Theatrical School was merely that of all secondary schools, whereas she was interested in everything and felt the insufficiency of her book-learning.

And our nomadic life did not give much opportunity for study. Of course, travel, constant change of environment, meeting with a variety of interesting people, discussions of value, contact with unfamiliar worlds, gaining insight into the souls of others, as well as the knowledge of experiences already gained by others, is in itself a great school of wisdom that is to be envied, an unaccustomed mental educational curriculum, which by broadening one's views gives far more than any school programme. And, in addition, Pavlova possessed the gift of intuition to an extraordinary degree. Her first impressions nearly always proved correct. More interested in the problem of the happiness of man than in anything else, she was deeply unhappy whenever she saw poverty, ignorance or lack of hygiene, all of which we unfortunately saw a great deal of in Egypt, India, Mexico. She was very indignant at the irreconcilable contradiction of people building huge "Palace Hotels" and liners of unprecedented luxury and at the same time calmly passing by without noticing them, cases of the most flagrant injustice and misery. Her schemes of help were sometimes wonderfully fantastic and naive. Figures and mathematics were not her forte, but her impulses were invariably towards goodness.

This wisdom of which I have spoken was united in her with an extraordinarily child-like nature. She was a child not only in many matters outside her province, but in all her psychology, by its directness and her way of looking at many aspects of life. Even when she was in the best and most peaceful of humours, some small outside matter would suddenly upset her to such an extent that before one had time fully to grasp the cause, tears would be streaming down her cheeks. Perhaps that was why she was so fond of children, being so near to them in spirit.

She was as meticulously scrupulous about other people's property, as she was in her art, and she was equally scrupulous in all details of her private life. A handkerchief lent to her, or books given to her to read would give her no peace until returned. She would be deeply distressed when anything of hers disappeared; it was not the actual fact of the loss that would cause her suffering, but the thought that someone had coveted the property of another. Of course in our frequent travels, in our constant changes of hotel and theatre, such things have happened, but not often. One had to make the best of them. Once when living in the same place for some time, we noticed repeated disappearances, until, finally, a valuable pair of earrings vanished. Pavlova was very upset and I went to my room to write out for the police a statement of what had happened. On coming back and approaching her for the signature of the paper, I saw her sitting in the same place, pensive and still. When I held out the paper to her, she shook her head and said in a low voice:

"Never mind. They probably need those earrings more than I do.".

Pavlova in a Costume 1830.
(Photograph by van Riel, Buenos Aires.)

A study of Pavlova.
(Photograph by Hoover, California.)

CHAPTER X.
PAVLOVA'S POPULARITY.

Considering how well she was known, it is extraordinary how much was said about Pavlova in the newspapers that was not true. Rumours of an incredible nature floated about, fantastic memoirs were published in this or that country and, what is perhaps more remarkable still, they were frequently marked "copyright". We found it very difficult to keep a watch on all this. When we were somewhere in Australia, we could not possibly know what appeared in the press of America, or in South America keep track of the publishing of "Memoirs" in France or Germany, all the more so as these very often appeared in second-rate magazines. And on our return to Europe it was generally too late to raise any protest against articles that had appeared several months previously.

But two years ago, when we were in Australia, a whole book written in German appeared, having Pavlova's autograph stamped in gold on the cover, Pavlova herself being cited as the author. This was too serious to pass without comment.

On reading the book, we saw that part of it consisted of reprints of interviews from various papers, the rest being purely the invention of the unknown author, who, keeping as much as possible to the tone of the interviews, made Pavlova say quite incredible things. Pavlova was all the more outraged as she had often been approached about publishing her memoirs and had invariably answered with a refusal, considering that this could not be done while she was still on the stage. And, in this case, words and ideas were attributed to her which she never would have thought of. In the end it transpired that a perfectly respectable firm of publishers had been led into error. Legal steps had to be taken. When they were convinced of their mistake, they agreed to do what was necessary to withdraw the book from circulation and published their explanation of the affair in all the leading papers in Germany.

One would imagine that there was hardly anyone who did not know Pavlova — or had not seen her photograph. Those connected with the press, at all events, should have known what she looked like. And yet, photographs of totally unknown persons purporting to be Pavlova would appear in the newspapers. Quite a short time ago some short-legged young woman in a ballet skirt standing near a big gramophone was depicted in an important French journal, with a note from the editor to the effect that this was the celebrated Pavlova learning a dance to a gramophone accompaniment.

After her death also, portraits of unknown persons have appeared with an explanatory note stating that they were Pavlova.

A sensational item of news appeared in the newspapers a short while ago to the effect that while dancing in Birmingham — a city which has the reputation of being an unnecessarily strict censor of morals, Pavlova had been stopped halfway through her performance for dancing without tights. This piece of news raised a storm of indignation in the whole press. The Birmingham press agency, which collects everything that is said about the town amassed 1817 cuttings from newspapers printed in English all over the world, as well as 26 leading articles. In them the Birmingham municipality was severely taken to task for its outlook on the art of Pavlova and unmercifully ridiculed. The local journalists used to say that it was the municipality itself that had inspired the news in order to advertise itself and get Birmingham talked about! The extraordinary thing is that it did not seem to enter into anybody's head to test the accuracy of the rumour, which would at once have proved without foundation. In all her life Pavlova never once danced without tights, not because she objected to it on the stage — on the contrary, she was a great admirer of Isadora Duncan's dances and was always telling excited rigorists that antique dances should not be performed in any other way than that followed by Duncan — but because being a classical dancer herself, she did not consider it permissible, if only for the reason that tights, by clinging closely to the legs, give them beauty of shape and the appearance of lightness and ethereality.

Audiences of different countries react differently. The most enthusiastic were always the Russian, especially when composed of young students. They were prepared to stand a whole night at the box-office of a theatre in order to secure a ticket to see some favourite, and would even go without food to pay for it. All foreign artists who have visited Russia, agree on this one point—Russian audiences are the most enthusiastic of all. In England, where the National Anthem is played at the end of each performance, a finish is thereby put to ovations. In other countries, where this is not the custom, ovations and applause sometimes go on interminably.

The youth of Russia considered it obligatory to meet their favourites at the stage-door, even in severe frosty weather, only, perhaps to catch sight of the wrapped-up figure of the artist hurrying into his or her carriage and driving away.

English audiences are also very responsive, ready to give an enthusiastic reception to an artist who is at all worthy of it. During the London seasons at the Palace Theatre, special ballet matinées were given on Wednesdays. The success of these matinées was unprecedented. The audiences consisted mostly of women, often accompanied by their children, and at the end of the performance, one can say without exaggeration that at least half the public waited at the stage-door for Pavlova to come out. The crowd was so large sometimes, that several policemen were necessary to hold it back to allow Pavlova to get into her car. This custom prevails also in the provinces of England. Wherever Pavlova danced, there was a crowd at the end of the performance hoping to catch a glimpse of her. She was always surprised at the patience of the people, standing about sometimes for a whole hour on end. It used rather to worry her. Being tired out after a performance, she would have liked to take off her make-up and change her clothes quietly and leisurely, but she knew that she was being waited for. When she danced at Covent Garden, there was always a large number of people round the stage door. There were days on which she gave two performances, when she did not go home at all between the shows, but remained resting in her dressing-room. But on learning that people sometimes stayed on for over an hour without dispersing, she decided to warn them in future when she was not going home. After such warning the majority would walk away, but a few of the sceptical ones, thinking this was merely a subterfuge, would still wait about for quite a long time.

The audiences of America, with the exception of New York, Chicago and California, are much more reserved, especially those of the Middle West,

A Study of Pavlova.
(Photograph by Hoover, California.)

A Study of Pavlova.
(Photograph by Hoover, California.)

where it is quite the ordinary thing to see the spectators in the front rows of the stalls or in the side boxes chewing gum and not applauding at all.

We were giving a performance in one of the small towns of the Middle West. On arriving at the theatre in the morning I witnessed the following scene.

In the office sat an old farmer, the ideal type of Uncle Sam as he is generally represented, who was bargaining obstinately with the manager, protesting that three dollars for a seat was an unheard-of price, that he never paid more than two, but was ready to go up to five dollars for two seats — for himself and his daughter — but no more. The manager on his side insisted that for Pavlova's ballet the price was not abnormally high as was proved by the fact that only very few tickets remained unsold. Eventually the farmer was talked over. When paying the money he said in annoyance: "I wish somebody would tell me what this Pavlova is going to do; they all keep on repeating that she dances, but she can surely not dance the whole evening. She must therefore be going to do some talking and singing as well."

On our way back through California we passed through this same little town and the manager of the theatre came to the station to see us. While we were talking I reminded him of the old farmer and he told us that he had had a letter from the old man in which he expressed his pleasure and his gratitude for a performance such as he had never seen before, remarking at the same time that for a show like that the tickets ought to have been not three but five dollars and that therefore he was sending an additional four dollars for his two tickets. The manager added that if we knew how mean this wealthy farmer was we should understand how pleased he must have been.

The university towns show their appreciation in a peculiar way. Here the performances are much frequented by students and they have a special system of their own of expressing approval — a simultaneous clapping and knocking at a given signal and at stated intervals. Generally the public joins in and the effect is very impressive.

Pavlova danced several times in the town of the Mormons, Salt Lake City. Our performances always took place in the old theatre which was filled with memories and stories of olden days when the prophet of the Mormons was the absolute monarch of this state.

When visiting the office of the theatre I always took the opportunity of going through the files of old programmes bearing dates of the '70s and grown yellow with age. In these programmes, under the list of prices of seats, it was stated that the management was prepared to accept grain or other agricultural produce in payment for the tickets at a certain stated price. Each programme invariably ended with a reminder to the public that guns and all other firearms must be left in the office of the theatre.

On her first visit to Sydney, Pavlova received a triumphant welcome. A crowd of more than ten thousand people assembled to greet her on the square in front of the station. Being extraordinarily simple and modest, such welcomes and departures were always rather embarrassing to her. She felt a kind of artificiality and advertisement in them. To walk between two rows of people kept back by the police gave her an uncomfortable feeling and neither time nor repeated triumphs all over the world could accustom her to pomp and ceremony: she only submitted to them from necessity.

Cinematograph operators were positively her enemies, bustling about, running from side to side, delaying progress and always doing their utmost to photograph her at the closest possible range and straight in the face.

Knowing by experience the awful results of such photography — when the newspapers appeared the next morning — she would often, if the importunity were too great, hide her face with her hand or with a bouquet of flowers.

Our arrival in Japan — we landed in Yokohama a year to the day before the terrible earthquake that wrecked the city — was a curious and amusing experience. Representatives of the press were there and an unusually large number of photographers. I think there must have been at least forty, perhaps even more. And if one can say of European photographers that they are importunate and fertile in expedients, their Japanese colleagues far outstripped them. Nimble, agile, small of stature, they climbed up the stairs, got on the backs of sofas, squatted on the floor and in fact gave a regular show of their own.

The Japanese, famous for their amiability, showed Pavlova unwonted hospitality and attention. On discovering that she took an interest in Japanese art, they did their utmost to make it easy for her to study it and the Japanese aristocracy were just as cordial in this respect as eminent Japanese artists. We received invitations to private houses to look at collections of Japanese dresses six hundred years old and more, collections of bronzes, china and drawings; concerts were arranged to enable us to become acquainted with their music from the earliest times. Pavlova was naturally most interested in Japanese dancing and dancing schools.

The public of Japan followed our performances with the greatest interest, filling the theatres even in the most remote towns where no Europeans at all are to be found. With the exception of Tokio and Kobe, which have European theatres, Pavlova everywhere had to perform in real Japanese theatres, which are very interesting and picturesque.

The auditorium is in the shape of a large square, the floor of which is divided by means of low partitions into smaller squares, about five feet by five feet. The public sits on the floor in these small squares, which each hold five or six people, and all are dressed in national costume. The upper tiers and the gallery are partitioned off in the same way. Only at the back of the hall are there one or two rows of chairs for Europeans, or for those Japanese who are accustomed to sit in the European manner. Little Japanese women hand round trays with miniature teacups and teapots during the performance. A number of coloured lanterns hang round the hall. But if the auditorium is a wonderfully picturesque and interesting sight, the stage of a Japanese theatre caused us much heart-burning by the peculiarities of its arrangement. It is of the same breadth as the hall, but quite devoid of depth. There is no curtain, its place being taken by specially constructed screens slowly coming together. But the main discomfort is that the Japanese theatre does not recognise suspended scenery, its place being also taken by screens. Consequently, our scenery, because of its height, would not fit and had to be folded approximately in half, nailed on anyhow and during the intervals taken down again for other scenery to be put up.

The Japanese liked our performances, but most of all they liked ballets of a dramatic nature and they showed this in their partiality for "Autumn Leaves" and the "Swan".

It was most amusing to hear their clapping. The majority of the audience were women, and their hands are so tiny that one would think the theatre full of children.

The Japanese are very interested in European music and all European musicians receive a warm welcome in Japan. There is a conservatoire in Tokio where instruction is given in all European instruments and the pupils are taught composition and the theory of music.

We found Japanese music difficult to understand. The most usual instrument, the samisen, something like our balalaika but with a long neck, seemed to us very monotonous. But another instrument, the koto, a long, slightly concave board, with strings stretched on pins, gives out a beautiful, sonorous sound, and the execution of the Japanese on this instrument at times reaches perfection. We had the good fortune to hear a celebrated Japanese musician, a blind man, who wished to play for Pavlova a composition of his own entitled "Autumn Leaves" on the koto. It was very beautiful and in no way resembled what we are accustomed to regard as Japanese music.

Our sojourn in Japan gave us great pleasure and also was not without its influence upon the Japanese. Our dances were so much admired, that they started schools for classical dancing. Russian dancers were found in Harbin

Pavlova in a Dress of 1910, Fashion.
(Photograph by Schneider, Berlin.)

and Vladivostok, who became teachers, and two months after our departure we received photographs of one such school during a lesson. Little Japanese girls of ten and twelve years old looked very sweet in ballet-skirts.

The popularity of Pavlova was enormous. And this is not to be wondered at, for she travelled several times all over the world and her photograph was constantly appearing in papers and magazines, year after year. She was always recognised in the street, in theatres, in shops, and she would often complain how tiresome this was. People were constantly approaching her and talking to her in her walks. When a member of the audience in a theatre, she was constantly stared at through opera-glasses. Once, when she was resting in Italy, we went to the local theatre to see a play. During the interval we noticed two women gazing fixedly at her. A few minutes later, they came into our box and began to say how happy they were at seeing Pavlova at last. Suddenly, plucking up courage, she told them that they were mistaken, that she was not Pavlova but Madame Dandré. The ladies retired in confusion.

On another occasion we were on a steamer on the lake of Geneva. Stopping at some small place, one of the "calls" of the steamer, Pavlova suggested that we should get off and take a walk. When we left the steamer and saw nothing but fields and vineyards before us, she exclaimed:

"Here at last there is nobody to recognise me and I am at liberty to do as I please."

She had not uttered the words before two ladies passed us carrying large bunches of flowers. One of them stared at Pavlova, seemed to hesitate, then ran forward, seized her hand, kissed it and giving her the bouquet, ran away.

All this was so unexpected and so sincere that Pavlova was touched to the depths of her heart.

If there were many people who showed Pavlova every attention, who desired and sought her acquaintance, invited her to their houses and gave themselves out as her close friends, there were also quite as many who expressed their adoration through the medium of anonymous letters and verses, through bouquets of flowers "from an unknown admirer". How many there were of these anonymous admirers in Russia, rushing to the gallery for her every performance, spending their last penny in the purchase of a ticket!

There were also enthusiasts of this kind in England. In the last fifteen years, whenever Pavlova danced in London or in some of the nearer towns, two young girls and a young man, joined later by another young man, invariably waited for Pavlova at the end of each performance. At first Pavlova paid little attention to them, disliking adoration and exaggerated compliments of every kind, but eventually she was touched by their constancy and becoming convinced of their unusual tactfulness, as well as of the depth of feeling which her art evoked in them, she grew to like them and they remained her friends ever after.

Talking to one of these girl admirers, Pavlova asked her laughingly:

"Tell me, Penny, do you know yourself how often you have seen me dance?"

"Certainly, Madame," came the unhesitating reply, "yesterday I went for the 287th time."

The inhabitants of northern climes have the reputation of being cold and calm. The Norwegians, however, did not live up to this reputation when Pavlova danced in Oslo after an absence of several years. The theatre was on the Esplanade, on the side opposite to the hotel where Pavlova was staying. It was only a distance of a few paces between the theatre and the hotel, and in the lovely spring weather Pavlova would return on foot to the hotel after her performances. Nearly the whole of the audience would wait to see her home. The crowd would be so great at the entrance to the hotel that mounted police were necessary to keep order. On reaching her room, Pavlova would have to go out on the balcony and bow to the people. A tumultuous cheering would be shouted to her three times and only then would the crowd disperse. And it happened thus on every day of the four that she spent in Oslo.

In addition to her immense popularity, Pavlova's name commanded unusual respect. Sometimes obstacles that were seemingly insurmountable would arise, especially during our constant moves in time of war. It must be remembered that in our company, consisting of sixty-four persons (we took our small orchestra of twelve musicians with us) no less than nine different nationalities were represented, and it is easy to imagine the difficulties that would arise at the inspection of passports and luggage when crossing frontiers. But the magic name of Pavlova smoothed our path. Steamship companies would consent to change their habitual routes for us and to call at ports other than their customary ones. The captains would also do all in their power to help us.

A detachment of American troops stationed near St. Jago, in Cuba once did us a great service. Arriving there from South America, we learned on landing that a general strike had been proclaimed on the island, affecting railways, telegraphs and telephones. Our luggage was taken from the steamer to the theatre by the crew, who being Frenchmen, paid no attention to local conditions. But no performances were possible and we spent a whole week in complete uncertainty of what would follow. We were supposed to have already begun our season in Havana, but could not even get into communication with that town as the telegraph was not working. Several times I addressed myself to the local temporary military governor, to whom extensive powers had been given, begging him to help us, but, alas, he too was powerless. The two attempts he had made to send off trains had been unsuccessful. At last one day he sent for me — a train was going to start for Havana at 6 a. m. the next morning, but whether it would ever get there or not, no one could say. Former attempts had failed because the strikers had taken away the rails.

"It's true," added the governor, "that the guilty caught on the spot were immediately hanged and the track repaired."

He suggested that we could go by this train if we cared to. He would put two carriages at our disposal, but we should have to go entirely at our own risk. After discussing the matter with Pavlova we decided to try our luck. The most difficult problem of all was getting the luggage from the theatre to the station. We made an attempt to organise this transport in wheelbarrows, but nothing came of it as the strikers interfered immediately.

Somebody told us that the American troops had some excellent lorries and that it was only with the help of these that we could hope to save the situation. The American colonel, whom I approached with my request, replied that, though he had not the right to make his soldiers work for the transport of private persons, he would permit it for Pavlova with pleasure. He was obliged, however, to leave it entirely to his men to decide, at the same time emphatically refusing to allow the labour to be paid for.

A few minutes later, the delegates of the soldiers appeared and said that for Pavlova, who was so much loved in America, they were quite willing to do anything that was required.

The strong, healthy American youth worked with such good will, that our luggage was taken to the station and very quickly loaded in the vans.

At six o'clock the following morning we started.

As a general rule, the train from St. Jago to Havana takes eighteen hours. Our train took forty-eight, but we arrived eventually, although with great difficulty. All the stations were closed, no food could therefore be obtained, and the train had to stop near a village, to which we went to get ourselves some bread, eggs and fruit.

The engine driver was a working man, who, for high payment, had agreed to take the train. When, however, we were within twenty miles of Havana and counted on soon being there, he stopped the train and declared that he would go no further, as he was afraid that the Havana strike committee had been informed and he would be killed as soon as he was seen. No prayers no promises of reward were of any avail; he climbed down from the engine and disappeared, leaving the train standing on the track. Eventually

A Study of *Pavlova*.
(*Photograph by Smirnoff, London.*)

a negro stepped out from among the mixture of passengers on the train and said that he had been a train fireman and thought he could drive us the rest of the way if he got ten dollars. This sum was gladly handed him and the train moved on.

On arrival in Havana at about two o'clock in the morning we discovered that the strike was in full force there too and that all vehicles were stopped. As soon as they heard of our arrival some friends of ours came to meet Pavlova in a motorcar, while the rest of the company had to make their way on foot in search of lodgings. In the hotel, where rooms had been reserved for us, we learnt that the kitchen was closed, all the cooks, waiters and the whole staff having struck and gone away. As we had been the whole day practically without food, we asked where we could buy something to eat. A little cabmen's eating house was pointed out to us, and there we managed to get some bread, cheese and beer. On our way back to the hotel, we met four of our girls and they told us in despair that they had been tramping about hungry for two hours, and had not succeeded in finding any rooms: owing to the strike, everyone was too frightened even to open their doors at night. We showed them where they could get some food and told them to come on afterwards to our hotel, but the rooms there proved to be all engaged, and eventually they had to make shift in one of ours.

On our return journey from South America, we put in at Panama. On the day of our arrival news had been received of the end of the war. The general gladness of us, Russians, was darkened by the knowledge that Russia, in spite of all her sacrifices, had been forgotten.

Expansive and excitable, the negroes were particularly delighted. There are many of them in Panama. It was here for the first time that we saw a big motor car with an organ installed in the place where the body should be. This contrivance, with its brilliantly polished pipes sparkling in the sun, manned by several negroes, does the tour of the town, blaring out cake-walks. This, we were told, is the favourite amusement of the negroes, and this machine is brought out on every solemn occasion.

Famished Europe demanded food, and President Wilson ordered the enormous stocks of foodstuffs collected in America to be sent hurriedly overseas. All the steamers of private American companies were engaged for this purpose and we found ourselves in an exceedingly awkward situation, for the only possible way to leave Panama is by steamer; and the only regular lines between North America and Panama, touching Cuba, where we had a season, on the way, were American ones. We had, consequently, to wait and this was by no means the simple matter it looks. Our company, as I have already mentioned, comprised sixty-four persons and they had to be fed. As at that time there were already several thousand soldiers in Panama itself, and several huge hangars for aeroplanes with many soldiers training for flying near Colon (the town at the Atlantic Ocean end of the canal), was suggested to us that we should give some performances in Panama and Cocossola. The conditions under which these performances were given were extremely original. I should explain briefly here how the wonderfully equipped Panama Canal is built at its Pacific Ocean end.

It is divided into two separate water-courses, each one with an outlet to the sea, in order that the incoming and the outgoing steamers shall not interfere with each other and can be loaded or discharged without delay. On the broad embankment dividing the two sections of the canal, big warehouses have been erected to contain the merchandise for transshipment from steamers coming from the Pacific Ocean and going to the Atlantic, or vice versa. A part of one such warehouse was divided off, a stage was put up, and somehow everything necessary for our performances got together. The work was very complicated. Our scenery and all the suspended accessories had to be fixed to iron girders at an enormous height under the roof. The company of sailors put at our disposal for the purpose, however, performed this task brilliantly so that everything was very well arranged. The facade of our improvised theatre was decorated with flags of every nationality, among which, at the suggestion of the sailors themselves, and to the great joy of Pavlova, were also our Russian flags.

The whole of the beau monde of Panama came to the performance as well as some officers and several thousand sailors. As it was hot, the side walls of the warehouse, which moved apart by a special mechanism, were opened, and the effect this gave was totally unexpected. Steamers of various nationalities, going from one ocean to the other, were moored along both sides of the warehouse, and their crews, astounded by the spectacle, turned into a most enthusiastic audience, crowding the bulwarks and the shrouds. A tropical moon illuminating the whole made of it a fairy picture.

In Cocossola our performances took place in an aeroplane hangar, also presenting an unusual sight.

All this brought some variety into our lives, but we had already been a fortnight in Panama and the matter was becoming serious for us. The governor of Panama had telegraphed about our case to New York, but had received a reply that nothing could be done for the present.

As the interests of Russian subjects were looked after by the French Consul, I turned to him for assistance, in the name of Pavlova. This very amiable and kindly-disposed man, considering it his duty to come to our aid, got into touch with all steamship companies and consuls, but with all his wish to help could do nothing either. Finally, a few days later, he rang me up on the telephone and asked me to come round and see him. It appeared that he had received a telegram informing him that a large French cargo boat (12 000 tons) leaving Chili with nitrate, would be passing through the Panama Canal in two or three days' time on its way to one of the ports of North America. On this steamer there was certain accommodation for passengers. I told the consul that we had to get to Cuba at all costs and that we must get the captain to consent to change his route and call at the island. He declared, however, that this was quite out of the question, as the steamer was under charter to the French Government, and that any talk of it was useless.

In the end, however, he agreed to cable to the French Government stating Pavlova's request and explaining the position of affairs.

To his surprise and to our great joy, Paris telegraphed its consent. As soon as the steamer arrived, I went on board to talk things over with the captain. He proved to be a perfectly charming Provencal. Showing him the wire from Paris, I asked him whether it was true that he had passenger cabins on board his ship. He replied in the affirmative and in his turn asked how many we were. At my mention of the number (sixty-four) he nearly had a fit, as the steamer had only two cabins for two persons each. The position, however, was so critical that something had to be decided upon. When I had boarded the boat, I had noticed the excellent wide deck. The question involuntarily presented itself — would it not be possible to set up tents? The captain said he would have no objection, but that he had neither beds, linen nor wash-hand basins, and the journey to Cuba takes five days.

I went off to the director of the American war stores and requested his permission to buy 64 beds, and a corresponding number of mattresses, sheets, wash-hand basins, etc. He was sorry, but it was not to be thought of, as the stores could not be sold to private persons. In the end, however, he consented to ring up the officer in command of the troops, who replied with an immediate order that everything we required be supplied us at the government price, explaining that an exception could be made for Pavlova.

The articles were received, delivered on board the steamer and a regular camp was pitched on the deck. With the help of tents and pieces of cloth we arranged ourselves there very comfortably, even cosily. Only once during the whole of the journey did we have a night storm accompanied by a downpour. All the rest of the time the weather was glorious, and everybody thoroughly enjoyed the voyage on the nitrate steamer.

Pavlova in Valparaiso 1918.

The captain did everything possible with the smallness of the stores in his possession to feed such a crowd and was constantly treating us to wine.

We did well to have taken the risk, for the first passenger steamer left Panama three weeks after our departure, and we had waited twenty-three days as it was.

Trading interests, always eagerly on the look-out for anything that a gullible public will greedily take up, made an extensive use of Pavlova's name — "Pavlova Perfume", "Pavlova Powder", "Pavlova Fashions for the year 1925", high "Pavlova boots" in America, "Pavlova Ices" in London, "Pavlova Cigarettes".

More pleasing and very characteristic was the letter received by Pavlova from the captain of a tug-boat accompanying the fishing fleet of one of the small English towns. He wrote to say that he had seen her on the stage and it would bring him good luck if he could call his steamer "Anna Pavlova". Pavlova gladly gave her consent and soon after we received a photograph of the boat with the name "Anna Pavlova" in big letters on its side.

It has happened, though rarely, that the fame and popularity of Pavlova produced no effect. When we were in Amsterdam, the management of the municipal theatre, wishing to be attentive to Pavlova, invited her and the whole of the company to visit the little town of Volendam, near Amsterdam, famous for having preserved all the characteristics of old Holland. Its population of fisherfolk wear the national costume and keep to all the ancient customs.

Arrived at Volendam, we strolled about the town, eventually coming to the quay, where there were a lot of children, looking very pretty in Dutch bonnets and wooden shoes. Some of the members of the company had their cameras and amused themselves arranging the children into groups in order to "snap" them.

Among those present was an old man, a very typical figure with a very typical face, and the photographers asked Pavlova to stand next to him. This she did, and taking his arm was thus photographed. Then the children danced in a ring and Pavlova joined in, taking the hand of the old man. When the time for our departure came, we noticed that the old man went up to the manager of the theatre and, pointing to Pavlova, was saying something to him. The manager, evidently surprised, began to explain, but the old man obviously insisted. We came up and asked what the matter was. It appeared that the veteran wanted to be paid for his trouble, "that lady" — Pavlova — having been photographed and having danced with him. When it was explained to him who "that lady" was, he replied that he cared nothing: she had been photographed with him and had danced with him, she must pay. Pavlova laughed heartily, but took the part of the old man, insisting on his being given the money.

* * *

Emil Ludwig, the celebrated German writer, the biographer of Napoleon and Bismarck, took up the question of who were the ten greatest women of our time, judged according to the services they had rendered mankind in any field of activity.

The list which he offers his readers comprises the celebrated scientist, Madame Curie, Joan Adams, the American pioneer in matters of social reform, Annie Besant, the head of modern Theosophy, Queen Marie of Rumania, and several others, among them Pavlova.

He prefaces his list with the following words: "The most beautiful sight that one has ever seen was a dancer, standing on the points of the toes of her left foot, barely touching her partner. Even the musicians stopped for one instant, so incomparable was this picture, so beautiful and graceful was this charming woman, almost a goddess, suspended, as it were, in the air, not feeling the weight of her own body...." "And the most terrible thing done by a woman, was when during the war I saw a woman run into a room, waving an evening paper and shouting, her eyes blazing 'A great victory on the Eastern front, five thousand enemy killed...'"

An Australian lady wrote to me a few days ago:

"Last week I went into the London museum to see Madame's costumes, and felt that I must tell you how very wise I think it was of you to put them there in their lovely case. For all time they will be a reminder of Madame's beauty and her art."

"While I was there a young policeman walked in and stood for a while looking at the costumes. Then he turned to me and said: 'Wasn't she wonderful! I am glad that this is my beat, because I come in all through the day and look at these.'"

"I thought it showed how Madame's art made a lasting impression upon the most unexpected people."

Pavlova in Valse Caprice.
(London 1910.)

Pavlova Painting Herself in "Chopiniana".

CHAPTER XI.
PAINTERS AND SCULPTORS.

It may seem surprising that in spite of Pavlova's world wide fame and the fact that she was a wonderful subject for painters-and sculptors, she was not more often reproduced by brush and chisel. The reason is to be found in her frequent tours involving ceaseless travelling and the nature of her work which left little time for sittings.

Her first portrait was painted in Russia by the artist Shmarov and is reproduced in this book. Next she was painted full length by Steinberg as a Muse, the portrait being an excellent likeness. She was also painted by the celebrated artist Serov, of whom I have already spoken. Both Pavlova and the artist were very busy at the time and by mutual agreement the sittings took place after 11 o'clock at night, when her rehearsals were over. Serov wanted to paint her in a long ballet skirt and "in the air". For this Pavlova had continually to leap, so that Serov should receive the correct impression of the position of the arms and body in movement.

In Berlin her portrait was painted by Professor Schuster Walden, unfortunately, not with great success, and in London by John Lavery. In this latter work she is shown in the costume of a swan lying by the side of a fountain. It is now in the Tate Gallery. Its considerable merits cannot be denied, but it fails as a likeness of Pavlova. More successful is the head in "Bacchanal" by the same artist. In Brussels her portrait in Syrian dress was painted by the artist, Aime Stevans, but this is rather a picture than a portrait. Bakst with whom Pavlova was on friendly terms, begged her in Paris to sit for him. She consented, but was disappointed in his work.

Seeing some works of the famous artist, Sorin, at an exhibition in Paris, Pavlova found them excellent as far as likeness was concerned and original in treatment. When he had made her acquaintance Sorin suggested painting her portrait. Although this was in the summer and Pavlova was free, Sorin feared that she would not give him the necessary number of sittings. I therefore proposed that he should come to London and stay with us, and I gave up my study as a studio. In this way Pavlova was able to chose the time most convenient for her.

To give Pavlova her due, she posed with such patience that I was quite astonished. Not wishing to interfere, I did not come to look at the work in progress, but casting a glance at it after four or five sittings I was over-joyed. It was Pavlova, so life-like, so spiritual, that a better portrait could not have been imagined. I called up the whole household in order to show them Sorin's work and they were all delighted. I told Sorin of the impression his picture had made on me, and he answered with a smile:

"Wait, it will be even better."

I could not help thinking how good a thing it would be to keep the portrait just as it was, unfinished.

The sittings continued. From a technical point of view doubtless the portrait was getting better, more finished, but for me it became nothing more than just a portrait: what had been put into it at the beginning and during the earlier sittings by the gifted artist, had vanished forever. Its good qualities nevertheless were so great that the French Government bought it for the Luxembourg Museum.

Sketches of Pavlova were made by the American artist, Troy Kinney, who specialised in sketches of movement and dancing. Each time Pavlova came to New York he was at the theatre, sketching all the while. Some of these sketches were very successful.

Some years ago, a very well-known London artist whom Pavlova knew, suggested painting her portrait. Pavlova consented, but on returning home after the first sitting declared that nothing would come of it, for the artist wanted her to dress in something vivid and to take up a pose which did not come naturally to her. Apparently her objections were not to the taste of the artist for there were no more sittings and nothing further was done in the matter. But there was an astounding sequel to the incident some seven or eight years later. We were touring one of the large towns of the British Dominions when Pavlova received a letter from a rich collector inviting her to come and look at his pictures. In the letter he added that she would probably be interested to see also a portrait of herself. This was certainly interesting and intriguing. We went, and to her astonishment Pavlova recognised this as the very portrait which had been begun in London. Evidently the artist had completed it later from memory. It bore a certain resemblance, but the general impression was not to Pavlova's advantage. One cannot help wondering how far the artist had the right (the moral right, of course, I mean) to sell this picture as a portrait of Pavlova.

She had a particular love for sculpture. When in Paris, she made daily visits to the Rodin Museum and to all the exhibitions. Constant study of the human body and of its lines, developed in her a fine understanding

A Group of Russian Artists with the painting of Pavlova by Sorin in the backfound.

Moskwin   Stanislawsky   Chaliapin   Kachalov   Sorin

of sculpture and a critical valuation of its works. The first sculptor whom she came to know was Cluzel, many years ago in St. Petersburg. He was very successful in his statuettes of dancers of the Imperial Ballet. He made a statuette of Pavlova and modelled her foot as well, which latter was afterwards cast in bronze. I have given this to the London Museum, where it is now to be seen.

Then the Russian artist Soudbinin came to London and modelled Pavlova in "The Swan", making also several small and very successful statuettes. Two statuettes were also made by Prince Troubetzkoy. These were very graceful and elegant, but do not give a very good idea of her. Another statuette in "The Swan" was also made by the Italian artist, the Marquis de Rosales, and in America she became acquainted with the very well-known American woman sculptor, Malvina Hoffman, who later became her close and devoted friend. Malvina Hoffman made a lovely statuette of her in "Gavotte". This was cast in bronze and found its way into many an American drawing-room. Following on that, she made a large bronze group of Pavlova and her partner in "Bacchanal". This group is now in the gardens of the Luxembourg Museum. Finally, the last big work by Malvina Hoffman

Pavlova Modelling a Statuette.

dedicated to Pavlova took the form of a life-size bas-relief of her and her partner in "Bacchanal". This bas-relief contains 58 different groups and is truly a remarkable work of art. In all probability it will be acquired by one of the American museums and will decorate some huge entrance-hall.

Several statuettes of Pavlova in various dances were also successfully made by the sculptor de Boulogne.

In all her life Pavlova never had a single lesson either from a painter or a sculptor, but possessed a quite extraordinary gift for drawing, and even more for modelling. Whenever she had leisure she would take to pencil and paints. This generally happened at Salzo-Maggiore in Italy, which she visited every year for treatment. I would go off early for a walk and bring back with me a large bunch of wild flowers, which she liked to draw better than anything. She always drew with such enthusiasm that it was difficult to tear her away from the task to go to lunch or dinner. She would be quite annoyed at being interrupted, declaring that work should never be stopped half way, for if not finished the same day many of the flowers would shed their petals and the buds open by next morning. Coping with the laws of perspective, of which she knew nothing, and trying to obtain shadow effects were tasks of great difficulty. Her despair in such cases was childishly touching. She used to say to me:

"You don't realise how difficult it is. I can feel it, but I don't know what has to be done."

And yet, she would get more or less what she wanted, and such work of her brush as still remains, naive and primitive, is full of artistic feeling. Her natural talent for sculpture was much stronger. Above everything she was interested in the body in motion, and usually took herself as a model. Though, here also, lack of technique was a serious handicap, she knew the body so well, was so sensitive to the poses and movements of dancing, that she made very rapidly and successfully, statuettes of herself in which her own image was correctly reproduced.

In Germany she made the acquaintance of the celebrated German sculptor, Professor Lederer, the author of the huge monument to Bismarck in Hamburg. Lederer was for many years her great admirer. He considered that in her art she created figures that were ideal for sculpture. He was quite enraptured when he saw her statuettes and suggested that she should come and work in his studio. It was very amusing to see Pavlova and the professor working side by side. Lederer had an enormous studio granted him by the State, for his works were on a very large scale. At the same time he was also engaged on a gigantic group, working on it standing on a high scaffolding, while below, at a small table decorated with flowers by the attentive hand of the professor, was Pavlova, modelling her little figures. Often she would ask him to help her or to show her how to put right some small detail, but he invariably refused, saying that her statuettes were so attractive just because they were made by an instinctive sensitiveness, and should not be corrected as they would then lose their charm.

Giving way to his insistence, Pavlova agreed to have her statuettes reproduced in china. In order to do this it was necessary to go to Thuringia to one of the old German factories. Pavlova was highly delighted with the atmosphere of the place. A tiny ancient town surrounded by deep forests and an old castle on a cliff overhanging the river, were wonderfully in keeping with artistic work. But most of all she liked the factory, which was unlike anything we could have pictured under that name.

It was built about 300 years ago and has not changed in any way since. The quiet buildings lying among gardens, the light rooms, the extraordinarily pleasant young artists — it was all very attractive. Certain details about the firing had to be discussed and Pavlova was given one of the gifted young artists to explain these matters to her. On one occasion when admiring a charming figure made by him, Pavlova suddenly noticed that he had only one arm. In reply to our question, he told us that when the had just finished his art school training and was given a post in the factory, he was obliged to go to the War, where he had lost his right arm. After the War he came back to the factory and with great effort of will and much practice, he had trained himself to model using only his left hand.

We used to arrive at the factory in the morning and Pavlova would set to work enthusiastically; then lunch with the artists and work again until the evening. As in the case of everything that she did, she was not satisfied with the statuettes which she made, and would not have them either put on exhibition or sold. But a year later, when all those who had seen them agreed that the statuettes were charming, she relented and gave her consent to the factory to sell them. In my opinion it is these statuettes that give one the very best idea of Pavlova; not by facial resemblance, for that she could not attain, but because she can be immediately recognised by the lightness of the figure and the grace of the movements.

Porcelain Statuette by Pavlova.

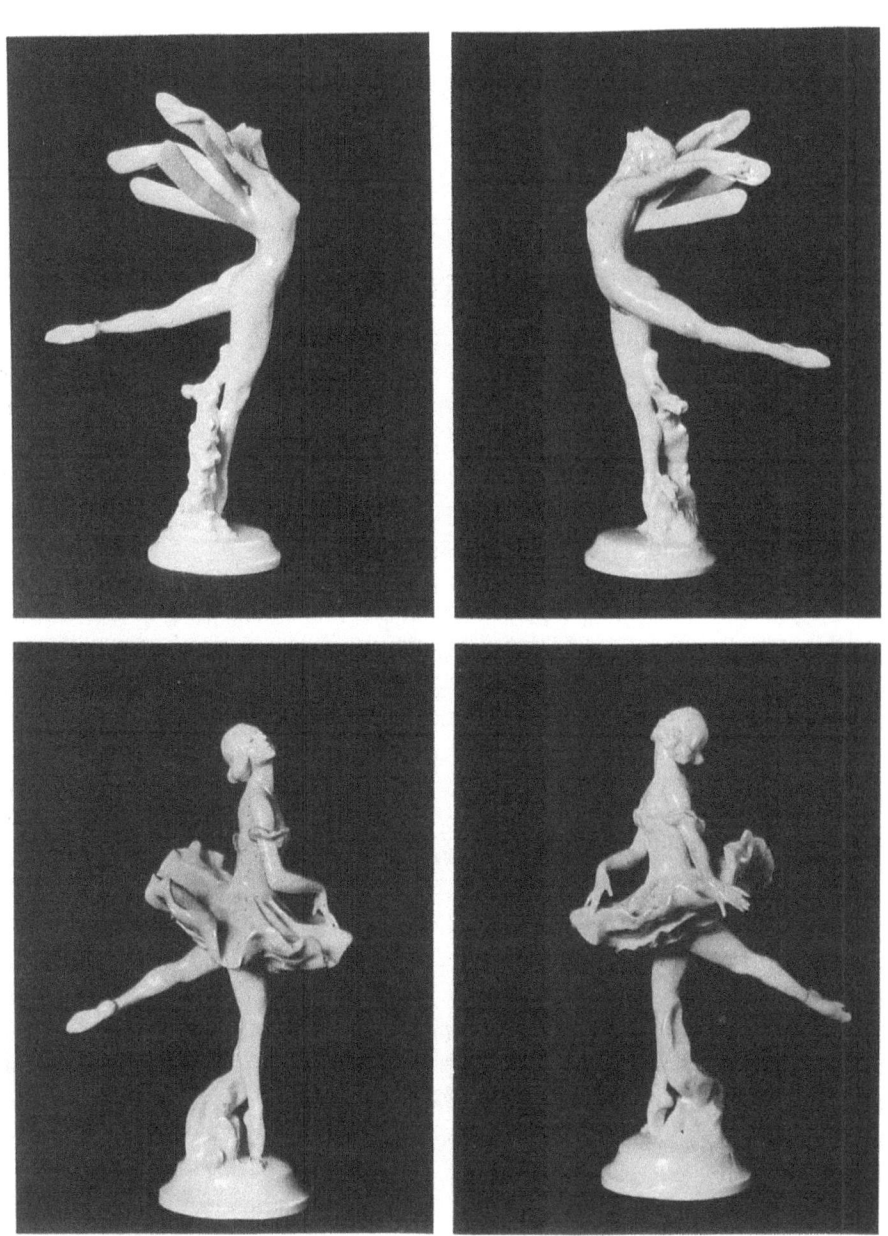

Porcelain Statuettes by Pavlova.

CHAPTER XII.

PAVLOVA AND DIAGHILEV.

I do not wish to enter into controversial matters in this book, but I feel that it is necessary to correct certain statements — as the actual facts are not known to many. A true light on them will be of value to future writers on the ballet and to the historian of the theatre of our time.

I have frequently read and heard it said lately, that Pavlova was introduced to Western Europe by Diaghilev; that it was he who first discovered her, and that to him she owed the beginning of her career.

This is not so.

Pavlova had danced in Sweden, Denmark and Germany the year before the first Diaghilev season in Paris, and Diaghilev's decision to add the ballet to his opera season of 1909 was only taken following the success of Pavlova's European tour and at her persuasive insistence.

My acquaintance with Diaghilev began at the St. Petersburg University, where we both belonged to the Faculty of Law. Our good relations continued ever after all through the long years. I always kept in touch with the various stages of his career from the time he took upon himself the editorship of the art journal "Mir Iskoustva", published at the expense of the rich art-patroness Princess Tenishev. Being on friendly terms with him, I also saw quite a lot of him when, as an official, he was attached to the Director of the Imperial Theatres and took a leading part in the publication of the "Annual". We used also to meet occasionally at the time of his remarkable exhibition of Russian portrait-painting and during his concerts of Russian music in Paris. Then later, I met him during the first Russian opera "Boris Godounov" and finally, the first combined season of opera and ballet.

I must here touch upon the position at that time of the Russian Imperial Theatres.

The Imperial Theatre in Russia was a huge organization, the only one of its kind for size and magnificence in the whole world. It had three theatres with four troupes and a theatrical school in St. Petersburg, and three theatres with three troupes and also a theatrical school in Moscow. Having been all over the world and having visited all the existing royal, state, municipal and private theatres, I consider myself fully justified in saying, that for lavishness of scale, artistic unity and model execution, there never was, nor is there today, anything approaching what was to be seen on the stages of the Russian Imperial Theatres.

The two opera-houses — the Marinsky in St. Petersburg and the Bolshoy in Moscow — had undoubtedly the first choruses in the world, not only for size and for the beauty and wide range of voices, but also for excellence of execution. The orchestras — of a hundred performers each — were not only composed of first-class musicians, but included well-known professors from the conservatoire as soloists. The ballet troupes of St. Petersburg and Moscow each had two hundred dancers.

The peculiar feature of the Imperial Theatres was that service in them was service under the State, and every artist, be he of the opera, drama, ballet, chorus or orchestra received a life pension at the end of his term of services (twenty years). Those who could still continue to work at the end of the twenty years, received a salary in addition to their pension both continuing to be paid even during the three months of the summer vacation.

This system, guaranteeing a livelihood for life, made a man value his service and the result was permanent orchestras, choruses and corps de ballet of exceptionally fine, harmoniously-working units.

The singers, the musicians and even the members of the chorus received their training in the Imperial conservatoires; the artists of the drama and the ballet in the theatrical schools, which were divided into two sections — the so-called "drama course" and "ballet course". This latter was open to children of ten, who received there a general education as well as a specialised ballet training.

On finishing the ballet school, the pupils were put directly on the stage, there to progress according to their natural gifts and their diligence: to become artists of prominence or to remain in the modest ranks of the c o r p s d e b a l l e t.

It must here be added that the Imperial Ballet School, founded as far back as the time of the Russian Empress Elizabeth and existing without a break for a hundred and fifty years, carried on the best French traditions, brought over to the banks of the Neva by a series of talented teacher-ballet-masters — Didelo, Perrault, St. Léon and Petipa.

The decorative part of the Imperial Theatres was also placed on a model footing. At one time the productions were in the hands of scenery-designers, who specialised in the subject, understanding stage conditions and stage perspective perfectly. Frequently their productions were very successful, but later they fell into a rut. In this matter also the Imperial Theatres stood on a much higher plane than others, executing all their own scenery and costumes having immense and excellently equipped workshops, and employing for the purpose the best scene-painters with a whole army of experienced assistants and workmen. Some of these scene-painters were true artists and the names of many of them are bound to find a place in the history of the Imperial Theatres. Lambin, Botcharov, Ivanov, Allegri who were responsible for so many fine productions, can never be forgotten.

Nevertheless, wishing to attain a still higher level of artistry in their productions, the management of the Imperial Theatres set out, in the first years of the century, to attract distinguished artists to take a leading part in theatrical productions, entrusting to them not only the designing of the scenery, but also of the costumes, in this way achieving a complete unity of impression.

Foremost among the artists whose help was so recruited were Bakst, Alexander Benois, Golovin and Korovine. The result was an ideal fusion of artistic setting with perfect execution. Foreigners visiting St. Petersburg were amazed at the performances in the Imperial Theatres and frankly admitted that Western Europe had nothing to equal them.

Diaghilev, who in 1907 under the auspices of the Grand Duke Vladimir and some French patronesses, had arranged a series of concerts of Russian music in Paris, quickly realised the great interest shown in this totally unknown music. He then conceived the idea, which proved successful, of showing Russian art on a broader scale, namely, as opera. In 1908, through the good offices of the Grand Duke, he was given the entire setting of the opera "Boris Godounov" by the management of the Imperial Theatres, and this was produced at the Grand Opera, Paris, with enormous success.

This success created so much interest among the people who were helping Diaghilev that they agreed to subsidise a whole season of Russian opera in Paris. This was in 1909. And it was in 1908 that Pavlova and her partner Adolf Bolm made a first tour in Europe.

A small, but well-chosen company composed of artists of the Imperial ballet, including such first-class dancers as Mrs. Legat, Bolm, Shiriaev, Obuchov, Mmes. Egorova, Wiell etc., accompanied Pavlova. The performances began in Helsingfors, then they were given in Copenhagen, Stockholm, Berlin, Dresden, Leipzig and a number of other towns. The success of the performances, as I have already said, was quite remarkable.

German critics frankly admitted that the appearance of Pavlova and this company was a revelation, for, looking upon the ballet as long since dead, they suddenly perceived that it was not only alive, but so beautiful that it must be given an honoured place among other scenic arts.

A Portrait of Pavlova by Shmaroff 1909.

The celebrated German critic Oscar Bie, who had just published an important work on dancing, wrote that unfortunately he had published it before seeing Pavlova. Had he seen her first, the book would have been different, but having seen her he understood that he had not been wrong in writing about the ballet, recognising in it an art full of vitality and worthy of high rank.

The Society of Berlin Artists gave in honour of Pavlova and her company a great banquet at which speeches were made by distinguished artists, saying that Pavlova's arrival had opened out new horizons of beauty in hitherto unknown movements and poses.

In the winter of the same year, 1908, Pavlova and Diaghilev lunched with me in St. Petersburg. He had just come back from Paris and he told us that a special committee had been formed there, composed of society women under the presidency of the Grand Duke, with the object of arranging the Russian season. Pavlova and I then tried to persuade Diaghilev to take advantage of this opportunity to show the ballet as well. He was terrified at our suggestion. He began to descant on the absurdity of it — the French were quite uninterested in ballet, nobody in Paris went to the ballet with the exception of a few old season-ticket holders, and the appearance of a male dancer on the stage would create a veritable scandal, as for thirty years Paris had been accustomed to seeing women dancers take the part of men.

We argued our point with heat, laying stress on the extraordinary success achieved by Pavlova's ballet in Sweden, Denmark and Germany.

Diaghilev, however, stuck to his opinion that Paris being the world's artistic centre, did not consider the opinions of other places, and that success in Berlin did not preclude an utter failure in Paris.

These conversations between us were renewed on several occasions. Eventually Diaghilev told us that he was returning to Paris to see the Grand Duke and the committee, and that he would suggest our idea of the ballet to them, but was convinced beforehand that he would get no support.

A few days later, however, we received a telegram from him stating that the committee had approved of the idea of the ballet, but had made it a condition that Pavlova should take part in it.

In spite of having signed contracts for that same time with Berlin and Vienna, Pavlova agreed to reduce the number of these performances and to appear during the Diaghilev season in Paris as well.

I have seen it stated that Diaghilev caused a revolution in the Russian Ballet, that he led it away from its antiquated, false forms and showed it to Europe in a new guise. Only those utterly ignorant of the subject can claim anything so absurd.

Diaghilev brought about no revolution and was not in a position to do so. Having no official position he could not influence the tendency of the ballet in Russia but, when he was arranging his first season of Russian ballet in Paris, in the position of impresario, he could certainly have chosen his own repertoire. However for his first season he merely took the ballets composed by Fokine ("Cleopatra", which had been given in St. Petersburg under the name of "Nuits d'Egypte", "Pavillon d'Armide", "Sylphides" — formerly "Chopiniana") and dances from the opera "Prince Igor". They had all been given on the Imperial stage. The scenery and costumes for these ballets when given by Diaghilev during his Paris season were merely done again by the artists who had designed them in St. Petersburg, and Fokine, who had originally produced ballets in St. Petersburg, now produced them in Paris.

Diaghilev took advantage of the summer season, when all the dancers of St. Petersburg and Moscow were free, to get together a first class troupe, inviting also the best soloists. To his surprise, the success of the ballet was greater than that of the opera. The ballet was a totally new spectacle for the Parisian public, and Diaghilev decided to confine himself to ballets only during the following season, entrusting their production to Fokine, while such men as Bakst, Benois, Roerich and Golovin were responsible for the decorative side.

The music chosen for the new ballets being by Russian composers — Rimsky-Korsakow, Borodin, Stravinsky and Tcherepnin, — Diaghilev was perfectly justified in calling that summer season in Paris "The season of Russian Ballet".

This fortunate collaboration of Russian forces in the persons of Fokine and famous Russian painters, to the accompaniment of Russian music, lasted for three seasons, during which such remarkable works as "Petroushka", "Coq d'Or" and "Carnival" among others, were produced. It was at this time that Diaghilev rightly decided to invite the collaboration of well-known French composers also, staging two ballets by Debussy, one by Ravel and also one by Laurent Schmidt, Rinaldo Hahn and the German composer, Richard Strauss.

This, one may say, brings the brilliant period of the Diaghilev Russian Ballet to an end.

In 1914 Diaghilev parted from Fokine, who had given him a series of masterpieces and was responsible for the success of the venture. Then he gradually drifted away from Bakst, who not only gave him the scenery for "Scheherazade", "Cleopatra", "Carnival", "Spectre de la Rose", but was also a great personal friend. Finally he also separated from Benois, who, owing to his remarkable erudition, his penetrating understanding in all matters concerning art, and his extraordinary critical sensibility, was a most valuable counsellor.

Diaghilev himself was a clever and very well-educated man, a great connoisseur of Russian painting and a wonderful organiser, who knew how to enlist the collaboration of necessary and useful people. He could also find sympathizers with his plans and people who gave him material support. Unfortunately, with the passing of the years, he became so dictatorial as to refuse to see any other point of view but his own. I have often heard him declare that in a business individuals were only a secondary consideration — that new people could always be found to take the place of those who left — that business had to be looked at as a whole, and therefore it was immaterial whether a certain dancer appeared today and quite another tomorrow.

Perhaps, if you surround yourself with mediocrities, this principle is right; in that case the exchange of one person for another is little felt and of no moment. But one should only exchange such man as Fokine, Bakst or Benois for others of a like calibre, and that is not possible. Their places were taken by such substitutes as Diaghilev could find, and these new people were incapable of creating original works that required, in addition to talent and knowledge, the ability to handle large numbers, and any attempts to follow in the footsteps of Fokine would only have resulted in feeble parodies of his productions.

In order to get out of this situation Diaghilev decided to seek out new forms of an original creative order, in no way resembling anything that had come before. When the first ballet of this kind made its appearance, the public found it amusing and the press, regarding it as an experiment, treated it with tolerance. But, to their surprise, the critics saw exactly the same kind of thing in later ballets which could no longer be regarded as experimental, but must be accepted as Diaghilev's definite new style; and this naturally raised protests. At first the critics condemned and later, simply said nothing.

While recognising the services rendered by Diaghilev to Russian art in general, and to the ballet in particular, during the first and unfortunately the shorter, period of his activity, I cannot refrain from pointing out the immense harm he did to the ballet in the second, and longer period.

He directed it along a totally false, artificially-constructed track of pseudo-originality and in the ceaseless pursuit of "novelty at any price" instructed his maitres de ballet to produce something so entirely new that it should in no way resemble what had been seen before — that was to be their fixed aim and objective. The result of this determination to break away as far as possible from the traditions of Russian classical ballet, soon made

Portrait of Pavlova by John Lavery.
(Tate Gallery, London.)

itself felt. It ended by making contortionists out of dancers by years of practising grotesques, by teaching them to make absurd, angular movements, not unlike those of eccentrics at a circus; it ended in fact in the troupe forgetting how to dance classical ballet. It was pitiful to see the tortures of really fine dancers, trained in the Imperial Ballet school, when occasionally they danced some classical dance, so affected by contortioning had their execution become. Diaghilev himself, when asked by Pavlova why he did not give "Sylphides", which was so popular with the public, replied frankly:

"But whom have I got to dance it?".

Pavlova, who had a great liking for Diaghilev and thought highly of the work he had done in his early years, was always very interested in everything he did, looking upon much of what he produced as merely transitional steps leading to something new and, possibly, successful. Whenever we were in London or Paris during Diaghilev's season, she invariably went to the performances, anticipating them with great excitement and interest, hoping to see some new revelation in art.

The first time after the war that she saw a performance of his in London, they were giving "Boutique Fantasque". She followed it all with keen interest, finding much in it that was good. And then, at the very end of the ballet, before the curtain dropped, eight men-dancers each picked up a woman-dancer in long skirts and turned her upside-down in front of the audience. The skirts fell down showing the legs to the waist. The spectacle was not aesthetic and in no way flowed out of what had come before. I was simply thunderstruck. Turning to Pavlova, I saw tears of mortification in her eyes. She was deeply hurt and murmured through her tears:

"What mockery!"

Being very sensitive and impressionable, she keenly resented anything that suggested profanation of, or lack of respect, for, art.

"Pas d'Acier" produced so depressing an effect on her that she left the theatre immediately and was quite upset for several days. Striving hard to understand what she saw, to find some explanation or excuse for it, or listening to arguments and opinions, she repeated again and again:

"Yes, but where is art in all this?"

Unfortunately, what so often happens in theatrical life, happened now.

Being considered an authority, having an important name and great prestige, Diaghilev contrived to make the public believe in him absolutely. The glamour of the first seasons — of "Scheherazade", "Sylphide", "Carnival" — enriched him with the public's confidence for the whole of his future career. He was looked upon almost as the founder of Russian ballet, and the public, and also to some extent the critics, especially the English critics, followed him credulously, considering him a prophet, whose mission it was to lead the art of the ballet to some new, enchanted lands. It must also be borne in mind that Diaghilev had something in the nature of a monopoly of ballet in most of the chief towns of Europe, being able to produce and present his performances as none other could. He had, after all, spent more than fifteen years between London, Paris and Monte Carlo, gathering a crowd of votaries around him. The Diaghilev season became almost the chief event of the theatrical year and aroused an enormous interest among the public, who never noticed that, if there was novelty in these spectacles, art had long since forsaken them.

Assisting at these performances on the Continent, I frequently and attentively studied the expressions on the faces of those present — invariably a cosmopolitan public: French people do not pay such high prices and rarely go to these performances.

In a little while one could see a look of perplexity, or simply of lack of comprehension, steal over the faces — what is all this? they seemed to ask. And then one became aware that each one, not quite knowing what his reaction to these productions should be, would watch his neighbours — if they applauded, when applause was necessary. Sometimes it seemed as if some witty man were having a joke, testing the public — saying to himself 'how much longer before they notice the hoax?'

In speaking of dances and ballet, one must come to some definite conclusion, some clear understanding, as to what is actually meant by the dance and what are the aims of the ballet.

Lamartine says that dance is mute poetry.

Théophile Gautier declares that dancing it nothing else than the art of showing off elegant and graceful forms in various attitudes favourable to the development of line.

Le Dictionnaire de la Danse defines the word dance as meaning the moving of the body in harmony with a certain rhythm. One can give another definition made quite recently: —

"Dance is the expression of human emotions and passions by the aid of measured movements; it is the making manifest of physical beauty through poses and rhythmical motions; it is the orderly arrangement of groups in decorative and harmonious design."

I will not undertake to solve the question as to which of these definitions is the most correct. But one and all they speak of poetry and grace of the body, and one thing is certain — dance must have beauty as its foundation. We go to the ballet in order to admire plastique and harmonious movements of the body. And the classical school worked out the principles of these movements. But apart from rigidly defined classicism, the design of Grecian dance, unhampered by any conventions of schools, is beautiful, as also are the national dances of various peoples. One must of course also allow the existence of dances based on the grotesque as a humorous element or as a characteristic of national dance. But such grotesque can only be inserted in a ballet as a short episode. It cannot be tolerated as the predominating theme.

The well-known French critic, Laloy, wrote a little while ago in the Revue des deux Mondes:

"The Russian Ballet of the later Diaghilev period has for various reasons — chief among them being in almost equal degree the blasé weariness of satiety, the advice given by certain aesthetes and the necessity for reducing expenses — condemned luxury and with an assumption of irony produced its geometrical groupings, flaunted exercise-tunics, gloomy choreography, reversed the purpose of the dance and abhorred all show of knightly gallantry. Bowed and rounded shoulders, arms like scissors, knock-knees, pigeon toes, somersaults, bow-legs, a veritable competition in contortion between the sexes, to the confusion of the fairer sex: these were the latest inventions of the Russian ballet, iconoclastic and misogynist. On reflection one arrives at the conclusion that this magician had bewitched us and now he is no more the spell is broken. When Diaghilev, nearly two years ago, was carried off by a sudden and incurable illness, even his most faithful friends came to realise that the enterprise which he had founded and supported with such tireless zeal and energy was not destined to outlive him. And this is true not only of the name he gave it of Russian ballet, but of the whole style he innovated, which is forever buried in his grave. Do not let us raise this ghost."

In his merciless words, Laloy is profoundly right. Diaghilev, who introduced Paris to a series of such marvellous productions as "Scheherazade", "The Fire-Bird", "Pavillon d'Armide", "Petrouchka", "Prince Igor", etc., gradually arrived at a negation of all colour and style, passing on to inadmissible simplification, and abolishing the decorative and costume part of the spectacle. At the same time he also began to drift away from Russian music, with the one exception of the works of Stravinsky.

But the greatest mistake he made was to allow that which is the very foundation of a ballet, namely choreography, to lose all connection with Russian ballet which is classical in its essence, and wilfully to go into direct opposition to it by creating movements, poses and groupings not permitted by any school. Quite involuntarily the question arises in one's mind — By what right did Diaghilev, forsaking the Russian school, Russian music and Russian artists, continue to call his enterprise "The Russian Ballet"?

Pavlova in 1910.
(Photograph by Schneider, Berlin.)

Between Pavlova and Diaghilev there existed a profound difference in their outlook on art. To Pavlova art was sacred. Never did she wish and in fact, would have been able, to allow of any compromises in it. All insincerity in art hurt her deeply. This does not mean that she suffered from a blind conservatism. Although she had absorbed the traditions of the Russian Ballet and always held them in reverence, she gladly went out to meet anything new and talented. She became one of Fokine's most enthusiastic and zealous collaborators, and in all his first attempts readily abandoned all the conventionalities of the old ballet, sacrificing herself to his wishes, submerging her individuality for the sake of the general unity of impression, although taking the chief part in all his ballets.

Fokine, a highly talented man, convinced of the necessity of reforming classical ballet, understood at the same time that an art with three centuries of glorious history behind it, built up by a whole galaxy of famous artists, should not be rashly revolutionised. He led it, therefore, very carefully along the path of evolution towards the new ideals.

As a result of this, Fokine's innovations never raised any protests and his first ballets — "Eunica", "Nights of Egypt", "Pavillon d'Armide", "Chopiniana" — became favourites with the public from the very outset. It is further interesting to note in this connection that even M. Petipa, who during the course of sixty years raised the ballet to its highest pinnacle and was the most prominent representative of the old classical ballet, far from being shocked at the innovations introduced by Fokine, attended the performances of his compositions, enjoying them and approving of them.

Diaghilev, on the other hand, looked upon art (speaking here of the ballet) in a much freer manner, adapting it, as he thought, to suit the taste of the public and those patrons whose help was necessary, and regarding his innovations as in harmony with the spirit of the times. Having once committed the fundamental error of parting with Fokine, Diaghilev found himself in a very difficult position. It was impossible to find someone to take the place of Fokine and his great gifts. Something had to be invented in a new realm and the public and critics convinced, that it was precisely along this new road that the future of the ballet lay.

In reality, however, Diaghilev did not invent anything new, but only followed the maxims of the Russian stage-manager-innovator, Maierhold, who had declared in 1910 that neither verisimilitude nor reasoned analysis were required in the theatre, and that the grotesque has been able to put an end to these old-fashioned conventions. Maierhold declared that at the root of the grotesque lay the constant aspiration to lead the public from one newly reached plane to the next, unexpected by the spectator and taking him by surprise. It was this absurd idea that was the dominant undercurrent of all Diaghilev's work.

Pavlova was fond of Diaghilev and, as I have already said, held him in high esteem for what he had done for Russian art in his first period, so that when in the course of ten years he twice held out an invitation to her to join his enterprise, promising to make a special repertoire for her, both times she came very near to accepting and I had much trouble in dissuading her.

On my side, I suggested to Diaghilev that Fokine be entrusted with the direction of the affair, but to this he would not agree, declaring that he had a sufficient number of talented maitres de ballet without Fokine.

Diaghilev's offer was, of course, from his point of view, one of great interest. With the inclusion of Pavlova, the whole Diaghilev venture would have been raised to a much higher level. But, in addition to that, the invitation to Pavlova had another significance. By signing a contract with him, she would be signing the death-warrant of her own enterprise, and Diaghilev would become everywhere abroad the ballet-monopolist. However, this never took place, and each went his own way.

Diaghilev directed his steps towards an imaginary cosmopolitan art which should gratify contemporary taste, going over ever more and more to acrobatism and buffoonish ugliness. Pavlova, on the other hand, remained true to the spirit of the Russian classical ballet.

Pavlova was never influenced by innovations or popular tendencies, nor did she strive for a cheap success with a public that often loses all conception of beauty, and no reproaches of conservatism ever made her betray the traditions of the Imperial Ballet.

Having once lighted her lamp she guarded its sacred flame with loving care throughout her life and carried it all over the world, and to the end of her days she was able to declare proudly that it always burned with the same pure brilliance as when she first kindled it at her native altar.

CHAPTER XIII.

THEATRICAL COSTUMES AND SHOES.

In private life Pavlova preferred simple, soft, clinging dresses to any other kind. Possessing a wonderful figure, she never wore corsets, either in private life or on the stage. When she became used to some dress, she would not part from it for a long while and frequently ordered another just like it.

She disliked visiting, never went to dances and avoided parties of any kind, but occasionally it was necessary to accept an invitation to some dinner or to a gala performance, where Pavlova would be recognised by everybody, and therefore it was necessary to have dresses suitable for such functions.

Whenever she was in Paris therefore she used to go the round of several of the big houses and choose the frocks she required. Some little scene like this would be enacted: Choosing a model, say, in blue, she would find it necessary to have it made in some other colour. In consequence, of course, all the trimmings would have to be changed. Then perhaps, in addition, Pavlova, would prefer the shape of the sleeve to be altered, or the cut of the bodice to be different, till at last the disconcerted dressmaker would cry out in sheer despair: "But, Madame, what is left of the model?"

A fitting was torture to her. The very thought that she had to go to one was enough to put her into ill-humour. Frequently the dresses, after so many changes from the original model, would prove a disappointment, but no protest could be made, as she herself had insisted on the alterations. Sometimes, too, after buying the dresses Pavlova would discover that she had no occasion to wear them.

During the tours in America, because of constant journeys and performances, Pavlova could never go out anywhere in the evenings. She set so much store by her one free day in the week, that she always preferred to spend it quietly at home or to take a run in a motorcar outside the town. She hardly ever accepted any invitations.

In the East, where more time was spent in the same place, Pavlova had to accept invitations from the Government representatives, the governor-general of Australia, the Viceroy of India. Such invitations, however, were usually to lunch.

Pavlova in her Dressing Room Preparing her Ballet Shoes.
(Photograph by Abbe.)

On her return to her London house for a rest after the constant travelling during the season, she always tried to remain at home as much as possible in the company of her close friends., If she ever did go to a theatre, she would say on her return:

"There was no necessity to dress, nobody dresses nowadays."

But in the matter of her theatrical costumes she was much more exacting. If her costume for a certain part were to the design of some well-known artist — Bakst, Benois or Korovine — she would allow no alterations to be made, keeping faithfully to the indications on the drawing and colours and shades suggested. But in those cases where the dance or the ballet did not call for a special design by an artist, Pavlova chose her own colours, and having very good taste, was most successful.

The chief part of the costume was the bodice, which had to conform to the main requirement, namely that of encasing the figure firmly without hampering the movements. A Russian dressmaker, Manya, who had been with Pavlova for many years, made her costumes and so accustomed was she to her requirements, that she could make them almost without a fitting. When it was necessary to have the costume made in Paris to the design of some artist, the bodice was always made at home and sent to the Paris workroom, to have everything else added and sewn on to it. And in the same way, all the headdresses were made at home. Pavlova insisted that, while being light, they should at the same time sit firmly on the head.

A very important part of a ballet costume is of course the ballet-skirt. One would think that the sewing of these is very easy just several skirts made of tarlatan, sewn one on the top of the other. But, as a matter of fact, there are several secrets connected with their making. First of all there is the important question of the material itself. It would seem that nothing could be more simple. And yet, tarlatan of the right quality cannot be obtained either in London or in Paris and several thousand yards had to be brought over annually from America. The chief merit of this tarlatan lies in its right degree of starchiness: it must be neither too soft, so that it hangs like a rag, nor too firm, so that it stands out stiffly.

The art of cutting out ballet-skirts was not arrived at all at once, but came gradually. In this matter, indeed, our Manya had attained perfection. She was very proud of it and though she received many tempting offers to teach the secret, or to sew ballet-skirts for others, she invariably refused to do so, even though Pavlova herself would have allowed it.

For every dancer the ballet-skirt is the most elegant part of her costume and the shape of it is of first importance.

It was often commented on that with our continual travelling, the frequent changes of climate, and dancing in dirty theatres, Pavlova's costumes looked as fresh as if they had just been made. Still greater surprise was felt at the freshness of the costumes of the company. This, of course could only have been achieved by the boundless love and faithfulness of our Russian wardrobe-staff, who where with us for so many years. Those modest and unnoticed participants in our tours did very responsible and troublesome work, not in the public eye, but behind the wings and in dressing rooms.

The senior, in years of service, was Kouzma Saveliev, who had been with us uninterruptedly for twenty years. He began his theatrical career in the work-rooms of the St. Petersburg theatrical costumier, Leifert.

Then there was Manya, of whom I have already spoken, or to give her her full name Maria Kharchevnikova, who was with us for eighteen years, coming to us first as an assistant superviser of the feminine wardrobe and eventually becoming headdresser, and responsible for the seamstress part of all Pavlova's costumes. She was a very diligent and conscientious worker and grew to be an excellent costume artist, making beautifully the most complicated costumes and decorating them herself with excellent taste.

The complement of Pavlova's permanent staff was nearly all Russian, but for many years, one Englishwoman, May Chapman, accompanied Pavlova as ladies' maid to North and South America, to the Far East and to Australia. May Chapman was an ideal worker, imperturbable, attentive and invariably dignified and tactful in her manner. Pavlova became accustomed and very attached to her and it was with great sorrow that she parted from her when May Chapman left to be married.

There was also Marguerite Letienne, who was in our employ for seven years, and during the last few years never left Pavlova at all.

Pavlova treated these employees as members of the family and when we were in London they lived with us at Ivy House.

Besides this nucleus, we were generally accompanied on our tours by additional seamstresses, for it must be remembered that our wardrobe consisted approximately of two thousand costumes, and some hundred to a hundred and fifty were required for each performance. All these costumes had to be taken out of the trunks or baskets, looked over, ironed and distributed in the various dressing rooms. The shoes, head-dresses, wigs, etc. corresponding to these costumes had also to be prepared. We invariably had our own hair-dresser, and latterly, we had to have a permanent mechanic and an electrician. All these, as well as the wardrobe-staff were Russians

If one is stationed in the same place for two or three weeks, things can be arranged and adapted quite quickly; but being constantly on the move, as we were for instance in North America, where sometimes we changed towns every night for a fortnight on end, much experience, energy and above all devotion are necessary in order to get through the work.

One is nearly always greeted with one and the same picture: in spite of repeated and written instructions, the theatre management fulfils only half, sometimes only a quarter of what has been asked. You arrive in the morning. The luggage has not been delivered yet. The dressing-rooms are apportioned; there are not a sufficient number and in the majority of cases they are badly arranged. I have often been puzzled to understand why it is that a company building a theatre spends enormous sums on the outside frontage of the building, on the decoration of the foyer, on the painting of the ceiling, on magnificent armchairs and carpets, so as to give the public every comfort, but never seems to trouble about the comfort of the artists, who have to entertain the public.

When I speak of comfort, I do not mean that I require dressing-rooms to be luxurious. I merely desire that those responsible for the building and decorating of theatres should also think of the artists. The system most frequently met with consists of dressing-rooms distributed on all the storeys of the building, two or three on each, and the artist who has finished acting or dancing has to run upstairs to the fourth or fifth floor. I say "run" advisedly because the interval between the acts is limited to a maximum of fifteen minutes and in that time the dressing-room has to be reached, the costume, head-dress and wig taken off, sometimes even the tights, and others put on, the make-up touched up or even made anew and the return to the stage effected. Constantly the changing has to be done very quickly during the action of the piece. When the stage is sufficiently roomy, temporary dressing-rooms are improvised in the scenery in the wings. But if not, the artist has to run upstairs and is frequently late in consequence.

In designing the plan of a theatre, it is always possible to arrange some combination whereby space is reserved for the dressing-rooms on the first two floors. Another just grievance is that a dressing-room quite often does not contain even the most modest of rugs. Dancers, therefore, when putting on their tights or changing their stockings have to stand with their bare feet on the floor. It is disgraceful that dancers, with their feet heated from dancing, should have to stand sometimes on a stone floor.

Very often the dressing-rooms are not heated at all or heated very badly. In South America, where the winter is short but fairly severe, there is no heating whatever, and we always carried twenty electric heaters for the dressing-rooms with us. The same thing has also happened in Australia. In new theatres, generally state or municipal, this matter of dressing-room accommodation is put on a sensible footing, but with the majority of private theatres it is a very serious defect.

Pavlova trying on a Ballet Shoe.
(This photograph shows her wonderful instep).

It is easy to understand what a business it is to get ready and carry round the costumes when the arrangement of dressing-rooms is so inconvenient. A ballet costume is usually a bulky object. Ballet skirts take up a great deal of room and must not be creased. In the smaller dressing-rooms, where two or three, sometimes more, dancers have to dress, there is hardly enough room to turn round as it is, not to mention hanging up costumes for two ballets and several separate dances. One is fortunate to find a room that can be put aside for the ironing of the costumes creased on the voyage, otherwise this may have to be done on a trunk in the corridor.

But all this could be borne if only the luggage arrived in time! Very often, however, it is late and is only delivered at the theatre at three or four in the afternoon, and sometimes even at six o'clock, — to all intents and purposes just before the performance. And then, there is real tragedy. All the doors of the stage part of the theatre are wide open for the carriage of the luggage, and the cold and draughts are terrible; people rush about from place to place searching for this box or that basket and pointing out where it should be taken. And if the dressing-rooms are small and there is not enough space in the corridors for the trunks, costumes have to be taken out on the stage and from thence distributed to the various dressing-rooms on the various floors. And this, when the dancers are already assembled and demanding their costumes, wigs, etc.

In addition to the ironing of the costumes and keeping them in order, frequently new ones have to be made in the course of a tour, more especially the tarlatan tunics, which wear out and soil very easily.

Consequently, as soon as we found ourselves in some more or less properly arranged theatre for several days, work-rooms would be immediately installed and new tunics and costumes prepared. We always carried two sewing-machines about with us, in order not to waste time looking for them in strange towns.

Though Pavlova considered her costume very important, her first thought, nevertheless, and quite naturally, was for her foot-gear.

Her thin and nervous foot with a very high instep, slender and beautifully shaped, gave, at the same time, great difficulty in the matter of choice and fitting of shoes.

Pavlova had a number of shoemakers — one in London, several in Paris, in Italy and everywhere where we stayed more than three weeks — in Berlin, Sydney, Buenos Aires, Calcutta, Johannesburg.

All these shoemakers, learning that they were serving Pavlova and fully aware of the value of the advertisement in having her for a customer, did their utmost to satisfy her. And this was by no means easy, for in nothing else was she so particular, as in the matter of shoes.

Her foot had one peculiarity — shoes that were perfectly comfortable to-day might be very uncomfortable to-morrow. Perhaps this can be ascribed to her nervous temperament, and to the great amount of work which she did. Sometimes, on walking along a street past a shoemaker's window, and seeing a pair of shoes, she would suddenly decide that they were exceedingly pretty. We would walk into the shop and the fitting would begin, then Pavlova would quickly decide that they were not suitable and we would walk out. Or perhaps, after the fitting, she would say that the shoes she had liked were exceedingly successful, and insist that the address of the shop be written down; but, alas, a day or two later, the new shoes would no longer be seen on her feet and she would explain that they were too tight or that they rubbed somewhere or had some other defect.

She always took with her a favourite little trunk that would hold 36 pairs of shoes, and when her casual purchases filled it to overflowing, she would give half of them away, making happy those girls who had a foot like hers.

The most serious question of all, however, and one that led to endless trouble and often frequent annoyance, was that of her dancing shoes.

In the old days, when dancing technique was far less complicated, when ballerinas did not even dream of what would be required of their successors, the form of the dancing shoe was very much like that of an ordinary ballroom slipper, minus, of course, the heel. They were of finer workmanship, the shoes of the dancers of old being famous for their elegance.

The traditional shape is adhered to by the French theatrical shoemakers, who makes shoes not so fine and beautiful as in former times, but still much more elegant than the Italian ones. The continual improvement in dancing technique, which was the outstanding quality of the Italian ballerinas, began to have its effect on the shape of the shoe and, therefore, on the craftsmanship of Italian shoemakers.

These shoes made the work of Italian ballerinas much easier, but the shape became completely spoilt by the blunt, squared-off toe. They make the foot look bigger and more clumsy.

I remember the following episode in St. Petersburg. Pavlova was summoned on some question to the director of the Imperial Theatres. There were several people in his room besides Pavlova — the head of the office staff, the manager of the ballet troupe and others. Noticing a beautiful pink shoe on the director's table, Pavlova asked to whom it belonged and the director told her that one of the aristocratic amateurs of the ballet had presented to the museum of the Imperial theatres a shoe of Taglioni's from his collection.

With a perfectly natural interest and a slightly beating heart, she examined the precious relic, so small and elegant. Watching her with a smile, the director remarked:

"Yes, that shoe can't be compared with yours. Nor the foot that wore it. You couldn't get on a shoe like that."

In an instant, Pavlova whipped off her own shoe and, to the general amazement, put on the shoe of Taglioni. Later she told me of the horrible moment she lived through — supposing she had failed to get the shoe on!

Italian ballet-shoes are made by several factories, but the best known are those of the shoemaker Nicolini Romeo.

His small workshop was remarkable for the fact that all the head men as well as the assistants were members of his family working under the supervision of old Romeo himself. Although the demand was far in excess of the quantity of shoes he could produce, Nicolini Romeo refused to enlarge his workshop or to employ outside people. From her very first years as a dancer, Pavlova wore shoes of Nicolini's workmanship, and as they had to be sent from Milan, it happened sometimes that mistakes were made in the size and as a consequence, a delay of weeks was then incurred.

On our very first visit to Italy, we decided to call on Nicolini in order to discuss certain matters personally with him. He proved to be a very nice old Italian. With his spectacles pushed back on his forehead while talking, he only answered with the one word "si, si", to everything we said. As he spoke only Italian and our knowledge of that language was limited, his son, who knew a little French was called to act as interpreter. But Pavlova's patience gave out and, putting on a pair of shoes, she explained what she required, demonstrating the defects of the shoes by performing various p a s.

Her quickness was marvellous: in the course only of a few minutes, she put on the shoe, took up some position, took it off again, pointed out what was wrong, put it on again and danced once more, and Nicolini watched as if under some spell and all he could do was to go on repeating "si, si."

In order to secure Nicolini's attention and make him careful in fulfilling his contract, we decided to guarantee him an annual order for a gross of shoes and to pay him rather more than the usual price.

All this was duly written down on paper and we took our departure,

*Pavlova's Partners Volinine and Novikoff watching
her with great interest as she breaks in her ballet shoes.
(Photograph by Abbe.)*

Pavlova saying happily to me that Romeo had at last understood everything. But this was rash and premature. We went at least ten times to his shop after that, and each time Pavlova explained everything, down to the minutest detail in the same eloquent way, but all to no avail! Invariably each delivery was not so good as the preceding one.

When visiting Milan on another occasion, we decided that it would be better to take an interpreter from the hotel with us so that Pavlova's instructions might be repeated exactly, but we had to regret that also. The interpreter, to whom everything was duly explained, took the matter up very energetically and warmly, and every ten words said by Pavlova were turned by him into a long speech — a torrent of words accompanied by a wealth of gesture, and it became quite obvious that more than half of what he said was added by himself. In the end poor Nicolini became so muddled that we had to revert to the old system of explanation. We were in Milan again the following year and there met the well-known dancer, Rosina Galli, the ballerina and ballet-mistress of the Metropolitan Theatre in New York.

Rosina Galli also had her shoes from Romeo and also had constant trouble with him. Pavlova was on friendly terms with Rosina Galli. The Italian dancer spoke good French and we decided to take advantage of the opportunity to go together to Nicolini. I think it was a long time before the old man forgot that visit. Both the dancers put on shoes and began to explain what they required, but there was so much of this explanation, the instructions were so numerous and so minute, that the poor old man was completely worn out, and Rosina Galli, in addition, kept on accusing him of ingratitude for not sufficiently valuing the custom of the greatest dancer on earth and the first ballerina of Italy.

Solemnly the old man swore, calling God to witness, that he would have everything done and would send the trial pairs to Salzo-Maggiore, where we were all going. Some days later the shoes arrived and to their horror the dancers found that Nicolini had completely muddled everything, doing for Rosina Galli what was required by Pavlova, and for Pavlova what Rosina Galli had asked for.

In addition to his lack of attention, or perhaps it was lack of proper understanding, Nicolini was very unpunctual. We could give him an order six months in advance, telling him exactly the dates, quantities and places of delivery; remind him two or three times, but all to no purpose. The first lot of shoes would arrive to time, the second lot would be a month or two late and the third lot would not arrive at all, and always it was the same. It is difficult to find a satisfactory explanation of why this man, undoubtedly proud of having a customer like Pavlova, was so inattentive to her wishes, making her suffer, and frequently leaving her without shoes altogether. The reason probably lay in the fact that it was a sort of family business run on "homely" lines. There were more orders than could be executed, and Romeo knew that a dancer, having once got used to his shoes, would never leave him. On re-reading these lines one is involuntarily reminded of the hundreds of times in Pavlova's long career when she was absolutely in despair over her shoes. The long-expected shoes would arrive at last, the parcel be impatiently opened, and a few minutes later Pavlova would discover that out of three or four dozen pairs, only two or three were of any use to her. Sometimes the order would fail to arrive at all, and then all our dancers, whose feet were at all like Pavlova's would bring her their shoes, from which she would choose a pair or two, or she would go through the rejected shoes of former unsuccessful consignments a second time. And there was an accumulation of these! The very natural question arises: why could not Pavlova in all these years find another shoemaker? After all, not all the dancers in the world have their shoes from Nicolini. Countless attempts were made, but without success.

I have purposely dealt with this subject at length, because so much of a dancer's success depends upon her shoes, the question is of vital importance to her, and here the shape of the dancer's foot must be carefully considered. Nearly all classical dances have the p o i n t e as basis, that is, dancing on the tips of the toes. Everyone can understand the expressions: "Such-and-such a dancer has weak toes, another has strong toes, or the famous ballerina so-and-so has toes of steel." By this short formula one defines the degree of strength in the p o i n t e s, not only that attained through constant exercise, but that which is inherent in the nature of the dancer's foot. Short, level toes are particularly helpful in this respect, for then the body has the support of all of them (I have known female and even male dancers whose short, perfectly even and naturally strong toes enabled them to walk, and even dance, on the tips with bare feet). Toes that are long and thin, on the other hand, following the angle of the big toe, are most inconvenient for classical dances and cause their owners much grief and trouble.

Pavlova's foot was precisely of this nature. The whole weight of the body had to be borne by the big toe. Naturally much effort and work were necessary to overcome this disadvantage and it is quite easy to see the important part played by the shoe and how much depends upon it being comfortable.

One must take into account the nervous strain felt by a dancer before her public, conscious that grace, charm and technical perfection are expected of her. An inspired dancer must be able to give herself up entirely to the character she is interpreting and not be distracted by the anxious thought as to whether owing to the discomfort of her shoe the pirouette will be successful or not. Consequently Pavlova gave much time to the preparation of her shoes. When by good luck they were comfortable and just right, the work was considerably simplified, but in the majority of cases a great deal of labour had to be expended in improving uncomfortable shoes to make them wearable. When shoes proved successful Pavlova would set great store by them and wear them as long as possible.

Before the opening of one of the seasons at Covent Garden the whole consignment of shoes received proved utterly useless. Pavlova made a round of all the shops where dancing shoes were to be had; all our dancers offered theirs, but only a pair or two could be chosen that were comfortable enough and we had a whole month's season before us, for which it was necessary to have at least two dozen pairs. Pavlova was in despair. Then

I remembered that one of our former dancers had a foot very much like Pavlova's and that her shoes used to fit better than anyone else's. I rang her up and suggested that she should go immediately to Milan, go through all the shoes that Nicolini had in stock and come back with those she considered suitable. She was successful in choosing about a dozen pairs and thereby helped us to scramble out of a very nearly hopeless situation. If all the letters and telegrams sent to Nicolini telling him that the shoes were too long or too short or too narrow or too something-else were to be collected, they would fill a thick volume.

But from the moment when Maestro Cecchetti went to live in Milan, our task became somewhat simplified. We wrote or telegraphed to him, and either he himself or his wife, who adored Pavlova, did all in their power to help her. On receiving our telegram Cecchetti would rush off to Nicolini, explain what was required, insist upon prompt dispatch, and see to everything. But this happened so often that we were quite ashamed to trouble the Cecchetti family in this way. The Maestro told us later that he once reproached Nicolini for the trouble he was causing a celebrated ballerina.

"Don't you understand what an honour it is for you that the great Pavlova has her shoes made by you?" he asked.

The old man thought awhile and then answered:

"Yes, it's a great honour that she is my client." And reflecting further, he added:

"Yes, but if I had two Pavlovas, I'd be done for."

Pavlova was often approached by shoemakers of all nationalities and in all parts of the world with an offer to supply her regularly, undertaking to provide her annually with any number for her own use free of charge, on condition that she would allow them to advertise that she had found their shoes to be the best.

She would give her own shoes as a model and they would make and deliver what seemed to be an absolute copy. She pointed out defects and a new shoe was made and so it went on. An American shoemaker in Los Angeles brought a new pair every day, altering them each time to her instructions and finally produced a pair in which she was able to dance once, but even they were not comfortable. It was Pavlova's opinion that this was because they were made by machinery; as she said "they had no soul", in other words, they were lacking in that indefinable something which Italian makers know how to put into their work, a secret that has possibly been handed down from generation to generation of shoemakers.

A Study of Pavlova.
(By Straus Peyton, Kansas City.)

CHAPTER XIV.

MUSIC

Musical critics at times reproached Pavlova for her choice of music, saying that it was behind the times, that she had become frozen in her repertoire, that she neglected to pay due attention to new ideas and new composers, and suffered from excessive conservatism.

It is perfectly true that Pavlova kept to a repertoire of her own, but to say that this was because she had no interest in music or lacked understanding of it is to make an unpardonable mistake. The character of her dances, and all that she put into them (for Pavlova's dances did not consist merely of technique, but were rather the expression of spiritual emotions, which she crystallised in the figures she portrayed) naturally required music to suit the mood. Consequently the music was nearly always lyrical to correspond with the dances. The melodies of Chopin, Tchaikovsky, Saint-Saens and Glazounov created the right mood, and once the figure created was blended with one of these melodies, she naturally kept to it. She preferred classical music to any other and her library contained all the distinguished composers. Nearest of all to her soul was the music of Chopin, for it responded more closely and accurately to the moods of her spirit. It stands to reason that she was keenly interested in contemporary music. Her constant travels prevented her from attending many concerts, but as soon as she came to London to rest, she would invite some good pianist to play whatever was new. From among these pieces Pavlova chose those she considered suitable. She liked the works of Debussy, Dukas and Ravel, who very kindly played her some of his compositions. Some of the pieces were extremely interesting from a musical point of view or original in form, but they were not suitable to the dance she had in view, did not fit in with her moods, she did not find in them what she required in order to express through music the particular idea that had to reach her public — to touch the heart of another. Could it be expected then that Pavlova, only to avoid the reproach of being behind the times, should take the music of modern composers for her creations, when it did not suit her moods and aims?

Take, for instance the works of Stravinsky. I do not consider myself sufficiently competent to subject them to analysis. It is generally conceded that he is a great musician who has done some wonderful things in the matter of new forms of orchestration. But it is an open question how far his music is suitable for ballet. One must of course agree as to what the ballet is and what are its aims. If the ballet is to be regarded as a serious and independent art, for which music, though a necessary element, has to be subservient to the rules of the stage and to the ideas of the choreographer then Stravinsky's music (with the possible exception of "The Fire-Bird" and "Petroushka") does not comply with these requirements. If, on the other hand, the grotesque is to predominate in ballet, as Diaghilev wished to think, then music loses all meaning. In this connection I think it is as well to quote an extract from an article by the musical critic of The London Times.

"The composer no less than the ballerina, is apt to forget the end and purpose of the art-form by becoming absorbed in his own virtuosity. In the earlier days of the Russian ballet Stravinsky appeared in the Fire-Bird and Petroushka to be the one composer most capable of realising what could be done with the ballet, and of bringing his music to the advance of its expressive possibilities. In these works he has visualised the stage, the swiftness of its drama through music and movement, and the particular kind of movement which his music would either accompany or generate. In "Le Sacre du Printemps" his music was getting out of touch with the stage. That work may be a greater musical achievement than its predecessors, but the subsequent juggling with its choreography shows that the composer was beginning to put the cart before the horse — to write music which somehow or other was to be made into a ballet, not ballet of which music was a necessary concomitant. His later works have shown him still further losing grip of the situation, and, as the technique of the dancers themselves inevitably deteriorated, cut off as they were from their original training ground, eccentricity took the place of that real virtuosity of the dance which had been the basis of the earlier exhibitions. There would have been no place for Madame Pavlova or her like in such things as Stravinsky's "Apollon Musagete", or the misdirected posturings of the young Parisians which were prominent in the repertoires of Diaghilev's last seasons. Most of the composers failed to realise that the ballet depended not on trying to make two rhythmic arts say everything, but on perceiving what things they were most fitted to say in consort."

Was Pavlova musical? A long time ago a well-known Russian critic, Andreevsky, called her "dancing music".

One would have thought that, for anybody who had once seen her dance, there could be no such question. So to feel music, so to unify oneself with it, so to express its every mood and fill it with a depth of meaning, can, surely, only be done by one whose very soul feels its secret and its spirit.

In his book about Pavlova, V. Svetloff says:

"As symmetry in static arts, so rhythm in dynamic only produces the impression of art when the separate component elements are united. The dances of Pavlova are an outstanding example of this. Various figures and choreographic pictures are made subservient to the clear and definite idea of rhythm. But even this, in its turn, is only the form that is the nearest approach to the expression of spiritual states. Each pose, each dance of Pavlova shows this rhythm, and the resulting impression is one of lightness and grace, in which no technical difficulties are reflected. In Pavlova this sense of rhythm is developed to its limit. It is the expression of her personality, her artistic sensitiveness. She has no need to know that a swan makes two strokes of its wings per second and a dragonfly twenty-eight. And yet, when looking at her in these two dances, you can see at once to what a degree of exactitude is this sense of rhythm expressed in them. Instinctively she unites, merges the rhythmical movements of the dance into the rhythm of her inner self, thus bringing the two rhythms into complete harmony. And therefore she gives to every emotion an extraordinary fullness and richness of sensation in the realm of rhythm."

The well-known French critic, Gaston Pavlovsky, writes in an article in "Le Journal":

"In what does the charm of Pavlova lie? Primarily, without a doubt, in her wonderful sense of rhythm. Pavlova was music itself, and it was precisely her movements that gave one the impression of music, whereas the majority of dancers follow the music, like an inexperienced conductor beating time while listening to the orchestra instead of leading it. This absolute synchronism between music and dance is what makes success, but is very rarely met with. One tenth, one-twentieth of a second between music and movement may escape our senses, but not our consciousness. We do not suffer any disagreeable feeling, but at the same time we lose emotion when this synchronism is not attained. On the other hand, when it is attained, our happiness reaches to ecstasy, though we are often not aware of the reason."

Recently the author of a book, himself a conductor, reproached Pavlova with lack of feeling for music, founding his accusation on the fact that she did not mind giving instructions to conductors changing tempos, introducing arbitrary pauses and thereby creating trouble with them.

Pavlova in her Dressing room at the Palace Theatre, London 1911.
(Photograph by S. Bransburg.)

Does the author of such views realise that the public came to Pavlova's performances quite indifferent to the conductor or his views on the right way of executing this or that piece of music, solely to see Pavlova; — and came in fact not only to see her execute certain dances to certain music, but also the wonderful beauty of the images she created? Pavlova wanted to express that which was of deepest value, that which brought tears to the eyes and drew thousands to her from all the corners of the world; and nobody ever cared whether she found it necessary to retard the tempo or to stop altogether in a place not foreseen by the composer, — who had not known when he wrote the music that Pavlova was going to dance to it.

It was in my presence that Saint-Saëns, coming into Pavlova's dressing-room after a performance of "The Dying Swan" said:

"Do you know, Madame, that it is only to-day after seeing your dance that I have understood what a beautiful thing I had written?"

Nikisch, her fervent admirer, who never missed a chance of being present at her performances, often made the statement that he would like to conduct for her dances.

It is only natural that the reproaches of certain conductors, wishing to show that from a musical point of view this or that piece should be performed differently, irritated and tried Pavlova's patience. Having known nearly all the contemporary conductors, I confess that I have rarely met one who could understand, or what is even more important, feel the dance.

Undoubtedly, the finest leader for the ballet was R. Drigo, the conductor of the St. Petersburg Imperial Theatre. He was the author of a number of melodious ballets himself, as I have mentioned elsewhere, also he was a splendid musician and a great friend of Tchaikovsky and Glazounov. Nikisch used to say that he had never heard a better rendering of Tchaikovsky's "Nutcracker" than at the ballet performance at the Marinsky Theatre under the leadership of Drigo. The reason for his outstanding qualities as leader is of course the fact that he had known all the dancers since they were school-children, was present at all the rehearsals and the whole career of the dancer passed before his eyes.

In South America, during the opera season, Pavlova put on a symphonic poem by Roger Dukas, entitled "Peri", a work requiring a large orchestra and very difficult to execute because of its constantly changing rhythms and tempos. Marinuzzi, a magnificent conductor of opera, led this piece after only two rehearsals without the slightest hitch and to Pavlova's complete satisfaction.

When conductors complain of ballet dancers arbitrarily changing or retarding the time, I always remember how one of our conductors at a rehearsal, during the dancing of a variation by Pavlova's partner, said to him:

"You come down after your leap too soon, I have a fermato at that spot in the score". To which the dancer replied quite reasonably that he could not remain in the air waiting for the end of the fermato.

A number of Pavlova's dances required such lightness, such rapidity, so many changes of mood on which the success of the dance depended, that it would have been absurd to make her slavishly follow the tempo. The moods of the music took entire possession of Pavlova and she interpreted them as if her body were a string vibrating in response to the melody. In one and the same dance she could be majestically stern, dreamily sad or touchingly gentle. How did she attain this? It cannot be explained by words; I should compare it to the play of chiaroscuro; clouds drifting across the sky alter the light and with it alter the appearance of the landscape. If her conductor had his eyes fixed on the score only, beating time, and not trying to understand what she was expressing by her dance, he, of course, could never understand her and they were bound to be at variance.

It is noteworthy that the higher the conductor stood as a musician, the more easily and quickly he understood Pavlova and grasped her requirements.

It would be pertinent here to quote the excellent remarks of E. Starck (who writes under the pseudonym of "Siegfried").

"The spirit of nature", says this musical critic, "comes to life in the rhythm of the dances of mankind, and the further they are from dry, academic artificiality in a return to nature, the more spontaneous, beautiful and powerful they are. In that form dancing is so attractive, because it is a manifestation of the divine in man, of his immortal soul — not of the cold, cunning, sly calculating mind, but precisely of the soul. In this it approaches music, which is also quite powerless to illustrate philosophical doctrines, but which on the other hand, possesses limitless possibilities in the matter of expressing the ecstasies of interior psychological experiences and all those complicated lyrical moods to which we are constantly subject, if, that is, we have not become walking lay-figures. The human spirit, the most precious thing in nature, manifests itself in dance in all its changeable moods and in all the peculiarities inherent in every separate individuality. And it is that which constitutes the most enchanting side of the art of dancing, for the spirit of man is infinitely interesting and attractive in the multitudinous variety of its moods."

Schumann once said to his pupils: "If you do not listen with your inner hearing and do not see with your inner eyes, you will not understand what I want to say." That could have been repeated by Pavlova.

CHAPTER XV.

PHOTOGRAPHY AND CINEMA.

Few people, I should say, kept photographers so continually busy as did Pavlova. The public was always interested to see a new picture of the great artist, whose life was given up so entirely to the beauty of movement, and everyone wanted to see Pavlova in a variety of surroundings and poses.

Before every tour Pavlova was photographed in various costumes, alone and with her dancing partner. These photographs were printed and sent round the different towns in which she was to dance.

But however many photographs, old and new, we sent ahead or brought with us, every newspaper wanted to have a special one taken by its own photographer. We would explain that our photographs, the work of first-class men and chosen by Pavlova herself out of a hundred or more, would certainly be better than those taken hurriedly by a newspaper photographer under unfavourable lighting conditions — it was no good, still the papers would insist upon having their own (perhaps their own photographers persuaded them to this end); and so cameras would click and on the following day the paper would appear with some dreadful picture labelled "The latest photograph of Pavlova".

In addition to the newspapers, the best local photographers would also approach Pavlova with a request for a sitting, so that they might exhibit her portrait and sell copies, if successful.

Pavlova never went to the photographers' studios, as this would have taken up too much time and been complicated. As it was important to take her in costume, it would have meant bringing her wardrobe to the studio, making up there, putting on tights and shoes, etc. She also realised that for the making of a successful picture of movement, it was necessary for the body to be properly "warmed up" and that meant preliminary exercise. She therefore asked the photographers to take her in the theatre during the performance. There are always powerful lamps on the stage and a studio could be improvised in some corner. At the finish of an act, in make-up and costume, "warmed up" by dancing, she could be taken in

Pavlova as Fenella in the film "The Dumb Girl of Portici".

two or three poses without any loss of time. This was repeated in the next interval and again after the performance was over. Such a method of work was not to the taste of photographers, but they had of necessity to submit to it. The majority failed to adapt themselves to it: they had no experience of work under theatrical conditions and their pictures were not successful; there and then their experiment came to an end. Others, quickly grasping the conditions and what was required, succeeded in obtaining some excellent results. One American photographer, who was constantly travelling round the world in search of interesting subjects (we met him in New York, in London and in Cairo) worked for a month in the theatres where Pavlova danced. Every evening he would settle down in his corner, rigging up a photographic studio with the help of two screens, and would try and catch Pavlova as she passed by, either on her way to the stage or on her return during an interval, or even in the wings in her moments of resting. His perseverance was crowned with success and he published a whole series of really excellent photographs.

It was very interesting to study the various types of photographers and their methods of work at these theatrical sittings. Some showed great energy, realising at once that Pavlova was at their disposal only for a few minutes and worked with great haste. Others, on the other hand, slow and clumsy, or flustered by the unusual conditions, losing first one thing, then another, never quite knowing what they themselves wanted were only irritating and wasted our time. In the best hotel of a big American town where we were once staying, a man came up to us and introduced himself as a photographer. His studio, he said, was there, in the hotel itself. The samples of his work which he had brought to show us proved that he really was an artist. Pavlova agreed to sit for him, warning him, however, that she could only give him half an hour. I shall never forget that sitting — the photographer and his assistants performed wonders of dexterity and quickness. The man himself in order not to waste time kept running across the room, and managed in the half hour to take more than thirty poses. Pavlova was quite enthusiastic watching his show of energy and his knowledge of the business. Nearly all his photographs came out very well.

When consenting to sit, Pavlova always insisted that proofs should be submitted to her before anything further was done: those of which she approved she permitted to be duplicated and sold, but those she did not pass, had to be destroyed. She was very strict about this, for many of these prints had faults, due either to the wrong position of the camera or the insufficient lighting. A leg or an arm would be foreshortened or the whole pose appear wrong and it was impossible to allow such photographs to be circulated.

Yet, this is what would occasionally happen. On returning to some town after an absence of a year or two, we would see in newspapers or in photographers' windows those very photographs that Pavlova had rejected on her previous visit. The explanation was simple enough: newspapers and journals wished to reproduce a photograph that had not appeared in any other periodical, and photographers, taking advantage of this, would offer at a good price these rejected pictures. It made Pavlova very angry when this happened, but it was impossible to do anything. Every time the photographers would swear that the negatives disapproved of at the time would be henceforth destroyed, yet here and there, now and again, reproductions appeared.

To a photographer having the slightest aesthetic feeling, it was a delight to take Pavlova, although catching her poses following each other in quick succession, was very difficult. Dressed in the costumes of some ballet, she would assume a number of different poses, would slightly change her expression, the turn of the head, the position of her arms, making each movement more entrancing than the last, but doing this involuntarily, as if unconscious of being photographed. This kaleidoscope of movements would send the photographer into raptures. But when he commenced taking the picture, he would be in despair, for to make her pause in immobility was exceedingly difficult. The photographer had indeed to catch the moment.

Now she would take a perfectly wonderful pose, and then suddenly, just as the photographer was ready, would change into another, quite unconsciously. We would beg her to resume the former pose once again, but she was no longer able to do so, for it had not been thought out, and was but a moment in a series of movements. There was only one way out of the difficulty, namely, to photograph her with a very sensitive camera with the minimum of exposure and to take a number of photographs, of which some were usually successful and some even wonderful in the results attained, giving the impression of finished portraits.

It is difficult to say who took the best photographs of her. Splendid ones were taken in Berlin in the first years of her career, then in Buenos Aires, in Paris and other towns. She preferred being taken in the midst of nature or at home, in her own garden.

Some three years ago Pavlova began to take a keen interest in the cinematograph. One of our dancers had a small camera, and during one of the tours he took various scenes and groups of people in our company, the results achieved being very good. In view of her forthcoming tour in the East Pavlova also resolved to buy one. Friends whom she consulted advised her to buy a camera with standard size films, for her future films might be extremely interesting and be much sought after. Such films can be demonstrated in any cinematograph, whereas Kodak's have a very narrow film and can only be shown on their own special apparatus. The camera that we bought, though excellent in itself, demanded rather more experienced hands than ours, and we were constantly having trouble with it. At the most critical moment it would suddenly stick and refuse to work; occasionally after a time, it would go on again, but more often it remained useless until we arrived in some big town, where it could be taken to pieces and put in order. Eventually Pavlova decided to buy a Kodak cinematograph camera, a very much simpler affair and practically always in working order, though reproducing everything only in miniature.

Pavlova was very enthusiastic about these "shots". No matter how great the number of films in reserve, there were never enough for her. In Egypt she took the pyramids, excavations, caravans of camels, the children of the fellahs; in India the bazaars, processions, temples, the palaces of Agra and Delhi, the sacred city of Benares. But most of all she was enchanted by Java, which we were visiting for the first time and where there is much that is unexpected and interesting — lovely landscapes, wonderful ruins, characteristic types. She was immensely pleased with a journey to the highest volcano in Java — Bromo. It made a great impression on her.

Java, as everybody knows, is a country of volcanoes, of which forty-two are active. To our surprise, we learnt that there is an official post — that of superviser of all the volcanoes. This post was honourably occupied by a Russian, an excolonel of artillery.

Bromo is the largest volcano in Java and in order to reach it one has to climb a pass of 8000 feet. One starts at two o'clock in the morning, traversing forests and ascending mountains on horseback for about three hours, and by sunrise the volcano is reached. The journey is tiring and not entirely free from danger, for the horses often stumble in the dark; but the beautiful view from the pass of the volcano a thousand feet below and of the surrounding ridges of mountains at the rising of the sun, make one forget everything and the hours spent there remain in one's memory forever.

On her return to Europe, Pavlova liked looking through her pictures in her leisure hours. Many of them, not being very successful, she cut out altogether, but nevertheless a number of most interesting films remained.

I will now pass on to the filming of Pavlova herself and her views on this matter.

A year before the War, while we were in Berlin, a society of German journalists asked Pavlova to take part in a charity evening entertainment in aid of the widows and orphans of journalists. Pavlova was not able to

Pavlova as Fenella in a scene from "The Dumb Girl of Portici".

consent, as it was to take place a month later and by that time she was due to dance in America. The committee then asked her to be filmed in one of her dances, saying that it would be an interesting experiment for her and a sensational draw — Pavlova on the screen — for their society. Pavlova consented and in the studio of some firm, the name of which I have forgotten, she danced "The Night" by Rubinstein.

The cinematograph at that time was in its infancy and this experiment impressed Pavlova most unfavourably. Probably this was due to the imperfect camera and to the fact that the triangular shaped area, with its apex towards the apparatus, which was marked off for her to dance in, proved to be very narrow. Pavlova was constantly stepping over the line and every minute she was told that her right arm was outside the camera or that the flowers fell outside the camera, and so on. And when she tried to alter her dances from across the stage into its depth, she was either suddenly very small or enormous when swiftly approaching the camera. She was left very dissatisfied with the experiment, but not wishing to deprive the charity entertainment of her support, agreed to the film being shown, on the condition that it remained in the sole possession of the charity organization, and should not be shown elsewhere.

The public nevertheless was perfectly pleased, as we heard afterwards, but Pavlova came to the conclusion that the technique of the cinematograph had not yet reached a stage when it was able to reproduce dancing.

In 1916 a huge American concern, the Universal Film Company, asked Pavlova to take the chief part in a big film entitled "The Dumb Girl of Portici", which was based on the libretto of the famous opera "Fenella". Pavlova did not wish to accept this offer, but it coincided with a rather difficult moment, viz. the War was on and Pavlova could not return to Europe with her company, fearing to take upon herself responsibility for the lives of others, as submarines were a very real danger. We had, moreover, already had two consecutive seasons in America and it would not have been policy to start upon a third one. At that time, however, there was a chance of buying the magnificent scenery and costumes of the Boston opera, and combining opera with ballet. A new tour could then have been undertaken in this way, attracting increased interest from the public. But to carry this out meant having substantial means at one's disposal, and Pavlova consented to be filmed, in order that her earnings on the films should help in organising this new enterprise.

The taking of this picture caused her much annoyance and many disappointments. From the very beginning of her career she had been accustomed to treat her art with great respect, paying close attention to every detail — the make-up, the costume, lighting conditions, etc. and here she felt herself completely inexperienced and helpless. The management of the company and the producer, it must be admitted, were extremely amiable and kind to her. Unfortunately, either they did not know, or were not able to direct her in these technical details. Finally she insisted upon seeing the results of the first pictures and when she did so, came at once to the conclusion that it was all very bad. The make-up, apparently, was not the only thing that was wrong, for being ignorant of cinematograph camera requirements, she found that some of her movements were too pronounced, too rapid and too jerky. Eventually, other artists playing important parts, seeing her distress, and out of their affection for her, came to her aid. They taught her what was required for cinema work. From that moment things improved and many dramatic and touching scenes came out very successfully. The picture as a whole, however, did not please Pavlova. She found it artificial and redundant. It was at the time when big firms competed with each other, each one trying to produce something more grandiose than its competitors. The public was thrilled by scenes of the Revolution, battles, the pillage of the castle, robberies, all was done very realistically. Horses, that fell under their riders were killed and lay about in pools of blood, beautiful, artistically made furniture was smashed to pieces; a crowd of a thousand people stormed a castle, got drunk, rioted and finally set in on fire.

This picture was shown everywhere and in some places it was successful; in my opinion thanks only to the name of Pavlova.

There were several good moments in this film, but on the whole it was not a success. One thing was certain — Pavlova came out very well on the films. The only problem lay in finding a suitable subject for her. But she was only strengthened in the conviction that the film was not her sphere.

Of late years she received several offers from Germany and America, but each time refused them. She was firmly convinced that, not having pronounced features, she was not "photogenic" and that, in addition, the screen cannot reproduce dance in all its beauty. With reference to this, she used to say that she would rather her name remained a legend for future generations, than that an imperfect reproduction should lead to disappointment.

She would argue —

"Think if we, to whom Taglioni is an ideal and the summit of art, should see her on the screen, and because of the imperfections of reproduction, should exclaim: "What, is this Taglioni?"

On one of our last tours in North America, a well-known American inventor suggested to Pavlova an experiment in his studio: he would photograph her dances in synchronisation with the music (this was his latest invention) and she should be sole judge of the result. If she approved, the idea was to be developed, if not, nothing more was to be said about the whole affair. At first Pavlova refused, but later, after seeing some of his films, became interested and agreed. The taking of the photographs was arranged in the studio of the inventor, a room quite unfitted for the purpose and not properly equipped in the matter of lighting. The inventor himself realised this, but said that if the experiment proved successful, everything would be properly arranged for the future.

Pavlova danced four dances to a piano and violin, and was in a greater state of agitation before the camera than she ever was on the stage before a huge audience. When we saw the results, our opinions differed. I was very pleased, and found in this trial confirmation of the view that a dance can, and should be reproduced on the screen; that it would only require a little elaboration and the adoption of the latest improvements. Although not denying that some parts had come out successfully, Pavlova found this film interesting only as an experiment; publication, however, was out of the question. The inventor accepted her decision without a murmur and handed the films over to us.

Pavlova was very friendly with Mary Pickford and Douglas Fairbanks and she invariably went to their beautiful home in the environs of Hollywood whenever she was in California. One day during dinner Mary Pickford told us that they had arranged a cinematograph in their house, so as to be able to look through new films quietly at home without having to go to the studio. And after dinner they showed us some separate scenes from a film on which they were just then at work. In the course of conversation Mary Pickford asked Pavlova whether she had ever tried filming her dances and Pavlova replied that she had, but without any success. And I told them about the latest experiment. They were both very interested and asked Pavlova to show them the films. To Pavlova's surprise, her dances on the screen impressed them greatly. They found that the photographic part was not up to the best modern technique, but they saw great possibilities in the pictures. They thought it was only necessary to find a suitable subject for Pavlova; one in which the dance came in as a part of the action, and not as an obviously super-added episode. They were so interested that they called in Charlie Chaplin, also a great admirer of Pavlova's, to look at our film. He quite endorsed their opinion and saw a great future in the experiment.

From California we went on to Mexico, whence we were to return direct to Europe. A few days later we received a letter from Douglas Fairbanks in which he said that the possibility of reproducing Pavlova's dances on the

Pavlova in "Rose Mourante".
(Photograph by S. Bransburg.)

screen seemed to him very important and very interesting. He offered his studio with all the personnel, the lighting and the photographers, and had prepared himself to help her with advice, if she would agree to return to Los Angeles for two or three days in order to have the film taken under suitable conditions.

Pavlova was tempted by this more than kind offer, and when our season in Mexico was over, she took a few baskets of costumes with her and we went off to make a new trial. Both Mary Pickford and Douglas Fairbanks were most attentive and gave Pavlova every assistance. Mary Pickford offered her the use of her own grimeur, a matter of great importance, for all new forms of artificial lighting require a special make-up. While making her own film in a studio next door, she used to come in to see how Pavlova was getting on, and Douglas Fairbanks kept a constant watch on the progress of the film. Several of Pavlova' dances were photographed, some of them two or three times over, and a few came out very successfully.

This time even Pavlova herself began to agree that with two or three months of quiet and thorough work during which the technique of film production and the lighting conditions could be properly mastered, great results might be obtained.

Mary Pickford and Douglas Fairbanks were very pleased that they had induced Pavlova to make this trial, for the results confirmed their original opinion. But Pavlova, although admitting that the advance in photography held out the possibility of considerable attainments, did not disguise the fact that she still thought it premature to photograph dances on a large scale, or whole ballets.

However, she found even the possibility very interesting and resolved to make fresh experiments for herself.

When our tour in Australia was approaching an end and the company was not so busy — for there were no more rehearsals — Pavlova decided to film a few scenes taken from "Don Quixote", "Giselle", "Invitation to the Valse" and "Fairy Doll".

Although we made use of everything that was available on the spot in the way of lighting, it was nevertheless insufficient and the film lacked the requisite clarity. Pavlova, however, tried it, though knowing perfectly well that a film taken in this amateur fashion could not possibly give really good results. As usually happened in such cases, she gave herself up completely to the work, acting as her own producer, rehearsing, dancing, etc.

Occasionally, looking through these films at home, at Ivy House, she would say that in spite of defects they were very interesting as well as educationally useful.

CHAPTER XVI.
CHARITIES.

Singers, actors and dancers of all countries are proverbially very generous contributors to charity, — to an extent that alas, is not always shown even by the richest of men. I hardly know of the case of an artist, even the most spoiled one, refusing to take part in a charity performance when able to do so. For some reason many people think that this does not cost an artist anything; a supposition that is totally without foundation, for all performers, and all the more so if they are celebrated, are very busy with their routine work, such as rehearsals and the learning of new parts. In England they have at least one sacred day in the week — Sunday — when, with the exception of concerts, performances cannot be given even for charity. In Russia, however, Sunday was the chief 'theatre' day, and, therefore, in order to take part in a charity performance, the artist would have to sacrifice this, very often his only free evening; or would have to appear at some charity performance after his own day's work was over. This often happened as late as one o'clock in the morning and it meant that after taking an important part, the artist, without any time for rest, would have to remove his make-up, put on evening clothes, drive across the town, perform and come home in the early hours. Very few people take into consideration that great artists cannot always appear in the same dress, that gloves and hair-dressers are necessary and that it is impossible to drive in an open cab in a ball-dress.

I should like to point out that it is often an expensive matter to take part in performances for charity. For men, it is, of course, much easier. But if the inconvenience and expense in the case of opera singers and actresses are great, they are even greater for dancers. Actresses and singers can put on evening clothes at home or at the theatre, whereas ballet dancers are obliged to bring the whole of their wardrobe with them and change on the spot, to put on tights, ballet skirts, bring dancing shoes and so forth. Charity performances are often given in halls which have no dressing-rooms and ballet-dancers are obliged to do the best they can behind improvised partitions or screens, or to dance on an uncomfortable floor, very often without any preliminary rehearsals. Nevertheless they rarely refuse. This willingness to take part in performances for charity resulted in the management of the Russian Imperial theatres forbidding its artists from doing so, as they considered it inconvenient for the name of an artist to be announced as participating in a performance of the Imperial theatre and also in a charity entertainment on the same evening. The publication of names had consequently to be stopped, the announcement of performances being limited to a statement that favourite artists of the drama, opera and ballet were to take part — three stars being used instead of the name.

And, knowing that they would see the best-known and most popular artists, the public went.

During the height of the St. Petersburg season artists were called upon to take part in charity performerces at least three times a week. Pavlova, who was particularly kind-hearted, took part in all the charity entertainments to which she was asked, continuing to do so even when she went abroad.

The war demanded sacrifices from everybody. Everyone did gladly whatever was possible to help those at the front who were sacrificing their lives. Concerts in aid of the Red Cross were being given wherever Pavlova went, local Allied consuls doing everything they could to ensure their success. The local charity organisations of the place also asked Pavlova to take part in their entertainments in aid of hospitals or homes for children — knowing how close to her heart was the welfare of the little ones.

When we returned from America to Europe at the end of the War we saw everywhere the ruin and poverty which it had left behind. But the hardest fate of all was undoubtedly that of the Russians, who after the horrors of warfare were destined to live through even worse — the revolution. They had to flee from their native land, completely ruined and having lost all their kith and kin, and become what is officially designated as "exiles".

Pavlova was shocked by the tragic situation of the Russians in Paris, especially that of the children, of whom many were orphans. From all sides she was besieged by prayers to help them. At first, tired out after her long journeys, Pavlova refused to start work again, but a stay of a fortnight in Paris soon convinced her how unbearably hard was the life of the Russians and she decided to begin again without delay. She consulted some friends, who were well acquainted with the position of affairs and came to the conclusion that help must be immediate, and not of a temporary nature. It was important to found something on a permanent basis, at any rate for those Russian children who were in danger of finding themselves literally in the street. They were already suffering terrible privations and it seemed as though there would soon be no means whatever to carry on their education. Pavlova resolved

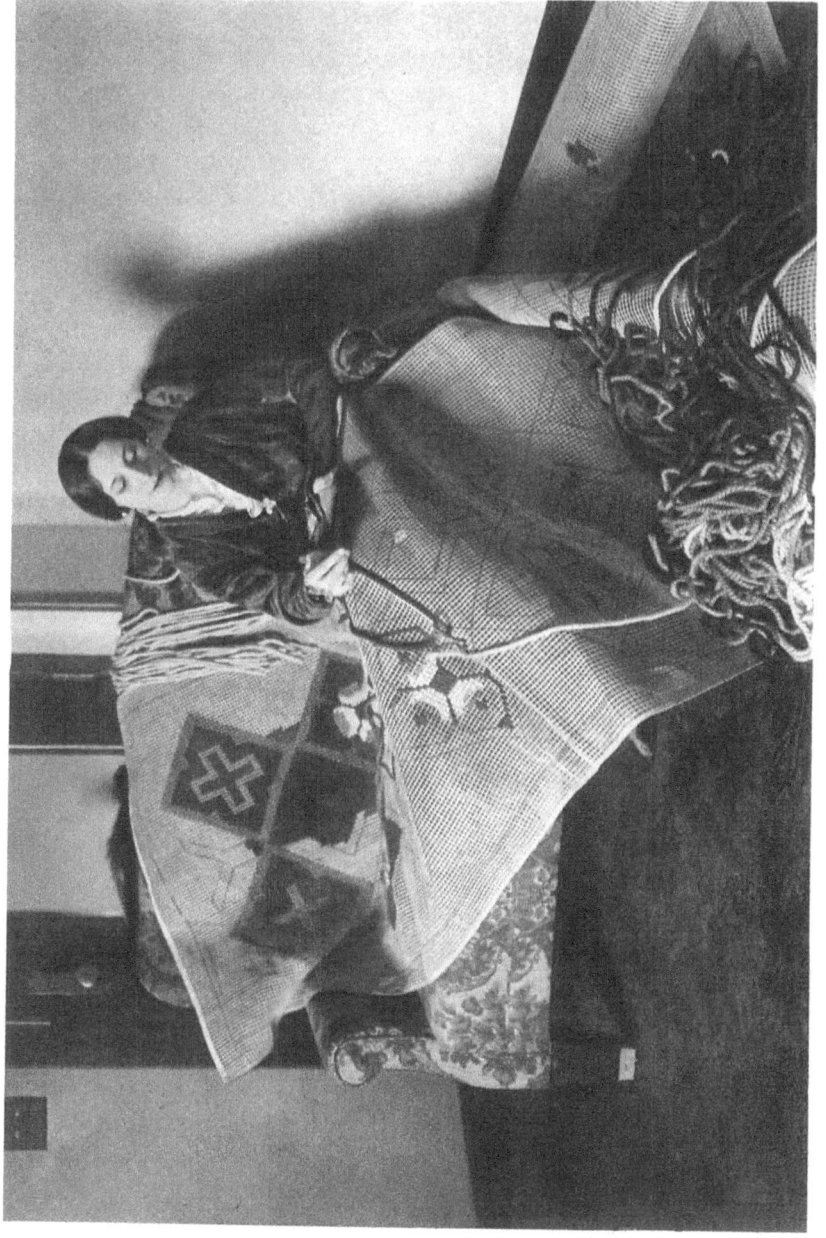
Pavlova making her carpet for the Ballet School church in St. Petersburg.

that a home for such children must be founded. The wife of the French President, Madame Millerand consented to be the patroness of a series of performances from which three-quarters of the profits were to go to the establishment of a fund to be known as the "Fondation Anna Pavlova", and one quarter to a fund for the orphans of French ex-service men. Four performances took place at the "Trocadero" with splendid results, and the fifth was arranged in the park of the Bagatelle palace, now a part of the Bois de Boulogne. In order that those who are unacquainted with this charming spot may have some idea of it, I should like to say a few words about its history.

The "Bagatelle" was first heard of in the year 1720, when its owner was the Marquis d'Estrees, and picnics and dances were given there. But it rose to its heighest fame in 1785, when it passed into the possession of the Comte d'Artois (afterwards Charles X.) He wagered Queen Marie Antionette that he would rebuild and completely refurnish the "Bagatelle" in six weeks and fixed beforehand the date of the great festival to be given in the renovated palace. In order to perform this tour de force he ordered detachments of Swiss Guards to seize all the consignments of stone on the road to Paris and convey them to the building place. The architects, Boulanger, Chalgrin and Bloikie, completed the work in 64 days. This whim cost the Comte d'Artois three million francs, but he won his bot of 100,000 francs from the Queen.

The festival was fixed for the 23rd of May 1786. A comic opera called "Rose et Colas" was given, the chief parts being taken by the Queen and d'Artois. It is related that the King whistled during the performance and that the Queen, walking up to the footlights, said to him:

"If you are dissatisfied, my dear sir, kindly leave. Your money will be refunded at the door."

In later years the "Bagatelle" was bought by Napoleon I as a hunting lodge. It then changed hands several times and was finally acquired by the town of Paris and opened to the public. With its lawns and beautifully distributed clumps of trees, the "Bagatelle" is without doubt the prettiest part of the Bois de Boulogne. It was in one of its loveliest spots that Pavlova's performance took place, and in the opinion of all present, it was veritably a fairy spectacle, so tastefully was the whole evening planned and so beautiful were the lighting effects arranged by the well-known architect, Doumergue.

This is how V. Svetlov describes this performance:

" . . . I recollect the "Evening Fete" in the historic park of the "Bagatelle" in Paris. It was a fairy-tale enacted on the banks of a lake. Anna Pavlova, "The Swan", died among the bushes and trees bathed in emerald light, or swept past in the wild dance of the "Bacchanal". The lake sparkled with fires; the trees resembled Christmas trees, decorated with innumerable many-coloured wreaths. Among those trees and bushes, Pavlova etherial in a gauze ballet-skirt, surrounded by her sylphides, transported the spectators into an atmosphere of romantic dreams. The strains of Chopin's music, the lights of many-coloured lamps reflected on the surface of the lake, the complicated design of the dance, always changing like a kaleidoscope — all this was mingled into one harmonious whole; nature "corrected and embellished" as Oscar Wilde would say, by the artists of this fete, and the art of Pavlova, which is so close to the life of nature, combined and gave a picture of poetic Fata Morgana."

Unfortunately, it had rained hard during the day and though the weather cleared towards the evening and the sunset was lovely, the public did not risk coming to sit in the open in low dresses. Consequently, instead of several thousands, only about one thousand persons were present, and the enormous initial outlay was not even covered. Fearing bad weather, the organisers had insured the performance for a large sum, but the insurance company refused to pay on the pretext that there had been no rain that evening. The total financial result of all the performances, in spite of the success they had met with, was not more than 50.000 francs. The whole of this sum Pavlova gave to the fund for French soldiers and started the scheme for her children's home independently. She succeeded in finding at Saint-Cloud, near Paris, a suitable house with a lovely garden, which she then and there decided to buy, leaving the organization of the home to our friend the Comtesse de Guerne, a Russian by origin. The house was bought and converted to its new purpose and fifteen Russian girls were adopted. The purchase of the house, its adaptation, the purchase of furniture and full household equipment, the future expence of feeding and clothing the children, together with the cost of their education amounted to a large sum which required serious consideration.

Pavlova was ready to give performances for the support of the home, but to count on a regular income from such a source alone was very precarious. Such performances require a great deal of preparatory work and it was impossible to organise them in America — where we were next due — while moving constantly from place to place. The impresario, again, invariably protested against such charitable performances. Pavlova thought however, that the object for which she was working was certain to meet with general sympathy, for, after all, was this not being done for Russian children, whose fathers and brothers died for the common cause, and was it not led by Pavlova, the great favourite of the American public? How, then, could one doubt the support of the Americans?

There exists in America a list of millionaires, their incomes being approximately known through their tax assessments. I succeeded in securing this list and we sent letters with Pavlova's signature to all the 7860 millionaires mentioned, thinking that if even five per cent responded the result would be excellent. Our reckoning, however, proved quite wrong, for only a few answered the call, some of whom, on receiving our annual reports, expressed a desire to continue their contributions. The most generous benefactor was Edzell Ford, who undertook to pay yearly for the support of one girl. I think the explanation of such indifference on the part of the American public lies in the fact that for two or three years after the war the whole suffering world begged America for help, and the Americans gave it generously, with both hands. Several committees were arranged and worked with extraordinary energy helping Belgian children and tens of millions of dollars were collected; a fund in aid of ruined Poland was worked very successfully (a committee presided over by Paderewski collected several million dollars; there were also several Jewish committees.) Among all these Pavlova's modest request passed unnoticed. If she had not confined herself to the dispatch of letters, but had put herself at the head of some sort of organization for collecting contributions for her home, if she had approached the millionaires in person, I have no doubt the result would have been different. However, anything of this kind was entirely foreign to her nature.

But if she was disappointed in American millionaires, she was given much happiness by the thousands of American girls who showed a deep interest in her home.

The idea of creating an organization to be called "Camp fire Girls" first came into the minds of leading American women as a counterpoise to the growing laxity of American youth under the influence of dance-halls and of the new theories preaching unrestricted liberty and complete independence to the younger generation. This movement, which had its beginnings some years ago, met with great sympathy from all classes of society and small groups were formed all over the country. There are now more than 10,000 local organizations having their own camps, the number of camp Fire Girls has already reached 500,000.

The aims of this movement made such an appeal to Pavlova, that she lost no opportunity in getting to know more about it, visiting their quarters in various American towns and being present at their meetings. On their side, the girls, learning of Pavlova's sympathy with them, also became her ardent well wishers and admirers, showing her every possible consideration. Whole detachments armed with bunches of flowers would meet her at

Pavlova being made an honorary member, lighting the 3 candles symbolic of the Camp Fire Girl's motto "Work Health and Love".

railway stations, deputations of the girls came to the theatre, and at a general meeting of their chief leaders, she was elected an honorary Camp-fire Girl having, according to the rules, to light a bonfire. She saw immense possibilities for good in this movement. The very idea of making it possible for girls to pass a few weeks annually in the country at very little cost, living in tents, learning to be independent, collecting firewood, lighting fires, carrying water, cooking, and growing vegetables in the environs of their camps, had all her sympathy.

During the War when it was necessary to send an immense amount of foodstuffs to Europe, all the centres of the "Campfire Girls" cultivated large plots of ground, supplying the government with enormous quantities of vegetables. The girls were taught to understand the great importance of economy, not only in the expenditure of their own small pocket money, but more important still, the duty of helping their neighbours by the saving of the produce of others and of the State.

But the organisers of this institution had other aims than these purely utilitarian ones. A love for their own hearth, the sentiments of friendship, mutual help and of love for their country, were developed in the girls.

Lectures were given in various branches of study and under the care of "guardians" the girls visited museums, national monuments, etc.

Pavlova launched an appeal to the Camp fire Girls on behalf of the Russian children in her Paris Home, saying that, though they were being educated in France, their whole upbringing was in the atmosphere of the Russian hearth, that they remained Russian in spirit and would prove useful pioneers when the time of Russia's renaissance arrived. They would then carry into Russia the noble aims and ideals of their American sisters. A reply came in the form of a cheque for 1000 dollars, collected among tens of thousands of girls, each one contributing a few cents.

As the hopes placed in American response had come to little the question of how to continue the support of the home by means of performances had to be again considered. Failing that, we realised it would have to be done out of our own resources.

Our next tour was in the East. It was of course out of the question to think of charity performances in Japan or China, but in India, where our audiences were largely English, we set about wherever it was possible, arranging "five o'clock teas" with Pavlova dancing at them, and also performances for charity. Although in this way some results were obtained, they amounted really to very little, whereas the cost of living in Paris was becoming higher and higher and the home needed considerable sums. Eventually it had to be arranged that the regular annual expenditure should be guaranteed from Pavlova's own purse, while the casual receipts from charity performances or benefactors would be used to reduce this amount.

Then came another misfortune—famine in Russia.

We were at that time again touring America and every letter that reached us from Russia spoke of this horror. The help that America organised proved remarkably beneficial. Those working in it gave evidence of wonderful self-sacrifice, and it was owing to their energy and tenacity that tens, if not hundreds of thousands of starving people were saved. Pavlova gave her assistance also to this organisation, but it was insufficient. She was particularly distressed and anxious about the terrible condition of the pupils in the St. Petersburg and Moscow theatrical schools. She resolved to give a performance at the Metropolitan Opera House, the entire proceeds of which should go to the two theatrical schools in the form of food-parcels. In order to increase interest and inspire confidence that the money would be used for this purpose, she asked Hoover, who was then at the head of the American Relief Committee, to be the honorary president. He willingly consented. The net proceeds were about 5000 dollars and 500 parcels were distributed among the St. Petersburg and Moscow schools and among necessitous authors. From that time Pavlova decided to send money regularly to the more needy artists of the St. Petersburg and Moscow troupes. She gave the management of this into the hands of artists whom she knew personally and in whom she had unbounded confidence. They, on their part, enlisted friends to help them in deciding where the need was greatest. Help was occasionally also given to former artists, many of whom were in abject poverty. She received many touching letters from the recipients of her assistance and both ballet companies sent her an address expressing their gratitude.

She received an intense shock when on her arrival in Australia in 1929 she was asked by interviewers whether it was true that the Bolshevik government had forbidden the distribution of the money she sent to Russia.

She replied that she knew nothing about it and was convinced that it could not be true.

On her arrival in Sydney she was approached by correspondents of English papers, saying that the editors in London were deeply interested in the news and had telegraphed to their representatives to see Pavlova without delay and verify the rumor. A few days later the information was confirmed by correspondents from Moscow, and then letters from Russia convinced her of it finally. The excuse put forward was that Pavlova was a favourite of the wealthy classes of Europe and America and that her money was therefore unacceptable to Bolshevik artists and would have to be used for the needs of the Red Army. Fortunately, the money had nearly all been distributed already and did not enrich the Red Army to any extent. Under cover of such an excuse to prevent a great Russian artist and one, moreover, who took no part in politics, from helping dancers of her own ballet school in sore need was so extraordinary, so absurd, that one cannot speak of it without the utmost indignation. The whole world without exception has stigmatized the Bolsheviks for this senseless and cruel order. Pavlova was, of course, profoundly distressed — why should poor dancers, who had been obliged to remain in Russia without fuel or food, and who had been accustomed to get food from her for several years, now have to be so sadly disappointed?

She began to form new plans. Something would have to be arranged to ensure that the money did, after all, reach its destination. It was quite clear that this could only be done with the help of third parties, but it had to be done with caution because after such a strict prohibition order, there was the danger that the intermediaries themselves might get into trouble.

Pavlova went to Paris every year and was happy to see that the home at Saint-Cloud was thriving, that the management was in excellent order, the health of the girls was good and that they were happy and in splendid spirits. From the very beginning Pavlova had been anxious that the girls should not only live within its walls, but should also be educated, receiving a practical grounding for their future life, in order to be able later to make a living. All the girls were taught either in the Russian school or in the French colleges, and on finishing each one was allowed to specialise in some direction and pursue her studies in the home. Thus, one graduated in the Higher Pharmaceutical School and received a post as a chemist's assistant; another in the Higher Book-Keeping School and so on.

The law promulgated in 1928 by which the real estate of foreigners was made subject to heavy taxation, placed Pavlova's home in a position of great difficulty. The aggravation of the financial crisis all over the world made all calculations with regard to donations and the receipts from charity performances exceedingly uncertain, whereas the expenses connected with the running of the home continually increased. And in addition there was a new and very heavy tax to be paid. We discussed the position with the Comtesse de Guerne and arrived at the conclusion that as all the girls had now reached an age (17—18) when they no longer required constant personal supervision, it would be reasonable to send them to live with their parents or relatives (most of the girls had some relations) and pay them the sum necessary for their support until they were in a position to become independent. With this in view (and in order not to have to pay the taxation)

Pavlova.
(Photograph by S. Bransburg.)

it was decided to sell the house. The capital thus freed was quite sufficient, as two or three girls started independent work every year. To Pavlova's great happiness many of the girls not only became independent, but married and had families of their own. In this way 45 girls passed through the home.

One of the most successful charity performances took place in Brussels under the patronage of the Queen of the Belgians. Russia was at the time without medical supplies The chemists' shops were empty of stock and hospitals were seriously crippled and even operations could not be performed owing to the absence of anaesthetics.

All the receipts of the performance were set aside for this purpose.

In addition to the customary programme, Pavlova herself staged a patriotic scene to the music of Tchaikovsky. She herself represented Russia and one of her dancers, Belgium. There were troikas and Russian bell-ringing and the whole thing was very touching. Many Belgians, who had lived in Russia, wept openly, admitting that it was long since they had lived through such poignant moments. This performance brought forward an unusual benefactor — someone, wishing to remain anonymous, had bought a seat and sent 100,000 francs in payment. We knew his seat to be No. 17 in the front row and awaited his appearance with impatience, but he did not come. Later it was discovered that this was a rich doctor, who had spent many years in Russia.

Japan greeted Pavlova so cordially and treated her with such universal esteem that when a year after our visit the terrible earthquake occured which destroyed nearly the whole of Yokohama and part of Tokio, and many hundreds of thousands of people were left without shelter, she naturally expressed a wish to be of assistance. She arranged a performance in Covent Garden, the whole of the receipts of which were to go to the victims of the disaster. The setting of the performance was very impressive. For the first time the programme included our ballet "Oriental Impressions" and Pavlova herself danced a special Japanese dance, entitled "Japanese Butterfly". The entire Japanese colony in London was present and the Japanese ambassador came on the stage during the interval, the curtain was raised and in front of the audience he expressed to Pavlova the greetings and gratitude of Japan. This performance resulted in a cheque for £ 600 being sent to the Lord Mayor, and it headed the list of contributions to the fund.

It is only natural that, considering the poverty of masses of Russians in different countries, Pavlova's arrival raised hopes in the hearts of her countrymen — for it was known that she could not refuse her sympathy for the misfortunes of others, but the number of appeals she received was so great that she was simply in despair. And in the meanwhile the theatrical business was declining every year, and with it declined Pavlova's earnings. A definite budget for charity therefore had to be fixed and not exceeded.

For a time it was possible to keep within the limits prescribed, but on arrival in Paris or Berlin, where the number of Russians is particularly great and where poverty is especially felt, the equilibrium of this budget would be at once upset, very much more being spent than was intended. Many were the cases in which help was imperative and people had every right to it. It was the duty of all who could help to do so. But there were also cases of disgraceful extortion under various pretexts. Persons having once received assistance to which they had no right, would come again the following year, insistently demanding money only because they received it before. Completely upset by such incidents and the huge number of appeals, some of which also I considered deserving, Pavlova would cry at times:

"I cannot help everybody. You know yourself how much we have already given away. Write to all of them that I can do nothing at the moment."

But, coming into my room a day or two later, she would suddenly ask:

"Did you send the money to those whom you spoke of as being in great need?"

I could of course only remind her that it had been decided not to send any, and then Pavlova, greatly agitated would say:

"But it they are really in want how can one not send it? Please do so as soon as possible."

Pavlova's Hands.

CHAPTER XVII.

NEW TENDENCIES IN THE DANCE.

ISADORA DUNCAN

The evolution of the Russian Ballet first began from within. Fokine, when still quite young and inexperienced, took the first steps in bringing about its renaissance. The first impulse from outside was given by the arrival of Isadora Duncan, the American dancer, in St. Petersburg. Her name was then almost unknown in Russia and her arrival very nearly accidental. The Russian Society for the Prevention of Cruelty to Children had asked her to come and take part in a big charity performance.

The first impression she made was mixed and contradictory. Part of the public was enthusiastic about her, seeing in her dances the beginning of a new era; others, rushing to the other extreme, denied her any good qualities and saw in her dances only an unsuccessful attempt at revolution. However, the interest she aroused was very great. When, a few months later, she came again, her twelve performances were all given to crammed houses.

Duncan came to Russia at a moment (1907) when the public began to be conscious that, in spite of all its merits, the Imperial ballet was growing antiquated. Petipa was eighty years of age. Something new, something fresh and young was wanted. Duncan was in the flower of her youth, her majestic, and at the same time wonderfully feminine and soft figure was admirably suited to Greek dances. She used her arms beautifully, she had fine shoulders, a wonderfully poised head and a charming smile, and had a naive and virgin expression. All this had power to captivate. Her costume seemed an extraordinary novelty. After the traditional ballet-skirt, tights and shoes made for dancing on tip-toe, one saw a dancer dressed in a short flowing Greek tunic, without tights and bare-footed. Another novelty was that this dancer had the unheard-of boldness to choose for her dances the works of the best classical composers. Her programme consisted of compositions by Gluck,

Schubert, Chopin and even Beethoven. Pavlova, and also Fokine were enraptured with Duncan's dances, those dances so full of feminity, so expressive and light, so irresistible in their charm and novelty.

Pavlova made Isadora Duncan's acquaintance and became her great friend, meeting her in St. Petersburg, in Paris and in New York. Duncan never missed any of Pavlova's performances, saying that it was always a sacrifice for her to look at a classical ballet, which she hated, and that she made up her mind to go only in order to see Pavlova, whose dances she adored. She used to say that she was quite indifferent to what Pavlova danced as long as she could see her movements.

After her first appearance she came to St. Petersburg quite often. She always received a hearty welcome, but the interest in her dances began to wane. Then she brought with her eight little girls from her school, and danced with them. These performances were immensely successful, the children being really charming. Later we saw Duncan and her girls, when they were older at the Century Theatre in New York. Then came the War and the revolution in Russia and Duncan's completely incomprehensible departure for Russia. Although she danced in Europe and America after this, we never saw her again.

It seems strange for me to write of these two great artists, Pavlova and Duncan, so different in every way and yet so sincerely admiring each other's talent, and to think that they are both no more.

Even during her life Isadora Duncan was the cause of much controversy; both those writers praising her and those belittling her were inclined to exaggerate, either raising her to unattainable heights or refusing to acknowledge any merits in her whatever. Now that fifteen years have passed since she really left the stage, the time has come in my opinion to give her her due. It can be said without fear of overstatement that she was a genius, for she discovered, worked out in detail and brought her own style of dance to perfection. It has been said that she copied her dances from Grecian vases. This is possible, but she put new life into them, did not produce slavish copies but inspired originals and was beautiful in them.

She has had a very marked influence on the dance in general bringing into it nature and simplicity to a degree hitherto unknown. It is also her great merit that by her example she showed the world that there is no irreverence in her experiments, that one may, and should, take the best musical compositions and dance to them if the dance is as full of dignity and beauty as were hers.

All this secured for her an honourable place in the history of the dance and the grateful memory of those who saw her. One cannot, however, but admit that Duncan, being entirely selfmade and having created her own art, has not succeeded in imbuing it with new enduring life, for, firstly, it was mainly dependent on her remarkable individual qualities, and, secondly, being founded on a few simple and elementary movements, her art was limited. One can allow that a man, never having had any musical tuition, can, nevertheless play well by ear, but he will never be a great musician. And so it was with Duncan. Her intuition prompted her to take the movements of Greek dances as a model, and in this she attained perfection. But this is not enough: the same movements, very little varied, cannot be repeated always and everywhere to different music. Repetition and monotony, **consequently**, resulted, and gradually the public lost interest. Although I admired Isadora Duncan, went to her performances very often, and knew her well, I was forced to admit to myself that this was so. On seeing her for the first time you were enchanted; the second time you were already beginning to be conscious of a certain monotony, and the third time you said to yourself "This is beautiful, but it's always the same".

It is very difficult to avoid monotony when the public sees the same dancer all through the evening, however talented she may be, and even if she dances different dances to different music. But this made itself all the more felt when Duncan embarked on the interpretation of a piece like Beethoven's Seventh Symphony. To be on the stage alone for about an hour can in no case be advisable, even from the point of view of physical stamina, if nothing else. After dancing for some time, to hide her fatigue, Duncan would sit or lie down on the floor for a while and then get up once more to dance to the musical score, to make rapid or slow motions. Finally, completely worn out and having wearied the spectators, she also failed entirely to prove that the dances added anything to the music of Beethoven — if anything, they had the opposite effect.

My opinion that Isadora Duncan owed her success to remarkable individual qualities is confirmed by the fact that, although she had a school for many years and pupils who went about with her for some ten years, studying and dancing with her, this school has only produced a few conscientious dancers, who reproduced Duncan's repertoire slavishly but failed to appeal to the public. But it is still more remarkable that Duncan created a whole bevy of imitators. I cannot recall any craze as widespread as that of "barefooted dancers". It can be explained by the fact that no training is necessary in order to make simple and natural movements, and yet it gives amateurs and quasi-dancers the chance of appearing on the stage and to be thus regarded as practising some sort of art. The result is that not one of these innumerable barefooted dancers ever achieved anything worth while or left any name behind her. They all disappeared forever and left no trace. When I think of Duncan, I see her as a wonderful artist, but limited in her creative work.

DALCROZE.

Pavlova, always interested in anything in any way connected with the dance, and hearing of the school of Jacques Dalcroze, wanted to make his acquaintance. Consequently while we were abroad, we visited Dresden to see the school and to learn something of the method of instruction and its application to the dance. In Hellerau, near Dresden, we saw a whole hamlet built round a central building — the school.

Dalcroze, who came to meet Pavlova, invited her to be present at two of his classes. One of these was chiefly devoted to the reading of musical problems, which Dalcroze wrote on a blackboard then and there, accompanying them with movements in rhythm. The second lesson took place in a large hall, beautifully illuminated by electric light through semitransparent walls of white material. The light, filtering through, gave beautiful, soft tones to the collection of variegated colours. There were here some thirty men and women, all dressed alike in short tunics, doing rhythmic gymnastics under the tuition of Dalcroze himself. Some of the exercises were very interesting — instantly catching the rhythm and rapidly transposing it into action, the pupils made spontaneous movements to any given rhythm, singly and all together.

The rendering of difficult and complicated passages gave evidence of a complete grasp of what was being done and a serious understanding of music. This produced a deep impression on Pavlova. She at once realized that this could be a great help in ballet, as one often meets dancers who have an insufficiently developed ear for music or a lack of the sense of rhythm. A musical understanding such as that possessed by the pupils of Dalcroze would naturally be of great assistance in the learning of new ballets.

When the class was over, Dalcroze took us over the premises of the school of which he was the creator and of which he is rightly proud. All was built on a large scale, well thought out and hygienic.

Then he invited us into his study and asked Pavlova what her impressions were, and she replied in enthusiastic tones. She was interested in finding out how far his system could be applied to ballet and asked him how long it was necessary to learn in order to reach the results seen in his class. But when he answered "not less than five years", she saw with dismay

Pavlova in ,,Giselle".

that nothing practical could be done, for it would have meant a double course of instruction for dancers, as Dalcroze's system by itself could do nothing to accelerate the teaching of technique.

Two years later we were again in Dresden and again visited Hellerau, being once more present at a lesson and carrying away the same admirable impression. There can be no doubt that the teaching of rhythmic gymnastics to children is bound to lead to good results for their future musical and rhythmic development and be very useful to them in after-life. And even the ordinary adult who has spare time and is interested in rhythmical development should profit much from the school of Dalcroze.

It was interesting to see his pupils. These were mostly young people of various nationalities, but now and then one came across the middle-aged and even elderly folk. Many of them proved to be teachers of rhythmic gymnastics who had come to Hellerau for their holiday in order to improve themselves under Dalcroze. On seeing these teachers of music coming here to learn to combine music with the rhythm of movement, involuntarily the idea came to us what a good thing it would be if composers writing music for the ballet or conductors playing it, would go through a course of rhythmic gymnastics. How much easier it would be for them to understand the essence and the secret of dance and rhythm, and how much more simple it would be for dancers to dance to their music!

MARY WIGMAN.

When at the end of the War we returned to Europe from South America, we found all theatrical affairs in a state of decline. This was only natural, for many of the actors and authors had to take part in the War and the theatres being doubtful of the new tendencies were unwilling to spend money on new productions.

The ballet was also affected. But even at that time there was talk of a new tendency in dance having sprung up in Germany, headed by Mr. Laban and Mary Wigman. The only explanation we could get regarding the fundamental principle of this new tendency was, that it consisted of a complete negation of classical ballet, involving the abolition of shoes and the simplification of the costume — or, to be more exact, one and the same costume for every dance. In the course of time, one came to hear more and more often that the influence of Wigman was increasing, as also the number of her disciples, that her teaching was very seriously considered and that the municipality of Dresden had voted her an annual subsidy.

When we went to Germany in 1925 for the first time after the War, every newspaper sent its interviewers to ask Pavlova her opinion on the art of Wigman. She, of course, could give no reply, having seen neither Wigman nor her school.

Arriving in Dresden she sent to Madame Wigman to say that she would like to see her school and received an invitation to visit it. We were present at a lesson. Fifteen girls, ranging in ages from eighteen to twenty-five, all dressed alike in long skirt, short bodice, and bare feet, were doing something in the nature of rhythmic gymnastics to the sounds of a gong. All the movements were performed with great precision in response to the orders given, the girls falling on the floor instantaneously, and so conscientiously that one became quite frightened for their knees; or else they were running about, continually changing the time.

Our impressions — Pavlova's and mine — were completely in accord. This Wigman movement was something like the Dalcroze method, but something much more feeble. When it became known that Pavlova had been to the school of Wigman, the interviewers crowded in once more. This time Pavlova had to answer that she had not seen the art itself, having only been present at a lesson in school. Until she had seen the results on the stage, she could express no opinion. Finally, in Munich, we saw it advertised that Wigman and her school were geving a performance. As it was given after some other show and did not begin until half-past eleven (as is very often the case in Germany), Pavlova was able to be present after her own evening performance. As always on such occasions, she was very excited, hurrying so as not to be late, expecting to see something new and interesting.

The curtain rose and we saw on the stage a piano, a gong and several barefooted girls in the same costumes as in the school. Among them, dressed in the same way, was Wigman. To our surprise and disappointment, we were soon convinced that the performance consisted of what we had already seen at the school, the only difference being that, whereas there everything was done simply, here the programme explained that such and such movements denoted grief and suffering, others triumph and so forth.

Wigman herself interpreted everything with increased energy, an emphasised assertiveness, with much more stressing than her pupils, but as for art, there was none. When the papers printed the news of Pavlova having been to Wigman's performance, the interviewers came for the third time, in order to find out, at last, what was Pavlova's opinion of Wigman's art. And this time Pavlova replied simply and firmly that she had indeed been to Wigman's performance, but could say nothing of her art, for there was no art, and what Wigman did must be considered an experiment, a quest after some new paths, which was not likely to end in anything really great because it lacked the chief element — beauty.

We asked ourselves the question — What was it all about? How could so strange a movement not only be born in cultured Germany, but subjugate the taste of the public, meet with success from the press and become the unquestioned arbiter in the field of the dance? But when we had been in Germany for some time and talked to many serious-minded Germans of artistic circles, we came to see that the phenomenon was purely accidental. When during the War Germany was completely isolated for several years, Wigman's appearances on the stage with her new ideas about the dance instantly received much support. Many thought that here was an original national art in the course of creation. Help was also given because there were no such things as proper ballet-schools in Germany, and such ballet as had remained in the Royal theatre dragged on a miserable existence. Wigman's school also carried weight by the fact that it was subsidised by the Dresden municipality. And then, the numerous pupils of the school, to their self-deceptive joy, thought that no great efforts and no long training were necessary for learning the art of the dance and that it was easy to become a dancer according to this simple method and make an appearance on the stage. There was no opposition and the "Wigman movement" rapidly spread through Germany.

When it was announced in Berlin in 1925 that Pavlova was coming for a few performances, the press pricked up its ears — How would Pavlova be received by the public after eleven years of absence? And then there was also the other question — How would Pavlova's classical dances be received by an audience swept away by the rise of the new movement? But after the very first performance it was perfectly clear, that Pavlova had not lost her fascination for Germany, and that, as heretofore, her arrival was a joy for all those who loved beauty. Once more the old truth was confirmed that classical dancing is not antiquated and that it deserves the most serious study, for it alone can serve as the foundation for future development. This became so obvious that the maitre de Ballet of the Berlin opera house, himself a rabid innovator in his productions and a man who did not recognise classical dancing at all, took to frequenting the Russian classical school assiduously, going through the full course there, and later he confessed to Pavlova that he now understood how indispensable it was for him.

The appearances of Pavlova kindled a great interest in the dance. Comparisons were made between her and Wigman. Opinions naturally

Pavlova in the "Invitation à la Danse".

differed. One well-known critic said that a single arabesque of Pavlova's was worth more than the whole so-called art of Wigman. Others said "Yes, the art of Pavlova is lovely, but it is the art of decline, while the Wigman movement is the rising sun".

There was once more an awakening of interest in the learning of classical dancing and the schools began to fill again. The friends of classicism were overjoyed for they felt that the tide had turned and firmly believed that in a very short time there would be a serious reaction in general sympathies. There can be no doubt that Pavlova's arrival and her subsequent tour in Germany played a very important role in the re-education of the public. Comparing her performance with those of Wigman the people could not but see the difference, and the success of the new movement began to diminish. The conviction that art cannot be furthered by the inventions of a few self-taught people and amateurs, but must have a solid and trustworthy foundation, began to penetrate deeper and deeper into the consciousness of all. Pavlova was always saying to the Germans:

"You must very carefully guard the flowering tree of the art of dance, always keeping in mind that its roots are-classical ballet. Everyone who is interested in this art must go through the classical school, and if he feels the necessary talent in himself and an urge to search out new paths, let him try to graft the new cuttings to this tree and possibly in the future some good fruit will result. But woe to him, who, for the sake of problematical reforms, in his efforts to give something new, begins by cutting down the old tree."

In the last two years the interest shown in Germany in Wigman's attempts has declined still more, and she has to a large extent transferred her activities to America, giving performances and opening schools there. Not only Wigman herself, but her disciples lecture on her art. M. Fokine was present at one of them and has sent me a newspaper report on it. It is so characteristic and interesting, that I think I have the right to quote it in full.

A melancholy Art.
(Novoe Russkoe Slovo, New York, March 1st. 1931)

When Margaret Walmann came to America to propagate the art of Mary Wigman, she referred to her teacher as a "Dark Soul". She explained that this art reflected the depressed state of the German soul after the defeat in the War.

When Stuart Palmer, the critic, wrote in the magazine "The Dance" about the art of Miss Graham he also called her a "Dark Soul".

America did not lose the War, so that I do not know, what the explanation of Miss Graham's depression is: the paper says that formerly she was "a normal and pleasant girl". I imagine it is merely the imitation of foreign influences. It is a transplanting of a diseased art from Germany to a healthy America.

But there is another explanation that suggests itself to me. The expression of grief in dance does not require much movement. It seems so easy. Whereas on the contrary the expression of gladness asks for a great deal. That is more difficult. The happier we are the more we want to be in motion.

The dance is mainly the expression of happiness, of Light, not of Darkness. Of course grief, like all emotions, is sometimes the subject of dance. But it was joy and not grief that gave it birth. And it is joy that leads it to continual development.

Pavlova showed us many swift dances — joyful, happy ones. But in this path she did not have many followers, whereas "The Dying Swan" is danced by everybody. It seems so easy. And therefore there is no dancer, no dancing child, who has not attempted "The Dying Swan". The great Isadora gave us the whole gamut of human emotions in her dances. But when I think of the "little Duncans", I can only picture to myself a girl with her hand on the crown of her head, like the figures in a funeral procession on Greek vases.

All amateurs throw themselves greedily on what is easy of achievement; follow the line of least resistance.

I was particularly convinced of the correctness of this view after going to several evenings arranged by Mr. John Martin, the critic of the "New York Times" in the "School of Social Research".

My last visit was on the 20th of February and it is about this that I want to speak.

Miss Graham was already speaking when I entered. Sitting on the floor behind her were two rows of young women in knitted jerseys. There was a platform for demonstrations in the middle of the room. All around was the public. Miss Graham has all the appearance of a fanatical prophetess. Apparently the whole of her exterior is against anything dainty, feminine or beautiful: a long chemise, hair that is demonstratively plastered back, a bowed back, elbows that stick out and shoulders thrust forward, either clenched fists or hands flatly outstretched ...... All denotes that she is above the "antiquated" concept of beauty, of grace, that she rejects it on principle.

While explaining her theory she often points to her chest and her stomach, where lies the centre and secret, I understand, of the something new in her art.

By a nod of his head and a smile Mr. Martin authoritatively confirms the indisputable truth of the new theory. Miss Graham constantly interrupts her speech with the phrase:

"Perhaps somebody would like to help with a question?"

Questions followed and the lecturer answered promptly. There were questions of this nature: must one be born for this art or can it be acquired without being expressly born for it? Miss Graham instantly reassured the questioner by saying that all her girls have very different temperaments, each one possessing a personality of her own, and they had all mastered the art.

I decided to ask no questions, though to me the whole thing was one large question.

Then came the demonstrations of the "dance". The young women lay, sat, walked on flat feet and .... that was all. Their arms either hung down helplessly or stuck out with the elbows up. Their chests were continually thrust forward or suddenly allowed to fall in.

These two movements constituted the whole dance.

The time was very slow and the expression melancholy, generally even aggressive. Clenched fists, a sort of barking movement of the body and the head.

"The barking girls ..... This is not only the cult of grief, but the cult of hatred", I thought. I was sorry for the girls, distorting not only their bodies but their souls also.

All that I saw was ugly in form and hateful in content. The feet were placed anyhow, with the toes turned in.

I looked round at the public. Everyone was sitting in easy, natural poses. Every woman, no matter of what age, seemed a type of beauty, ease and truth compared to what I saw in the middle of the room.

At that moment a woman asked Miss Graham what she thought of the ballet.

I pricked up my ears. Miss Graham answered that she approves of the ballet as one of the forms of dance; that, for instance, she liked Pavlova, especially when she bowed after each one of her dances. "She bowed very well ..."

It is not difficult to imagine what I felt on hearing this opinion of the greatest of dancers, one just dead and dear to us all, Pavlova .... That is the best that Pavlova had done ... she bowed well ....

Then the lecturer continued:

"But when the ballet attempts Grecian dances, the result is horrible!"

She never explained why it was horrible. The audience took her at her word and some clapped.

"I can't keep silent," said I to myself — but kept silent.

Others began to put questions. I said nothing. But my face was evidently more expressive than I should have liked, for Miss Graham turned to me herself.

"You, sir, apparently want to ask something."

"Yes," said I, "if you will be kind enough to explain what I ask you: have you in view, when working with your girls, a desire to develop natural movement or are you against the natural in your art?"

A long pause.

All other questions were answered instantly.

"Has one to be born or is it not necessary?" — that question was answered without any hesitation. But this question of the relation between dancing and natural movement was followed by a long pause.

The reason of this embarrassment was quite clear. All that had been demonstrated was so unnatural, so against nature, that there could be no mention of any link between life and this "art".

After the pause came long, vague explanations, quite irrelevant to what I had asked.

I repeated my question, and to make it clearer, asked for permission to illustrate my idea by gestures.

"In order to raise the arm, your girls first raise the shoulder, then the elbow and only then the arm. One does not do that in life. If I want to take my hat off the peg, I don't first lift my shoulder and then my elbow ... No, I just raise my arm and take what I require. According to your system I ought to be doing something quite different."

I showed how an ordinary, everyday movement had to be done according to Miss Graham's method. The result was comic. Every one laughed — the public, I think Miss Graham also, and I, myself.

"But you do lift up your shoulder to raise your arm," she said.

"I? Never."

Again she pointed to the spot between her chest and her stomach.

"Don't all your movements come from here?"

Then I too pointed to my stomach and assured her that nothing particular happened there when I took a book off a shelf.

"But you breathe?"

"I always breathe," I said with conviction amid general laughter.

I have treated this question at length and put it to the lecturer first, because it is impossible to define more clearly the difference between a beautiful and a hideous movement, between a clumsy and a graceful one, than the example of a gesture in life.

If it is necessary for a man to sway his whole body in order to take a step, we call him clumsy; if in order to lift an object that is not very heavy he must strain his neck and the muscles that do not come into use in the action, we feel his lack of agility, the insufficiently trained body; if in order to shake you by the hand, he has to raise his shoulder and then his elbow, and to lurch from side to side, then he most decidedly produces a very ugly impression. A movement is the more beautiful, the less we feel strain in its execution.

Such is the aesthetic of the ballet, such is the aesthetic of any dance, of any people. The teaching of dancing very largely consists of constantly doing away with unnecessary movements.

The theory of Wigman and Graham, however, is exactly the reserve. It can be expressed thus: strain as much as you can.

Without throwing light on the question of natural movement, Miss Graham suddenly and unexpectedly said:

"You know nothing of the movements of the body."

On receiving such a compliment from the young dancer I assured her that it had been my occupation for over forty years. Then I said:

"May I ask another question?"

Consent was given rather less willingly.

"Have I understood you correctly, that you divide all movements into two categories — those with the chest thrust out and those with it fallen — in?"

"Yes."

"The fallen — in chest expresses according to you anger, hate?"

"Yes."

Then I illustrated how, when approaching the bedside of an invalid or a dying man, we let our chest fall in. In that case it is sympathy or grief not hate.

"May I ask one more question?"

"No, you and I will never agree. It is not very nice of you to keep everybody with your questions."

I asked my question however, in spite of this second compliment.

"Why is the ballet 'horrible'?"

I put the question although the lecturer's unwillingness to talk to those of different opinions was obvious.

The ballet is called horrible and no explanation is given.

After I had repeated the question with insistence, Miss Graham took up the "fifth position", apparently under the impression that it was very ballet-like.

"How can Greek dances be danced like this?"

"You know very little about the ballet", said I. "You do not seem to know that there are a number of ballets in which there are no "five positions", ballets that are constructed entirely on natural movements, on the purest lines of Greek style. You criticize the ballet without knowing it."

Mr. Martin was already looking at his watch.

"Mr. Fokine," he said, "we cannot continue this argument. The ballet has its own field and so has modernist dance. The ballet has had the chance of saying its say for three centuries. Modern art will perhaps say it in three weeks."

Everything in this reply is wrong. The ballet did not talk, but danced for three centuries. Whereas modernist dancers talk more than they dance, and have not been doing so for three weeks but several years. Nobody stops them. On the contrary, it is I who am stopped.

Naturally, rather than talk I would prefer to compose and stage ballets, as I did on the Imperial stage, in Diaghilev's and in Pavlova's companies.

But ... Diaghilev is dead and the Diaghilev ballet died with him; Pavlova is dead and with her died her ballet. Many years earlier, Russian ballet died in the country that gave it birth.

But the ballet has already done so much. I, myself, have composed 57 ballets, many of which are Grecian, such as "Daphnis and Chloe", "Narcissus and Echo" and others. Nijinsky composed his archaic "L'Après-midi d'un Faune", Pavlova has become famous in her "Bacchanal", and so forth. Surely this gives me the right to ask why the ballet is " horrible" when it treats of Grecian themes. Why should the monopoly of Greek dances be given to the dilettante?

In Mr. Martin's reply the contrasting of the ballet and modernism is also false. It is not logical. For how can one set up one against the other such concepts as music and modernism, painting and modernism, ballet and modernism?

The ballet is a form of art. Modernism is its temporary condition, a period in the evolution of an art.

The ballet has lived through classicism and romanticism as well as modernism.

Diaghilev's ballet of its last period, for instance, or the Swedish ballet of Rolph de Maré went so far to the left, that neither German dancers nor modernists of the type of Miss Graham can ever come up to them.

But Miss Graham knows nothing of this. Neither of modernism in the ballet nor of the Greek style in it.

We are not surprised if critics know nothing of the art about which they write. That occasionally happens and we are used to it. But it is quite incomprehensible that a dancer, and an "intellectual" one at that, who speaks more than she dances, could not spare the time to study, say, the history of the art, has never learnt what has been done in that art before her and imagines the ballet to be five positions with contorted legs.

After Mr. Martin had called me by name, Miss Graham said, adressing me:

"I did not know that I was talking to Mr. Fokine."

How she would have spoken to me had I previously been introduced, I do not know, but the fact remains that she preferred not to speak any more at all and cut short both the lecture and the demonstration.

"We shall never understand each other," she finished.

As far as I was concerned that was no answer to my questions.

I know and love the art of the most distant peoples and of the most distant times. Why, then, should I not have been able to understand the theories of Miss Graham, if they contained even a germ of truth?

No, it is not to discover the truth about the art of dance, not to make clear some verity, that the School of Social Research arranges these evenings every Friday. No, that is not the reason. They know nothing because they do not want to know anything.

To say that Pavlova is good mainly because she bowed well, to say that Fokine even without recognising him, knows nothing about the movements of the body, to say that a Grecian ballet is built up on the five positions, is to show impertinence and ignorance.

These traits unfortunately are characteristic not only of some solitary dancer (in which case they would not have been worth mentioning), but of a whole tendency in art. This tendency is called modernism, the new art of the dance. It may, of course, be fashionable (fashion gets hold of all sorts of whims), but it does not contain anything new. Ignorance and dilettantism are not new. They have always existed. Only in our time they have flourished more profusely.

M. Fokine.

Pavlova in Italy.
(Photograph by Moreschi.)

CHAPTER XVIII.
PUBLICITY.

Advertisement is a necessity of the theatrical business. It was perhaps made least use of and was least required in Russia. The public in Russia was so fond of the theatre and of music, that a mere notification of the forthcoming arrival of some famous singer or pianist was generally sufficient for all the tickets to be sold within the next two or three days. No huge signs or posters were hung up. Interviews with foreign performers were also very rare, and when there were any, they were of a serious nature — about new rôles, the position of contemporary art, etc. Serious newspapers never printed any absurd or sensational rumours or anecdotes about artists, who, in Russia, were treated with too much respect to allow of such flippancy. People frequented the theatre not for amusement only, but rather for the intellectual pleasure they would receive from seeing a good play, opera, or ballet excellently performed. There were careful and thoughtful critics, who could analyse not only the acting, but also the psychology of a play and the artistic value of its setting.

In pre-war Germany the position of the theatre was somewhat akin to that in Russia. There, the theatre was also taken seriously, as an art necessary in the life of an educated people. But after the War all this was greatly altered. Nowadays all over Germany as well as elsewhere the theatre is merely a place of amusement, and if the public does not find the amusement it requires it simply does not go to the theatre.

The opera also is passing through a difficult period: public interest in opera is on the decline, so much that — a perfectly incredible thing — such a pillar of the opera tradition as the Metropolitan in New York has included Offenbach's "Belle Hélène" and "Orphée" in its repertoire.

This view of a theatrical performance as an amusement is also to be seen in the methods of advertising it. The simple, quiet notification of a performance or of an artist appearing, has given place to shrieking, cajoling posters of the same nature as those advertising a cinematograph, cigarettes, chocolate, soap, etc. The incredibly noisy and bustling life of modern cities, with the rush of motor cars, motor busses, underground railways, and the perpetual ringing of telephone bells, tends to distract the mind. And in order to make the public react or remember, the most obstrusive methods have to be employed. Advertisements are hung up in tramcars, on the walls of the Underground, on the outides of busses, the hoardings of houses under construction are pasted over with glaring posters; enormous electric signs in the centre of the town flash advertisements in coloured lights. When already seated in the theatre, we have an advertisement staring at us from the curtain.

However, one gets used to everything and our eyes have become so accustomed to advertisement that we have almost ceased to notice it. But formerly when one first arrived in some metropolis of Western Europe, coming from the quiet atmosphere of a town like St. Petersburg, where advertisement was unknown, the contrast was staggering and not in favour of the West.

When Pavlova came to dance for the first time in London in 1909 and saw on the top of an omnibus in huge letters "ANNA PAVLOVA", she was so shocked that she burst into tears. It seemed to her a sort of humiliation to the dignity of an artist. The same was felt by other dancers who came with her.

Later it was inevitable that, during the London season, one should come across posters bearing her name next to those of fishermen in sou'westers carrying a fish on their backs or cheerful gentlemen drinking a special brand of whiskey or beer.

America has gone even further in this matter. One can easily understand the expression "advertisement on the American scale". There, the bustle of life has long reached its zenith and advertisement in its most aggressive forms is a part of life.

In New York one is at first struck by the complicated grandiosity and the skill shown in light advertisements. One could not fail to notice a huge chariot drawn by four horses made of thousands of lamps rippling against a dark sky, or the advertisement of chewing-gum, consisting of a bunch of roses with butterflies hovering around. Such advertisements cost fortunes and, presumably, attain their end and bring in fortunes too. And as for the more modest ones, they are in such numbers that they merely form part of the general illumination and are scarcely noticed.

The performances at theatres and even the concerts of well-known artists are also blared out by corresponding advertisements. Huge posters in the most vivid colours, tens of thousands of portraits, pasted up wherever possible and exhibited in the most insignificant of shops, advertisements in coloured lights, notices in the papers — all this is said to be necessary to draw the attention of the American public. It is difficult to verify the truth of this theory, but still the fact remains that although it costs immense sums of money it is done by all the theatres and the impresarios.

On our last journey to America however I came to the conclusion that advertisement does not always attain its aim.

We started our tour by a three weeks season in New York. Our impresario said to me that, as we had taken a very big theatre holding over 3,000 people, and because the result of the New York season would affect the whole tour, he had decided to advertise on a larger scale than usual this time. And, in effect, posters were pasted up at every step, the papers were constantly printing notices and electric signs were placed in three of the best sites in the town. All this cost him about 30,000 dollars.

Our three weeks in New York passed off extremely well and we were about to continue our tour. On the day of our departure we went with the impresario into a large art shop in the centre of Fifth Avenue, where reproductions of some studies of Pavlova by an American artist were on show. We chatted for some time with the owner, a pleasant and educated man, said goodbye and were on the point of leaving. Just as we reached the door, he suddenly stopped the impresario and said:

"Tell me please, when do Pavlova's performances in New York begin? I am so fond of them that I should not like to miss them".

The poor impresario clasped his head in despair — he had spent 30,000 dollars, Pavlova had danced in New York for three weeks, all the papers had been full of notices of her performances and here was a man with a shop in Fifth Avenue who had heard nothing about it.

When a tour is being organised, some eight months before it begins, a special press-agent starts preparing "printing material". This preparation consists of his looking through the existing literature about the given artist, criticisms of past performances and all that is known about his or her new productions, and from this he prepares a series of articles and paragraphs.

But the main thing is to discover, and if they do not exist, to invent, some stories or anecdotes, which are better liked and remembered by the American public than any serious article.

Sometimes among these press-agents there are very able men who can invent something new and not necessarily inane. In the majority of cases, however, these "stories" are made up to one and the same prescription. A paragraph is put into the paper that such and such an artist has been robbed of jewellery worth a very large amount. All kinds of dramatic details are invented. That such and such an operette or music-hall celebrity, having the most beautiful legs in the world, has insured them for some fabulous sum, and a photograph of the legs (belonging to quite another person) is reproduced. Then the next article would contain a picture purporting to be the legs of Cleopatra or Phryne, and the paper would go on to state that according to expert opinion, those of the visiting celebrity were much more beautiful. And such nonsense is printed and by it the artist will be remembered.

When the material is ready, cheap cardboard clichés are made from it in order that the local papers should not have to waste time and money. With this "material" and thousands of printed reproductions of photographs, the advance-agent goes off some four or five months previous to the beginning of the tour.

He makes a round of all the towns included in the tour, calls on the editors of the local papers in each town, hands them the prepared "material", leaves a number of photographs and proceeds to the next place.

Six weeks or so before the tour another such agent, repeating the same work, with some additional material, starts off. Eventually the troupe arrives and with it is yet one more agent, who arranges interviews, sees that editors have not forgotten to put in the notices, etc.

Pavlova in Venezuela.

Pavlova hated the advertising part of the business. She was specially indignant in the case of a poster showing lack of taste, but whenever we tried to get an artist to undertake them, nothing ever came of it. I think that the demand for really artistic posters, such as were still in existence some twenty years ago, has been killed by the striving after size and vivid effects. The only really beautiful poster for Pavlova was made by the late Serov. The figure of Pavlova in charcoal and white chalk, very light and graceful and at the same time an excellent likeness, was drawn on a pale blue background. This poster was used by Diaghilev for his season of 1909, and at the time produced a great impression. But when we hung up this same poster in Paris a few years ago, it was completely lost among the enormous commercial advertisements.

When passing through American towns, it was truly an ordeal for Pavlova and she would constantly turn away in order not to see pictures of herself. Very much in fashion at one time was a poster depicting a flying Pavlova about five times her natural size. Because of the scale on which it was drawn she was shown with such ample curves that the figure bore not the slightest resemblance to her. It was nevertheless very popular, and in spite of her protests the impresario was always ordering it.

Another showed a gigantic head of her, and one of perfectly monstrous dimensions pictured her standing in an arabesque on a terrace with a mosaic floor, with a volcano emitting flames and lava in the distance.

The last year, in our tour in Europe, we made use almost exclusively of a beautiful reproduction of a well-known photograph of Pavlova in The Dying swan, surrounded by a wreath. This poster was so artistic and at the same time so striking that it was given the second prize at the International Exhibition in Cologne.

Our press-agent, well aware of Pavlova's dislike for all kinds of advertising dodges, did not risk making up any absurd stories; he did however insert a paragraph to the effect that Pavlova took 10,000 pairs of shoes with her on her tour, and that she used up about a dozen pairs at each performance, changing them after every dance. This resulted in her receiving hundreds of letters from dancers and youthful amateurs imploring her to let them have at least one pair, as in any case she threw them away.

An incident that really did happen at the ballet performance in Braunschweig in 1914 was given great publicity.

After the performance the Minister of the Court came to Pavlova and said that the Emperor Wilhelm wished to see her. She came out in the Russian dress in which she had danced her last dance. The Emperor and Empress and the Court stood in the foyer. Wilhelm was very amiable and paid a few compliments to her and the Russian ballet in general. As she was taking her leave the Empress gave her her hand, which in accordance with etiquette Pavlova had to kiss. To her horror she saw that her make-up had left a scarlet spot on the white glove. When the War broke out, this incident was given a sort of symbolic meaning, as if foretelling blood, and many were the articles written about and around it.

More often than anything else interviewers were anxious to have Pavlova's opinion on contemporary dances. She always said she well understood their origin in the general desire for gaiety after the War and their popularity could be explained by their simplicity, whereas old-fashioned dancing required long tuition, grace and elegance. But though understanding them, she found them ugly. Moreover, they were often danced with too much abandon.

At the same time as she said this the Pope issued an edict condemning modern dances, and brought forward the dignified, graceful old Italian dances, such as the Furlana, as examples to be followed.

This coincidence gave all the papers an opportunity of having articles on the subject, newspaper sellers in the streets shouting "Pavlova and the Pope."

Quite frequently our press-agents would ask Pavlova to help them in their inventions or, at any rate, if she were asked, to refrain from contradicting any sensational story which they might have thought of themselves. But invariably she firmly refused.

Only a short time ago, during one of our last tours, the impresario asked her to go with him for a motor drive in order to stage an accident. He was very insistent upon this, because of the huge advertisement that would result from the newspaper reports of Pavlova in a motor accident.

In spite of all his prayers, however, Pavlova would not be persuaded.

During one of our journeys from America to Europe we lost a trunk containing music, and as some of the music could not be bought, it had to be orchestrated from the piano score. Out conductor set to work, but luckily the music was found and everything was in order.

The papers, nevertheless, produced a photograph of the conductor sitting before a pile of music paper working at the orchestration. At the same time they mentioned in an accompanying paragraph that poor Mr. Stier had to prepare twenty-four ballets for the orchestra and that he worked day and night in order to be in time for the opening of the season.

An incident, more like a newspaper story, actually happened to us in the small town of Fresno, in California. During the performance all the lights suddenly went out and we were obliged to stop. We were told by telephone from the central generating station that the damage was serious and it was quite impossible to say when it could be put right. There was a large garage adjoining the theatre and our manager was seized by a brilliant idea. As the stage was on the ground level four big motorcars were brought, two of which were placed on each side. Then their large lamps were lit and the performance was continued, to the great joy of the public, highly delighted at being present at so original a performance.

On one occasion Pavlova lost a basket containing her ballet-skirts. It should be remembered that we travelled with more than 400 pieces of luggage and it is a matter of surprise that not one single basket, not one trunk was ever permanently lost. It has happened that a basket or a trunk would be mislaid temporarily. Needless to say this would create great excitement in our wardrobe world, for if the basket were not found in time, all the costumes would have to be quickly made anew. In this case, however, the basket was found, but from the papers next day we learnt that a basket of costumes had been stolen in some mysterious way and that our wardrobe woman had stitched away for 24 hours on end, and that it was only thanks to her self-sacrifice that the performance was able to take place. Pavlova would be very angry when such sensational stories were printed, but was of course quite powerless to put a stop to it.

Is advertisement useful to a theatre and can a minor artist be raised to the level of a great one by its help?

Reasonable advertisement is helpful to every artist, because it makes his or her name known even in the most obscure places of the globe. In the case of opera singers and musicians it plays an important part. The more popular a singer or a musician is, the more gramophone records are sold. But with the contemporary public's lack of discrimination in matters of art, advertisement can play a very harmful part by pushing to the front a complete nonentity. Such advertisement as a rule only continues to have any effect as long as it is paid for. As soon as ever it is discontinued, the inflated reputation of the so-called celebrity bursts like a soap-bubble.

A foolish and ignorant advertisement can at times be very dangerous even for a good artist. I was personally acquainted with an excellent young tenor, whose reputation was completely ruined by an advertisement calling him a second Caruso. Serious critics, and the public as well, were irritated by this and he did not even enjoy the success he had the right to expect. Eventually he vanished entirely.

Many a time have bassos appeared pretending to rival Chaliapin, and not one of them has ever attained anything. In our day, not even the most celebrated and admired of artists can compete in popularity with the stars of the cinematograph and the reason for this lies in the size of the cinematograph organisation with its thousands of theatres all over the world and its boundless facilities for advertising.

Pavlova at the Taj-Mahal in India.

CHAPTER XIX.

NATIONAL DANCES.

Pavlova was always greatly interested in anything connected with the art of dancing. No matter where she happened to be, if some performance were being given of which ballet formed a part, or even if dances were merely incidental she invariably went to see it, and if I tried to dissuade her from wasting her evening, saying "Why look at anything which is almost certain to be indifferent or bad", she would reply:

"I must see everything. What is bad is also very useful, for it enables one to see more clearly what should not be done."

And in every new country we visited which had its own national art, schools and traditions, its own national dances, we did our best to enable her to see them.

Undoubtedly the first country in which the cult of the dance is held very high, where school traditions go back for more than a thousand years, is Japan. According to the custom there the school passes on from father to son, and in cases where there is no direct descendant, then to the favourite pupil, keeping, however, the name of the founder. In Tokio we visited a school that had been in existence for six centuries and bore the name of its founder.

Japanese dances are extraordinarily difficult and complicated. Their technique and their meaning involve a number of movements of the head, hands or fan, which are often without significance to a European. These dances, sometimes very long, interpret in minute detail all that is being enacted by the people on the stage. The Japanese public follows them with the greatest interest, understanding all that is being "related" by the actor. For us, however, it was long drawn-out and monotonous.

But there are also other dances — comic, and national. They are much more simple in meaning and fully accessible to our Western understanding. A Japanese dancer (in Japan female parts are usually taken by men) is very heavily made-up and in consequence his face assumes a mask-like appearance. Whether it is for this reason or because such is the tradition, there is absolutely no play of facial expression. On one occasion, however, when paying a visit to a school, the teacher asked Pavlova's permission to show her one of his pupils, a girl aged about twelve. She acted and danced for us a whole story, the plot of which was that an invalid mother sent her son to the bazaar to buy a fish, and on his way home he was attacked by a big bird, which carried away the fish. The boy tells the bird that his sick mother is hungry and is waiting for him to return and threatens to bring his bow and arrows and shoot it unless the fish is given back.

The little girl acted this story so perfectly, that it was possible to understand it almost completely. The child played without make-up and her mimicry was wonderfully expressive, her little face alive in every feature.

For a European to learn Japanese dancing is very difficult, perhaps even impossible. In any case it would be necessary first to learn the language. A simple imitation of the gestures would be meaningless.

While in Japan Pavlova conceived the idea of staging a Japanese scene, which was later incorporated in a ballet called "Oriental Impressions". She took lessons herself in Japanese dancing and suggested that some of our dancers should do likewise. As soon as this desire of hers became known, all the most prominent teachers offered their services and — lovingly and with great patience — gave lessons to our dancers. Certain movements of the legs, however, are so contrary to the fundamental principles of classical dancing, that some of our dancers considered these lessons harmful and stopped them. Pavlova was taught one dance by the famous Japanese dancer and actor Kikugoro and another, a comic dance, by a Japanese female teacher. She worked at them very hard and we were glad when her enthusiasm for them was over, for we did not think they were doing her any good. When the lessons were finished the Japanese teachers not only refused any fees, but gave a little present as a souvenir to each one of their pupils.

The dances of mysterious India were a great disappointment to us. Who has not read of the bayaderes, so graceful and of such incomparable beauty, dancing sacred dances in temples and secular ones at feasts? None of those living in India to whom we turned could give us any definite information, but we were told that there were certain temples in some of the faraway places where bayaderes were still to be found. Those Hindoos who had seen these dances spoke of them without any particular enthusiasm. There are no schools of dancing in India and it is an art in which nobody is interested.

The management of our theatre in Calcutta, which is the property of a huge company owning about seventy theatres in India, Burma and Ceylon, knowing that Pavlova was very anxious to see some local dances, collected together what they could and made up a company of some forty persons, including several soloists.

The management itself warned us that we might be disappointed and their fears proved to be only too well grounded. What we saw was a parody of Oriental dance, or so it seemed to us, with an obvious admixture of contemporary European influence, the whole without even the redeeming feature of good taste.

In Bombay Pavlova was invited by some rich Parsees to see a celebrated Hindoo dancer. This dancer had a high reputation and was often invited to weddings and other festivities. She was not very young, but was a fine, rather stout woman, more a singer than a dancer. She accompanied her singing by rhythmic movements of her arms, occasionally of her head and, very rarely, of her body. There were undoubtedly some interesting moments from an artistic point of view; she was certainly an artist, but that was all.

We saw another famous dancer in Calcutta. She was younger and although she also sang while dancing, she showed a greater variety of movements. And that is all the dancing we ever saw in India.

I must mention that this dancing was to the accompaniment of music on very strange instruments, most of them string ones, but with an indispensable participation of drums, hung on the belts of the musicians. The musician generally struck the drum with his thumb, which resulted in a deep and pleasant note. Nearly everywhere these orchestras also comprise singers.

We heard Indian music several times and could see that a considerable interest is still shown in it. We were told that most towns in India have their good musicians, self-taught, in the majority of cases.

The Rajah of the province of Baroda, who has the reputation of being the most enlightened ruler in India, has built up a permanent national orchestra and also a school of music, inviting a European musician to take charge of it.

Pavlova was very interested in India, particularly in its women, sinuous and graceful in their beautiful, soft, clinging costumes. She was anxious to find somebody to help her stage some Indian dances. After our return from our first tour in the East, we decided upon a ballet to be called "Oriental Impressions". The first part consisted of Japanese dances, those which our dancers had learnt in Tokio, danced to real Japanese music, but arranged for a European orchestra. The next two scenes were Indian. The first was an exact representation of the ritual of a wedding in a wealthy house, such as we had seen it ourselves in Bombay. The subject of the second was taken from the adventures of the favourite Hindoo god, Krishna, and his beloved, Rhada.

We were fortunate enough to find in London a young and educated Hindoo, who had studied dancing in his own land and was doing all he could to popularise it. Through him we made the acquaintance of an Indian woman musician, who had finished her studies in the Paris conservatoire. She agreed to write the music for our two scenes, making use almost entirely of existing native melodies, of which there are a great variety in India. But, as the character of these melodies lends itself with difficulty to pure European orchestration, our Indian friend found one of their professors of music and in conjunction with him solved the problem with complete success. All the costumes and the properties we brought with us from India.

Much more difficult was the question of scenery. In Indian theatrical art there is no scenery, and what we saw was in a sort of pseudo-Moorish style and very bad. Then the idea came to me of utilising the splendid collection of Indian miniatures in the British Museum and in the library of the India Office. After we had chosen the most suitable of the miniatures of the XVII century we asked Allegri, the artist, to come to London, copy them and make the scenery, preserving the style and the ornamentation of the originals. In this way the music, the dances and the costumes were the work of Indians, while the scenery was borrowed from the pictures of the best period of Indian art. "Oriental Impressions", however, met with an indifferent reception in London, where it was first produced, except from the Indians, who came assiduously to our performances and each time

Pavlova with her Japanese Teacher Kikugoro.

went behind the scenes to invest Pavlova with a wreath of jasmine petals, the national form of greeting and respect.

In America, on the other hand, "Oriental Impressions" had a great success. The pictures of India shown by us were quite novel for the Americans, whereas the English after some two hundred years domination were well acquainted with the country. Indian journalists in America said that Pavlova had performed a national service to their country by popularising it and arousing an interest in it. These performances were also popular in South America. But we were thoroughly surprised by the Germans, who said that "Oriental Impressions" was a copy of something, but of what they did not state.

When we went on our last tour of 1928—29, I suggested to Pavlova to take "Oriental Impressions" with us to India. The idea quite horrified her. I took the scenery and the costumes nevertheless, and when we arrived in Bombay I told the press representatives about it. Next day the papers were full of it. Pavlova was besieged on all sides by requests and entreaties to show the ballet. Very unwillingly she consented and was, of course, very nervous about the result. To show the Indians their own dances and customs to their own music, set to the orchestra, however, in the European way, to represent the dreams of their favourite legends, must indeed have seemed a bold idea. But "boldness captures cities" and to Pavlova's infinite satisfaction the success achieved was enormous, so that we had to give this ballet at every performance.

This was in Bombay and in the Calcutta the same thing happened. I must now explain why I was not afraid to give "Oriental Impressions".

Although art in India at one time stood very high, it is now completely neglected. It seems incredible that in this huge country there is absolutely no interest taken in creative art. I am not referring to the lower classes, generally quite uneducated, but even among the highest, among the numerous rajahs, who possess untold wealth, boundless territories, countless palaces, dozens of Rolls-Royces, there is no wish to do anything for their own national art and no interest is taken in it. Many rajahs go constantly to Paris and London, travel all over the world, and yet they rarely spare a thought to the art of their own native land. It is only the English who keep alive any interest in Indian art. They have founded and support an important archaeological commission, whose duties are to look after ancient monuments and carry on excavations. They have also established art schools in Calcutta and Bombay. When we visited them on our travels, after making the acquaintance of the director, we came to the conclusion that, intelligently handled, the youth of India show great abilities and a discriminating taste. Both schools support the national trend in art, and much of the work exhibited by them shows how successful is their reproduction of ancient painting.

But this good beginning has not yet touched the Indian theatre and what we saw in this direction was extraordinarily naive and bad. When she was contemplating the production of "Oriental Impressions", Pavlova realised that it was almost impossible for a European to absorb the spirit of the East, as the difference between the races is so great, but she and her collaborators strove to reproduce the atmosphere of India as perfectly as possible.

Pavlova made an enchanting Rhada, a complete reincarnation of the tender and loving girl who is, at the same time, proud of the love of her god. And the work of the others taking part in the ballet was also worthy of the subject. The Indian public was full of appreciation for this reverence shown to their country, for this desire to represent it in its best and most attractive colours. Indian critics were loud in their praises of the attempt we had made and said that it would be impossible to gauge the measure of gratitude which India owed to Pavlova. She, a foreigner, had seen the necessity of breathing new life into their moribund art and had pointed out the right path, which lay through the study of national customs and legends.

The great interest aroused by our ballet showed itself, among other things, in the fact that all the Indians who came to see Pavlova after the performance to express their opinion and gratitude thought it incumbent upon them to give her some sort of hints concerning the ritual of a wedding. One man declared that during the ceremony the bridegroom ought to hold a coco-nut in his right hand. Two women pointed out that the veil of jasmine petals covering the bride in the first part of the ceremony was not made correctly, being, so they said, too thick and completely covering her face. Because she was so conscientious Pavlova accepted this advice, and at the next performance the bridegroom held a coco-nut and the bride had her veil altered. But other Indians came along after the performance and energetically protested against the coco-nut, saying that it was the custom of one small state only and certainly did not apply to the whole of India. They also said that the veil was right in the first performance — that all the corrections, in fact, suggested by other Indians the day before indicated modern tendencies. This sort of thing went on for several days and eventually Pavlova decided to end it and, thanking each newcomer for his advice, continued to give the ballet in its original form.

I have had several opportunities of discussing our performance with highly educated Indians, whose frank opinions I was anxious to have. They entirely approved of the production, explaining to me that as India is so large, nearly every province has its own traditions and customs which are often quite unknown in other parts of the country. The only criticism they had to make referred to the make-up and appearance of the Buddhist priests who came to the wedding, but that was not easily altered.

In Burma, which resembles India closely in religion and many of its customs, a great interest is shown in the national dances of the country and we had two opportunities of becoming acquainted with them.

The first time we arrived in Rangoon was on the European New Year's Day, which coincided with the local holidays. According to custom, a whole camp of stalls and booths was pitched in a large field near the town. A theatre was erected and one can judge of its primitive state by the fact that the people sat on the bare earth under the open sky and the wonderful light of the moon. In the orchestra, composed of several instruments, the chief person was an artist (there was no other name for him) who sat in the middle, in a place partitioned off, and played on a dozen drums of various shapes and sizes. The rapidity and sureness with which he did this was wonderful although the performances lasted right through the night.

It is difficult to say whether this was one play or a series of plays, for we understood nothing. It was a purely native, humorous performance of an extremely realistic character. Judging by the ceaseless laughter of the audience, the actors must have been saying very amusing things. The play was constantly interrupted by dancing, also purely native, rather coarse, but very interesting and original. These dances contained much boldness and humour and were executed, apparently without any effort, but undoubtedly with great mastery and very rhythmically, and were in parts technically very difficult. Pavlova was so pleased with this performance that we came again the next night, after our own.

When we passed through Rangoon in 1929, the management of the theatre gave in Pavlova's honour a performance, consisting of dancing, music and juggling. The dances differed considerably from those we had seen before. Their origin was also popular, but they were more studied and sophisticated. The costumes of the dancers were not of any assistance to the performers, but rather a hindrance, consisting as they did of a buttoned-up bodice with sleeves and a long skirt with a train, so tightly drawn round the body that squatting in them was quite difficult, though this action was particularly frequent. There was not much beauty in these dances, but considerable dexterity, exactness and crispness of execution, with sudden turns of the body, all done so rapidly and with such irreproachable rhythm, that involuntarily the question rose in one's mind—how long a period is necessary to master all this?

Pavlova with Spanish Gitanas in Grenada.

Pavlova was even of the opinion that it could not be learnt, but was rather some inherited quality, the result of racial customs. The dances were cut short by music, in which the loud, noisy notes of the drums were prominent, and by the appearance of very clever jugglers.

Our next tour took us to South Africa.

Johannesburg, the centre of the gold-mining industry, is full of black labourers (about 300,000) belonging to various African tribes. They live in separate camps and their favourite recreation is the arranging of competitions between dancers of different tribes.

A large gold-mining company, having more than 60,000 natives in its employ, in honour of Pavlova organised a display on a large scale. There was a large open space, on one side of which a platform had been erected for the guests, and on the other was the orchestra composed of at least one hundred musicians, seated before huge drums and instruments something like our xylophones. Some three hundred Zulus in war-dress, with feathers, shields and spears were assembled.

The solo dancers were two chiefs, one — the more important — had fox brushes hung all over him and immense feathers on his head, while the other was almost naked, showing a splendid athletic torso. The former had the reputation of being the best dancer on the Johannesburg gold-fields. The rhythm of the musicians was truly amazing. Without any leader, apparently by some instinct, all would start playing instantaneously and stop as suddenly. We were told that the secret lay in the chief opening the performance with a song which gives them the necessary directions. The same extraordinary rhythm was afterwards shown by the hundreds of black dancers, who made the earth shake under the stamping of their feet.

A deep impression was made by the wildness and strength of these warriors, who looked as if they had really worked themselves into a fury that was almost madness.

How realistic the effect could be is shown by the following incident. A cinematograph company made a film dealing with the history of the Transvaal. There was a battle scene in the picture showing a group of white people attacked by an army of Zulus. The former, according to the plot, victoriously repel the attack. Some 3000 Zulu warriors were collected for this episode, and when, entering wholeheartedly into their parts, they charged with fearful yells, brandishing their spears, everybody ran away — the camera operators as well as the white defenders!

Before the dances in honour of Pavlova commenced one of the company's head men summoned the chief who had the reputation of being the best dancer, and asked him to tell his people to do their best and bade him show what could be done by the first Zulu dancer.

"For, you know", he continued, "you are going to be looked at by the world's greatest dancer."

To which the native replied with great dignity:

"How can she think that of herself never having seen me?"

At the end of the dancing, both chiefs asked Pavlova to come out to their people, who were drawn up in military file, and in their presence invested her with an honorary shield and spear.

In New Zealand we made the acquaintance of some representatives of the Maoris. They were the original inhabitants of these islands and are an independent and comparatively civilized people. When the English invaded New Zealand, the Maoris resisted, but were worsted in the war that followed. However, they gave evidence of so much knightly valour and chivalry, that the English granted them full citizen rights and even certain privileges which they do not enjoy themselves. The Maoris proved to be a very intelligent people and soon accustomed themselves to European civilisation. They graduate in the university, enter Government service and sometimes attain the very highest positions. We made the acquaintance of a former Prime Minister, who was of Maori blood. The Maoris are rather dark skinned, like young Italians or Spaniards, with regular features and pleasant manners. They have preserved their national architecture, of which handsome carving is a distinguishing feature, certain of their customs, their songs and their dances.

In order to show attention to Pavlova, deputies from the Maoris offered to give a display of their dances and to let her hear their music. To do this they were prepared to come to the theatre at any time. It proved extremely interesting. Everything that they did amazed us, for we had never seen anything like it. Some of the melodies are very attractive and remind one of the Hawaiian music; the dances were purely war-like. They represented the preparations of a warrior for battle. The foe is frightened by facial contortions which are all done in concert. It was strange to see these same people, who a few minutes previously had gone through the actions of genuine savages, chatting to Pavlova of the impression made on her by their art. The majority of those taking part in the performance were students at the university.

After Japan, Java has the highest reputation for its dances, of all the countries of the East. Javanese dances are carefully tended and loved and their traditions reverently preserved. As is of course well-known, the island of Java belongs to Holland and the Dutch have left some of the sultans in full possession of their former rights. Among the many petty, unimportant sultans, there are two possessing large territories and many subjects, having their own Courts and their own ballet-dancers.

The chief and the richest sultan is the ruler of the province of Joksha. Our arrival in this town happened to coincide with an event which we had longed to see, namely the reception of the sultan. To this festivity the Dutch governor, various local authorities and visiting strangers were invited. On this day there is usually a ballet performance. On receiving an invitation Pavlova and I duly set off for the palace. This consisted of a huge open square in which were a number of separate buildings connected one with another. The particular building in which the reception was held had a large hall with many pillars surrounded by a verandah. There were about a hundred guests present. The master of ceremonies led each guest up to the sultan, introduced him by name, the sultan shook hands and the guest took a seat. The sultan's appearance was highly interesting. He was of middle height, rather stout and with a yellowish face, dressed in a European general's uniform, with red stripes down his trousers, and his head was bound round with a coloured handkerchief in accordance with native custom. But the most remarkable thing about him was the number of orders he wore. So great a number of stars of all kinds we had never seen on anyone before, and as there was no room for them all on his chest, some were even hung below his belt.

When the Dutch governor arrived the sultan went to meet him, took the arm of his wife and sat down between them. Next to the governor sat the favourite wife of the sultan, a pleasant modest young woman. A little further off, but in the same row, sat five or six of the sultan's former wives. The guests took their places on three sides of the hall. Behind the columns on our side was the sultan's orchestra of some eighty Javanese musicians. Many of the instruments, we were told, were more than 600 years old. Considering their great number and variety we expected much of the orchestra, but were disappointed, probably because the monotonous music of the dances did not give the musicians any chance of showing their powers or doing justice to the sonority of their instruments.

Pavlova, having so often heard and read about the dances, waited for them with enormous interest. And here, as is so often the case in such circumstances, we were again doomed to disappointment. Most people are satisfied with the spectacle of something novel and having local colour. But Pavlova looked for and expected more. We thought we should see something unusual, the product of an exotic, original culture, legendary figures of local epics come to life, but we only saw eight young girls in rich, ancient costumes with trains and impassive and expressionless faces showing us slow, flowing dances, in which the trains seemed to play an important part, being thrown from side

Pavlova with Zulu Dancers in Johannesburg.

to side with a swift movement of the foot. Each dancer had a woman attendant, who at the necessary moment placed the train in the required position. Very dexterously, sometimes on their knees, at others squatting on their heels, these attendants caught the train at the right moment and arranged it in position. These dances were very complicated and for the Javanese probably very interesting. For us, however, they were unintelligible and monotonous. At the end of ten minutes or a quarter of an hour it seemed to us that they were always repeating one and the same thing.

The Court ballet is composed of princesses of the blood, for the sultan with whom we had the honour of becoming acquainted, had had about fifty wives. His progeny are so numerous that filling up the ballet presented no difficulty. The music, accompanying the dancing, had also no message for us. It was a great pity that so large and full an orchestra played nothing apart from the ballet.

Cooling drinks, cigars and cigarettes were handed round in the intervals. It was interesting to watch the etiquette, established many centuries ago. Anybody wishing to speak to the sultan, went down on his knees and, bowing his head, put his hands to it. Having spoken to his sovereign and received his orders, the man slowly stepped back. Drink and food were handed to the sultan in the same way. The servant on his knees held the tray above his head. This etiquette was observed not only by the servants and the courtiers but even by the sultan's favourite son, a very pleasant and elegant young man in the uniform of a hussar regiment. The sultan gave him several commissions, and every time he approached his father, the son went through the same procedure.

It was also interesting to watch another orchestra, that of some local regiment, seated on the floor behind the columns on the other side. The soldiers were sitting completely at their ease and smoking in the presence of the sultan and their officers without the least constraint.

The end of this reception was extremely prosaic. When the ballet had gone and with it the orchestra of Court musicians, a ball began. To the sound of the military band, the sultan and the wife of the governor danced a fox-trot. The sultan is said to be intensely fond of modern dances.

A few days later we saw Javanese dancing in a garden just outside the town of Solo. The performance consisted of a play with scenes of a pantomimic character and of dances. Some of it was interesting — there was certainly more life and expression here — but nothing either very vivid or very characteristic. We were told that there is in Java a wonderful dancer, who presents the types of old gods and heroes in an artistic manner. He is very celebrated and highly respected; unfortunately we never saw him. Then there is also a marionette theatre of a special kind of Javanese dolls with inordinately long arms and legs. Although this theatre is rather waning in popularity, it is nevertheless still be to seen at all fairs and popular festivals.

Now that I have spoken of the dancing that Pavlova saw in the East, I will proceed to what we saw in South America and Mexico.

We began our tour in South America from the Pacific Ocean side. In Peru, where Pavlova had one of her greatest triumphs, some friends, who were always very attentive to her, wanted her to see some Peruvian dancers, who re-created the stage and the dances of old Peru in the time of the Incas. In order to represent the heroes in these plays they drew upon historical material; but for the rest — the customs, costumes, dances — these presented no difficulty, the Indians of to-day having preserved in their integrity the outward appearance and the customs of their distant ancestors.

The organisers of these performances gave a very accurate and interesting reproduction of historical Inca types, but the Inca dancing was rather poor. To a great extent this is the fault of the thick and heavy costumes worn, for the huge plateau on which the Incas lived has a very severe climate. One can say that the South American republics of the Pacific coast have created nothing new in the way of dances.

On the other hand in Argentina the people are very fond of dances. They are not of local origin, it is true, being of a purely Spanish character, but they are imbued with so much of the spirit of the Argentine that they can be regarded as national.

We never succeeded in seeing the dances of the real gauchos and their womenfolk. Among them, it is said, are some wonderful amateur dancers. But several times we saw the tango danced by professionals in Buenos Aires. They were good dancers, but there was nothing original in their performance; it differed in no way from what may be seen in Paris or London.

In Brazil the matchiche is danced splendidly — with much chic and elegance. Here for the first time, we saw it danced as it should be.

We spent Christmas in Porto Rico and there saw the negroes performing their national dances, some of which they still preserve. They were brought over from Africa a long time ago and have not quite lost their mystical and ritualistic character. We were told much that was interesting about the cults and customs of the Porto Rico negroes, particularly those of Haiti; much of it bordered on black magic. A great deal of research work has been carried out in this direction, but all the facts are still not clearly known.

All that it was our fortune to see was not very interesting. The negro dancers, with huge feathers on their heads, went through varied motions with the characteristic body-swaying that is usual with them, performing it all in marvellous rhythm, and ending in a wild dance. There was nothing original in it all and we even had the feeling that much of it had been borrowed from the negroes found in North America. The difference was only in the costumes worn. It is possible that we did not see the real ritual dances, for these are performed secretly, the authorities not regarding them with any favour. Certainly it would be difficult to give the name of dancing to the wild "hopping" that we witnessed. But as mystical ritual it may of course be very interesting.

Pavlova was greatly impressed by Mexico on our first arrival there. The country itself has a character of its own, unlike anything we had previously seen. But of all things she most liked the people, tenaciously and carefully preserving their national characteristics and costumes, which in the case of men consists of picturesque sombreros and coloured cloaks, and for women dresses of the most vivid colours. The feeling which these people evinced for music and art, the artistry with which they make various nicknacks of wood and straw, their taste in colouring their home-made cloths in amazingly beautiful shades with dyes obtained from the juices of plants and fruits, their sly good-nature like that of our own Ukranians, their natural gaiety and love for dances and music, make the Mexicans a very likeable people.

Pavlova liked going to the markets to make the acquaintance of the various types of peasants who brought their fruit for sale. Everything in these markets was bright, picturesque, colourful. On returning to Mexico five years later, we were sorry to see that the picturesque figures of the men and women vendors, carrying on their heads baskets of fruit, flowers and local sweetmeats, had vanished. The reason for this change, we were told, is the socialist government's dislike of any evidence of nationalism, even in dress.

Pavlova made up her mind to go the market, hoping that perhaps something of the past might have survived there, but here too, it had all been swept away. The police would not allow people to come into the town in national dress. When this decree was first promulgated, the peasants not knowing of it, came as usual from far off with their baskets of fruit and vegetables, but because of their dress they were not allowed inside the town boundaries and were obliged to return home with their merchandise. This made Pavlova very indignant, for nothing, one would have thought, could be more reverent and touching than this preservation by the people of their national characteristics, and consequently of their love for the fatherland, its antiquity and history; but no, in the name of some abstract idea, the

Pavlova in Japan.

people are deprived of this right. In the name of a vaunted freedom the peasants are forbidden to wear the dress that was worn by their ancestors and which was their pride. It became known later that the Government had found yet one more sphere for its activities: religion was gradually being thrust out and churches were being closed.

The love of the Mexicans for art was shown in the triumphal reception which they gave to Pavlova. A classical ballet had never been seen in Mexico before and it made a tremendous impression. In accordance with an existing custom, all artists arriving in Mexico City usually give a weekly performance in the Plaza de Toros, that is to say, in the arena where bullfights take place. This huge, circus-like building holds 40,000 people. It has no roof, but the acoustics are so good that both Caruso and Titto Ruffo sang there, and we ourselves were present at a concert given by Casals. It was consequently arranged that we should also give our performances there.

A platform was built at one end of the arena, beams were put up to carry the scenery and strong searchlights were installed; a place was also divided off for the orchestra. The performance though beginning at five o'clock did not end till eight.

One point was doubtful: how would the people receive our performance? Would they come, and how would they like it? The more expensive seats were in the stalls and the lower boxes. Of these there were about 2,000. The remainder of the theatre was given up to cheap seats. When the public was already collected, I called Pavlova and persuaded her to look through a slit in the curtain. She received quite a fright at the sea of people before her: 32,000 had collected. Our impresarios (there were three in view of the heavy expenditure entailed) were terribly agitated.

I thought they were anxious about the prospects of success of the performance, but, it appeared, their minds were busy in another direction. The time of year was February, a month when it often rains in Mexico, and I learnt it was the custom that if the rain comes down before the performance starts, the money taken has to be refunded; on the other hand if the performance has started before it rains, no matter how hard the downpour may be, the money is not returned. As on this particular day the weather was dull, our impresarios implored us to start earlier than arranged. This, of course, could not be done and we began exactly at the appointed hour. The curtain went up and the impresarios breathed freely once more!

Pavlova and our other dancers were amazed to see how these simple people followed the whole performance with bated breath. There was at first a dead silence, and it was only later, by the thunder of applause, that one was made really aware of the size of such an audience and felt its impressiveness.

Among the many people in artistic circles whose acquaintance Pavlova made in Mexico were some painters, who accompanied her to museums and national schools, where the national trend in art was at that time still followed. She had several opportunities of hearing Mexican music and seeing local dances, all of which pleased her greatly. When the public learned of this, as a special and gracious show of courtesy to Pavlova, they presented her with the scenery, costumes and full orchestration of the music of Mexican dances. Men and women teachers offered to teach these dances.

She was asked to learn them before her departure and dance them in public. Pavlova took this matter up very enthusiastically and having chosen two couples to take lessons also, she herself began to learn the dances.

She found this not so easy, however. The peculiarity of Mexican dances is that all of them, being of a popular character, are based on turning out the instep, and Pavlova's legs, trained for classical dancing, were bound to be unpleasantly conscious of a certain difficulty in this direction. She decided to "classicise" them and dance them on the pointes. Our other dancers did them exactly as the Mexicans themselves.

The lessons progressed very successfully. Our dancers liked these dances and they could soon be included in the programme. Their success was very great, a favourable reception gradually taking on the proportions of a great ovation. The Mexicans are wont to express any particularly strong approval by flinging their sombreros, which they value very highly, on the stage. At the end of the dances the stage was strewn with more than a dozen of these sombreros.

The following incident, causing Pavlova great pleasure, occurred during our stay in Mexico City. Our arrival in that town happened to coincide with the visit there of the famous violincellist, Pablo Casals. He was giving a series of concerts. After one of our performances he came to see Pavlova, whom he had known before, in order to express his pleasure; then he said to me he was sorry to see that our 'cellist was not apparently quite up to his task and did not play "the Dying Swan" as it should be for Pavlova. He added that he would like to play it himself for her, but in such a way that she should know nothing about it, and it should come as a complete surprise. We decided between ourselves to arrange this for the very next day and accordingly Casals brought his precious instrument and we hid it in my room. And so that Pavlova should not see him, he went away, coming back only a few minutes before the beginning of "The Dying Swan".

We placed him in the wings on the side opposite to that from which Pavlova started her dance.

Our mysterious preparations took up a few minutes and Pavlova wondered what was the matter. But at last the blue lights were turned on and the dance began — the heavenly execution of the great musician combined with the art of Pavlova. As I watched her, I saw her open her eyes wide at the very first sounds. Then as she danced she slowly came nearer and nearer to Casels, until that moment knowing nothing of the change we had arranged. He told me afterwards that when he saw her approach with wide-opened eyes, he had to close his own lest in his agitation he should not be able to continue playing.

Pavlova danced as she had never danced before and when she came to the end, she ran to the greatly affected Casals, embraced him and led him out before the audience, who greeted them with wild enthusiasm. The impression produced by this co-operation of two artists of genius was certainly an ineffacable one.

In Cuba we saw several times the great public balls which are arranged in the opera house. The stage and hall are made into one and the space thus obtained is enormous, giving room for thousands of dancers. These balls are very popular with the people, but the better classes never attend them, or only look on from a box. The music of the dances is highly original, melodious and unmistakably Spanish in character. It is performed by a negro orchestra and one notices a very peculiar sound that is unfamiliar and is produced by the rubbing together of two pieces of some particular kind of wood. The dances themselves, somewhat resembling modern fox-trot, are indulged in more than boldly. During one of the performances at which we were present, there was a sudden shriek, the dancers parted, and on the floor we saw a woman who had been stabbed. Then the ball went on. It is said that such occurrences are frequent.

On our return journey from Australia to Europe we put in at Colombo, and the loading there detained the boat for two days.

Ceylon has the reputation of being one of the most beautiful places on earth. We were advised to take advantage of the steamer's stay and visit the ancient town of Kandy, a hundred miles from Colombo. This was the capital of a small local kingdom, but its chief attraction for the Buddhists lies in its temples, which are very interesting architecturally.

According to tradition one of them contains a very holy relic, the tooth of Buddha. The main interest of Kandy for non-Buddhists is the marvellous beauty of the landscape. A small lake, surrounded by a low stone wall, is picturesquely shaded by wonderfully luxuriant greenery. All

Pavlova in Egypt.

round are steep hills covered with meadows and flowers and rich villas snuggle in the uplands. The chief temples lie on the shores of the lake. No description can convey an idea of the loveliness of this spot. An extraordinary calm takes hold of one here, all cares seem to drift far away.

Pavlova was enchanted with our stay in Kandy and breathed deeply of its perfume-laden air. The Buddhist temples are interesting for more than their architecture, in that they seem to convey a much deeper religious feeling than any we had yet visited. Pavlova liked going into them. The mysterious semi-darkness, the scent of jasmine petals strewn before the altars, the lights of the candles and the figures of praying Indian women on their knees before a statue of Buddha — all this touched her to the depths of her heart and filled her with ineffable peace.

A great and pleasant surprise awaited us in Kandy. A local religious Hindoo festival takes place there annually. It is accompanied with great pomp. Our arrival happened to coincide with this festival. It begins by a grandiose procession, which seems to stream out of the temples and proceeds round the whole town. An enormous crowd of people, gathered from the entire neighbourhood, lines the route several hours beforehand. The most convenient place from which to view the procession was the balcony of our hotel: it looked out on the lake, along the shores of which the procession passed. This opened with several priests carrying images; following them were more priests of superior rank and then came richly caparisoned elephants mounted by officials.

The elephants had to walk along white cloth spread out before them by specially appointed servitors. They moved slowly and haughtily along this white path and immediately after their passage the cloth was rolled up by the servitors, who ran on in front and spread it out before them again.

There were more than twenty elephants taking part in the procession. In front of the main part of the cavalvade were some dancers doing special wild dances to the sounds of drums. Among those taking part were warriors in ancient costumes. The whole picture, on the background of the lovely landscape, was so fantastic, that for this alone it was worth while to come to Ceylon. After the solemn march had passed the hotel, we mingled with the crowd in the company of the local doctor who had kindly offered to act as our guide, and we wandered about the town and the town square, which on the occasion of the festival had been turned into a sort of fair.

Fruit, local sweetmeats and various trifles were sold, but nothing of any special interest. The types of vendors and purchasers, however, were worthy of notice, for Ceylon has a great variety of races.

On our way we met a man, whom the doctor presented to Pavlova. He was, it appeared, one of the chiefs of the local administration, and spoke English very well. When he learnt that Pavlova was interested in the dancers whom we had seen in the procession, he suggested that we should go with him and after walking through several side streets we again met the procession. But this time it seemed new and unrecognizable. Darkness had set in and everything moved forward to the light of torches, and this made it appear even more strange. Our new acquaintance summoned the chief dancer and told him to come with his dancers after the procession to a certain spot, which he named. Invited by him, we went into a sort of garden, where the dancers were already waiting for us and there, to the light of torches, on some firmly beaten earth, we were given a whole performance consisting of five or six dances, which were very original and did not in any way resemble anything we had seen before.

It was explained to the dancers who Pavlova was, and they examined her curiously. When the performance was over and Pavlova was about to take her leave, the head dancer, coming up to her, kissed the hem of her dress and said a few words. They were translated to her. In the names of his fellows and himself he paid his respects to her as their great sister.

The next day we went to look at the famous Botanical Gardens, considered among the finest in the world. The most valuable and the best collections are supposed to be in the gardens of Rio de Janeiro, those of Java and in Singapore, after which come those of Ceylon. The variety and magnificence of the trees is really wonderful. This garden is remarkable for having a large mountain river flowing through it, on the banks of which grow the trees particularly in need of moisture. Not far from the Botanical Gardens we came across the elephants which had taken part in the procession of the preceding day. They were bathing. Needless to say Pavlova made friends with them.

From there we went back to Colombo. The road is so beautiful from beginning to end that to travel along it is a joy in itself, even if it did not lead to Kandy. It runs through palm groves all the way and for many miles is bordered by rows of tropical trees. Going up the slopes of the mountains, the ricefields give way to huge tea plantations. Everywhere picturesque villages are dotted about and one gets glimpses of tiny Buddhist temples.

Work is still done by elephants in Ceylon and we often came across them. It is very amusing to see this huge animal standing submissively inside a little enclosure of bamboo twigs. This pen, which any child could destroy in a minute, is amply sufficient to make the elephant understand that it must stand quietly within it.

Pavlova with the Elephant at Hagenbeck Zoo in Hamburg.

Pavlova with the Elephant at Hagenbeck Zoo in Hamburg.

The road ran alongside a little stream. Our Indian chauffeur pointed out an elephant lying in it and damming up the flow. The water ran over it, and the animal was gloriously happy. We decided to photograph it, but wanted it to get up. Our Indian shouted at it and called it, but the elephant, evidently understanding that he was being needlessly disturbed, only moved an ear and made no attempt to rise.

On our drive back to Colombo, we met a huge elephant with an Indian perched on it. It was so fine a sight that we stopped the car and asked the mahout to stop also while we photographed him and the elephant. We then drove up to the elephant and it good-naturedly put out its trunk. We happened to have some biscuits, which it sampled with relish. The mahout, who spoke English, suggested that one of us should climb up and go with him for a short distance. We three men who were with Pavlova, refused but Pavlova herself expressed a wish to do so, and walked up to the animal in order to mount. I noticed at once that it seemed to get into something like a panic and stared round anxiously. The mahout said with a smile to Pavlova that she could not mount, and when asked why, told us that a male elephant will never allow a woman to get on its back. This seemed incredible to us, but the chauffeur confirmed it. I have never had the opportunity of verifying the correctness of this, but it is an indisputable fact that the elephant we met would not allow Pavlova to mount.

In Europe, Pavlova saw some interesting dances in Sweden. When we were there before the War, we were present at a congress of dancers from the various provinces. The dances, of a purely popular character and very varied, were executed with much zest and feeling.

When Pavlova was contemplating the staging of Don Quixote, she resolved to go to Spain and see there the real and not the "classicised" national dances. Spanish dances of the classical school she danced very well. Marius Petipa, who spent some years of his youth in Spain and who, it is said, danced them extraordinarily well himself, very often inserted them in his ballets. Pavlova, however, wanted to see the real dances of the people. As we were spending the summer in Italy, we took the boat to Barcelona, and from there began a tour of the towns where we hoped to see something interesting.

We learnt in Barcelona that all the small theatres and cabarets, where dancing was to be seen, did not open until two in the morning. We therefore went to bed at ten and rose again at two in order to visit these places. We asked ourselves in surprise: when do the people of Barcelona sleep? It is apparently the only town in the world where the shops in the main street are open all night. All these little theatres and cabarets also do not seem to close before five or six in the early morning and when we left after 4 a. m., the people apparently still stayed on.

But all that we saw was extraordinarily poor. These dances were performed by Spanish men and women to Spanish music, and yet there was not a sign of the passion, fire and elegance that should be in their dances. In one of the most popular places, on an open stage, the Spanish dancers finished their turn with a Russian dance. We were very disappointed with the result of our first two days, and went to call upon a very old, but still very active lady-teacher of Spanish dancing. She is much admired in Barcelona, and at one time, some sixty years ago, was a well-known dancer and later the choreographer of the "Liceo" Theatre. The old lady flung up her hands in surprise when she heard that Pavlova had come to see her, and was highly gratified that we had approached her. When she had heard our impressions, she affirmed that the real Spanish dance was dying out. At one time it was danced in the manner of classical dance, and this was beautiful and graceful, but of late years nobody wanted to do any serious work, for it would have required years of training, whereas now-a-days the wish is to learn something quickly. If a girl is at all pretty, she gets an engagement immediately though her danceng may be very weak. In her opinion the real native dancing could still be seen in Granada, where gypsies keep up the purity of the dance — Flamengo — but as for the rest of Spain, the real Spanish dances can only be seen there by chance. She named a young dancer, one of her former pupils, as the most talented and possessing a good style. Unfortunately she had received an engagement and left shortly before our arrival. As the teacher wanted to show Pavlova her school and her method of instruction, she invited us to be present at one of her lessons, which invitation Pavlova accepted with pleasure.

The lesson took place in a large room hung round with photographs of men and women dancers of the last century. To our surprise this teacher's instruction of classical dancing was perfectly correct. She showed us three or four of her pupils doing Spanish dances. The little girls were still very inexperienced, and it was difficult to say what they might become. It was interesting to watch the mistress herself, who, in spite of her years, very energetically and very correctly showed all the necessary poses and movements.

From Barcelona we went on to Madrid having heard that a Spanish dancer was appearing in one of the local cabarets there. She proved to be the very one who had been spoken of by the Barcelona dancing mistress. We went to see her and were very pleased. She was a graceful and stylish dancer, who did the genuine Spanish dances excellently, but who, to our great surprise, had absolutely no success.

Then we went to Seville, once famous for its dancers. I was in Seville some twenty-five years previously with the late Alfred Bekeffi and at that time we saw an excellent school, which showed us eight or nine very fine performers. This time however we made the acquaintance of the only serious teacher of the place, and he repeated word for word what had been said by the old lady in Barcelona. He added that everyone was running after the fashions and preferred learning the Fox-trot and the One-step to Spanish dance. The two or three cabarets which we visited while in Seville, proved to be extraordinarily bad.

In Granada we of course went off to the gypsies, who live on the outskirts of the town in caves dug out by their ancestors in the sides of the mountains. These gypsies form a very exclusive caste and are allowed to marry only among themselves. The men engage in trade and various petty industries, and the women busy themselves with household matters and dance. When we arrived only the women were at home. When they learnt of our desire to see their dances, they asked us to wait, going off to put on their best clothes and to send for the musicians. In half an hour everything was ready.

The performance was given on the clay floor in one of the more richly decorated caves. Eight of the women performed six or seven different dances. The men, who came back later, also joined occasionally in the dancing. These Gitanas were not beautiful and their costumes were quite lacking in originality. Each one had flowers or rather long stalks stuck in her hair in a peculiar manner, so that they swayed on their heads while they were dancing. They were something like our Russian gypsies, but much coarser and more common. Judged from the point of view of expressiveness and temperament, two or three of them danced well. And that was all that we saw in Spain, the country that was once so universally famous for its fandango and bolero.

We were again in Spain in 1930, when we had a season in Barcelona. There was an international exhibition there at the time and, owing to the place being filled with foreigners, many small theatres and cabarets were opened. Spanish dances were to be seen in all of them. Pavlova's curiosity and conscientiousness made us visit these places once more. In two or three of them, we saw quite tolerably good dancers, showing considerable temperament, but there was little variety and it very quickly became boring.

Pavlova's visit to the Sphinx.

CHAPTER XX.
PEOPLE WHOM PAVLOVA MET.

In the course of her travels Pavlova made the acquaintance of many crowned heads and presidents of republics. Outside Russia the first monarch she met was the King of Sweden. He went to her first performance in that country, and was so interested that he never missed any of the others. He invited her to the palace and presented her with an Order for artistic merit.

A court carriage was sent to take her to the palace. She was shown into a room in which were glass cabinets filled with many curios. Pavlova was so lost in contemplating these that she did not notice the king entering the room. She was very much embarrassed when she became aware of his presence and noticed him watching her with a smile; but he was so simple and kindly, that in a few minutes she found herself talking with him as to an old friend.

The next crowned heads with whom Pavlova had the honour to converse were King Edward VII and Queen Alexandra. Lady Londesborough gave a dinner-party at her house, St. Dunstan's, Regents Park, in their honour and asked Pavlova to come from Paris to dance before the august guests. A stage was specially constructed. Pavlova brought Mordkin and together they did a number of dances, finishing with the Russian dance. For this she wore a costume and a kokoshnik (Russian headdress) made to the drawings of Bilibin, the artist. When the dances were over, the king expressed a wish to have her presented to him, and she was asked to step down from the stage into the room. Although the stage was not very high, her movements in descending were hampered by the heavy dress and the huge kokoshnik. Noticing this King Edward himself came forward and helped her down. Court etiquette was disregarded. The King asked her how she liked England and Pavlova replied that she found it difficult to express an opinion as she had only arrived in London three hours before the performance began. The Queen mentioned that she had heard from the Brazilian minister how well Pavlova danced the matchiche. She had indeed danced it just before in Paris with great success. The Queen expressed a desire to see it danced by her guest, but Pavlova explained that she had not the costume with her.

Owing to the Queen's insistence, however, she had to dance it in Russian costume, minus only the kokoshnik, and her hair tied up with a handkerchief.

The good-natured charm of King Edward quite conquered Pavlova's heart and it always gave her great pleasure to remember that evening. Until then, her name had been quite unknown in England, but on the following day she received four offers from various London theatres. She signed a contract with the "Palace", where she appeared consecutively for five years, having each year a four months season there. These were perhaps the happiest years of her work.

Quite a different impression was produced by the emperor Wilhelm, who never forgot that he was a monarch. In Brunswick, in 1914, the first child of the emperor's only daughter who was married to the Duke of Brunswick, was baptised. The Emperor expressed a wish to be god-father to his granddaughter. Representatives of all the courts of Germany came to Brunswick for the occasion. A gala performance was arranged for which the Duchess of Brunswick wanted to show something new and it was decided that the performance should consist of Pavlova's ballet. At that time Pavlova was contemplating a tour in Germany, so that the invitation fitted in very well with her plans.

The setting of the ballet was magnificent. The ancient Brunswick theatre, one of the best in Germany, was beautifully decorated. But at this performance Pavlova had, for the first time, to undergo a very unpleasant experience, namely, the total absence of applause. At first she was rather frightened at this, but later it was explained to her that at a gala performance in the presence of the emperor no one dared to applaud until he first set the example, and he applauded very rarely. This continued during two acts and only after "The Swan" was the emperor heard calling "bravo". The applause then broke out and gradually became a veritable ovation.

At the end of the performance, the Minister of the Court came to inform Pavlova that the Emperor wished to see her. She was taken to the foyer, where the emperor and the empress stood surrounded by the Court. Wilhelm II expressed his pleasure and told her that he had also seen the Imperial Ballet at a wonderful performance given in his honour in Peterhof. He told his suite how unusually this had been arranged, and how at this performance, given on the water, the ballet represented nymphs, and little girls were wreaths of water-lilies. And turning to Pavlova, the emperor repeated that it had given him much pleasure. Pavlova replied that she knew it, as she herself had taken part in the performance. Wilhelm was greatly astonished and asked her how that could possibly be, for the Peterhof performance took place in 1896. She replied that she was then one of the small water-lilies.

The emperor and his court produced an impression of brilliance, one was conscious of power and organization, but everything was very stiff and cold. A breath of warmth and simplicity was brought in by Wilhelm's daughter, the Duchess of Brunswick. As Pavlova was leaving, the Duchess impulsively embraced her and kissed her, thanking her for the success of the performance.

I take this opportunity to say a few words about the occasion on which Pavlova was a water-lily. I fancy there is no other court which was as lavish and as clever at arranging receptions and gala performances as was the Russian Court. When the emperor Wilhelm visited Russia in July 1896, a gala performance was arranged in his honour on the Olgin island at Peterhof, which, as is known, was built by Peter the Great and later became the favourite residence of Catherine II. The palace of Peterhof is one of the most beautiful in Europe. It is surrounded by an immense park, which has a whole system of fountains; in number, size and beauty rivalling those of Versailles. The gala performance of which I speak took place on the lake, in the middle of which lies an island, and on the island is the theatre made to look like ancient ruins overgrown with trees and bushes. The audience sits on the raised shores of the lake over the water. At a distance of 25 or 30 metres there is another small island surrounded by rocks. This island was the stage on which the performance was given. The orchestra was on a pontoon, hidden away under the shore of the island and quite invisible to the audience. This added to the illusion. The background of the lake, the wonderful lighting, the rising moon — what a beautiful performance it was, all the ballerinas and the huge corps de ballet taking part.

For the effective entry of the ballerina Kshessinskaya, a special device, much appreciated by the audience, had been invented. She had to appear from behind the island and land on the shore. In order to produce the impression that she was moving upon the water she stood on a mirror which was placed on its surface. This moved slowly forward, pulled by ropes under the water.

When Pavlova returned to St. Petersburg after her triumphs abroad, she danced at the Marinsky Theatre. At one of the performances the Emperor Nicholas was present, and during an interval she was approached by the Director of the Imperial Theatres who informed her that the Emperor desired to see her. As Pavlova was at the time already changing for the next act, this invitation created great excitement.

A few minutes later, however, she appeared before his Majesty. This was her first and last meeting with him. He was extremely amiable and presented her to the Grand Duchesses, his daughters, and told her that from all sides he had heard of Pavlova's triumphs and was very glad that she presented Russian art abroad with such honour.

Then he added:

"But don't desert the Russian stage altogether. Give me your word that you will return."

As Pavlova was taking her leave, he said regretfully:

"They all tell me how wonderfully you dance "The Dying Swan", and I have never had the opportunity to see it."

Pavlova was greatly struck by this sincere modesty. She would have liked to say: "But you have only to order it, your Majesty," but did not dare to.

During one of her performances at the London Palace Theatre, she was warned by the management that the nearest box to the stage had been reserved for some illustrious personage, who wanted to remain incognito. Later she was told that this was the King of Spain. Next morning she received a beautiful basket of orchids with the card of King Alfonso.

She was destined to see him twice, at the time of her performances at the Teatro Reale in Madrid, when she was invited into the Royal box. Both the King and Queen were very fond of the dance and very gracious to Pavlova.

Within the last few years Pavlova was twice in Denmark, and on both occasions was invited to the palace. The King was a great lover of her performances and was nearly always present. At her first interview he presented her with a Danish Order. According to the impressions she received in conversation with the King of Denmark he showed much insight into art, and his manner was so unaffected, that she felt as if she had known him for many years.

A few steps away from the royal palace at Copenhagen, on the opposite side of the square, stands the palace in which the Dowager Empress of Russia, Maria Feodorovna, lived. She also expressed a wish to see Pavlova.

Pavlova used to say that she was amazed at the freshness and vigour of the Empress, who had at that time already reached eighty. The Empress recalled memories of past times, performances at the Marinsky Theatre, the Theatrical School, etc. and made Pavlova cry.

In South America Pavlova met the presidents of most of the Republics. She met those of Peru and Chile, and on her last arrival at Buenos Aires, she made the acquaintance of the Argentine president Alvear. This highly cultured and educated man was present at most of Pavlova's performances. He invited her to his house and showed her every attention. When lunching with him, I was always surprised at his remarkable knowledge of all that was connected with the theatrical business, how correct and to the point were his remarks and how quickly he grasped details that were often not understood by professional critics.

In Venezuela, Pavlova made the acquaintance of president General Gomez. He was (I believe he is still President) I think the only South American president to retain so much authority and power. He lived on his large estate, and had there a camp of some twenty thousand men, who kept guard over him.

We had heard a great deal of his despotic character and his drastic decrees and on one occasion we had convincing proof of this. The general grew to like our performances and was very often present, instructing his A. D. C. to find out what the next programme would be.

For a certain Sunday "Coppelia" had been arranged and the president was duly informed. He promised to be present. At the end of the orchestra rehearsal on the Saturday, our conductor came to me to say that one orchestra rehearsal would not be enough and he had fixed another for Sunday morning, but found the musicians refused to come, as on Sundays they played in church.

It should be noted that the orchestra playing for us was the only one in the whole town and consisted of local talent, and it certainly was very poor. For the first time in our experience there was no cello in the orchestra, its place being taken by a wind instrument called a bombardino. The manager of the orchestra was an Italian. I asked him what the matter was and he confirmed the statement that the musicians played in churches on Sundays and that it was quite impossible to force them to come to a rehearsal. We consequently decided to postpone giving "Coppelia" and dance one of the ballets already given.

I sent instructions to the printer to make the necessary alterations on the programme. On my way home I met the A. D. C. of the president and told him the reason why "Coppelia" could not be given that evening. He said nothing, but an hour later the frightened manager came running up to say that there would be a rehearsal on the following morning after all, and that the printer must be advised accordingly, so as to avoid a possible misunderstanding. When I asked him how everything had been arranged with the musicians after all, he replied:

"Arranged? Orders, that's all."

"But suppose the musicians disobeyed and did not appear at the rehearsal?"

He looked at me in surprise.

"But who would dare not to come? That would mean six months imprisonment, and possibly not simple imprisonment, but in chains."

The custom of having benefit nights for the artists has survived in South America, and when Pavlova had a benefit in Caracas, the president of the republic presented her with a large velvet box and on opening it, we discovered her name and surname formed in 20-dollar gold pieces. There were exactly one hundred coins, and though it was not remarkable as a work of art, it certainly proved very valuable, for as things were not going any too well, the present had there and then to be used as money.

Being on the point of leaving Havanna for Mexico, the Americans whose acquaintance we had made told Pavlova of all sorts of horrors that were taking place in Mexico, where revolts were constantly springing up against Carranza, the new president. Our friends even expressed surprise that Pavlova was bold enough to take a whole company of young girls there. This upset Pavlova and she began to waver. I suggested sending a telegram to the president asking him to let us know whether Pavlova could consider herself perfectly safe in Mexico and whether he would take her and her company under his protection. A day later we received a reply from Carranza saying that he guaranteed complete safety and had already given the necessary instructions to the authorities at Vera Cruz.

On our arrival there we saw that instructions had indeed been given, for all the custom-house and passport formalities were over in an instant. And when we took our seats in the train we saw a number of bare-legged ragamuffins with rifles seated on the roofs of our carriages. On asking who they were, we were told that they were two hundred men sent to guard us against bandits. And when I asked what, then, the bandits looked like, I was told that there was not much difference. However, we arrived in absolute safety.

As I have said, elsewhere Mexico produced upon Pavlova and upon us all an enchanting impression. Her performances were an enormous success. She was told that the president desired to make her acquaintance. We went at the appointed hour and, a few minutes later, were ushered into his presence. But we were very surprised and disappointed when we saw Carranza himself. We had imagined that the president of the Mexican Republic would be a dusky Mexican, with a cruel, tyrannical face, dressed in an exotic uniform covered with gold lace, but instead, we saw what looked like a German professor, bald, with a long silvery beard and wearing spectacles.

The president proved to be a very good-natured man; he told Pavlova how much he enjoyed her performances and how he regretted not being able to be present more often. Then he asked her how she liked Mexico, to which she replied enthusiastically.

"And what pleases you most?" he asked.

"That you have forbidden bull-fights," she replied without hesitation.

In further conversation Pavlova expressed her regret that the unrest in the country would not allow us to visit other towns, of which we had heard so much. She added that she would not have minded the risk herself, but in view of the American consul's refusal to give some Americans in our company permission to travel, the trip had to be abandoned.

"Wait a couple of years", said the president, "and you will see that Mexico will have become the most peaceful of countries. Then you, Europeans, will come here for a holiday and rest."

Alas, within two years of that interview, president Carranza had been killed and bull-fights had again been permitted by the new president.

Meeting with crowned heads always gave Pavlova great pleasure, especially in her younger days, and she was happy if any one of them was present at the performance, as it brought back to her the atmosphere of her native Marinsky Theatre and the agitation she lived through as a little girl when, making her earliest debuts, she saw the Emperor and his family in the end box nearest the stage.

In the course of her artistic career, Pavlova made the acquaintance of many prominent people in the most diverse professions and positions. It was only natural that she was most impressed by those who had reached the highest positions thanks to their own brains, energy and talents, or those who held up service to humanity as their ideal.

Some seven or eight years ago, at the time of our stay in New York, friends offered to introduce Pavlova to Thomas Edison. We arrived in West Orange, the small town in which the great inventor lived, and visited him, first in his home and then went to the building where his laboratory and his workroom were situated.

There we made the acquaintance of his three permanent assistants, who told Pavlova how Edison worked, how every hour of his life was carefully mapped out, and how when one of his experiments in connection with his inventions drew towards the end, he moved entirely into his workroom, eating and sleeping there. We were shown the modest sofa on which he slept for a few hours a day during the sixteen days in which he was finishing one of his last big inventions. Pavlova expressed to Edison her amazed admiration at his energy and tenacity in attaining his goal, the strength of will required thus to give up ordinary comforts at his age. Laughing gently, Edison said:

"And don't you do the same thing for your goal?"

Fritjof Nansen produced a great impression on Pavlova. He came behind the scenes at one of the performances in Oslo, made her acquaintance and asked us to his house, which was surrounded by a garden and was situated on the shores of a fjord. As he was not very well at the time, he apologised for not being able personally to do the honours of the garden. Pavlova was greatly interested in the conversation which she had with him, touching on his travels, Russia and the work he did there.

Another great man Pavlova was anxious to meet was Rabindranath Tagore, whose personality and altruistic work had long and seriously interested her. When she was in Calcutta she wrote to him asking if there was anything in his poems suitable for the subject of a ballet, as it was her intention to stage one of Hindoo life.

Tagore very kindly sent her one of his poems, which he thought would be appropriate and asked her to come and talk it over with him personally. Unfortunately he lived and had his school at a place some hundred miles from Calcutta, and Pavlova was not able to go there.

Among great artists on the stage, Pavlova had the highest admiration for La Duse. Her sincerity, simplicity, profundity and the power of her acting always produced a deep impression on Pavlova. I take this opportunity of quoting what Eleonora Duse said about Pavlova.

In reply to the words of a man who saw her (Duse) after a performance and said that her voice had carried him into a fairy world, she answered, "Ah, perhaps because I had seen that fairy — that most exquisite artist, Pavlova, yesterday and think of nothing else."

Of all the great musicians Pavlova was most impressed by Nikisch. She was keenly sensitive to the force of his personality, which he succeeded in transmitting to his orchestra. She met him several times, both in Russia and abroad. They had the kindest feelings towards each other and were always glad of an opportunity to meet. I remember that once at a performance of "La Fille Mal Gardée" Nikisch came into Pavlova's dressing-room and said that he had been doubly affected that evening.

"First" he said, "by your dancing and acting, and second by memories."

"What memories?" asked Pavlova in surprise.

And Nikisch replied:

"Many times have I played this ballet when I was still a second violin in the orchestra in Vienna." Then he sighed and added:

"I was young then."

Pavlova in her Garden.

CHAPTER XXI.

FLOWERS.

Pavlova had a very special love for flowers. One could not find a pleasure more subtle than watching her making a tour of the garden. The extraordinary grace that distinguished her in dancing was never absent in ordinary life. Each movement of hers was full of beauty, charming because in her it was wedded to simplicity. She had an inimitable way entirely her own of kissing her favourite flowers, just lightly touching the others with her hand.

What were her favourite flowers?

Without a doubt the wild flowers of the field, perhaps through association with the days of her childhood. But owing to our constant wanderings, to our life in large cities, she rarely saw a genuine meadow, but when she did, she was as happy as a child.

In 1928, after a rest in Italy, we decided to go across the Garda Lake to the Dolomites of the Tyrol. Near the tiny lake called Carresi, at the height of 2000 metres, there is a magnificent hotel surrounded by dolomite mountains of extraordinary beauty and wonderful colour effects. Pavlova admired everything enthusiastically, but the greatest joy for her was still to come. We went for a walk in the mountains and found ourselves among meadows covered with wild flowers. I have read somewhere about the famous American naturalist Mure, who did so much for the study of American flora, and after whom one of the national parks is called. He was sent out by the American Government to Alaska, and on arrival began carrying out his investigations. The assistants who accompanied him on this journey wrote in their notes that, when high up in the mountains he discovered flowers of his own native fields, he went on his knees and kissed the ground. I was reminded of this when I watched Pavlova's happiness. She flitted from spot to spot, recognising and calling by name her native flowers, which she had not seen since the days of Ligovo. Here was a particular kind of bell and there a small pink flower — daisies and forest violets and many others. She knew the names of all.

While walking in the forest, we came across a little white flower growing in the moss and having a delicious scent. Pavlova took such a fancy to it that she insisted on taking it to England. Consequently we got some large biscuit tins, filled them with moss and earth, and in these put some of the flowers dug up by the roots. In this manner we took them across the whole of Europe, arousing the curiosity of all the custom-house men. When we arrived home, Pavlova planted them, selecting what she thought the most suitable corner in the garden at Ivy House. They lived through the winter and then unfortunately died.

She also preferred the simplest among garden flowers. She admired lilies and roses, their beauty and the perfection of their form, but they did not touch her heart. She did, however, make an exception in favour of orchids. Their exoticism and "orientalism" attracted her. She liked carnations less than any other flower.

When we were in Costa Rica, wishing to show some attention to the wife of the president of the republic, who had come to the station to meet her, Pavlova decided to pay her a call and take some flowers. In the windows of the finest flower shop, she was delighted to see some beautiful orchids. She went in, picked out a large bouquet and asked for it to be tied up. Seeing that we were foreigners, the owner of the shop asked Pavlova for whom the flowers were intended, and was horror-struck when he learned that they were for the president's wife, for, as he explained, orchids were the most common of flowers in Costa Rica. Something better would have to be chosen and he suggested a bouquet of carnations as being the choicest and most suitable. Private taste had to yield to Costa-Rican etiquette.

On her last journey to Australia, Pavlova took a great fancy to some beautiful little flowers with an exquisite scent, called "Boronia". We decided to take a few pots back with us and went to a nursery garden to pick out some plants. There we saw some other plants that Pavlova also fancied. Among these was an enormous bush of marvellously coloured purple bells. Pavlova expressed a wish to buy it and had it transplanted into a huge tub. The gardener said that he doubted whether so large a plant would stand the long journey, but consented to let us have it, provided we took the risk. Then we chose a few other plants as well. On leaving Adelaide, I went on board the steamer to see where we could lay out our garden. The steamer officials very kindly gave us the free run of the boat on condition that the other passengers were not inconvenienced. Looking about I came upon an extremely suitable spot in the bows of the vessel: it was not used by the passengers and, at the same time, was well protected from the wind. The place belonged to the male nurse of the steamer hospital ward.

I asked him for permission, rather expecting a refusal, but he very kindly granted it. He proved to be a great lover of gardening and very willingly undertook the trouble of looking after the plants, and for five weeks guarded and tended them. Later, he told me very indignantly, that the people who occasionally came there picked off the last purple bells "as a souvenir of Pavlova". When the trees were first put into our greenhouse, they began to wither, for we had taken them during the Adelaide spring and brought them over to an English autumn. We were afraid that they would die, but they recovered and to Pavlova's great joy the big bush flowered once more, as if in its own native land.

Pavlova had a special way of her own of bowing to the audience, doing it so gracefully and with such dignity, that she deserved to be applauded for this alone. She received presentations of flowers with the same elegance. At times the stage was completely filled with immense floral baskets and a dozen or so bouquets lying on the floor, but Pavlova manoeuvred very cleverly among them, never disturbing anything, leading her dancers to the footlights, pulling out a few flowers from some bouquet and presenting them to her partner or to one of the other members of the company. One well-known opera singer said to me once that while watching Pavlova, she tried to imagine herself in her place.

"Believe me," she said, "I am sure I should have knocked over those baskets and then probably fallen myself."

Though Pavlova herself received nothing but pleasure from flowers, this feeling was not always shared by those around her. They gave a great deal of work to those at home when Pavlova brought back from the theatre an unusually large tribute of flowers, for whatever the hour, Pavlova had them immediately put into vases. Unfortunately most bouquets are wired, and this she considered barbarous, insisting upon the flowers being immediately relieved of their "manacles", and this was by no means a pleasant task. But as she would not go to bed until all the flowers had been liberated, we all helped most diligently. Her maid, who had been with her for many years on all her journeys, was the chief sufferer in this work and often said:

"If only those who sent these flowers knew what I wished them!"

The most beautiful basket of flowers that I have ever seen was one Pavlova received on her first visit to Amsterdam. It was so huge that it was brought into the stage with difficulty. It consisted entirely of hortensias. the colours wonderfully well chosen: tender pink at the top, gradually merging into darker pink below, then mauve, and finally a rich blue at the bottom.

Pavlova was greatly distressed at the thought, that, because of the size of the basket, the flowers could not be carried into the hotel, especially since on the following morning we had to journey to another town.

At that time we had our own luggage car and I told the chauffeurs to put the basket into it and try to take them carefully to the theatre of the next town. When we arrived there I was happy to see that the flowers were in excellent condition, and Pavlova had the pleasure of receiving them for the second time on the stage. The same thing was repeated the next day, and owing to the fact that the flowers were in pots, Pavlova received this basket on seven consecutive evenings and it invariably produced the same effect. Those who gave it to her probably never even imagined that it would travel all round Holland with us and give Pavlova so much pleasure.

I do not know if the fashion for a certain rose called "American Beauty" still exists in America.

The flower itself is an ordinary dark red rose, but it has an extraordinarily long stalk, and the longer the stalk the more expensive the rose. A bouquet of such roses is very often five feet in height and each flower costs three dollars. When she received huge bouquets of these roses Pavlova used to exclaim in vexation: "How much more pleasure it would give me if instead of these flowers which are so artificial, the money they represent were given to my charities."

When these floral offerings were too numerous — on first or last nights — Pavlova would send all the bouquets to one of the hospitals.

The flowers in her own garden at Ivy House were often a source of disappointment to her. There were many reason for this. She only lived there for short spells and intermittently and could therefore hardly ever supervise the planting herself. Another reason was the shadiness of our garden, so that the flowers did not get enough sunshine — at no time very abundant in England. Whenever she found that she had not enough flowers, Pavlova remedied the defect very simply and decisively by going early in the morning to Covent Garden, coming back laden and enthusiastically seeing herself to their planting and distribution.

For a length of some 200 yards the garden at Ivy House runs alongside Golders Green Park — one of the London municipal parks. By the will of the former owner, who bequeathed it to the municipality, a small, walled garden called the "Shakespeare Garden" has been arranged in this park. As its name indicates it is dedicated to the memory of the great dramatist who was such a lover of nature. His works are full of references to various trees, plants and flowers, and the owner of the garden had the beautiful idea of collecting in it all the flora mentioned in the works of Shakespeare. This was Pavlova's favourite spot.

She was also fond of aquatic plants of every description. Several times she tried planting water-lilies in our small lake, but the swans pulled them up by the roots and it had to be done again every year.

About two years ago she had a small basin and fountain made in the garden and in this she planted lotuses which took root excellently. Near this spot we pitched a tent in the summer and put the garden furniture into it, so that we could drink tea there in fine weather. A hammock used to hang here and Pavlova, resting in it, could watch her favourite birds taking a bath in the fountain.

When we made our last Australian tour, we arrived there from Java approaching the country from the northern side. This part of Australia is in the tropics and is remarkable for the profusion of its vegetation. In the country around Townsville, the first town in which we arrived, our chauffeur stopped the car on the summit of a little hillock and pointed to distant fields of a sky-blue colour. This was very beautiful and at the same time quite incomprehensible. When we drove up nearer, we saw that what we had taken to be fields, were huge bogs covered with light blue lotuses. I recollect that in our journeys in Japan, we saw a number of small ponds covered with these flowers, but they were white lotuses, not the pale blue variety. Pavlova poetically imagined that the Japanese were so fond of these flowers that they cultivated them near their villages. Apparently, however, they grow them for another, more prosaic reason, the roots of lotuses being used for food.

Our trip to Sochemilco, a place about 30 kilometres from Mexico City, left us with one of the most picturesque of our Mexican impressions. A small river flows there, dividing into hundreds of branches which enclose a number of little islands, and on these the local peasants grow flowers. A national characteristic of the Mexicans — their love of vivid colours — also comes out in the flowers they make their favourites. Nowhere else can such colours and varieties in poppies be found — scarlet, pink, yellow. Whole islands are covered with them. The only means of locomotion in Sochemilco is by flat-bottomed boats, which are to be seen continually gliding in among these flowery islands. An added beauty to this picture is given by the local genus of poplar growing on the banks. At every turn one meets a boat laden with flowers and steered by a woman in national costume. The hours one spends in Sochemilco remain in one's memory for all time. The impression is fairy-like, and the scene is made even more picturesque by the enormous, snow-capped volcano in the background.

Pavlova's first visit to Holland coincided with spring and, therefore, with the blooming of the tulips. She was to dance in Haarlem, a town which for many centuries has been the centre for the cultivation of this flower. A special love for the tulip is a national trait of the Dutch, but it is only in the last few years that the fashion for tulips has spread all over the world and the export of bulbs from Holland now constitutes an item of importance in the national exchequer. This encourages the Dutch horticulturists to be constantly producing new varieties. As the result of long and costly experiments in cross-breeding some very wonderful and hitherto unknown types have been evolved. Pavlova was happy when asked to make a motor car tour to see the fields of flowering tulips. The impression was that of a huge brightly-coloured carpet spread for many miles around Haarlem.

During a performance of Pavlova's the representatives of the Haarlem Society of Horticulturists asked permission to make a presentation to her on the stage of a bouquet of white tulips. In one of the intervals, therefore, while Pavlova was bowing to the public, they handed her a huge bouquet of snow-white tulips tied together with white gauze and the president of the society said that only after years of experimenting and much crossbreeding had the Haarlem horticulturists succeeded in evolving this particular white tulip of great beauty and size, which connoisseurs considered the most rare of all the varieties produced in the last hundred years. It is indeed a specimen so costly that it can only ornament the gardens of American millionaires, for no ordinary person can afford the luxury of paying 500 florins for a single bulb. The Dutch flower-growers wished to give this queenly flower a queenly name and so called it after the queen of the dance — Anna Pavlova. If ever it should happen that the memory of Pavlova's famous dance, "The Dying Swan", fades with time, this most gorgeous and lovely of all tulips will recall by its name the greatest of dancers.

CHAPTER XXII.

PETS.

From her childhood Pavlova loved all animals. Her mother told me how once they had a lot of mice in the house and, as is usually done in such cases, a number of mouse-traps were set. It appeared, however, that the mice were too well-fed to be caught. A few days later the cause was discovered — little Niura was found secretly feeding them.

When she had finished at the school she was given a magnificent, huge Leonberg, for which it was difficult to find room in the tiny flat. Its stay there gave rise to some unfortunate incidents. On one occasion when Pavlova was playing with it in her bedroom, the dog swept everything off the dressing-table with its enormous tail. The mirror, the bottles, everything was smashed to atoms. On another occasion Pavlova asked some friends to supper after the theatre, but when they were about to sit down to table, they discovered that the Leonberg had supped first. A more serious incident occurred when Pavlova wanted to wash it. It did its utmost to escape being bathed and finally when she took it by the scruff of the neck in order to push it into the water, the dog fastened its teeth in her leg and would not let go. She was saved by her presence of mind, for, in spite of the excrutiating pain, she did not attempt to tear her leg away or beat the dog, but spoke caressingly to it until eventually it loosened its hold. She carried the marks of the teeth on her instep for a long time.

Later she was given a splendid Eskimo dog, brought from Nova Zemla by the polar explorer, Sedov. The dog was a very beautiful specimen, but wild and quite unsuited for life in a house. Most of all it liked to be taken out driving with its mistress and on one occasion, when the winter had set in and the Neva was frozen over and covered by a thick layer of ice, the dog jumped out of the sledge at the sight of its native element, tore madly about on the field of snow and eventually disappeared forever.

Pavlova's next dog was a beautiful white English bulldog called "Bull". I have never seen a kinder, cleverer or more original animal. He was known to everybody and was very popular in St. Petersburg. She kept him for many years, until at last he grew too old.

Pavlova with her Siamese Cat.
(Photograph by Lafayette, London.)

Fond as we were of dogs and great as was our disinclination to part from them, to have them with us on our tours in various countries gave a great deal of trouble. Sometimes, though not very often, an hotel would not allow any dogs at all, but occasionally the magic name of Pavlova came to our rescue and the management would agree to make an exception, provided the dog did not accompany us in the lift but used the back staircase. At times, however, the management would be inexorable, and then one of the members of the company, living in a less pretentious hotel, would be asked to take charge of the animal. There were many dog lovers in the company, who would undertake the care of it with pleasure.

In Los Angeles, California, in the house of some friends, Pavlova saw a beautiful Boston terrier and liked it so much, that she went to the kennels it came from and bought herself a puppy, to which she gave the name of "Poppy". This dog accompanied us on our travels during the five years of the war, both in North America and two long tours in South America.

On the way from Argentina to Venezuela we had to spend a day on the island of Trinidad, so as to take the French boat going from French

Pavlova with her Boston Terrier.
(Photograph by d'Ora, Paris.)

Guiana to Martinique and calling at Trinidad. When disembarking and landing from the launch to the quay with our Boston terrier, the Customhouse authorities immediately stopped Pavlova and told her that, Trinidad being British territory, dogs were not allowed. As the French steamer had not yet arrived and the English one taking us to Trinidad had already sailed, the position was tragic, but we were saved by the owner of the launch, undertaking to keep our "Poppy" on his boat. The dog lived on the launch for two days, then the French ship arrived and it was transshipped.

"Poppy" became so accustomed to a life of constant change, that he bore everything with equanimity and with an apparent recognition of the inevitability thereof. There is only a narrow-gauge railway with small carriages across the Andes, in which dogs are not allowed and in the luggage van the cold is so intense at that altitude, that any living creature runs the risk of being frozen to death. A hamper had consequently to be purchased and "Poppy" was hidden in it, and so was carried from place to place in order that there should be no difficulties with the porters. The crossing of the mountains lasted fourteen hours and during all that time "Poppy" showed absolutely no sign of life. On crawling out of the basket after a journey of this kind, the dog had to stretch his limbs for quite a long time in order to regain their use. We were so tenderly attached to this dog that we did not wish to part with him on coming back to Europe after the War. We therefore brought him to England with us. The six months' quarantine only expired three days before we started on a fresh tour, so that poor "Poppy" had only these three days in which to admire England. When we came back from the tour, we decided not to repeat the experiment and each time after that we left "Poppy" with friends in Paris.

Pavlova's last dog was a French bulldog called "Duke", whom I bought in London. He was a very handsome and very comical animal with his pink muzzle and his one white ear and one black one. Pavlova grew very fond of "Duke", who was a very loyal and intelligent, but obstinate animal. He had one great misfortune and that was his snore. So dreadful was this, that there was no possibility of sleeping in the same room. Soon after I had given "Duke" to Pavlova, she went on an English tour and took the dog with her. In towns that had large hotels, where two adjoining rooms or at any rate a room with a bathroom were obtainable, "Duke" could be accommodated. But in most of the smaller towns it was only possible to get single rooms, and this made the situation very difficult, for "Duke" prevented Pavlova from going to sleep. She used to say that next morning her neighbours would look at her askance, wondering how she could snore so. The situation was saved by one of our male dancers who slept so soundly that nothing could awaken him. He only begged of "Duke" not to start snoring until he was himself well asleep.

When we had to go to South Africa, Pavlova was very anxious to take "Duke" with her and we took the necessary steps to get a permit. The officials would have been pleased to do Pavlova a kindness, but had to explain that the dog would be allowed into South Africa only if it were itself an "artist" and took part in the performances. It was suggested that Pavlova should sign the necessary guarantee, on the strength of which the dog would be allowed in and later, when the animal was in South Africa, nobody was likely to be very interested in whether "Duke" took part in ballets or not. However Pavlova, who hated all ways of getting round the law, was obliged unfortunately to refuse the proferred plan.

With the exception of England and her colonies, dogs were allowed into all countries without any difficulties, and it was, consequently an unpleasant surprise for us when, arriving one morning in Copenhagen from Berlin, we learnt that dogs were not permitted to enter Denmark. After many negotiations and conversations with the Ministry by telephone, we received permission to place "Duke" in a private veterinary hospital outside the town.

On leaving Copenhagen we wanted to take the dog with us to Sweden, but apparently there were some restrictions in that country as well and we were obliged to leave "Duke" in hospital in Copenhagen. Arriving in Hamburg from Norway, we asked some friends of ours in Copenhagen to send "Duke" on by aeroplane. The Copenhagen papers made much of this incident, and caricatures appeared showing "Duke" leaving by aeroplane and being seen off with great pomp by the local authorities.

"Duke" is still alive and well, being in the custody of some friends in Paris.

From our American friends we had often heard of the wonderful beauty of American parks, especially of the National Park called "Yellowstone", after the river that flows from it. The "park" is about 9000 sq. miles in area and contains a marvellous variety of natural beauties — waterfalls, mountain forests, canyons and geysers. The American Government, having declared this place a reserve, has constructed enormous hotels in four of the most interesting spots which, from the point of view of the sightseer, embody every comfort. Moreover the Government gives permission to anybody wishing to visit the park to camp where he pleases and to live there for any length of time. People are permitted to use the fallen trees and branches, of which there are large quantities, to pick flowers and berries and to catch fish with which the waters abound. But they are not allowed to fell trees or bushes, to trap animals or birds, to carry firearms or to make any changes in the landscape.

For fifty years now the animals in the park have been unmolested and allowed to live their own lives freely, with the result that they have lost all fear of man and, curiously enough, of one another. The forests and mountains contain a large number of bears — black, brown and grizzly — elks, deer of every kind and numerous wild birds.

Knowing Pavlova's love of animals we went in the summer of 1917 to spend a fortnight in "Yellowstone Park", and from the moment we entered it we found ourselves in a fairy kingdom. As a conveyance we hired a sort of jaunting-car harnessed to two horses.

They were very beautiful, these unhurried drives through boundless virgin forests, never touched by axe, along the banks of rushing mountain rivers (the Park is situated at an altitude of 7000 feet and some parts are even 11,000 feet in height) over hills and through valleys, covered with wild flowers — whole stretches of the one species — it seemed like miles of blue or red or white flowers. What we took at first to be a snow-capped mountain turned out, at closer range, to be fields of white flowers, and on another occasion we thought we were approaching a beautiful blue lake, only to discover a valley covered with a sea of blue flowers. Pavlova, who had never seen such quantities of wild flowers, and she loved all wild flowers, was enraptured and happy, and picked large bunches of them. Her delight was further enhanced by the number of small animals which we met on the road, squirrels, badgers, martens, all afraid of nothing, and paying no attention to us.

At a turning in the road we saw a magnificent deer with huge antlers calmly watching our approach. We passed probably not more than ten paces away, but it did not exhibit the least sign of fear.

But the greatest thrill of all was still to come. About half a mile or so from the hotel there was a small clearing and daily at about eight o'clock a cart would come along containing the food remains that had accumulated in the huge hotel kitchen during the day. The bears knew this and often followed the cart to the clearing. On one occasion we saw a bear on its hind legs walking with the cart and holding on by one of its huge paws. Often some fifteen to twenty bears would collect to partake of the feast, but they seemed to obey some order of precedence, for when two grey bears — grizzlys — appeared, the others made way for them, evidently knowing that the grizzly temper is uncertain and best not aroused.

When Pavlova took to bringing the bears pieces of sugar and chocolate, they became not only friendly, but quite bold. I felt very uneasy when one of them, dissatisfied with some sweetmeat, rose on its hind legs, towering

Pavlova with her Cadilan.

over Pavlova and held her with its paw by one shoulder to prevent her going away. Had the huge paw scratched the shoulder under the thin muslin frock, what might the reaction of the animal be at the sight of blood, I asked myself. But Pavlova never felt any fear of animals and treated these bears much as she would dogs.

It is a matter of common knowledge how dangerous a she-bear is when she has her cubs with her. I was not at all delighted, therefore, when a she-bear came up to us with her cub one day, and left the baby with us while she went off to dig among the food. At first the cub was perfectly happy in our company, but presently, like a child, it began to cry. On hearing the cry, the mother rushed to the defence like a whirlwind, but seeing no one was harming her child, she merely took it away with her.

I took a number of photographs of these bears, but unfortunately they turned out badly, as this bear-feast did not take place until sundown.

Truly the animal kingdom of this place reminded one of the Garden of Eden before the Fall. One would see a fawn lying quietly with her young one on the grass. A bear passes a few paces off, and neither animal takes the slightest notice of the other.

I remember, in the days of my childhood, in Russia, how annoyed our coachman was when we came across performing bears in any village we were passing through, as our horses would shy and rear and show signs of panic—but in Yellowstone Park horses and bears pass each other daily without paying attention.

Our stay in Yellowstone Park made an unforgettable impression on Pavlova, who always retained the happiest of memories of the days we spent there.

One of the reasons why Pavlova chose "Ivy House" was because of its large garden adjoining the park of Golders Hill along the whole of its length, thereby giving the impression of being separated from other houses by an enormous expanse of green. We were also attracted by the singing of the birds when we first walked into this garden. The house had not been inhabited for some years and the garden had been completely neglected. The birds had made a sanctuary of it. We cleared the garden and even replanned it once or twice, but the birds did not desert it. Hearing their chirruping in the mornings one could imagine oneself far out in the country. There were a profusion of berry bushes in the garden, and in consequence Ivy House was a favourite haunt of blackbirds, starlings and a variety of small birds. They felt free from the intrusion of cats here and multiplied largely.

Soon after we moved to Ivy House Pavlova was given two swans. Jack, the male, was a splendid big bird, but rather bad tempered and unapproachable in spite of all Pavlova's attempts to tame it.

I warned her of the danger she might be running, knowing how powerful the blow of a swan's wing can be. A friend of mine had a very valuable sporting dog, whose leg was broken by a blow from the wing of a swan. My fears proved well-founded. A short while later, a workman doing some repairs in the house went into the garden and carelessly approached the pond. Jack flew at him, hit him in the back, knocked him over and continued striking him until some others ran up. Fortunately there were no serious results, beyond a few bruises. One day, taking advantage of the fact that his wings had not been clipped, Jack decided to try flying. He did not however correctly gauge his strength and, not rising sufficiently high, hit a neighbouring chimney-pot with his chest and brought it down. But in spite of the force of the blow Jack had enough strength left to fly away. The chimney pot cost us five pounds, while Jack, having flown some twenty miles, alighted on a strange pond. The owner of the pond having read in the papers about the disappearance of Pavlova's swan, communicated with us and our gardener brought the fugitive back. After that his wings were clipped and little by little he grew accustomed to his abode and gradually became less wild; so much so, that eventually he would take bread out of Pavlova's hand.

Feeling that the swans were cramped for room on the little lake and hoping that our swan family might increase, Pavlova had the lake considerably enlarged, and to her delight, one day while she was away, she received a letter from our gardener to say that the swans had built a nest and were sitting. This old gardener had been in Pavlova's employ for many years and was a great drunkard. She had long had it in mind to dismiss him. Once however, he sent her a Christmas card with the words "Nature first, art second" written on it, and whether this meant that he considered his vocation superior to hers or not, I do not know, but this slight incident softened her heart towards the old man and induced her to bear with his failing.

When we returned home we found the swans still sitting and a few days later Pavlova came running up excitedly to tell me that the swans had come down on the lake with a cygnet. Unfortunately the cygnet died a couple of days later.

When we came back after the War, following an absence of five years, Pavlova found that the swans no longer knew her and did not come to her call. Talking with various press representatives of her impressions on her return to England, she mentioned among other things how grieved she was at being forgotten by her swans. A few days later Pavlova received a letter from a complete stranger saying that he was a great lover of swans and wished to give her some valuable hints. He had studied swans and fancied he could tame ours once more. We asked him to call, and made his acquaintance. He proved to be a very nice and interesting man, and we were soon convinced that he was really fond of swans, knew how to treat them and very quickly gained their confidence. We named him the "Swan Professor".

His love for swans was quite extraordinary. He came to Ivy House each day whatever the weather, brought fresh grass for the swans and remained with them two or three hours. He told us that every day he used to visit several of the neighbouring parks, where there were swans, in order to study the habits of the birds. The results of our acquaintance with the professor soon showed themselves. Jack became quite tame and his family increased rapidly from two to eight. But this was rather too much. I said to Pavlova, that when later they were all grown up, we should have more swans than water. The little ones grew up, however, and the "professor" undertook their education. He trained them so well that they would come to meet him when he arrived.

After that we went abroad and did not see the professor again when we came back. The result of his training, however, was so remarkable where Jack was concerned, that Pavlova could be photographed with him in various poses. She would take him on her knees and twine his neck round hers and Jack would bear it all without the slightest protest. Knowing how wild swans are as a rule, I consider this a wonderful achievement. Dissensions, however, soon began in our swan family. Jack took a dislike to one of the young ones, who, choosing a mate, flew over into a neighbouring park and founded a new dynasty of our swans. Another pair we gave away to friends. Shortly afterwards, while we were away, Jack, the patriarch of the family, died. On our return we found three swans, but soon after Jack's wife also died and the nest again contained only two. Young Jack soon became quite tame and his gentleness was a source of great joy to Pavlova.

One day in the street, in Italy, we came across an illustrated paper, containing an extraordinary picture in colours — it depicted a London crossroads, a great block of motor buses and cars, a huge crowd of people and in the middle a policeman struggling with an enormous swan. We became interested and discovered from the caption that this was our Jack, who had escaped from Ivy House, but had got no further than the cross-roads by Golders Green station, where there is always a good deal of traffic. And he actually did cause all the traffic to stop. The policeman who bravely tackled Jack could do nothing until another one came to his assitance. Between them

Pavlova with Poppy.

they put the swan in a taxi and took him to the police station. Later he was restored to Ivy House.

After the death of Pavlova, our female swan also died and Jack was left all alone on the lake. He received offers from three different people who wished to adopt him and give him a new home. An Englishman wrote saying that he had a large lake on his estate and would gladly put it at Jack's disposal. Another man, also an Englishman, asked me to let him have Jack in order to install him on a lovely small lake on his estate near Biarritz. He even showed me a photograph of the lake. Lastly, the third offer came from a great friend of Pavlova's, a lady in Holland, who had a beautiful house in an ancient park. A canal running through park formed several lakes. I am of course convinced that in memory of Pavlova our Jack would be made comfortable wherever he went, but until Ivy House is sold, the swan will remain on his own lake and afterwards, I have decided that it will be better for him to remain in England, where he was born.*

On moving into Ivy House, Pavlova lost no time in starting to keep pigeons. They thrived so well and multiplied with such rapidity that we had to give many away. Nevertheless, when we came back to Ivy House last year and counted them, we found that there were more than sixty. This year there are already eighty-five.

At first Pavlova used to choose well-bred specimens, but later, during the years of the War, they became mixed, and though some have still kept their distinctive colouring, on the whole they have reverted to the common type. When we stayed at Ivy House for any length of time, the pigeons grew to know Pavlova quite well and gave her a great deal of pleasure by flying to her, perching on her and taking food out of her hand.

When speaking of birds, I cannot help mentioning Pavlova's wonderful sensitiveness when dealing with them. She had observed them so closely, understood them so well, that every anxiety, their chirrups and other — sometimes barely noticeable — signs, told her what had to be done, and when they received what she considered was required, they would calm down and become perfectly happy again.

Many people knew of Pavlova's love for birds, with the result that numbers of birds were brought or sent to her. When we arrived in Hamburg, the brothers Hagenbeck, the owners of the famous zoological garden, decided to make her a surprise present. When the performance was over, two men carried onto the stage on a bamboo stick an Ara of enormous size. We had never seen anything resembling it either for the richness of colouring or for size. After the performance the Ara was delivered to our hotel and then rose the question as to where to keep it. There was a large chandelier in the drawing-room and to this we attached a ring, and there the parrot took its seat. But it was so huge that its tail touched the floor.

Early in the morning the parrot woke us by its cries and I had to move it into the bathroom. In the end we had to ask the Hagenbecks to take the bird back. At the same time Pavlova suggested that it would give her great pleasure if they were to send instead a flamingo to Ivy House. When we returned to London, she was delighted to find there a couple of beautiful pink flamingoes, perfectly familiarized with our small lake and the swans upon it. We had them for three years.

---

* Ivy House having been recently sold, Jack is in his new English home.

Quite extraordinary was the impression which the parrot made on Pavlova's French bulldog. When it first saw the Ara it stood in front of it as if carved in stone, its eyes bulging out, like one under a spell.

When Duke recovered himself a little, slowly and fearfully he drew near the tail of the bird, but the Ara gave such a wild shriek that the dog rushed away as if he had been stung and after that only looked at it from afar.

In the neighbouring Golders Green park were two peacocks. One fine day they both decided to pay us a visit. Pavlova received them very kindly and gave them food, after which they became first our frequent visitors and eventually moved over to us altogether. In spite of the gardener's energetic protests at the birds' lack of consideration for his beds and their habit of pecking the flowers out of the vases, and the maids' complaint at their soiling the balcony, Pavlova found their beauty so attractive that she would not allow them to be disturbed. On our return from a tour in 1930, we learnt that the peahen had made a nest and was sitting. She chose a most extraordinary place for this, on some stones, quite near a path. She sat very patiently and, as she never left her nest, Pavlova used to put a bowl of water and a plate of food next to her, and when it rained made her a shelter of waterproof paper. All our efforts, however, came to nothing. One morning she suddenly gave up sitting; one egg lay on the bare ground and we saw that she would not return to it. And so it all ended.

How fond Pavlova really was of birds and animals can be seen from the following slight incident. While the pen-hen was on her nest, her husband did not come near her, but always flew up on the walls and squawked from there.

He was probably dull and was calling her. This cry would sometimes last for hours, and every time that I wanted to chase the bird away, Pavlova would implore me not to do so, saying that she was certain that, hearing the squawk, the hen knew the whereabouts of the cock and was not anxious.

Birds were always Pavlova's weakness, but her continual voyages made it impossible for her to devote much time to them.

When we were in the East for the first time in 1922 she saw in Singapore, some delightful little birds, known in Australia as "painted finches".

The colouring of these birds is wonderfully bright and beautiful, a black head, a vivid purple neck, a striking yellow breast and blue wings. We bought two. They proved to be most charming and intelligent little birds, quickly becoming domesticated, losing all fear of us and taking food out of Pavlova's hand. It is a peculiarity of these birds that, when courting, the cock places himself before the hen and not only chirrups, but dances, if one can so call the rapid hopping on the perch. Very soon Pavlova decided that the birds wanted to make a nest. Unfortunately we did not know the kind of nest they needed. We bought all sorts of things for them — half a coco-nut, woven and every other kind of nest, until someone had the bright idea of hanging up a small cigar-box with an opening cut in it. This pleased them at once. But now it was also necessary to find the material of which the nest could be made. Pavlova gave them cotton-wool, ordinary wool, strands of silk, but nothing seemed to suit. When driving in the fields near Cairo one day, she saw some tall plants, with some fibre sticking out of them. We gathered some of this fibre, but even that did not prove to their taste. Eventually somebody brought us fibre of some local plant and the cock-bird accepted it at once as suitable, and began immediately to carry it into the nest. Pavlova was overjoyed, but when the male bird had taken it all in, the female followed and threw it all out again. This was repeated two or three times and there the matter ended.

On our return to London we discovered that these birds could be bought there, though they are rather expensive, and we acquired several couples. Of all the small birds that we possessed these painted finches by their disposition, their fearlessness and their intelligence were the most attractive.

On our arrival in South Africa for the first time in 1926 Pavlova was quite enchanted at the variety and originality of the local birds. Our hotel in Kimberley stood in a garden, and outside our window was the tap for watering the flowers. The water oozing from the tap attracted the birds, and their beauty and variety was a wonderful sight. In Pretoria we made the acquaintance of the director of the zoological gardens, and asked his advice as to the best place to buy birds, for there did not seem to be any bird shops. He very kindly told us that he was expecting some Kaffirs to bring him birds for sale in two or three days and that he would buy a few for us at the same time. A couple of days later Pavlova received a cage containing about twenty delightful little birds and a bill for ten shillings. This started our collection of birds to which we added wherever we found ourselves. From Africa we went on to Australia, and soon became convinced that the variety of birds to be found there, exceeds that of any other country. This observation of ours proved correct, for there are up to 40,000 different varieties of birds in Australia. As our tour progressed our collection grew and the question of its transport became serious. Pavlova herself invented folding cages which took to pieces for travelling, the birds being then transferred to special small ones. When we arrived in a place in which we intended to make a stay, the big cages were put together again and the birds turned into them. The next improvement, also invented by Pavlova, were fountains in

Pavlova in the mountains of Java.

Pavlova by the Temple of the Sacred Monkeys.

sections for bird baths. All this entailed a great deal of trouble and worry, but the birds gave Pavlova much happiness.

From Sydney we went to New Zealand, and the climate there being considerably colder, we decided not to take our birds with us, but to leave them in Sydney. On arrival in Auckland we went — as was our wont in every new place — to see the zoological gardens, which were just finished and magnificently planned out. The director, advised of Pavlova's coming, conducted us round in person. We went into the bird section and there saw a big cage containing several very quaint birds of about the size of an Egyptian pigeon. These birds were covered with red, black and white spots, and had crests which they were continually either raising or lowering. They turned out to be some very rare species of Mozambique woodpecker.

Pavlova took a great fancy to them and began to play with them and talk to them, and the birds willingly came in answer to her call, pecked at her fingers and generally exhibited the most friendly feelings. Watching the scene attentively and noticing how delighted Pavlova was with the birds and how intelligently she treated them, the director offered to make her a present of one. The next day we received the bird and Pavlova named it "Khokhlik".*

The more I grew to know about birds the better I understood Pavlova's love for them. "Khokhlik" proved a delightful little creature. He grew quite accustomed to us at the end of a few days, allowing himself to be handled and would fly about the room examining everything with curiosity. He had one queer habit: when he wanted to sing (though it could perhaps hardly be called singing) he emitted a prolonged, vibrating note for two or three minutes, meaning thereby that he required something high up, to perch on — usually my head or the head of somebody present would be selected. He would then lift his crest and start singing, giving one the impression that a vibrating tuning-fork was being held to the ear. There would be quite a tragedy if he saw his reflection in the looking-glass. This would make him savage and he would hurl himself against what he thought to be his enemy and often hurt himself badly. We took "Khokhlik" back with us to Europe and he lived another two years with Pavlova. His death was due to the carelessness of some friends who fed him with too many grapes without removing the pips.

At the end of our Australian tour we had about 120 birds and the complicated business of their transport to Europe had to be considered. Ordinary passengers are only allowed to keep birds in the butcher's quarters and on big boats one finds whole aviaries there. But of course this

* Russian for a little crest or tuft.

arrangement is not very satisfactory. In hot climates draughts are specially arranged and these are very dangerous to small birds. Pavlova obtained the captain's permission to turn her bathroom into an aviary. A large cage was built and during the whole journey we did not lose more than five or six birds.

While Pavlova was making her collection, she had a huge cage made in London to be ready for her arrival. It took up the whole centre of our greenhouse. The frames were made of thick iron and plate-glass, while wire netting was put on the inside to prevent the birds hitting the glass. The upper part was only netted so that the air could come into the cage. In their new quarters the birds thrived exceedingly well. But by an immutable law of nature all these small birds do not live long; they die very soon when brought to another climate, and they seem to die very suddenly. One day the bird appears perfectly happy and feeding well, next morning it is found sitting helpless somewhere on the floor of the cage and a few hours later it is dead.

Once we talked to a great lover of birds and he told us that, when in the East, he grew quite enthusiastic about buying birds and had had a considerable collection, but gradually the birds began to die off and at the end of two years there were none left. After that, he swore that he would buy no more. Our birds seemed to be somewhat longer-lived. Perhaps the conditions of their life had something to do with it, for Pavlova gave them every comfort. Bird-baths with running water and an electric stove for cold weather were installed. The most longlived were the African birds, of which two, brought over in 1926 are still alive, while the Australian ones are all dead.

In the summer of 1928 we went to South America and in Santos market saw some birds of wonderful beauty. They were like precious stones, — vived red, blue, green, purple. There were quantities of them. When we asked the price we were told that they were sold at one milreis apiece, which is equal to about sixpence. Pavlova and I were astonished that, considering the low price, they were not seen in Europe. One of their distinguishing traits is that they soon become used to people and take food from the hand almost immediately. We bought sixty and arranged them on the steamer in such a way that they were always in the open air and in the sun and yet protected from the wind. For the first few days, while we were still in the tropics, they got on extremely well, but when the steamer approached more northern latitudes, though it was only September and still quite warm, our birds began to die. We succeeded nevertheless in bringing eighteen to London. When turned out into the cage they seemed to be perfectly comfortable, but by the end of a fortnight, only one solitary bird remained, and this one lived but a few days longer. Then we understood why these birds were never seen in Europe.

In that same year we moved on to the Far East and the winter of 1929 found us in Java. When we arrived in Batavia, we went to the market to see if any birds were being sold there, but to our surprise found none there of any interest, with the exception of some rather extraordinary doves. Such big and fine doves, with such wonderful feathers, we had never seen before. But they were only kept in cages and must not be let out. When we were on the point of leaving, Pavlova, very disappointed at having found nothing, suddenly noticed a small bird, about twice the size of a sparrow, with a black head, a grey and brown body and bright yellow under the tail. She remarked on its bright, intelligent eyes, and decided then and there to buy it. Our purchase proved very cheap, costing one gulden (1/6 d) including the cage. We took it home and Pavlova put the cage on the balcony. It should be mentioned that in Java, because of the heat, the hotels are built in such a way as to have no windows in the rooms, thus keeping out the rays of the sun. An hotel apartment consists of a large balcony, where one passes one's time and has one's meals, a reception room and finally a bedroom. Next to the bedroom is a bathroom; not a European bathroom, however, but one resembling our Russian bath — a wooden floor with holes, a huge tank of water upon it and a jug. Because of the heat hot water is not necessary. All this was so arranged that the window of the bathroom looked out on the opposite side of the building, thus ensuring a constant movement of air. The following morning Pavlova cleaned the cage, but forgot to close the door and the bird flew out. Greatly distressed she called me and pointed out where the bird sat on a large mango tree, where it was quite out of reach. A Malay servant went by while we were debating what to do and grasped what was the matter. He came up to Pavlova and told her in broken English that the bird — a cadilan — (presumably its Malay name) would return to its cage. We did not believe him, thinking that this was merely said to comfort Pavlova, but, to our surprise, some two hours later, the bird flew down and perched on the cage, and when Pavlova opened the door the little cadilan calmly hopped back to his familiar perch.

This seemed to have confirmed the words of the Malay, but Pavlova feared to repeat the experiment. After Batavia we gradually toured the whole of Java, finishing our tour in Surabaya where we stayed about a fortnight. During this time the little bird showed itself to be quite tame and very charming. Pavlova had grown so attached to it, that she resolved to acquire several and at the Surabaya market we bought some more.

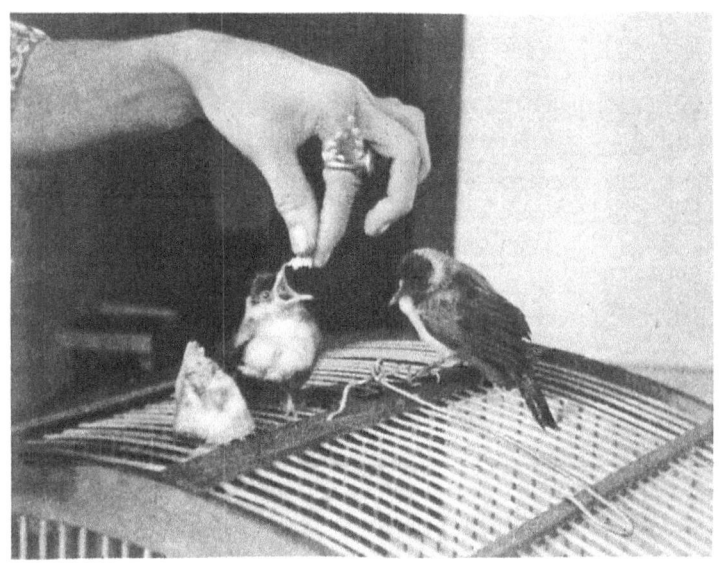

Feeding the young Cadilan.

On one occasion Pavlova and I were drinking tea in the hotel garden, having the cage with the bird near-by. A friend of ours, who knew of the incident with the cadilan, came to see us and, without warning Pavlova, opened the door of the cage. The bird flew out. Pavlova was very frightened, for she thought that this time the bird would not come back. Two or three hours later, however, it returned and we then believed that this must really be some special trait of its own.

From Surabaya we went to north Australia and then toured the whole country, ending at Perth in the west.

This time we learnt that the Australian Government had issued a series of very strict regulations against the export of birds. This was a great blow to Pavlova, who wanted to buy some more of her favourite painted finches, diamond finches and others. I petitioned for permission for Pavlova to buy some of these birds and this petition was granted. We therefore bought twenty or thirty pairs. When we took them with us to Sydney, I had to petition the federal government to be allowed to take them out of the country. But here I came up against the most unyielding obstinacy. The people were quite well aware that Pavlova wanted the birds for her own personal pleasure, that they are not rare, as there are millions of them, and yet the authorities refused us. But that was not all, for as Pavlova has brought over many birds from India and Java, the authorities demanded a full list, declaring at the same time that they would send one of their agents to verify it. Pavlova became alarmed, thinking that perhaps owing to some misunderstanding her favourite cadilans might be retained and confiscated. She was in such a state of agitation that I bought a box of the kind used for food on a journey by car, removed all the dishes and tins and had it divided into three compartments by means of light partitions. In each compartment I put a little cage of which the outer side was protected by an apron and the lower contained a sort of light valve which let in the air. The birds were perfectly quiet. They were in complete darkness. Nobody could have imagined that there was a living creature inside the box. The officials sent by the government to look at the birds arrived, and though personally I never feared any difficulties, Pavlova was triumphant at the success of our ruse and the escape of the birds.

While still in Sydney Pavlova decided to let her cadilan out to fly again. Our house stood in a garden on the shore of the bay. I was against this experiment, fearing lest in a different climate and different surroundings the trusting bird should meet its death through its own carelessness, all the more so as there are in Australia several kinds of birds of prey and they are very numerous. My fears, however, proved groundless, for the bird returned, and every day after that, having gained Pavlova's entire confidence, came back to its cage just before sundown. We grew more and more attached to it. On one occasion, however, the bird was let out too late and apparently not having had its fill of flying, it was caught by the darkness and lost itself. Pavlova was terribly anxious; she went to the theatre in a greatly agitated state of mind and wandered about everywhere when she came back, searching for and calling her cadilan. She did not even want to go to bed. She was particularly anxious because the nights were very cold. We decided not to shut the window in the drawing room, where the cage stood, and also to leave the door of the latter open. Early in the morning the maid came to say that the cadilan had returned. Knowing how anxious Pavlova was, I brought the bird to her into the bedroom. Shortly after I came back, and found it lying on her bosom covered by a downy Orenburg shawl, literally purring like a kitten. Pavlova put her finger to her lips:

"Hush. He's telling me...."

On our return to England we were again afraid that letting this tropical bird out to fly about would be risky. But the cadilan had become so accustomed to us by this time, had grown so attached to Pavlova and showed such fearlessness, that, knowing what happiness it was for him to fly about at liberty, we decided to make the experiment again. The cadilan proved extremely sensible and developed a new trait — answering Pavlova's call.

When she grew anxious at its prolonged absence and called, the bird, sitting somewhere on a high tree, replied. The other two young cadilans grew up, and though they never became quite so tame as our favourite, would nevertheless allow themselves to be picked up and would eat out of one's hand. The cadilan was truly delightful when Pavlova let it out to fly about the room, as she always did during lunch. It was very inquisitive and tasted everything, its favourite dishes however being butter and jam.

In their own native land cadilans prefer feeding on a fruit called "papaya", something like our melon, which grows in immense quantities on low trees. We were very much afraid that the absence of this food would be a source of great difficulty, but our cadilans ate every kind of fruit and were besides fed on a special food that is sold here for insectivorous birds. A great delicacy for them were flour worms, which are especially bred in bran. It was however perfectly plain to me that these charming little birds were not destined to live long. One can realise that a bird born near the equator and having lived there, could not long stand the climate of England and being fed on artificial food. They were with us, nevertheless, for nearly a year and a half. Then the young ones began to sicken. For no obvious reason and apparently while still eating normally, they grew weaker and weaker and finally died both on the same day. During the first year the old one showed no symptoms of approaching death, though we kept a very close watch on it. But when the second winter came round it grew gradually more and more melancholy. We called in a vet, who thought it might be the beginning of anaemia, and told us to increase the portion of worms and also to give it a little meat. At times the former cheerfulness would return, but it was obvious that the bird was fading away. Pavlova was away on a tour, I was alone at home and tended it and every evening covered it up myself.

One morning I found it in its usual position on the perch, but with its head under its wing and already rigid. This was a great grief to Pavlova. We buried it under her favourite tree and, returning late in the evening from the last performance of the tour, she brought a large bunch of flowers to put on its grave. Pavlova herself only survived her bird by two months.

CHAPTER XXIII.
TAGLIONI, ELSSLER AND PAVLOVA.

I have often been asked my opinion on the question of comparison between Pavlova and her two great predecessors — Taglioni and Fanny Elssler. It is very difficult to give an answer to this question for there is no one among us who has seen either of these dancers of the middle of last century.

One way only then remains — to study such literature as exists on the subject of Taglioni and Elssler.

I take the liberty of giving here the opinions of three of the best-known critics, men who devoted a great part of their time to the study of the history of the ballet and its greatest representatives. In their articles they touch upon this question of comparison.

All the three critics are Russians, but that is not to be wondered at, for in Russia the ballet was a highly respected and much loved art. A. Plescheev, the well-known ballet critic, counted among his friends and old ballet acquaintances several people who had seen Taglioni and Fanny Elssler at the time of their sojourn in Russia. I will begin with his views:

"Pavlova was the possessor of an exceptional and fortunate combination of incomparable exterior sculptural forms of the dance with its inner illumination and spirituality. A combination of incomparable feminity and grace with an ethereal lightness. A combination of a profound sense of the dramatic and a child-like playfulness, gaiety and vivacity. A combination of lyrical poesy with bacchanalian frenzy. The rarest of all harmonies of contradictory choreographic elements.

Those who have seen the tragic, the poetic or the carefree figures created by Pavlova on the stage, cannot but admit that such figures have never yet been equalled. In the course of centuries, perhaps, they may be seen again, just as Taglioni and Fanny Elssler were both represented in the person of Pavlova.

But she stands higher than they do, for they did not posses her complex combination of gifts. Taglioni was only etheral and spiritual, while Fanny

Elssler was human and passionate. But Pavlova combined in herself the romantic, ethereal Taglioni with her opposite — Fanny Elssler.

The gamut of Pavlova's talent (as we see by her artistic creations) was greater than that of her greatest predecessors."

Valerian Svetlov, who has produced a whole series of works on the ballet, devoted many years to the study of Pavlova's dances, the result of which was a beautiful volume entitled "Anna Pavlova." In his article on her death, he writes:

"She was often called, and is still called, 'The Taglioni of the XX century'. But this is no definition, rather does it disparage the work of Pavlova. We know that Taglioni could not have had the same perfect mastery of dance as Pavlova, for the simple reason that the dance of her time had not reached the same level of expressiveness as that of our day. All its conceptions, its romanticism, its inner spirituality were not the same as those of our time. Persons of different generations feel differently and react to the surrounding world each in his own way. Even nature changes its appearance with the change of an epoch, for where will we now find a landscape of the romantic age-weeping trees overhanging the steely waters of a lake under heavy, melancholy-filled clouds? At the time of Taglioni, the technique of the dance was different and the spirit of it as expressed by this technique was different. Besides, why these comparisons? And how can we compare when none of us has ever seen Taglioni? Description alone is not sufficient; neither dance nor melody can be described in words, they require to be seen and heard. Let us give Taglioni her due, not in any way belittling either her talent or its value as an artistic phenomenon of her time, but it is this very age in which she lived that confined her within the frame-work of a vague romanticism, putting narrow limits to the possible emotions and to their outward interpretation. There can be no comparison between Taglioni and Pavlova's range of expression. Pavlova's was extensive and profound. All the complicated gamut of human moods and feelings, with all their psychological shades have found in her an interpreter without an equal."

And finally, the third of these critics, is André Levinson, who for a number of years collected material about Taglioni, analysing the critics of her time and studying the epoch, before writing his remarkable monograph of her. This is what he says:

"The tradition of Taglioni does not suffice to express or explain the revelation of Pavlova. We know that this tradition contained first of all the idea of ethereal lightness, of virgin innocence and of forms free from all that is earthly carnal. Taglonism is of course only one of the many facets of the art of Pavlova, the art that showed itself in metamorphoses without number. "Comparaison n'est pas raison" says an old adage. But the use of analogies gives so much convenience to ideas by prompting definitions, that we are often obliged to measure the present by measures of the past (to adapt the present to past scales). We define the genius of an artist, our contemporary, by recalling the name of some distant and famous predecessor. We are more willing to attach the idea of greatness to the past than to the present, and by reason of its distance, the figure of a great man becomes heroic, and at the same time the memory of it becomes fixed for all time. He receives an aureole and the credit of a doubtful legend. By recalling Pavlova's predecessors we gain a deeper insight into her art. We know that she had no rivals in our time. The greatest wish of every dancer was to be compared to her, even if only distantly. But if we are called upon to give Pavlova herself a place in the hierarchy of stars, we can find nothing better than to assume that she was in our time what Taglioni — Marie pleine de grace — was in her own epoch. Having in view the forthcoming publication of my book, I studied with all possible care the relics and signs left us by the "Sylphide" by which one could get an idea of the anatomy of her body and the reason of her fame. And the more I study them the more I arrive at the conclusion that the definition of a "modern Taglioni" does not appear to me to be sufficient for Pavlova. The more I collect the evidence of contemporaries, sift documents and ponder over other information, which allows me to study dancers who were celebrities in their day and whose names we find in madrigals and the dedications of Victor Hugo, the more I come to a conclusion to which it is at first difficult to grow accustomed. We have in our midst the greatest dancer of all times, or to be more exact, of all the historical periods of dancing which admit of analysis. All that we know of Camargo, Sallet, Fanny Elssler, Grisi or any other 'marvellous angel of the heavens of illusion' does not make any one of them the equal of Pavlova."

When we read the articles of French and Russian critics, we see that they all agree as to the unequalled lightness, spirituality, chasteness and grace of Taglioni. Fanny Elssler, on the contrary, had a passionate temperament and was cheerfully realistic.

Taglioni possessed extraordinary qualities as a purely classical dancer. She acquired these by indefatigable labour under the severe guidance of her father.

Her contemporaries relate that after the daily lesson she would often fall swooning to the ground; that she was undressed and dressed in other clothes without gaining consciousness. But the perfection of dance which she reached remained fixed and one cannot imagine that any new tendencies could have been within her reach.

On the other hand, Pavlova while conserving all the rigorous severity of classicism and classical traditions, for she had no equal in the old ballets like "Giselle" and "La Bayadère", was at the same time the ideal ballerina for the new ballet of which Fokine dreamed.

It was very justly said of her, that in her frail, slender body, so full of inexpressible grace, she carried all the treasures collected by the labours of the past centuries as well as all the possibilities of the ballet of the future.

Pavlova was born ethereal, whereas Taglioni, having acquired her ethereality and added severe classicism to it, seems to have remained fixed there. She subordinated her art to these dominating qualities of her dance without giving it any inner meaning.

It has been my good fortune to talk about Taglioni with two of the most competent persons, namely, Marius Petipa, the maitre de ballet, who saw Taglioni many times and Johannsen, the well-known dancer and choreographer, who danced with her.

With regard to Taglioni I consider Marius Petipa's opinion the most valuable of all. Being an artist of her time himself, he lived through the history of the ballet of the second half of the XIX century. This maitre de ballet of genius worked in turn with all the famous ballerinas, Italian as well as Russian, and could therefore judge of them better than anybody else. And this is his definite opinion: 'Taglioni would not have been admired so much in our day.' He considered that of the two, Fanny Elssler was the more likely to gain popular favour. He thought that if the Italian dancer, Limido, who was famous in the eighties and was considered the greatest technical dancer of our day, had lived in the day of Taglioni, she would probably have had just as much success.

My opinion that Taglioni remained "fixed" in the perfection of her etheriality is confirmed by the fact that even in St. Petersburg, where she probably reaped the chief laurels of her life, it was said towards the end of her five years' visit that she no longer produced quite the same deep impression as before.

By the very character of her art, Taglioni was extra-ordinarily well-suited to the romantic era, in the full bloom of which her scenic career was passed.

Nothing could have suited the ideals of the age better than her etherealness and chastity, and it was the romantic school that worshipped her and set her up on an unattainable pedestal, without considering that her talent, though perfect as far as it went, was after all not very wide, and certainly not deep.

Quite different was the versatility of Pavlova's gifts. Her genius made it possible for her to vary her rôles without end. Possessing, like Taglioni, ethereal charm for ballets of a romantic nature, she was equally without rivals in dramatic subjects, as well as in playful and coquettish ones. The characters which she created were not only remarkable for their perfect beauty and lightness, but were imbued with such a depth of feeling and spirituality, that they could never become fixed, and the public constantly wanted to see her in the same rôle, knowing that in every case she would be different.

This versatility of Pavlova's gifts may be well illustrated by quotations from certain well-known journalists. M. Ofrossimov writing in the "Rul" said, —

"That which in the genius of Pavlova, lends itself to expression in words was, I think, her ability, each time she was on the stage, to create and feel her creations anew, and so great was her power that she made her stage impersonations talk, sing, laugh and weep by her dancing, her marvellous technique and her power of acting.

Pavlova's types? They were many and varied. From the ecstasy of "beautiful death" in the "Dying Swan" when with graceful movements of the arm-wings and wide open eyes she gazed at the vision of death, to the playful charm of the French idyll, "La Fille Mal Gardée". From the deep emotion of "Giselle" and the tragedy of "Amarilla", to the rosy cloud of "Christmas" and Beethoven's "Rondino" with her fan of ostrich feathers completely covering her body in her last solemn bow to the public, to the lightness of the "Dragon-fly", where she fluttered out and stopped instantaneously stretched yearningly towards a ray of sunlight as if she were merging her body into it and longed to begin her airy game, so that we at once felt that this could not be a painted canvas or a projector which we saw, but a green meadow and a real sun. From the pensive Chopin valse with its wonderful soaring in the air on the first chord, to the "Bacchanal" where she danced the pagan worship of the body."

Oscar Bie, one of the most prominent-German critics and the author of a book about dancing says: "The mad-scene in Giselle is one of the most remarkable creations that has ever been realised in the art of choreography. Despite the fact that no word is spoken, this scene holds us enthralled, and we understand the enthusiasm of the French in earlier days for the intense pleasure of a well-acted pantomime, rather than the more materialistic impression of the spoken drama.

Pavlova achieves the union of two elements, that of 'the dance acted', and 'drama in dance'. She makes the old art live again by re-animating it with the breath of contemporary life. Behind her perfect naturalness we see the traditional foundations of technique.

Her silent body is a rhythmic symphony, there is melody in the movements of her arms, harmony in the movement of the torso. She brings before us an image of a great tragedienne. In the space of a few seconds she awakens and releases such a whirl of rhythms that one can only sit and marvel at the wealth of plastic, musical beauty which this artist's body contains."

Of "Papillon" and "Libellule" V. Svetlov wrote:

"These two masterpieces of choreographic imagery are, to a certain degree, in complete contrast to the Swan. In the latter we have a picture of suffering and death, in the former images of light-hearted happiness. The artist has chosen her colours and plastic forms so as to make of the care-free, joyous lives of the Butterfly and Dragon-fly true songs without words, creations of indescribable beauty. I remember one evening in Moscow when the people, enraptured at the sight of the Butterfly hovering in the golden motes of sunlight, made her repeat this little piece three times.

"Pavlova's dancing breathes the joy of living; it is a hymn of benediction to the spring sunshine, to the love of life which its warm rays enkindle. Her lovely 'songs without words' are certainly more mere dances. They have in them that which speaks directly to the soul and requires no analysis nor scientific understanding. Their aesthetic value is immeasurable. There is no need to search for a definition of the beauty of her dancing; each finds it for himself immediately without trying to explain it. And how, indeed, can one ever explain the meaning of beauty?"

Later he speaks of the impression created by Pavlova's appearance in "La Péri".

"I am convinced that no modern dancer brought up to disregard the principles of the classic dance, whose artistic education would consequently tend in the opposite direction, that is to say beginning by abjuring the "old" aesthetic traditions, no such dancer, as I have said, will ever be able to show an understanding of the beautiful and of the new ideas, to equal that of Pavlova in Dukas' La Péri. The score is very difficult. The rhythms are constantly changing. The time is complicated, yet the phrases are full of melody. The dance, original and intricate, corresponds to the spirit of the music. And Pavlova is unbelievable in it. She so transforms herself that one is utterly amazed. For this artist, a supreme classical dancer, almost changes the very principles of her dancing. And it is her gift of penetrating to the very soul of things to give them birth and expression, which enables her to undergo such a metamorphosis."

And finally we have the closing words from an article written after the death of Pavlova by the well-known critic P. Pilsky:

"How amazing was the versatilily of this artist! Her wonderful creative power, her subtle and delicious humour, her noble pathos, the sensitive psychology of her dances, her magical transformations, the crispness of her execution, the poetry, the spiritual exaltation, her magnificent presentation of heroism, of the spirit of flowers, of Bacchism and legend — what a treasury of creations, a flock of fairy birds shining in the sky with a rainbow of glorious colours, grieving for the eternal in art and its living dreams."

And Pavlova's epoch was different.

If the beginning of her carrer was passed in Russia under the familiar roof of the Imperial Theatre and in work with her teachers, all the rest of her service to her art was passed on the stages of the wide world, under difficult and unfavourable conditions, at a time when new tendencies in art arose, traditions were being undermined, a pursuit began after cheap effects, jazzbands blared and one was acutely conscious of the decline of the taste of the public, which understood art less and less, and was less and less interested in it.

This was very justly remarked by an American critic who writing of Pavlova, said that in order to remain the undisputed queen of the dance for twenty years under modern conditions, and to meet invariably with great success in the course of all that time, as well as with the worship of people in every country of the world, to oblige charlatanism and triviality to beat a retreat, before her, Pavlova possessed something greater even than genius; she had shown herself to be one of the purest lights of civilisation.

When Pavlova danced "Giselle" in Paris, the grandsons of Théophile Gautier, the author of the ballet (who borrowed the subject from Heine) and the grandsons of the composer of the music, Adam, were present at the performance. In these families the traditions of their famous ancestors were held sacred and many exist about the earlier dancers of "Giselle". It is interesting that in their letters to Pavlova, expressing their admiration, the descendants of both Gautier and Adam, write that the interpretation of the role of Giselle was such that their grandfathers could never have dreamed of anything approaching it.

If legend has remained of Taglioni as Sylphide, it will remain of Pavlova in the mystic image of the swan awaiting its liberation in death. She alone has attained in art what may be called the mute breath of the divine.

Last photograph of Pavlova with Mme. Doubrowska in Monte Carlo, January 1931.

CHAPTER XXIV.
LAST DAYS.

There was nothing to give warning of the terrible days drawing near.

We had finished our last tour in Europe. Pavlova began it in January 1930 in Spain, then toured the South of France, Switzerland, Germany, Denmark, Sweden, Norway and completed the season on the 12th of May in Paris. After that she took a prolonged rest. Part of this time was spent at home, at Ivy House, and later we went to Plombière (Vosges), where she took the baths.

When her course of treatment was over, she came back to London at the end of August feeling very well and began to prepare for the English season, which opened on September 8th and went on until December 13th in Golders Green Theatre, only five minutes' walk from Ivy House.

During this tour Pavlova had again begun to complain of pain in her left knee. Massage and diathermy did little good this time. As our continental tour was not due to begin until January 19th, Pavlova decided to take advantage of this interval to go to the sunny south of France, stopping in Paris on the way to consult a doctor about her knee. She saw specialists in Paris and they agreed that a rest of five weeks would put matters right. On her arrival at Cannes, Pavlova began a treatment of iodinization (a process of getting a preparation of iodine into the system by electrolysis). She walked a great deal and felt very well. A fortnight after commencing the treatment, she began a little practice, going for this to the local theatre. At first she was anxious as to the effect of the treatment on the leg, but gradually became more and more convinced that a considerable improvement had been effected. By the end of our stay at Cannes, she was doing her full course of exercises with absolute ease. Before beginning the tour in Holland she wanted a few days' rehearsal with Vladimirov in Paris and we left Cannes on the 10th January in consequence.

While travelling, about nine o'clock on the morning of the 11th while Pavlova was still asleep, we felt violent shocks and the train came to a standstill. Pavlova woke up in a fright, but raising the blind and seeing that we were at a station and the day was beautiful and sunny, she started to dress calmly. We then came out of our carriage. It was quite unharmed, although the neighbouring ones had suffered, but it was only when we went near the engine, which was surrounded by a group of mechanics and workmen, that we realised the extent of the catastrophe from which we had escaped. The engine was completely wrecked. It appeared that our train had run into a shunting goods train. We returned to our carriage to await the coming of another engine to take us back to some junction, whence we were taken on to Paris by another route. This incident had no effect whatever on Pavlova's health.

In Paris she went to Dr. Zalevsky. He was quite satisfied with the result of the treatment and Pavlova began her preparation, first alone and later with Vladimirov, who told me that he was quite surprised to see how much better Pavlova was, and in what excellent condition for the beginning of the new season.

Business called me to London and therefore during those days I was not with her in Paris. I was told later that having one day come to do her exercises, she found the room unheated and very cold. In spite of this however, she stayed on to work and it is possible that when changing after getting heated by dancing she caught a chill. It is also possible that she caught cold at Cannes, where the weather is very treacherous. She never coddled herself, never wrapped anything round her throat and usually wore open necked dresses. As her powers of endurance were very great, it is probable that she did not heed the first symptoms of illness, and had already caught cold before the day when the room was unheated, and that perhaps caused the chill to get a thorough hold upon her.

Her first feeling that something was amiss came on the Friday evening and she complained of fatigue. She left Paris on the 17th of January at 9 o'clock in the morning. She felt rather worse in the train and took to her bed immediately on arrival at The Hague. The doctor who examined her diagnosed pleurisy in the left lung.

The same day I arrived at The Hague, and found her in bed talking to some members of our company. She greeted me with the words:

"Just imagine, I must have been poisoned by something I ate in Paris, and the doctor, instead of treating me for that, says that I have pleurisy."

On the Sunday morning I called in another doctor, who was considered the best at The Hague (Dr. de Jong, the Queen's physician). He confirmed the diagnosis of the first doctor. They both drew my attention to the weakening of the heart action and insisted that she should take a little alcohol in some form, but Pavlova at this time began to feel a strong distaste for alcohol and refused to obey the doctors' orders. I tried giving her a little rum in her tea and wine, but it was of no use, for she declared that it was disgusting. She always bore slight illnesses so easily, that the idea that there could be any danger never entered anybody's head. Dr de Jong said to me that in the case of pleurisy great care was necessary even after recovery, for another cold could easily produce a relapse. I took him into Pavlova's room and asked him to repeat the warning to her, and tell her how she must take care of herself. She answered:

"But doctor, how can I possibly do all that when I have to start my season to-morrow?" and looked at me in surprise when we said that there could be no question of this.

On the following day, Monday, she complained that she had slept badly and experienced some difficulty in breathing. She was constantly given warm milk, which she drank in small sips. After the consultation on Tuesday, I noticed for the first time with some anxiety, that a doubt as to the possible outcome of the illness had crept over both the doctors. I am immeasurably grateful to Dr Zalevsky, who arrived at The Hague on the Wednesday. Pavlova had grown accustomed to him during the last years, was very fond of him and trusted him implicitly. Having examined her immediately on arrival, he expressed great anxiety. He said that there could be no doubt that Pavlova had caught a severe chill some days before the illness had developed and had continued to work when her lungs were already touched, without knowing it. In this condition of lowered vitality she evidently caught cold again and the pleurisy spread with alarming rapidity.

On Wednesday evening I was left alone with Pavlova. She was sitting up in bed and signified a desire to talk to me. I bent towards her and she questioned me about our business, rehearsals, repertoire and so forth. It was the first time that during her illness she led the conversation round to the theatre, and all that she said, all her ideas and instructions, were absolutely logical and reasonable, showing how well her brain was working. This conversation filled me with joy, for it seemed impossible that a person who was dangerously ill could speak of business affairs so clearly and in such detail.

Next morning, however, the doctors discovered that the inflammatory process had spread to the right lung. Dr. Zalevsky decided that an injection of antipneumococ serum must be made, and on the Thursday morning her back was pierced in order to remove the fluid that was hampering her breathing. This was quite successful. Then the serum injection was made. All sorts of measures had also to be taken to improve the action of the heart, which was noticeably growing weaker. But obviously her strength was failing and at six o'clock in the evening she lost consciousness. She was no longer aware of anything that was happening round her.

Various remedies were continued, but nothing had any more effect. All the time she was breathing oxygen. In spite of the unusual rapidity of the development of the illness which carried her away in six days, I am happy to say that Pavlova did not suffer much. I am of the opinion that she did not realise her condition, for she did not once refer to it all through her illness. Her maid, Marguerite Letienne, never left her for a moment. Pavlova was very fond of her and Letienne tended her with touching gentleness and unremitting care. Pavlova's breathing grew fainter and fainter. About midnight she opened her eyes and with difficulty raised her hand as though she wished to make the sign of the cross. A few minutes later Marguerite looked up and saw that she wanted to say something. She bent down and Pavlova said:

"Get my 'Swan' costume ready."

Those were her last words. At half past twelve at night on Friday the 23rd of January Anna Pavlova breathed her last. Dr. Zalevsky, Marguerite Letienne and I were present at her death.

Pavlova's Resting Place.

Instructions were given immediately and in a few hours the coffin arrived. In the meantime Marguerite and another nurse dressed Pavlova in her favourite dress of beige lace and we placed her in the coffin. I also put in some sprigs of lilac.

The illness had altered Pavlova's features and although asked I would not allow a mask to be taken. The Russian priest came at seven o'clock in the morning and, according to the custom of the Orthodox Church, a mass for the dead was celebrated. During these few hours since her death, the features had softened and a slight shadow of a smile appeared on her lips. At 7.30 a. m. we carried the coffin from the hotel to a chapel belonging to a Catholic monastery, where the body remained until taken over to England, pending a decision of the question of the place of burial.

This was a difficult question for me to decide. The numerous Russian colony in Paris wanted Pavlova to be buried in that city, but personally I desired that it should be in England. I know how beloved Pavlova is in England, I know that at any rate during the life of this generation she will not be forgotten and that there will always be fresh flowers on her grave. I have no doubt whatever that she would have been given a magnificent funeral in Paris, but I am not at all certain that there she would have been surrounded for long with the same love and devoted reverence as in the country where she lived for many years and where she used to come "home" to her own house.

On the same day, the Friday, I left The Hague for London to make all the necessary arrangements. It was my great wish that Pavlova should be buried not far from the house in which she had passed twenty years of her life and which she loved.

The best place in London, designed on quite a new plan, is called "The Garden of Rest" and belongs to the Golders Green Crematorium. Pavlova had more than once expressed her approval of the principle of cremation and, after consultation with some friends and the Orthodox priest, I decided on this. If in the future a possibility occurs of taking Pavlova's remains to her native land which she so loved, it will be easier to move the urn with her ashes.

The body arrived from Holland at Gravesend, on the Thames, on the morning of the 28th of January, and was taken in a special carriage to London, to Victoria Station. From there it was transferred to the Russian Church, St. Philips, where it was met by the clergy and the choir. A mass for the dead was said and there the body remained during the whole of that day, Wednesday the 28th.

After the mass and until the closing of the church at nine o'clock there was an unceasing stream of people who, wishing to honour her memory, filed slowly past the coffin to the reading of prayers. There were both rich and poor, famous and unknown. They would pause for a minute in front of the coffin to offer up a silent prayer. Even after nine o'clock and until eleven p. m. those in the church had continually to open the door to let in the late-comers who wished to offer their last respects to Pavlova. The many thousands who came that day to honour her evidently considered that she belonged as much to England as to Russia.

The church was opened again at ten in the morning of the 29th, and again came the procession of people. At half past ten, the beginning of the service, the church was packed. Flowers were being brought or sent all the time — wreaths, small bunches single flowers — these were countless.

A mass was celebrated after the liturgy. When this was ended again the streams of people filed past the coffin.

The body was removed from the church at 2,15 p. m. On the way to the crematorium the motor carriage containing Pavlova's remains and all the cars accompanying it, stopped for a minute in front of her house. Eventually, at 3.30, the procession reached the crematorium, the body was taken into the chapel, and in the gallery, in place of the organ, sang the Russian church choir. A few minutes later, to the singing of funeral chants, the coffin slowly moved towards the door dividing the chapel from the inner apartment and disappeared from view. Over these doors are the words "Death is the Gate of Life".

Mr. E. Sablin, the former diplomatic representative of Russia at the Court of the King of England, covered the coffin in the Russian Church with the Imperial flag, saved during the evacuation of the Russian Embassy in London. This flag remained on the coffin to the very end, being removed only when the coffin slowly disappeared from the view of those present.

CHAPTER XXV.

THE ENIGMA OF PAVLOVA'S ART.

So much has already been written about Pavlova — in so many brilliant pages have talented critics and writers analysed the perfection of her technique, of her acting, of her marvellous sense of rhythm and all other aspects of her art — that one may be permitted to pass over these questions here. But what I want to do, and indeed feel I must do, is to touch upon that which made her different from all the other dancers whom it has been my lot to see. Looking back on her career as a whole, it is only now that we are beginning to understand the hidden reason and the real meaning of the world-wide love for this dancer. All the obituary notices as well as all the articles inspired by her death, have emphasised one important, outstanding fact: Pavlova was verily the best-loved person of her time, was truly idolized. And the surprising part of it is, that it was only through her art that she could call up this feeling for herself. She never wrote, took no part in politics, rarely went to any gatherings and, one may say, never into society; in fact had practically no personal contact with the public. Her charities were also little heard of. Consequently she was known only through her art. It aroused admiration, this admiration turned to love and finally became adoration. And this love and this adoration supply the true key for understanding her charm, that of the **human being revealed in art**. The feeling she evoked was the response to some call, some deeper call than that of art alone. It was a response to that something almost unique that dwelt secretly, yet tangibly, in her; I can only say — Pavlova's was no ordinary personality. She was given from above the gift of radiating beauty around her, not only through the form and movements of her body, but also through her spiritual self that touched, one knows not how, the depth of the heart and soul, and left there a feeling of joyous beauty and fond gratitude to her who gave such happiness.

The more sensitive and understanding of Pavlova's Russian critics, by virtue of their Slav temperament, were the first to feel this peculiar quality of Pavlova. In his article "La Mort du Cygne", Levinson writes:

"Twenty, thirty times I spoke of her when she was alive. And always at the moment when I thought I had captured the miracle of her art and the mystery of her personality, words failed me. Technique can be analysed with perfect calm, talent can be examined from every angle, but before the revelation of genius, the manifestation of the divine in a human being, one is left in a state of bewildered delight."

In another article "Le Genie d'Anna Pavlova", he writes:

"How many times have I, during Pavlova's life, attempted to solve the enigma of her art — an art unequalled, unapproached. Folly and self-deception! Each of her appearances on the stage was in the nature of a miracle, which cannot be rationally explained.

Now that she is no more, now that the swan of former days has broken away from its exile in our midst, we have no hope of penetrating this secret. Forever have we lost the formula by which this blending of soul and body was achieved. Suddenly Pavlova disappears from amongst us, dies, passes beyond our reach: and then we realised that she was given to us, not to keep, but only to gaze upon, to be taken again. We had always suspected that this being, soaring upwards on the mighty wings of the soul, did not quite belong to this world and certainly not to this age. One recalls the feeling that one had, on seeing her dance, as of something not of the same stuff as our era, old-fashioned if you like; or, one might say, not of "our day". This had to do with her quality of soul, and also with the visible part of her, charged with spirituality to the utmost. In a world more and more devoid of mystery, some of her gestures bordered on the supernatural. She was as much out of her element in our modern cities as would have been a peri or a fay, or any other legendary figure kneaded together of reality and the stuff of dreams. Each of her gestures was not only an arabesque traced with extreme grace, but also a symbol of the ineffable: and by symbol I do not mean some obscure hieroglyphic but an image, clear, concrete, arresting, of the inner life. This implies that her art was of the essence of poetry. Théophile Gautier wrote in a Paris newspaper a century ago that Taglioni was one of the greatest poets of her time and that she was "a genius in the same measure as Lord Byron or Lamartine." How much more isolated does Pavlova stand, who alone in our day, carried in her slender frame this power of lyricism, this flame of poetry, this élan towards the hidden beyond."

Another Russian writer, Piotr Pilsky, in his article "On the Death of Pavlova" says: "One may analyse Pavlova from the point of view of technique, one may be lost in admiration of her arms, of the marvellous curve of her wrist, of the wonderful arch of her instep, the delicacy of her shoulders. There was magic in the beauty of her pure classicism, in her acting with which were combined such a depth of wisdom and lightness of spirit, such artistry and quiet simplicity, where all was illumined, enveloped by tenderness and touching lyricism. One may dicuss and weigh, estimate and define, but what has never been, and never can be done is to solve the mystery of the spell with which she held her audience. This secret slipped away, not to be caught by definition, by a flood of the most beautiful words or their mathematical precision. A breath of the holy spirit embodied in the earthly forms of the highest art, hovered over the audience, gently finding a way into the soul and ever remaining in the memory of a perturbed but grateful heart. But no formula could be found, not one of the spectators or of the critics ever succeeded in commemorating the miracle that appeared to him, the sacrament that passed before his eyes of that loveliest of the dreams of art."

And just as the Russian critics, so also did the French feel this unearthly quality in Pavlova. The critic of Le Journal, Monsieur Gaston Pavlovsky, describing his impressions, writes:

"Her superb talent embraces in itself the art of all ages. To stir the emotions by a hollow semblance of reality is nothing; but so profoundly to move the soul that it becomes aware of the principle of Beauty lying dormant there,—that is a gift approaching the divine."

At the end of an analysis of Pavlova's art, another French critic says:

"Anna Pavlova is not a dancer: she is a direct manifestation of the divine."

English critics in admiring Pavlova, in analysing her as a dancer, in extolling her grace, elegance and technique, invariably confess their inability to explain the artistic phenomenon which is Pavlova.

"We can understand", one of them writes, "that Pavlova is a marvellous dancer, that her extraordinary success is wholly merited. But what charms does she use so to conquer her public? Why do we who follow the performance with interest, who see the scenery, the costumes, the dances and the play of the others, from the moment of Pavlova's entry on the stage cease to see anything else and all our interest is centred in this small frail woman? We live in what she represents and when she vanishes into the wings, we only wait for the moment when she reappears and floods us all again with that feeling of happiness."

There is a word in the English language — p e r s o n a l i t y — meaning the possession of those qualities which give a man special characteristics that differentiate him from others. The English critics presumed that the impression made by Pavlova was the result of such personality, exceptionally strongly marked in her case. But if the English critics found only this explanation of the enigma of Pavlova, English audiences, or at any rate the greater part of them, immediately felt Pavlova's spellbinding, though unsolved secret. In her very first season in London Pavlova received a letter from a young woman, a stranger to her, in which she wrote of a drama in her life and of the hopeless melancholy that had possessed her for many years. On the advice of her mother, this woman had come to see the dances of Pavlova and after that came every evening for several consecutive weeks owing to the inexpressible sensation of happiness she received from these performances, and after she had experienced the peace-giving effects of beauty, she had again the wish to live. Again, a young couple, who wanted to be married, asked Pavlova to bless them. The bride and bridegroom explained their wish by saying that Pavlova's art was the most beautiful thing they had seen in their lives and they believed that the blessing of the creator of this beauty would bring them good fortune in the future.

I have often seen in houses whole rooms dedicated to Pavlova. Countless photographs, collections of programmes, theatrical albums, cuttings out of newspapers, dried flowers given by her, the ends of ribbons from her bouquets, everything was kept, like holy relics. In some cases there was even an admixture of religious feeling, for according to the words of these people, Pavlova's art by its pure beauty brought one nearer the divine. When looking at her dances, they lived through the emotion and the joy of gazing at something not of this world. It is noteworthy that this was felt by people differing widely in religion, nationality and position. An Englishwoman from the provinces wrote to me: "You know that for fifteen years I have had a place in my bedroom which I call the altar. A photograph of herself which Pavlova gave me stands there, and I have always fresh flowers before it. Now one more relic has been added — the candle which I held in my hand in the Russian church at the funeral service. I shall light it once a year, on the anniversary of her death."

An artist in California sent me a photograph of his studio, a part of which is given up to photographs of Pavlova and flowers. I have received many such photographs from New York, Berlin, Melbourne, etc. Two women in Chile, who for many years have had a strange, unworldly love for Pavlova, have arranged an altar where a photograph of her has been placed near a picture of the Virgin Mary. A woman in Holland had an addition built on to her house, so as to make in it an exact copy of Pavlova's bedroom, gathering in it everything that could in any way remind one of her.

By my whole turn of mind, I must number myself among the people of a positive type of thought. I am inclined to look sceptically on the rhapsodies of others. But, in the course of years, psychological reactions of this kind caused by Pavlova's personality and art occurred so constantly, that at last they became habitual. It is possible that the reason of this lay also in what Pavlova herself had lived through in these years. She had torn herself from Russia, to which she was passionately attached, in 1914; she had lived through the War and the death of friends and had felt deeply the tragedy of her country — the revolution. At first she allowed herself to be carried away by the ideas of liberty and equality, and the awakening of the people. For the attainment of such ideals she considered no sacrifice too great. But then came disillusionment. Nearly all the friends who had lived through the War, perished of privation during the years of revolution.

The vague melancholy and the equally vague longing for the "far-away", which was part of Pavlova's nature, grew acuter at such times of trial. As I was with her in all her travels and met the numbers of different people who wished to see her, it was my task to make their acquaintance and talk with them so as to find out what they wanted, saving her thereby from fatiguing visits and conversations; and also to read and answer their letters. And ever more and more often I heard the expression of a reverent adoration, which many thousands of people from all the ends of the world and of all nationalities laid before her as their tribute of gratitude for what she had given them. Many people have told me that from the day on which they first saw Pavlova dance, all that they later saw which was beautiful and pure blended in their minds with the thought of Pavlova. The beauty of nature, music or of works of art conjured up images of her. What were the means by which Pavlova implanted these emotions so deeply in the hearts of people that they remained there burning with the pure and gentle flame of love and happiness? Certainly not by her dances alone. They were only the beautiful forms in which her immaterial self manifested itself, penetrating into their souls like a breath of the divine.

Chopin believed in the divine origin of all artists of genius. He claimed that art was nothing else than the manifestation of the divine principle on earth and that therefore it was the greatest power in the world.

Someone else has said that the divine in man, though present in him in the form of "cosmic dust", is in some persons condensed into a "nugget". Was not the soul of Pavlova perhaps such a "nugget"?

Her teacher, Cecchetti, used to say:

"I can teach everything connected with dancing, but Pavlova has that which can only be taught by God."

Pavlova was religious in the best sense of the word. Accustomed as a child to go to the village church with her grandmother, and later, brought up in the Theatrical School where all the pupils went to church every

Sunday, she loved to attend Divine Service, especially in quiet churches conducive to peace and a reverential mood. She was especially fond of the Easter midnight service in the orthodox Church. No matter where we were, she always tried to attend this service and it has frequently happened that, quickly changing her dress after the performance, we would hurry across a whole town in order to be in time for the first "Christ is risen". She never liked to go to those churches which the congregation turns into a meeting place with their friends. Such disrespect for religion hurt her deeply. She was also hurt by sermons on political matters. She looked upon this as so contrary to the true meaning of religion, that at one time she even gave up going to church at all on that account.

For her favourite old church in the Theatrical School she ever preserved a special tenderness, and each time that she found herself in St. Petersburg, she went through her preparation for the Sacrament in it. Once, when in the church, she noticed that the carpet leading up to the altar was worn and she decided to work a new one. But its dimensions proved larger than she had thought and the task she had undertaken seemed gigantic. Pavlova, however, gave up every free hour to this labour of love, embroidering many hours every day in railway carriages during our daily journeys in America. And yet, in spite of all her diligence, the work did not progress with sufficient speed, as she wished to finish the carpet by her return to St. Petersburg. Nevertheless it was finished in time with the help of the dancers of the company, who considered it an honour to take part in this task, and Pavlova brought it to St. Petersburg and herself placed it before the altar. It would be interesting to know what has since become of it.

Her faith in the Divinity she identified with her unusual love for nature. In nature and in her own life Pavlova saw the manifestations of the Divine in various forms. Her religious feeling manifested itself also in her dancing. She showed an example of this in the ballet from Gluck's opera "Orpheus", where as Eurydice, clad in a Grecian tunic with a light-grey veil, of which the ends were held up by four girls, she moved forward slowly, with bowed head, occasionally pausing as if in an ecstasy of prayer.

Another moment of profound emotion which she made the audience share, is to be found in "Giselle", when she appeared holding a white lily and, scarcely touching the floor, glided across the stage with an expression on her face that made the audience hold its breath for it seemed as if an angel had come to announce the birth of a Messiah to our unhappy world.

It is remarkable that this spirituality of Pavlova's dances was also felt by ministers of the church. When we first arrived in one of the big towns of South America where the Catholic religion is particularly strong, one of the well-known priests told his flock when Pavlova and her company were about to arrive that he knew nothing about the nature of the performances to be given and did not advise anybody to go until he had himself seen one. A few days later, he ended his customary sermon by saying:

"I allow you to go to the performances of Pavlova. I have seen her; she is worthy to dance before the altar."

After Pavlova's death, a symposium in her honour was held in the church of St. Mark-in-the-Bowery, in New York. The famous American dancer, Ruth St. Denis, said in her speech that an artist such as Pavlova lived on the threshold of heaven and earth as an interpreter of the ways of God. The rector of the church, the Rev. William Norman Guthrie, declared that it was only such an expression of religious experience as Pavlova gave in her art that would bring back the old-time vitality to religion.

But the most remarkable acknowledgement of the spiritual beauty of Pavlova's art was made in the speech of the Orthodox Bishop Tikhon at the memorial service for her in Berlin, held at the Russian Church there on the 24th January, 1931. Here are his words:

"In the name of the Father, the Son and the Holy Ghost.

We are gathered here, beloved brethren and sisters, by the untimely death of the world-famous Russian ballet-dancer, Anna Pavlova, the servant of God, to send up our fervent prayers for her to the Throne of the Most-High.

Every time when prayers for the dead are read here for an artist of the theatre, and particularly of the ballet, a feeling of doubt and perplexity assails the devout. On the one hand, we know of the disapproval of the canons of the Church of the theatre, and on the other there is a widely spread belief that the Orthodox Church is inimical to the human body and to all earthly pleasures. It is said that Orthodoxy inculcates the merciless warfare of man against his body, an extreme, fanatical asceticism, a subjugation of the flesh, and recognises the right of life and development in the soul alone.

It is in refutation of this error that I should like to say a few words of the deceased b a l l e r i n a, Anna, the servant of God.

No single religion, no single system of philosophy preaches such a lofty doctrine about the human body as the Orthodox Church. The human body, it teaches us, is the most perfect organism coming from the hands of the Creator, the crown, the marvellous flower of all visible nature, so fine a form of matter, that it indissolubly merges into the thinking, free and immortal spirit, into the higher world of the soul and contains in it a spark of the Holy Ghost. "Know ye not that your body is the temple of the Holy Ghost which is in you?" (I Cor. 6 v. 19), "The members of Christ" (v. 15). What in this visible world can be higher than the spiritualized temple of the Holy Ghost, or the members of the body of Christ Himself, the Son of God?

But such a lofty doctrine of the human body requires a correspondingly elevated conduct in respect to it. "The body is not for fornication," says the same apostle, "but for the Lord" (I Cor. 6 v. 13). "Shall I then take the members of Christ and make them the members of an harlot? God forbid." (I Cor. 6 v. 15).

A man must work for the Lord, then, with his body, serve to the glory of God. "Therefore glorify God in your body and in your spirit, which are God's", says the holy apostle Paul.

But how is one to look upon the disapproval of the Church canons for the theatre and theatrical dances? For, after all, the deceased was a ballerina.

But if the body is given us for the glorification of God, as we have seen, so also can the dance as being a form of the body's existence be made, and should be made, to lead in the same direction. It is an expression of the emotions of the spirit, of thoughts, feelings and moods, and in accordance with the nature of these thoughts, feelings and moods can serve God. For is the dance not compatible with prayer? We know from the Bible that at the triumphal transportation of the Ark of the Covenant the king and prophet David leaped and danced in religious ecstasy.

Even in the Divine Services of the Orthodox Church religious dances are possible. The Abyssinian Orthodox Church, cut off from other churches from the first centuries of the Christian era, developed its ritual of service independently and has given a place in it to religious dances. And even in our Easter service, does one not feel it almost a religious dance when our priests, dressed in vivid, many-coloured robes, and to the joyous singing of the Easter hymn, quickly, almost at a running pace, go in turns round the church with a censer greeting the congregation with "Christ is risen?" The whole of this service is full of rhythmic movements that remind one of dance. And the solemn services of the archbishop with numerous priests, deacons, sub-deacons, candlebearers, wandbearers, etc. each of whom in the solemn pacing performs severely defined movements and routes. Does this not remind one of a religious dance? In verity are the words of the apostle thus obeyed "Glorify God in your bodies, which are God's."

Rhythm, dance, therefore, like verse, is one of the natural ways of artistically expressing our feelings, thoughts and moods. Consequently the dance of a true artist is his form of service to beauty. And as true, absolute beauty is God, the dance, therefore, can serve God. And the service to God, as absolute beauty, is so high and so fruitful, that our writer, F. M. Dostojevsky, says in a prophetic ecstasy before beauty: "Beauty will save the world." And in truth, what lofty and noble feelings, thoughts and moods can be called up in the spectator by a true artist-dancer in a beautiful and dignified dance! And what a high spiritual enjoyment can such a dance be for the spectator. It transports him out of this vale of tears and vanity to the high heavens, to eternal beauty, to God.

Such talent of a great artist "by the grace of God" was given to the deceased servant of God, Anna; and to it, to this gift of God, she gave up her beautiful life; towards this eternal beauty she called her spectators. And as an artist cannot summon up emotions and moods that he is not himself living through, there can be not doubt that the deceased herself lived chiefly in the atmosphere of these lofty feelings, thoughts and moods, striving to forget this vale of misery and reaching after the eternal beauty of heavenly life. And that this was so, many traits of her private life bear witness. Who is there who does not know her boundless love and sympathy for the poor, the suffering? How many children, chiefly orphans, were educated at her cost? What queues of petitioners were at her door and none left without help! What nobility, elegance and charity surrounded her! Verily hers was a pure soul reaching after heaven with such strength that even her body in those marvellous dances, dances in the service of beauty, seemed to spurn the earth in its flight to God, drawing her spectators with her.

Let us, therefore, send up our earnest prayers for her to the Throne of Beauty Eternal and Absolute, and may the Lord have mercy on her for sins voluntary and involuntary, for "no man liveth and sins not", and may He give her rest in His realm of Eternal Beauty. He endowed her on earth with a great talent. Not one talent he gave her, but five talents, and she has not buried them in the ground, but multiplied them. To her may there be spoken the words of the Merciful Lord to the good servant who, when giving an account of his stewardship, reported that to the five talents he had received he had added another five by his labours: "Well done, thou good and faithful servant; thou hast been faithful over a few things, I will make thee ruler over many things; enter thou into the joy of thy Lord." (Math. 26 v. 21). Amen."

SUPPLEMENT.

SUPPLEMENT.

1. Theatrical Museums.

2. Extracts from the Press of Different Countries.

3. Extracts from Letters
   (received by the Author after Madame Pavlova's Death.)

4. Anna Pavlova's Repertoire at the Imperial Theatres St. Petersbourg.

5. Anna Pavlova's Repertoire Abroad.

THEATRICAL MUSEUMS.

The majority of cultured people are interested in theatrical artists and nearly every member of an audience has a favourite singer, musician or actor. Very often the name of some great performer is connected with a cherished memory of youth, and yet how very little, one might say practically nothing, is done to preserve for posterity the memory of those who often devote the whole of their lives to the art they serve.

The best way of preserving the memory of stage artists is by the establishment of theatrical museums, in which may be gathered portraits and photographs of the artist in various rôles, their costumes, and the literary material such as criticisms, memoirs, articles by their contemporaries, books of critical analysis, etc. It is only under these conditions that it is possible to re-create in one's mind the figure of the actor, to understand wherein lay his gifts, or what were his interpretations of the parts he took. It is quite impossible even for the most talented of historians to re-create some far-away figure from fragmentary, scattered or accidental material, which he can only trace with great trouble in theatrical or private collections.

The difficulties encountered by the well-known critic, André Levinson, in compiling his book on Taglioni confirm this. One would have thought that considering the immense popularity of Taglioni, who only died in 1884, it would not be difficult to collect material about her. As a matter of fact, it has been discovered that there is nothing about her in the museums, and though some portraits of her are in existence, it is very difficult to re-create even her physical likeness.

The best theatrical museum that I have seen is that in Moscow founded and arranged by A. Bakhrushin, a wealthy man sincerely devoted to the theatre. To this museum he gave up the lower storey of his house and in it he collected with tireless zeal everything he could find in any way connected with the theatre. His scheme at first met with indifference, but little by little both the public and the artists grew to understand the importance of what he had started, and from that time onward he was constantly receiving relics of all kinds. Some of these he bought, but the majority were given to the museum. When I last saw this museum, it truly amazed one by the number and diversity of the objects it contained, although the whole collection was made in the course of only about twenty years. Under the Bolsheviks, Bakhruskin's house has been nationalised and he himself has been given the post of keeper in his own museum.

The best theatrical museum in Western Europe, as far as I know, is the one attached to "La Scala" Theatre in Milan. Several rooms leading out of the foyer of the theatre, are devoted to it, so that the public can visit it during intervals between the acts. It is very well arranged, all the objects are conveniently disposed and the catalogue is excellently compiled. This museum consists of an extensive collection of objects connected with the art of the stage in all its forms. There is also a library in connection with it. There are two museums in Paris one attached to the Grand Opera and the other to the Comédie Française, there are also small collections in some cities as well as the private collections of connaisseurs, but of real museums there are hardly any. Last year the well known amateur of the art of the dance Rolf de Maré has founded in Paris an institution bearing the name of "Les archives de la Dance" and has built for that purpose a beautiful house. The aim of this institution is the organisation of a library, an archive and the collection of various materials relating to the art of the dance. It is further proposed to organise conferences on ballet and Demonstrations of the dances.

A great deal of material dealing with Pavlova has remained: albums, critical articles in all languages, programmes of performances, collections of illustrations, photographs, addresses, medals, presentations, etc. There is also her large theatrical wardrobe, head-dresses, tights, shoes and various small ornaments — all this would make quite an extensive catalogue. I should, of course, like to give all this to a Russian theatrical museum, but have decided meanwhile to give the objects which, because of their memories, are the most valuable, to the London Museum, which is intending to form a theatrical section.

The photograph of the glass case, in which all the articles I have given have been placed, gives an idea how everything has been arranged. This glass case contains a "Swan" costume, the costume worn in "Christmas", a Russian costume made to the design of Bilibin, her dancing shoes, her tights, her head-dresses and ornaments, a mirror, a make-up box and all the trifles that invariably accompanied her on her travels. I have been told in the museum that this glass case has increased the number of visitors who take a great interest in and closely examine these relics that are so precious to many.

La Scala Theatre Museum has asked me for a few small articles and the newly formed museum in San Francisco for others. This latter wants to have a room dedicated to Pavlova's name.

Some years ago Pavlova received a charming letter from a lady in London who told her that she was a pupil of Taglioni's who had been a friend of her grandmother's and a frequent visitor at their house. Taglioni had long given up the stage by that time, and had a school in London. During the years of Taglioni's friendship with this family, this lady had managed to collect a good many letters and engravings of the famous dancer, and when Taglioni left London for Marseilles, she had given her pupil several objects, which she had since treasured. This lady had never seen Taglioni on the stage, and only on seeing Pavlova had she realised that Taglioni must have danced just as wonderfully.

We made her acquaintance and she proved to be a very interesting and cultured woman and told us a great deal about the great b a l l e r i n a. Two years ago she wrote to Pavlova that she had decided to make her a present of all the relics in her possession — artificial flowers, a spray of b o u l e s d e n e i g e from Taglioni's skirts, a small p o r t e - b o u q u e t that she carried about with her, a pair of black ballet shoes, which she wore during the lessons, a p a p i e r m a c h é form for wigs, which she took about with her everywhere, several letters and a questionnaire filled up by the celebrated b a l l e r i n a herself.

All these things are in my possession and will perhaps find their way some day into a museum.

Relics in museums, portraits and literary material collected in libraries, are very valuable, one might say indispensable, for the future historian. But the activity of the dead artist's friends and admirers in supporting and developing his beloved art, is what makes his memory a living one.

In this connection, the aims of the Anna Pavlova Society, founded in Berlin after her death, are very interesting. (Anna Pavlova Vereinigung E. V., Eisenacher Str. 36, Berlin.) They are as follows:

1. Taking as their motto the name of Anna Pavlova, to aid in the development of cultural attainments in the realm of the dance.
2. To found a centre for a joint service to the art of the dance, in practice as well as in theory.
3. To encourage the development of youthful talent.

Having taken the name of Anna Pavlova, the society has as its sole object the desire to keep the art of dancing at a high level, and its statutes forbid any kind of commercial or political interests.

On the anniversary of Pavlova's death the society intends to arrange annually, in her memory, a private or a public performance.

In order to create a central institution for service to the art, the society has in view the organising of soirées and performances, in order to acquaint the public with little-known dancers of various nationalities.

In addition to performances, the society intends to arrange lectures and debates. Very animated was the evening arranged a short while ago in the auditorium of the State Art Library in Berlin and devoted to questions of stage dancing in connection with German modernist dancing, which was seriously criticised.

For the coming season the society is to organise something in the nature of a faculty of dance for pupils of all schools and for anyone in the audience wishing for a fuller knowledge of the problems of the dance, and from October 1932 it is intended to institute regular lectures on the following subjects: Anatomy (Prof. Peshkovsky), the history of the Dance (Prof. Sachs), style and costume (Prof. Sheurich), the encyclopaedia of dance — general instruction — (Laban), the system of dance notation (Laban and Fischer), legal questions (Chaslinde, lecturer in the dance section of the Prussian Ministry of Public Instruction), the basic instruction of music (Schlee), the history of choreographists from Noverre until the present day (Levitan).

The goal which the society has in view — the encouragement of youthful talent — is at the present moment very difficult of attainment, for in order that the endeavour should not remain entirely platonic, money in necessary for premiums, for the organisation of competitions. etc. In this matter the society hopes that people will be found in various countries to support it.

It is my opinion, that for all dancers, irrespective of their aims or the school to which they belong, as well as for all those studying the dance, the existence of this society and its future success should be very desirable, not only because this is the first attempt to create an organisation with so wide a cultural programme, wholly dedicated to the problems of the dance. but also because, if dancing is to be recognised as a serious art, the consciousness of this fact must penetrate not only to dancers and pupils but also to the public.

I am well aware that the task the society has taken upon itself will require time and labour, but the founders' energy and love of their work, as well as the motto chosen, the name of Anna Pavlova, will succeed in accomplishing this highly useful, cultural work.

The Glass Case with Pavlova's relics in London Museum.

EXTRACTS FROM THE PRESS OF DIFFERENT COUNTRIES.

1. Australia . . . . The Telegraph, Brisbane
2. Belgium . . . . Nation Belge, Bruxelles
3. Canada . . . . S. Morgan-Powell, Montreal
4. Denmark . . . . Haagen Falkenfleth, Nationaltidende
5. ,, ... Anker Kirkeby, "Politiken", Copenhagen
6. England . . . . Alan Parsons, The Daily Mail, London
7. ,, ... The Referee, London
8. ,, ... Manchester Guardian, Manchester
9. France . . . . Maurice Brillant, Paris
10. ,, ... Emille d'Arnaville, Radio Adress, Paris
11. ,, ... Julie Sazonova, La revue Musicale, Paris
12. ,, ... Florian Delhorbe, Paris
13. Germany . . . . M. Charol, Börsenzeitung, Berlin
14. ,, ... Volkszeitung, Berlin
15. ,, ... Acht-Uhr-Abendblatt, Berlin
16. Holland . . . . Henri Borel, "Het Vaderland"
17. ,, ... W. Buning, De groene Amsterdammer
18. India . . . . The Bombay Herald
19. Russian Press . . . . André Levinson, "The Renaissance", Paris
20. ,, ,, ... J. S. Derniéres, Nouvelles, Paris
21. ,, ,, ... The Rul, Berlin
22. ,, ,, ... Piotr Pilsky, "To-Day", Riga
23. ,, ,, ... M. Fokine, "Novoe Russkoe Slovo", New York
24. ,, ,, ... G. Grebenchikov, "Novoe Russkoe Slovo", New York
25. ,, ,, ... M. Siegfried
26. ,, ,, ... M. Lubowski, Berlin

The Telegraph. Brisbane (Australia). 24. Jan. 1931.

.... The people of Brisbane were able to enjoy fully the experience that Pavlova provided — an experience in which were blended the highest satisfaction derivable from physical perception and the spiritual exaltation without which the lives of men would be as "earth's decaying leaves". The opportunity of rising above the commonplace through the influence of beautiful music is given to almost everyone; and the prominence of sculpture in the world of Art obtains for plastic masterpieces a growing appreciation; but the union of music and plastic, as was manifested by the genius of Pavlova, is a rare and lovely flower by the road of Time. The dancer's artistic greatness lay in her power of expressing her emotions through music and of expressing music through her emotions. Whether she was poised, her beautiful body vibrating with the tension of her balance, or moving, the embodiment of grace, across the stage, Pavlova was music made visible, and as such she brought ineffable gladness to those who find in many of the rhythms of modern ballroom dancing no more of the poetry of motion than existed in the crude movements that formed a great part of the language of primitive man. And just as all great sound music reflects the personality of the composer, so did the visible music of Pavlova reveal the warm sympathy and the creative strength of an inspired artist. Seeing Pavlova was like hearing a great symphony — the more performances one attended the more was beauty revealed and art glorified.

Nation Belge. Bruxelles. 23. 1. 1931.

.... How can one find words worthy of her? A French critic wrote of her recently that she was the Dancer and the Dance. It would be difficult to give a better description of the impression which each of her appearances created. Her technique had reached a point of perfection which defied all comparison. She identified herself with the art to which she had devoted her life. Her first steps upon the stage lifted us from the earth and led us into a hitherto unknown world wherein the laws of gravity fled before her all-conquering power, and we were borne to the very heights of thought and feeling. Those who did not see her in "Giselle" and the "Dying Swan" will never realise how precious is the memory of certain moments when the very march of Time seemed to be stayed to allow the realisation of an unearthly masterpiece.

She danced even as one breathes or sorrows or loves. Never, even in the midst of her most difficult feats of technique, did one have any sense of conscious effort. She seemed like a force of nature, an emanation from the breezes which blow across the plains and through the forests, a reflection of the sky and the waters imprisoned in a human form. Her dancing spoke to the heart the language of the heart, and when she disappeared after each dance it was as if we had suddenly been bereft of something essential, and we would applaud until our hands ached, to draw her back again to satisfy the insatiable longing which consumed us.

All through her life she was unaffected by the caprice of the moment. She remained faithful, without any compromise, to the classic conception of the dance which she had been brought up to reverence. Though Russian by birth and temperament, she knew the meaning of self-control. A romantic, yet she kept herself from all over-expression of emotion. In her all things met in such a state of harmony that it is no exaggeration to say that we were confronted by the sublime.

Anna Pavlova is dead. With her has vanished a source of deep emotion that we shall not find again.

S. Morgan-Powell. Montreal (Canada).

Once more Pavlova is here, with her ballet, to charm us by the magic of her incomparable art. There are other dancers of skill, not lacking inspiration, beauty, mastery of their chosen medium, and pantomimic powers. But there is only one Pavlova — there is only one dancer who can intoxicate the senses, and fire the imagination until one sees her as an ancient statue come to life, embodying all the grace and all the loveliness that Praxitiles and his like wrought in marble. Every movement that she makes is instinct with expression. She is the past mistress of rhythm utilized to give poetic expression to definite ideas.

When at the close of "Le Cygne" she flutters slowly to the ground, and after the last final quiver collapses, it is a stricked swan that has died before your very eyes, not a dancer posing as a swan. When, in the exquisite "Dionysus" ballet, she stretches out adoring arms to the impassive statue it is a vestal who is stirred by the flame of passion before the altar, not a choreographic artist presenting a calculating study. She lives the elusive, fleeting, irrecoverable moment. It passes swift as a swallow's flight, — passes and is gone, leaving behind a tremendously vivid picture of beauty caught and drawn to earth while a solitary lark sings. But you have had the moment and vision, and you would never willingly part with either.

I have seen her dance the "Swan" many times, but never, I believe, so exquisitely as she did at St. Denis last night. One of the chief charms of her art is that she never does anything twice in exactly the same way. Always there is some new beauty discoverable, some new and lovely light discernable some new and ineffable grace imprisoned for a moment in a pose. So in the "Swan" dance it seemed that she had never danced it just that way before. Assuredly it seized the imagination of her audience and drew from them, after the last faint note had died away, such a tempest of applause as rarely greets even a great artist here. But she would not do it again. She is too great an artiste for that.

Haagen Falkenfleth. Nationaltidende. Denmark. 23. 1. 1931.

.... Hers was an enchanting personality and it was this, perhaps, even more than her extraordinary virtuosity which enthralled the people of Europe, America, Australia, Japan, Java — every country in which she appeared. Because of the perfection of her technique, she could change, in her dance, to a figure of fairy tale, light as a bird, a spirit, a sylphide, a butterfly, a dragon-fly and then her famous Dying Swan in the mimed drama composed for her by her comrade of the Ballet School, Michel Fokine. But neither her wonderful lightness nor her extraordinary musical sense would have been enough so to enchant the most critical audiences of the whole world, if she had not imbued all her interpretations with that spiritual beauty which was like a reflection of a perfect soul. There was almost a religious ecstasy in her dancing and it is that which threw a spell over us and made one of her compatriots, looking at a picture of her, say,

"That is she whom the whole world loves."

Anker Kirkeby. "Politiken". Denmark.

The present generation considers it a great thing to have lived through the world war, but how much deeper an experience it is to have lived in the century of Anna Pavlova.

She was not only by far the greatest dancer of our time and after the death of Sarah Bernhardt and Duse, the greatest genius of the world stage, but choreographic experts maintain that she outshone both Fanny Essler and Marie Taglioni. The greatest conoisseur of the history of the ballet, André Levinson, once assured the writer of these lines that Anna Pavlova surpassed the greatest dancers of all time for the sole reason that choreography had never been so highly developed as in this age in which she reigned, the supreme queen of the dance.

It is true that she was technically perfect. Her body was sylph-like, but the slender fine limbs were taut as springs of steel. She had been brought up in the strict Russian school at the Imperial Theatre at Moscow, and during her twenty years of travelling there was no day on which she did not practise — in ever — changing theatres, hotels, railways, steamships. The expressiveness with which she endowed her art transformed her dancing into poetry. She was the inexplicable, the mystery, the eternal. How are we to express what dancing is, how are we to explain to later generations how she danced before our eyes, how radiantly she soared, exulted, despaired, fainted and was crushed, as for instance in the "Dying Swan"? Critics all over the world have attempted it, poets have attempted to form her soaring into rhyme and rhythm; but I know no better description of Anna Pavlova's dancing than that given by a little Norwegian girl when she saw her at Oslo for the first time: — "It is like dreaming something that will never happen." To us who are now alive the wonder actually happened, and now is no more. We who have seen Pavlova dance will never be able to forget it.

.... At the head of her admirers in our country was the prima ballerina assoluta of our ballet, Elna Lassen, who, with a deep reverence, presented Anna Pavlova on the stage with an enormous laurel wreath at her farewell performance when she received twenty seven calls. The last impression which she received of Copenhagen which really (and this is more than a mere phrase) was close to her heart, was from the Hans Christian Andersen festival in the City Hall where in the sunshine of an early spring day, in the midst of thousands of cheering children, she saw herself surrounded by a pageant of all the fairy-tales of that famous writer and was forced to a seat among them to drink chocolate with Thumbelina and the Emperor dressed in nothing but his shirt. When Pavlova bent over the little eight-year old Thumbelina at her side and asked the child, "Do you know who I am?" she unhesitatingly answered, "You are the greatest dancer in the world, Anna Pavlova". A tear shone in the eyes of the dancer, she bent over the child and kissed its brow. She understood that in this town she was not only known but loved.

It is true that we loved her, and it was well that she was told of it through the mouth of a little child. To a unique extent the world's greatest dancer had succeeded in enchanting Copenhagen with her art.....

Alan Parsons. Daily Mail. London. Jan. 1931.

"Whatever she touched she turned to beauty."

It was with a sense of almost personal loss that I read of the death of Pavlova. I seemed suddenly to live over once again a certain night in the Palace theatre some twenty years ago and to see it all as clearly and vividly as if it were yesterday. We had been sitting impatiently through a variety show, waiting only for the moment when her number should be shown on the board. At last it came and a strange hush fell on the house as Pavlova fluttered on in her "Swan" dance, seeming lighter and less substantial herself than a handful of swansdown. There was no applause — just an audible sigh of wonder and gratitude for a thing so essentially and elementally lovely. Even when the Swan's final flutter had died on the air there was a full minute's pause before the audience could recover from its trance.....

There are moments in the theatre when silence is a hundred times more eloquent than applause.

.... Whatever Pavlova touched she turned to beauty. I can think of no higher praise, no lovelier epitaph than this.

London Referee. Jan. 1931.

Anna Pavlova danced through life to achieve a beauty of rhythm which was the very perfection of human grace. From every great stage of the world she shed the light of her art and touched the most materialistic audiences with radiance.

.... To see Pavlova dancing was to partake in an art of passionate abandonment. The whole spirit of the gracious woman animated her every movement, and her face became a blind mask of ecstasy. Scholars hold that the dance was the first of the arts, and certainly the primal force of human creation was manifested in a dance by Pavlova. Like all great artist she was impersonal, a reed to transmit the music of the spirit, the embodiment of her creative ideal.....

To give so much pure joy as Pavlova gave to the world is to partake considerably in the sum of human good. Her devotion to her art must have brought an inner serenity to which the generality of men and women is a stranger. To deplore her death is to commiserate with the world for the loss of a thing of beauty, and to pay tribute to an art which was, in the last analysis, an expression of supreme unselfishness. It may be that the next few generations will not see the like of Anna Pavlova, but she has left behind her a lovely legend which will be handed down to them as an artistic heritage.

Manchester Guardian. Jan. 1931.

It is superfluous to set down the mere itinerary of a life that was a continual procession in the search for beauty and in its service. Wherever she went there were those who felt of her as the old Russian general did when she left St. Petersburg for the first time. "The best be with you," she said. "When you are taking away the best we have known?" he answered.

She was seen in Manchester not so often as one would have wished, and her last visit was in 1930. But the memory clearest in the mind of the present writer was of 1925, when she appeared with Novikoff at the Hippodrome. She was dancing a dance called "Dragon-fly" to music by Kreisler. Before your very eyes the wings flashed and flamed, the lithe body quivered, almost still, then darted on a new caprice. Tier on tier, the dim audience, with not a gap in its ranks, held its breath in bewitched silence. Suddenly in a corner at the back of the stage, Pavlova's foot slipped. Perhaps it would not have been noticed had it been anyone else. It was so small a slip — the ball of the foot seemed to slide along an excessively planed surface, for just the space of a heart beat out of control. Instantly throught the dim audience went a sound as though the wind had suddenly lifted the arms of spellbound trees. It was a sound of sheer surprise, forced out by the incredible. Pavlova's foot had slipped!

That afternoon we saw her, seized and held aloft by Novikoff, come down again to earth with such contact as a butterfly makes with a flower; we saw her body, like a stream over pebbles, a flux of beauty, never, except for its beauty, the same for two moments. We heard her cheered again and again; but the gasp of surprise from a thousand rigid throats was the afternoon's true laurel — the most significant tribute we ever laid before the incomparable art of Anna Pavlova.

Maurice Brilliant. Paris.

Not one member of her former audiences, had he only seen one of her radiant appearances upon the stage, could have helped feeling a sense of personal grief at the sudden premature death of this dancer who possessed something greater even than genius, who transformed the vigorous discipline of the classic dance, already so beautiful and etherial in itself, into an art most profoundly human and at the same time glorified by its spirituality. This marvellous union, which has never been equalled, as André Levinson has so aptly noted, consisted of a perfect technique, a body which was the ideal of the ballet school and predestined for its service, a spirit which animated and illuminated her body and a soul which made a glory of her least gesture. She did not try to dazzle or astonish with feats of brilliant technique but the harmonious beauty of her dance revealed itself to the most casual spectator and enthralled those least capable of analysing the pleasure they received.

We know that, famous already in Russia, as soon as she appeared in the first Diaghilev ballets at Châtelet she gained universal fame. However, she did not stay long in that famous company for her soul was filled with a desire to travel the world over, and with the company which she had formed, she the high priestess of Terpsichore, revealed in every country her ephemeral master-pieces and gave new birth to the old for she had a mission to reveal these to mankind.....

.... Alas this lovely spiritual being is no longer with us. When we saw her less than a year ago who could have believed that this precious light would be put out so soon by a pitiless fate.

I shall always hold sacred the memory of that last spring when I had the honour of meeting her, She was an exceedingly charming woman 'and if it ware not necessary to speak of her art, I should love to talk of the great heart of this artist and her wise inexhaustible charity.

Her art was entirely classic in the deepest sens of the word. Never was anything seen more clearly and strikingly filled with the ideal of perfection — living perfection — than certain of Anna Pavlova's steps and above all the development of her marvellous arabesques. She will leave in history the same radiant memory as Taglioni. Levinson who understands the dance better than anybody, who had a marvellous insight into the art of Pavlova, and has spoken of it beautifully, dedicated to her his book on Marie Taglioni in this manner, "To Madame Anna Pavlova, the dancer in whom for our enchantment, the genius of Marie Taglioni lives again." Later he says, "She is without question the greatest dancer of our time — perhaps of all time." — It is not I who will contradict him.

An extract from a memorial adress given from Radio Station L-L in Paris on the 30th of January 1931.

Emile d'Arnaville. Paris.

"Anna Pavlova who was known over the whole world and loved as much as she was admired, is no longer of this world over which she threw an immeasurable enchantment, but she has left a radiant dazzling memory which will not easily fade.

She, the greatest, the most noble dancer of our time, often passed through Paris — somewhat like a shooting star — between two voyages from West to East there to have set more firmly upon her pale brow the crown which proclaimed her queen over millions of subjects, a crown which had been offered to her by lovers of the choreographic art and which no one was ever able to take from her.....

.... This evening it is not the life of Anna Pavlova — that life so entirely devoted to art and the creation of beauty — that I wish to call to mind, nor shall I speak of the boundless charity of this artist, a trait which showed her full of loving kindness and nobility.

No, this evening, if you will allow me, I wish to say one simple farewell, to fling it far and wide above the city and across the world, in the name of all those who admired her, and this farewell will be like a flower thrown out into the void to seek the winged soul of the dancer who was herself the flower of the world. Let our homage to her be quietly paid, and secretly be accompanied by a prayer for the peace of her faithfuf soul, which lives now more radiantly freed from its delicate covering, from that body so fragile, graceful and supple, so aristocratic of line, so characteristic of her race, so full of movement that one cannot imagine it lying still and cold in death, when once it was movement personified. ....

Wishing one day to make an incarnation of Beauty, God created Anna Pavlova and said to her quietly, "You will dance. Here are your wings which no one will ever see. Now, fly to earth."

"Lord, I am Thy servant", said Anna Pavlova obediently as she tried her first step. And behold it was a miracle, for even now she had nothing at all to learn. Even the butterflies were shamed as they watched her.

Poets and musicians of genius, tuning their lyres, quickly strove to serve her. Imagination and music united to accompany each gesture of this divine creature in whose smile lay such beauty.

O, dreamer, see, Anna Pavlova has taken her position. —

This was the moment when the painters and sculptors came to her. Each one believed that the beautiful adventure of Pygmalion had happened again, such was the allue of the least movement of this wonderfyl being and to such admiration were they moved by the perfection of her line. Galatea had come to life again for their enchantment.

For a breath Anna Pavlova held her pose. ....

Now physicians and doctors stared in amazement at this unearthly being who could play with the laws of equilibrium, who cared nothing for the force of gravity. For a long time they watched this goddess poised beautifully upon her toes as though she were preparing to leave the earth and with one movement lift herself to the very sky.

Anna Pavlova smiled.

Then the crowd drew near, folowing the elite, the people whose desire to feast their eyes, upon beauty in silence and stillness, without any effort of thought, she understood so perfectly.

Then Anna Pavlova danced.

A clamour arose from the amazed enchanted people. This anonymous crowd with its unknown longings, its endless conflicting ideas, had suddenly become united in unaffected joy.

Trembling, glowing, overjoyed they greeted the appearance of the dancer who trembled even as they did, filled with the ardour of sublime passion, which is all too often checked and suppressed. They had now a new idol, an idol of flesh and blood, whose every movement created beauty.

Because of her fervent love of her art Anna Pavlova experienced every triumph. Her beauty accomplished the miracle for which God had chosen her.

She alone united in the same outstretching towards the ideal those who longed to find it again, those who were drifting away from it, those whose hearts were full of song, those who wept, wise men and foolish, the powerful and those whom fate had flung aside, the bourgeoisie, the artists, those who passed by, those who talked, those who thought, and those who loved or would be loved.

Lightly she touched, but never betrayed, our most secret thoughts. In a gesture, a step, an attitude, a smile, a glance, she could show all the joys, all the sorrows of life, and watching her dance, we forgot the three-fold troublous mystery of Life, Love and Death.

Wishing one day to make an incarnation of Beauty, God created you, o Anna Pavlova, You whom, alas, we shall not see again. You whom we shall see forever.....

Florian Delhorbe. France.

There are times when a dancer is inspired and among all dancers there are those who shine more brilliantly than others. But Pavlova is the Dance itself. Upon the stage she becomes transformed. She is no longer free. She is not a woman of the earth as she was even a moment ago, as are those still who surround her. They are people of flesh and blood, she is an aerial being. When at the grave-side she portrays the soul of Giselle, she ceases to be of the earth and becomes a spirit. When we see her uplifted by her partner she seems to swoon and die. Her gestures continue beyond reach, grow and impress themselves upon the mind as sounds when they die away into the distance. She is rhythm made visible. Vibrating in every fibre of her being, yet she is a magical harmony.

She has made of her body a perfect and beautiful instrument. Though her legs and exquisite feet seem fragile, yet she is lightness with muscles of steel. For her every technical difficulty becomes a happy game. When she leaps she makes no effort to lift herself from the ground, but rather is she drawn into the air as a little doll may be lifted by a thread, or as in Hans Anderson's fairy tales, the little paper dancer is whirled across the room by a breath of air.

Because she has become complete master of technique she is able to abandon herself completely to the emotion of the moment. She is entirely beneath its sway, she forgets herself and her public and a smile which comes from her soul, lights her face. She forgets herself that she may express her innermost thoughts.

She has come from the midst of the people of Russia, she is the East itself, without its heavy sensuality. See her in a minuet or gavotte, she is a coquette to her finger-tips. Now she is a little statue made in porcelain, now a Bacchante, now a dragon-fly and we hear the sound of its quivering wings, now a swan in the twilight beating its wings in agony upon the blue waters — ah, what a long sigh of repressed emotion whispers through the audience. Every feeling which can be sung in music finds expression in her.

Because she has conquered her art she is its sovereign, and from her it comes to birth afresh. She has the air of inventing every step of an old ballet. Before she appears there is a sense of expectancy, when she comes she alone possesses the stage, and going she leaves a void behind her. She makes us love Russia, and awakens our desire for perfection.

Julie Sazonova. La Revue Musicale. Paris.

.... She was one of those happy geniuses who, while they hold us enthralled with their own personal gifts, are at the same time representative of an epoch of art. .... Those who confuse the dancing of this school with its technique, who count with satisfaction the number of fouettés exeduted by a dancer, who believe that the b a l l o n , the p o i n t e s d ' a c i e r , and the ease with which a dancer surmounts technical difficulties, constitute the whole art of dancing, would realise their mistake when they saw the simple etherial grace of Anna Pavlova. With her, technique took its proper place, it was a means, not an end.
.... In her art it played the same role which the rules of versification play in Dante's Divine Comedy.

The latin flower of classic dance, transplanted to Russia in the 18th century came to fullness in the art of Anna Pavlova. Just as Racine illustrated and crowned the work of his predecessors, so Anna Pavlova was the incarnation of the highest ideals of the creators of the Russian ballet, from whom, through almost two centuries of work and thought, she has essentially descended. Her art — entirely individual as it was — showed the result of the long road which had been traversed by millions of little winged feet of unknown dancers...

.... The young Anna Pavlova, then in the very flower of life, won admiration on all sides. She was the crown of all dreams, and in her the contending parties in the Ballet School could see a solution. Being outside all contentions and disagreements, belonging to no party, she represented at the same time a proof of what had been best in the past, and a hope for the future ....

Pavlova was the very essence of lightness, but more than that, she gave a new beauty to the t e r r e à t e r r e dance. Her almost superhuman p o i n t e d ' a c i e r never revealed any physical effort, nor did she suffer from that over development of the muscles common to dancers. All forms of the dance were equally familiar to her. She could be of heaven or of earth, she could sparkle with coquettish joy, she could show us a being pierced to the heart with mortal sorrow; within her were all the multiple elements of the classic dance.

Not only could she fly into the air as if her body were composed of aetherial atoms and scorned the earth, but there were moments when she knew how to fill this transparent matter with all the sadness and bitterness of the law of gravity, and then what an expression of tragedy was hers as her body was forced back to the earth by the unconquerable power of mortality and death. For her, to fly was life itself, to be chained to the earth, death.

.... To future generations she will be a legend, an example of what the plastic art can attain. To ensure that the art of choreography wile live one will only need to evoque her name at every difficult moment in the evolution of the ballet.

But for those of us who saw her, the tragedy of our loss is too poignant for us to find consolation in memories. Like the lover of Giselle we long to touch the now intangible shade, to rejoice in the living warmth of her art, to see again the wonderful ligth of her eyes, to hold her image which is fleeting from us. But where are the words which will stay her flight?

Reading that brief notice, "Anna Pavlova is dead." one had almost the physical sensation of seeing a light extinguished. Our world has become a grayer, sadder place.

Anna Pavlova is dead.

When we say her name which only lately filled us with such happiness and has now become a symbol of sadness and loss, we do not think of the little childlike body which has gone back to the dust from which it came and against which it battled so victoriously all through life, but rather of the images freed from Time and Death which her mortel body created and which live, triumphant forever, through her genius.

M. Charol. Börsenzeitung. Berlin.

....Pavlova is the highest expression of an art of dancing, which is not ours, which belongs to the centuries gone by, but which through its ideal perfection, is beyond the reach of time and will outlive all schools and all styles of dancing. Those to whom the ballet no longer makes an appeal, who regard this school of dancing as artificial or meaningless or think that it has been outlived — all those should see Pavlova, and then will be as fascinated and uplifted as was the crowded house at the Kroll last Sunday.

....It did not matter what she danced because the highest in the art of dancing is only a foundation with Pavlova, a means by which to attain what she wants to express. What did matter was the finished perfection of every movement, of every step, of every gesture, beautiful and noble, even in the most rapid changes, and to the very end, controlled throughout by a strong power which enables her to give expression to her ideas and emotions.

VOLKSZEITUNG (Berlin).

The Russian miracle is once more with us. Motorcar after motorcar draws up before the „Des Westens" Theatre. The whole of elegant Berlin, fills the stall and boxes.

The ballet, which attained its bloom in the time of the Tsars, was formally the monopoly of the privileged ten thousand. The art of Anna Pavlova has freed it from rule, social boundaries and mapped-out directions, it has destroyed all class-distinctions, charming all equally by its magically alluring atmosphere.

When the curtain went up uncovering to the eyes of the spectator a vision of a slender, infinitely graceful being, bathed in the light of a searchlight, everything was forgotten. At the sight of this fairy-like lightness, liberated from anything that is earthly, this amazing certainty, which has roused the enthusiasm of the peoples of the whole globe during the last two decades, one sits spell-bound.

We must make a confession — we thought that the culminating point in the art of even such an exceptional woman must sooner or later be reached. But Pavlova is better, more wonderful than ever.

Since the days of Laban, Wigman and Palucka we have lost the habit of the old forms of classical ballet. But Pavlova is superior to all technique, above al forms; she is a great, spellbinding artist; a creation of movements, of aromatic fluctuations freed from all physical laws, from the weight of earthly matter; a miracle, the limit of which she reaches in the inimitable tragic beauty of "The Dying Swan".

ACHT-UHR-ABENDBLATT (Berlin).

There are people who say: "Pavlova, her art is of course very fine, but it does not touch us, it is not modern." Such people are as much in the right as one who should say: "A chamois, certainly very beautiful, but it does not suit our time. The leap of a gazelle, the flight of a bird, the sun, the sky, Mozart, Cupid, Psyche, Renoir — all are beautiful, but not modern." One is tempted to ask, "And what does this 'modern' look like?" I confess I prefer not to see it.

Anna Pavlova comes on the stage and everything is forgotten. That is the summit of the art of the dance. All comparison with Pavlova is ridiculous. Any one who carelessly compares his idols with her kills them.

It is doubtful if the spirit of genius will ever be manifested with such clearness, with such exceptional mastery of technique, as in Pavlova. Her dance is the perfection of technique and at the same time the victory of genius over technique.

There is nothing that is not in her power.....

Where everything else comes to an end, begins, the rising of her star. She is the last solitary star of a departing world.... and so infinitely beautiful that one is inclined to be sceptical of the coming worlds.

Henry Borel. "Het Vaderland".

The luminous star has shifted in a glorious orbit.... The Swan is dead now, never to rise again in beauty. The slender flower lies broken...

An epoch of the dance is closed with her, that of the ballet, which without her would have been declining already. It is true we still have great dancers of the classical ballet, which has still some time to live, but the most beautiful supreme expression of it departed with Pavlova.

Her life in this sober, business-like, matter-of-fact world, was a fairy tale. As a "danseuse noble" she glittered in the old St. Petersburg of the Tsars, when the ballet there was still Imperial, she witnessed its downfall, and, far from her country, she went roaming about the world to ravish it with the beauty of her dancing elevated above all technique. It is only a short time ago since I wrote about her. I cannot find new words to match the unutterable beauty of this Apsara from Indra's paradise. I am thinking of all that is pure and brilliant and serene — of flowers, of swans, of bending reeds, of waving cornstalks, of rocking butterflies, of twinkling stars, of fluttering dragon-flies, of gleaming snowflakes, of moonbeams dancing on rippling water, of diaphanous elves — when I think of Anna Pavlova.

.... So long as the dance remains an art, so long as rhythm and measure and melody can seize a human being to dance his raptures and anguish in beauty, so long will Anna Pavlova live, she who has not died, because beauty is immortal.

W. Bunning. "De groene Amsterdammer".

....The realisation of the loss, the appreciation of this sublime dream, which with Pavlova lost its embodiment, was consciously or unconsciously, felt by everyone who had the art of dancing at heart. An art perished with her, her art: the world of the dance remains in bloom, but the heaven of the dance has become empty.

....Through....the truly great artist the world becomes brighter and nobler. His departure is a vanishing of light, a darkening of the world, an augmentation of the incomprehensible. When Pavlova danced it was one of the ideals of humanity dancing; humanity disembodied, enraptured, inspired and harmonious. To her the dance was a religion, a true world-accepted, world-surpassing religion. She ennobled the world of the dance and made it the true world; she restored heaven.

All this was lost with her and its loss was realised. This realisation rises above all schools, above art and the dance; they are mere means, changing and inconstant, to embody for us and to display what she embodied and made visible to us; dancing humanity in its noblest form, of old related to the gods.

We shall miss in future, as in the case of every great artist, the standard to measure the growth of all that is smaller, we shall miss an example in which humanity saw itself lifted to the ideal.

An Indian Poona Dancer. "Bombay Herald".

"I never, in all my dreams, imagined that there was a person in this world who could dance like that. Her limbs are as soft and as supple as velvet. She can do just what she likes with them, as well as with the hearts of her audience.....

When the curtain fell for the last time I left the theatre thoroughly agreeing with a certain Frenchman, who, when mentioning three people as the greatest dancers in the world, and being asked, "But what of Anna Pavlova?" replied, "La Pavlova! She is not of this world! She is on a plane all by herself!"

André Levinson. The Renaissance, Jan. 1931. Paris.

The Lyric of Pavlova.

The dear ashes have not yet been deposited in a foreign land when I write these lines. Like a light Elysian shade the image of Anna Pavlova is still hovering over us before departing forever. For those whom her dances enchanted the time has not yet come for a passionless appraisal, while for those who had the happiness of knowing her personally it is difficult to forget our sorrow. I see sincere grief all round. But are there many who have even an inkling of what we have lost? "Heavens, how strange, Russia without Pushkin," wrote Gogol when he heard of the poet's death. Heavens, how strange, the stage without Pavlova. Everyone knows and is able to understand that a celebrated Russian dancer, whose fame resounded the world over, whose name even life was wrapped in legend, is no more. We were proud of this fame, but all that there is of the vain and perishable in theatrical success and the applause of the crowd, screened from us at times the other, the higher nature of her artistic mission. The incomparable external grace and the brilliant craftsmanship of a classical dancer are concepts too narrow, too superficial, to contain the glad tidings of her art.

Pavlova is, "an exceptional, perhaps unique manifestation of the Russian spirit." I well remember and have carefully considered by whom these words were said and about whom. But the priest at the funeral service, after all, had the courage to quote the words of another great poet, that "the world will be saved by beauty". And never have we felt so strongly, as when we were in the church amid the funeral grief that, "that touch of other worlds" of which Dostoievsky never tired of speaking, was clearly manifested in the dancing of Pavlova.

.... She was taken from us suddenly, and yet the angel of death has constantly accompanied her in her triumphs and in her travels for twenty three years. I can well remember the Christmas concert of the 27th of December 1907 in the Hall of the Nobility (in St. Petersburg) when first she danced the "Dying Swan" arranged by Fokine to one of the pieces of the suite of Saint-Saëns. Always and everywhere audiences demanded this dance, that they might feel to the depth its lofty melancholy. For the audiences of the whole world the living face of the artist was identified with the symbol of the wounded bird. And every evening therefore, Pavlova, smitten by an invisible arrow drooping her poor pale brow with its head-dress of feathers, and her slender frame, her nerveless arms crossed on her outstretched leg, prepared to receive death in a pose so full of inexpressible beauty that the most indifferent, most turbulent hall, grew silent in sorrowful adoration. And from San Francisco to Sydney, from Java to the Argentine Pampas every person, planter and Samurai, a London dandy or a cowboy, felt equally, even if he did not understand, the tragedy of the imprisoned soul in the earthly envelope, yearning for the heavens and yet unable to make the upward effort. And now the wings have beaten for the last time and they have opened. The white swan has vanished from view. Let no one in future dare to attempt this wordless poem, with which for us is merged the memory of Pavlova. It is a shrine of beauty and must not be touched.

.... She felt, or thought herself primarily a ballerina, a classical dancer. But nothing was more foreign to her than academic correctness. The ordered system of this dance of pure reason with its strict statutes, its algebraically checked harmony, she filled with such a fire of life, such ardour of fancy, such flights of imagination, that every dance of hers gave the impression of being impromptu. It would be impossible to be more alive in this most abstract of styles or more original within the limits set by the school. In moments of tempestuous ardour she seemed to tear the "canon" of conventional beauty from her inner self and in moments of gentle calm she illumined it with an inner light. Thus, it was possible to be amazed at Pavlova, but vain to try and imitate her. There was only one Pavlova, there is no other — and never will be.

Dernières Nouvelles. Paris. Jan. 24th. 1931.

J. S.

.... She was undoubtedly the world's greatest dancer. No one ever disputed the crown with her from the moment when, as a seven year old girl she stepped over the threshold of the majestic building of the St. Petersburg Imperial Ballet School, which occupies most of Theatre Street. None ever doubted that she was the incarnation of all that for centuries had been collected in the magic word "ballet". In her the classical school produced its finest, never-to-be-repeated flower. Love, enthusiasm, adoration, followed her everywhere. When her dances were criticised they were compared to others which she executed, for there could have been no other comparison. Anna Pavlova was outside school, outside theoretical arguments. She was equally enthusiastically admired by zealous upholders of tradition and by ardent reformers, by partisans of "school" and by "Duncanists". She was unique. She was for all. She was the incarnation of all that is least definable and most beautiful in choreographic art. All in her was unique — the eyes shining with mysterious expression, in which joy was united to pain, and the delicate body that concealed magic power, and the exceptionally beautiful and expressive arms. But her most wonderful gift was her power to vivify and spiritualise by the help of a poetic feeling which never left her. He who searched and could not find an abstract formula to define the ballet, could have said — it is what Pavlova does in her best creations, and he would have been understood.....

The "Rul". Jan. 24th. 1931.

.... For those who saw Anna Pavlova even once she cannot die. For it was a unique, a peculiar pleasure — to see Anna Pavlova. Not only to see, but to hear, the singing of her body, to hear (there is no other word) the vibration of each of her movements, each muscle taughtened like a violin string, the wonderful hands, the finger-tips..... This vibration in the dancing of Pavlova, the scattered beads of slight movements, gave the impression of genuine music, into which the spectator let himself be drawn, for which he listened and which drowned the orchestra.....

Anna Pavlova is dead..... How is that possible? Are then harmony, joy, not immortal? And did we not commune with immortality every time we saw her on the stage? And now she is dead..... No, that cannot be, it is impossible.

For it is also in a harmony like this that Pavlova the artist, was one with the human being. I remember coming to her once at an unseasonable hour, the hour of rehearsal. There was a long line of people at the stage door, people who were obviously not artists. With what veneration, with what gratitude did they pronounce the name of the great artist. These were all people whom quietly, without any fuss, she helped. Sometimes her name was only discovered by accident, so delicately was this help given.....

Pavlova, the artist, and Pavlova, the woman, unite in one beautiful radiancy.

Piotr Pilsky. "To-Day." 24th Jan. 1931. Riga.

At this moment I am bending over an album of portraits of Pavlova. Here she is as if alive (how difficult it is at such a time as this to say the word "alive"). There was something fragile and unearthly in this woman and artist, something which showed itself in her eyes, in the soft bend of the head, in the direct and intelligent look — a shining soul and a splendid personality. It is with a peculiarly poignant sadness that one looks at the half length portraits of the young Pavlova; there is trustfulness in the smile, the slightly parted lips, beauty in the high headdress, the waved hair. She looks like a charming girl going to a dance. And here is another picture. In it Pavlova's face breathes the calmness of deep melancholy, as though much had been experienced in life, the worth of everything discovered and only a kindly, but deep pity for people, their sad hearts, their uncertain fate, their hard everyday life, had remained.

But however different the portraits may be, first showing the girl, then the young woman, and later the woman of riper years, in all of them, in the features, in the eyes, in the position, there was one thing that specially captivated and charmed — the deeply meditative, inspired penetration. This may be given another name — an instinctive and sensitive understanding and sympathy.

Pavlova's sensitiveness was twofold, ethical and aesthetic, moral and artistic. She passed along her road in the halo of human — divine beauty and in the brilliance of her own wonderful radiant genius. In her every-day life, as well as in her dances, she carried a fragrance of sanctity. I know how much this word means, but it is the only one to define that which lay in this wonderful servant of art — the truth, goodness and exalted happiness.

To the majority, naturally, only the artistry of Pavlova was evident. It overshadowed her humanity. Now when she is dead, both these forces shine equally, blazing with their brilliant flame. They have been united by the noble spirituality of the works which this wonderful woman created.

It seems as if no one ever thought so little of the decorative surroundings of her dance as Pavlova. This does not mean that she scorned it or avoided it or placed insufficient value on the harmony of the whole, the artistic combination of its parts, — no, but this was for her a secondary, an incidental element, on which she was not dependent. Her own line the transforming changeable face of her dance, its grace, were in themselves decoration enough. And this side of her gift was remarkable for artistic unconsciousness, the beauty of an artistic flowering upon the stage. In Pavlova's "La Bayadère" it was not the local colour which was striking, nor the patches of vivid Eastern colouring but the beauty and spirit radiating from her sensitive understanding of oriental mysticism.

In her picture of the East, the earthly was blended with the heavenly. Only an inspired understanding of the part, and an exceptional power of instant transformation could have produced such a vision.

Very few have done such great historical service to mute pantomime as this incomparable artist. She succeeded unconsciously by the power of her genius in making it not only live, but speak, endowing it with an eloquence not inferior to that of drama, filling it with warm living blood. From the mute body of this dancer came forth the celestical music of motion. Each movement of her arms seemed like a song, so that one was enchanted by the harmony of her body and awed to silence by the superb tragedy which her body could portray.

M. M. Fokine. Novoe Russkoe Slovo. New York.

My heart is heavy. Indescribably heavy.

Pavlova is dead.

Who did not know her? Who did not love her?

None. Russians were proud of her. For the ballet, for all who danced, she was the ideal. For painters, composers, and masters of the ballet she was an inspiration.

We admired Pavlova in the Dying Swan times without number. Her representation of death stirred the emotions and brought tears to the eyes, and yet, at the same time, there was lightness and happiness in the heart, for it seemed that beauty was immortal, great art was immortal and should never die.

And now death had come, death real and cruel, snatching away from life its wonderful creation, robbing art of its most perfect attainment.

Pavlova is no more.

Her marvellous art is no more.

It will be talked and written about. It will be dreamed about. But can the dancing of Pavlova be described, be expressed in words?

No. Neither photographs, nor pictures, nor the descriptions of contemporaries will ever be able to define her art.

Pavlova is no more, her art is no more. But her influence has remained. Pavlova will be the dream of many generations, a dream of beauty, of the gladness of movement, of the charm of spiritualised dance.

Pavlova never uttered any catchwords, never battled for any principles, never wanted to prove any truths, and yet she proved one, that the chief thing in art is — genius. Neither new nor old, neither classical nor modern, but only the art of a gifted personality. Therefore in the unanimous and enthusiastsic estimate of Pavlova the representatives of the most varied tendencies unite. Painters, composers, writers, choreographists, dancers of every school. Both the classicists and the modernists are at one in their praise of her.

But she danced in works of the most varied values. Sometimes a naive, antiquated composition, unbearable it would seem, to a modern spectator, would acquire in her execution a meaning and a special charm.

She has rendered a great service to the old classical ballet. At a time when many were prepared to condemn the whole art because of the obsoleteness of some of its forms, she was able to show in the old ballet things of value, which without her would have passed unnoticed.

Pavlova has also rendered an unforgetable service to new ballet. She was the first ballerina in reformed Russian ballet. Nearly all the first experiments in new productions were made with her collaboration as chief dancer.

I remember Pavlova from her childhood. I remember her as a pupil of the Imperial Theatrical School. In those days it used to be said about this thin, frail little girl, in her blue uniform with white tippet and white apron, and a tightly bound little plait, that she was a "capable child". Then I remember her a young solo dancer. Many a pas de deux have we danced together in old, at times absurd, ballets. At that time she was Pavlova II and "very promising". Later I remember her as an acknowledged ballerina. Also many ballets, many scenes and many dances have we danced together. But my happiest recollections are of our joint work on new productions in St. Petersburg and our appearances in Diaghilev's Paris performances. She was already a celebrity then. Pavlova in "Armide", in "Cleopatra" and especially in "Sylphide" was already the joy and pride of the new Russian ballet.

Then I remember Pavlova when she travelled all over the world with a company of her own, taking the art of the Russian ballet to the uttermost corners. By that time she was "Pavlova, the incomparable".

And thus, from the tiny pupil Pavlova, I saw her become the greatest of dancers.

She did not remain long in Diaghilev's ballet. The big artistic ensemble strangled her, distracting the attention of the audience from her personal art. The ballet was necessary to her as a background, nothing more. With a ballet of this nature she worked for nearly twenty years. Although as a rule she had good partners, the meaning of the ballet to her was but that of a frame for a picture.

The variety of her roles and dances was infinite, from the coquettish variations in short ballet skirts to the drama of the mad-scene in "Giselle", from the tempestuous "Bacchanalia" to the poetic Chopin valse of the Sylphide fluttering in the rays of the moon, from the national dances of all races to the sorrowful tremor of the dying swan.....

If one had to say what it was she best portrayed, in what she was really beyond all comparison, I should say her sphere was melancholy. Not drama, but lyric. In her very physical conformation, her slight figure, long neck and slender arms, there was so much sadness.

And there, in addition to the "Dying Swan", "Giselle" and "La Bayadère" were her greatest achievements. Unearthly, of another world were the figures she gave us and they made a profound impression on one's heart.

Pavlova united the deepest sentitiveness with virtuosity, with complete mastery over technique.

Now, when in the pursuit of the "new" in the art of the dance, the art of ballet is treated more and more carelessly, when mastery, knowledge and technique are replaced by dilettante experiments of the self-taught, the death of Pavlova is a particularly sad loss for the ballet. By her appearance alone she proved the beauty, the seriousness of this art better than a whole volume of theoretical arguments.

More than twenty years ago when composing the ballet of "Sylphides" Pavlova and I dreamed of the renaissance of the romantic ballet of the times of Taglioni, of replacing the gymnastics of the ballet by the poetic dances of this ballerina. Taglioni was Pavlova's ideal.

Did Pavlova attain her ideal? Is it not possible that she surpassed it?

In any case Pavlova will remain the ideal for future generations.

In her fame, in the love for Pavlova lies the pledge of the future development of the ballet.

G. Grebenschikov. Novoe Russkoe Slovo. New York.

.... I am completely ignorant of the technique of the ballet. But as every really perfect art is equally intelligible to men of wisdom and to little children, I dare to think, that the fairy-scene of lights, colours, movements and music, which was the ballet of Anna Pavlova, says no less to me than to any connoisseur.

I was even a trifle sorry for the specialists, who would necessarily have poisoned their mood by a too conscientious knowledge of merits and faults. While I, like a child, was free from any criticism, for, being one of the enthralled spectators, I only saw and heard beauty, that same holy and heavenly beauty, which comes down to us on earth in rare moments of joy.

Dare I, or more correctly could I, write of anything else but the rapture? No, because even rapture cannot be described it is impossible and unnecessary to talk of it, for it is a sacrament, a reverent prayer. The average man would not understand it, or would understand it in his own way, and the over conscientious critic would even pervert it. While the rare friend the reader, would understand what is meant even if it were unsaid.

Especially I dare not take upon myself to speak of Pavlova. I will only say that she is truly a goddess, immaterial, light as swan's-down and her every movement is gladness, song, a paean to beauty, a psalm to the universal longing for flight into eternity. When a dying swan beats its wings in the sky, it is not death it is awaiting, but liberation for further flight from the wounds dealt by this world.

.... And this is the thought that comes to me: some day beauty will rule the world. And then people will be chosen for sovereignty who have attained something, as Pavlova, has done. Here is one who would be acknowledged by all, outside all laws and contests, a queen who has attained sovereignty by her own tireless work, her own immense love for beauty. For truly she is a queen and it is a joy to be among her subjects.....

M. Siegfried.

Once upon a time a poor family celebrated the christening of their daughter. Fairies come from a magic world, approached the cot of the child to bestow upon her their gifts. The first gave the little girl beauty, the second intelligence, the thrid noble spiritual qualities, the fourth gave her vitality. Finally the last, pale of face and with great black eyes, bent over the cot and said: "I will give you the best that any human being can possess: to be imbued with the harmony that permeates the universe. It is everywhere. You will hear it in the murmur of the stream, in the spring-time song of birds, in the barely audible whisper of the grass, in the noise of the storm; you will find it in the light of the moon, in a mountain gorge, in the crowded streets of a town. It is the sweetest and at the same time the most enchanting music. You will learn to understand it. I bring you the gift of penetrating the great harmony of the cosmos. You will incarnate it in the poetry of your body, in the rhythm of your movements. You will build your magic castle on inaccessible heights in the glory of golden rays, and there will not be a people who, filled with ecstasy, will not bow down to you."

The years went by and the prophecy of the fairy came to pass, for the child grew up and became the poet of the dance. The entire world bends its head before the beauty which she revealed to it.

The Dying Swan.
Something Seen and Felt. M. Lubowski. Berlin 1925.

The stage grows darker and darker, gradually assuming a mysterious gloom. The audience is stilled, hushed. There is such a silence in the hall that one hears the beating of ones own heart and even the repressed breathing of ones agitated neighbour. A soft, gentle, rather dusky moonlight steals over the stage and is mysteriously reflected on the dark cloth of the curtain which serves her for background. The air seems filled with legend, with magic. One feels the nearness of something unearthly, of something supernatural. Now no one in the hall seems to breathe any more. All eyes are turned towards the stage. Everything has changed, has merged into vision. Something amazing white floats slowly into the stage. It is drowned in the soft, tender blueness of the misty moonlight and takes on a fairy aspect. Something marvellously graceful and at the same time strikingly majestic moves on the stage. Heavens, what movements. But these are not mere movements. Here is a soul living through noble tragedy. It is the incarnation of a fragment of the complicated, varied life which always and everywhere surrounds us, but which we pass by unheeding, as if blind. It is the incarnation of the last phase of that august and mysterious thing we call life, which is brought to an end by that even more august and mysterious thing which we call death. Before us is a swan of wonderful beauty. It feels the approach of death and is seaching for a quiet, hidden corner far from the clamour of life, in which to droop its heavy head and hide it under a wing outspread for the last time. Fearlessly it gazes into the implacably calm face of approaching death. It battles courageously against it until life is finally extinguished knowing though it does that the struggle is useless and that its moments are numbered. It falls from exhaustion, but quickly rises again. The enfeebled wings droop lifelessly, but with a mighty effort it raises them once more and beats them with such solemn majesty that it would seem as if the life so gallantly fought for were bound to triumph in the end. But more and more death weighs down its victim. More and more often, it falls, its risings grow ever weaker and of shorter duration. The beat of the wings becomes feebler. The marvellous line of the bend of head and neck is no longer there. The swan's legs tremble and give way. Finally it falls, never to rise again. The wings are spread along the ground, lifeless, immovable. On one of them, slightly hidden by it, rests the head of the noble creature, fallen in hopeless but heroic contest. A few more convulsive shudders pass like waves through the body and all is over. That which, only a few moments ago, was a swan, is now nothing but a white formless shape, illuminat ed by the rays of the monn, and round it the sounds of the dying orchestra weave a fadeless wreath of gentle sorrow and deep suffering for a lost life which was perfect beauty.

Anna Pavlova. Grief, heart-ache and despair envelop us all at the thought that inevitably a day must come when the whole civilised world, sorrow-laden, will stand at the death-bed of the swan, the death-bed that has become a cruel reality. The blood runs cold in ones veins at the thought that divine poetry, having once taken the form of a human body, cannot avert from it in spite of its divinity, the doom, of all things living, and make it immortal.

Anna Pavlova. Infinite is the number of those who at the fatal moment would be glad to give their lives for the swan, which has flown over the whole world and has everywhere spread life-giving joy. May the knowledge of this universal love, this universal adoration and these universal ardent prayers continually rising to the Throne of the Almighty to grant the swan long life, continually pour new life-force into its veins, so that ever new generations may see the Immortal Dying Swan and understand its heavenly beauty.

EXTRACTS FROM LETTERS RECEIVED BY THE AUTHOR AFTER MADAME PAVLOVA'S DEATH.

1. Ruby Ginner . . . . London
2. M. D. . . . . London
3. D. W. . . . . London
4. D. H. . . . . London
5. Troy Kinney . . . . New York
6. M. M. B. Wilson . . . . Australia
7. N. W. . . . . Geneva
8. C. M. . . . . Chile
9. X. S. . . . . Chile
10. I. B. . . . . Berlin

LONDON. February, 1931.

It was in 1911 that Anna Pavlova first came into my life and lit that flame of inspiration which has led me ever since and will lead me to the end.... It was not till I saw Pavlova that I knew that art of the dance could be one of the great arts of the world. In her art I found all that I loved and lived by, wind and wave, fire and flowers and starlight. Her dancing carried one away from the little petty lives of men to the truth, the beauty, the passion of life.

Since that first revelation of her art I never missed a performance of hers if I could help it. She used to say to me sometimes that I went too often, that one should not see the same thing many times. She did not know, I suppose, that her art was one of the great beauties of the world. That as lovers of beauty will never miss watching the daily glory of sunset, or the wonder of moonrise, so one went always to watch Pavlova dance.

As years went on she gave us greater works, she grew in power, and I think that her art was never so beautiful as in the last few years when her woman's soul was mature, and the fullness of her experience of life, of joy and suffering flamed in everything she did.

To me her art was supreme because of its intense vitality. She seemed able to portray every human emotion, and in her hands each one became a living flame.... In all her dances she made us almost unconscious of her technique, and so proved herself to be a supreme artist. Standing before the masterpieces of Michel Angelo one does not ask how the colours were mixed or the brushes used, the soul is too deeply moved. So it was when Pavlova danced. We did not question how it was done, we accepted it as one does the perfume of flowers or the light of the sun. ....

Whenever Pavlova came upon the stage she gave us not only the perfection of her delicate flower — like body with the muscles of steel, but she gave us always unstintingly of the white flame of inspiration in her soul.

Of herself the woman, it is more difficult to speak. The artist belongs to the world and is shared by all humanity, but how can one speak of the woman who dwels in the innermost places of ones heart? What was it that made her so lovable, so inexplicably and unspeakably dear? Her humanity, her sympathy, her great and simple sincerity. And how tender she was towards all hurt things, and how angry towards all things untrue and unjust.

.... I think that I never came away from a conversation with her without some gem of humour, of beauty or tenderness. In all the years that I was privileged to know her I never received anything but tenderness, understanding, sympathy and encouragement. In spite of the wide, wide difference of our lives, there always seems to have been an intimacy of spirit which can only have come from the generous sympathy of her understanding heart.

In the years that lie ahead we shall see her dance again whenever our eyes rest upon a flower in the sunlight, or the flash of wings in the air, when we hear the ripple of a child's laughter, or the falling tears of humanity. Her dancing cannot die, it lives in the elements of life. And for herself, she is enshrined in our hearts till we may be permitted to meet again, and in that day she will come forward with outstretched hands and take up the thread of intercourse just where it was broken.   Ruby Ginner.

February, 1931. London.

.... Anna Pavlova was the greatest artist I ever saw. There was so much of the elemental in her art — so much of air and fire that I cannot think of her apart from light — light in all its many manifestations. Light of flames, of starshine, of the sun and of the moon, of eventide and of dawn. Light seemed to flow and flame in her, and illumine her lovely art with an imperishable purity. It was something incandescent — utterly unimpeded, and all her dances shone with it. ....

It is certain to me that of all great artists Pavlova kindled the imagination to a keener glow, disturbed the memory with a graver beauty than any other. The dance may have lasted only a few moments, the memory of it was to remain for a life time..... Her art was so winged and luminous, so unimaginably pure, that to praise such perfection would seem an impertinence, were it not that praise is akin to prayer, and there were times when such beauty made one want to pray.

.... I met her only once but for twenty years she has been the most beautiful thing in my life and the idea of her the one that has seemed the most worth thinking about. And always, not only during those too brief London seasons, but in the long years when she was away from England, always, I think, she must have been subconsciously in my mind, for the flash of any sudden beauty — birds in flight, blossoming trees in spring, — any vision that was rare and lovely, would at once make me think of her. ....

Like Cleopatra she was composed of "fire and air" and o, of what "infinite variety"! Fire and air which seems to bring my retrospective wheel full circle and may help to pluck out, if not the heart of her exquisite mystery, some little matter towards its solution.

For the miracle of Pavlova was, I think, not so much the outward miracle of movement of which we were radiantly sensible, but the inner and greater miracle of the spirit which we were only permitted to divine.

M. D.

LONDON. February, 1931.

The world knew her as a dancer, and as such she was worshipped and adored by peoples of all nations, young and old, rich and poor alike, yet not everyone in that vast multitude realised and understood what made Pavlova the "Incomparable," a title she has so truly and so richly deserved. Many can become notable dancers by dint of hard work, and be feted and upheld, but as long as this world lasts, there can never be another Pavlova and one feels grateful and thankful that such a thing cannot happen — the memory of her is sacred unto all time.

Why was she unique? .... It was the beautiful soul of Pavlova, reflected in her work, which set her alone, on the highest plane attainable. When watching her it did not occur to one to look to see whether she was executing this or that "pas" with technical brilliance — it mattered not, instead one was absorbing the message she had to give, never was her work mechanical, she lived every moment. She had at her command every emotion, one moment it might be gay light — hearted roguishness, the next, pathos enough to tear out ones very soul.

By her glorious work she elevated the standard of dancing and showed us to what degree of beauty this new art could be brought. She came to us with her loveliness of form and mind, possessing an etherial fragility which one felt belonged to another world. She seemed to have floated from Heaven, to rest a while on this earth, teaching the glories of another world. She has been taken from us surely as she would have wished, having lived and died for her work. Her task in this world having been faithfully accomplished she has gained eternal peace, but the world who mourns her, though richer in beauty for her life in it, is an emptier and sadder place to-day.

D. W.

February 1931. London.

....Bernard Shaw has defined a miracle as an event which creates faith. Anna Pavlova is the greatest miracle that ever happened to me because she awakened my faith in and love for beauty. Whatsoever things are pure and lovely will always remind me of her, for until she came I was blind to them — and now I see. Since the night she danced into my life, this world has seemed a fairer place to live in.

I loved her slender body, her perfect limbs, her tiny hands and feet — but most of all I loved the gracious poise of her head and the long line of her graceful neck. Her form was perfect, her face was beautiful and her dancing was divine. Had I the pen of an angel, I could scarcely do justice to Pavlova's art, for she did not merely dance, but was herself, the Spirit of the Dance.....

Anna Pavlova was to me the very soul of beauty — the embodiment of all purity and perfection, and to watch her was the greatest joy I have known.   D. H.

March 1931. New York.

...To this unequalled scope she added the exceedingly rare power to create at will the illusion of dematerializing herself. This refers not only to the comparatively familiar devices of appearing lighter than air. It was rather a command of sculptural style carried to a point that denied physique, created the impression of a disembodied spirit. Such knowledge of sculptural form is rare even among sculptors. It was this knowledge, or instinct, that enabled her to modify classic conventions without violence to their beauty or basic intent.

Her technical riches in the classic alone, if they might conceivably have been divided, could have furnished several dancers with ability sufficient for as many successful careers. In this sense: provided a danseuse is acceptable in all departments of technique, high development of one department alone brings her distinction. Anna Pavlova, unique in her time, was distinguished in all departments.

....Now, all this glorious ability was not a master, but a servant; a servant to a poet; the poet that was Anna Pavlova. She loved the drift of a thistledown, the sparkle of crystals, the spring of a Teledo blade. She exulted in the leap of flame, grieved for the wilting iris. Her heart laughed with the cherry blossoms, beat high with the skyward lift of the Cathedral spire. Such things she studied. She learned in what forms the wild flower plays, and the mountain proclaims its grandeur; and those forms she incorporated into her art. And just as her movements were governed by decorative taste, so was the sequence of her moods directed by an equally infallible instinct for dramatic fitness.

Instances of her study of the relation between mood and form I had the privilege of seeing during some of those too-few half hours I spent with her outside the theatre. Her manner of drawing in the air the growth of a flower or the character of an edifice, meanwhile stylizing this aerial sketch into movement suitable for the dance — clearly this practise revealed a source, if not the source, of the eternal underlying significance of her art, the endless range of her moods, her instantaneous command over the moods of others...

But there was something even greater. Her conceptions, always lofty, were expressed in terms of beauty, so exalting, of harmony so enchanting, that we others were lifted out of the theatre, freed from our own spiritual limitations, elevated to a realm where all is good, and strong and noble.

In the glimpse of such a realm, has she not given us a reasonable promise that such a realm exists? It seems to me she has. And that, I think, is why a doubting world, though not conscious of the reason, give her its love; and why to love, it added the reverence called forth by that which is divine.   Troy Kinney.

January, 1931. Australia.
"cosa bella mortal passa, e non d'arte." (Leonardo da Vinci.)

It was in 1926 that I first saw her at her Majesty's in Sydney, but it is of that last time in 1929 that I should prefer to speak, for then my impressions were keener and finer, though I could never wholly lose the feeling that here was another dream by intense longing created in this perfection. To find words in which to describe such beauty would challenge the rare genius of a Shelley, a De le Mare or Lafcadio Hearn. Now I find myself envying those who write of technicalities, who can talk of pirouettes and entrechats, of pointes and arabesques. They at least have something concrete of which to speak. They know how and where to commence. But to try, as I would, to give a glimpse of that loveliness which was the quintessence of her rare spirit, is like trying to capture the sunlight, or to hold between my hands the scent of primroses or lilies of the valley. There are some beautiful words in which Lucio Settala in D'Annunzio's finest play, describes the Gioconda Dianti:

"She is forever changing like a cloud which appears to be different from one moment to another, without one following the transformation. Every movement of her body destroys one harmony, only to create another still more beautiful. When you beseech her to be still, to remain immobile, then through that very stillness there rushes a torrent of some unknown power like the passing of thoughts into the eyes."

And it was even so that we saw her. In every movement there was such heart — catching beauty that with Lucio we prayed that she might for a moment be still, for here in this or that gesture was the consummation of all our dreams. But the arresting was for no longer than a heart's beat, and she was away, tugging at our little bound spirits until for the space of a few short hours they had kicked themselves free of the earth and were away in the worlds which were theirs before this material incarnation. That she was not thus for everybody, I know. There were these who thought of her as a great dancer to be seen and admired, and — if they could — forgotten. But for these people Blake was no more than a poor dreamer, Chopin the lover of Georges Sand, Botticelli a name of the Middle Ages, the coming of spring but the ordered sequence of the seasons, and the first opening of a dragon fly's wing but a definable law of nature. For them there are no magic casements to swing wide at the sound of a laugh, a remembered scent in the darkness, the brush of a moth's velvet wings, the stars drowned in a hushing lake or the fall of a swan's feather upon the water. For them each hour has its appointed task and they have no time to sit and dream with stilled body and wandering spirit. So we cannot wonder if they do not know beauty when she comes to them on magic feet, and must live and die and never know the answer to that yearning which, however much it may be stifled, will beat and stir uneasily far below in the dark subconscious.

As we watched her we asked ourselves. Wherein lies the secret of the spell she weaves? Into what crook of fairy has she dipped her hands to scatter its gold dust upon the world? The only answer must be that the subtle secret lay within herself. Behind those shadowed eyes was something which was not of the world as we know the world. Something rarer and finer that made of her all her life an intangible elusive spirit, so that when she died, despite all our grief, we felt that she was here still, changed only in element. And that we could no longer see her was the fault of our own dulled vision which demands always the earthly tangible. She lived beauty all her life, she created it in every movement, and now she has left us such a heritage of memories that we who knew her must surely live more beautifully, and so pass to generations yet unborn the magic of her spell. . . . .

Young and old alike were caught in the golden net of her enchantment. At a performance of "Fairy Doll" I remember one little auburn — haired child sitting tense, her golden eyes wide with delight. At the interval her mother asked her had she liked it. The child lifted her flushed face. "O, so much it makes me nearly cry." Like that baby we too could have wept — wept for sheer delight for that one of the dreams of childhood had come true. When after all the other dolls had been carried away the tiny curtain was drawn by the old shop-keeper, I have heard a gasp of delight from every child in the theatre. There she was — the Fairy Doll which we never possessed but of which we dreamed, and in Anna Pavlova was that which made each of us feel that she had known our dream and come into life to dance for us that we might have its realisation.

It is rarely that we see perfection achieved just here or there it may be so that we pause in our breathless haste to stand wide — eyed and silent as ever the Athenians before some wonder-work of Pheidias. But from a gold-enamelled buttercup to the majesty of a mighty bridge there may be such beauty that we beholding feel its completeness. And in her "Autumn Leaves" Pavlova gave us an image of perfection. A little choreographic poem to the music of Chopin and such the delicate artistry of its creation that it seemed as though she and the composer had between them some subtle link — the kinship of sentient souls..... When we remember that we shall never again see her, pale and fragile, dancing the Chrysanthemum, it is as though someone had told us that there will never again be primroses or swallows flying down across the sky. M. M. B. Wilson.

April, 1931. Geneva.

"What was it that we sensed in her? She was a genius and her art absorbed her whole life, by untiring, unremitting work she had made of her fragile body a perfect instrument for her art. But other dancers have done that too and yet how different they were from her. Rather it was that she had in herself and showed in her dance a spiritual quality which distinguished her from all others and which by its very presence showed the essential depth of her soul. In rare moments when our mental vision is clear this quality reveals itself to us. We sense it when we see the leaves silhouetted against the night sky, or the sea stretching to the wide horizon. Behind the mere outward visible form we divine something which in our hearts we have always known to exist, a power which springs from eternal flux and change. The schooled mystics say there are moments when their souls reach the highest point of ecstasy and the Truth is revealed to them, and they declare that the Truth appears like a little flame. When there is a perfect balance between intellect and human genius, this flame, this power, shows itself in a capacity for untiring work. And Madame had made her art a light and an instrument for the expression of her soul.

I have only found this same divine flame in one other, Eglantyne Jebb the founder of the Secours Universel de l'Enfance, a woman who devoted her whole life to this great work. Her resemblance to Madame was very striking; one immediately felt in both of them a great strength and a wide humanity.

..... As a child I quite simply connected all my ideas of beauty, poetry and truth with my idea of God. To-day perhaps when certain words come more rarely to my lips, the idea of a spiritual being has become more remote, less naively personal. So I realise that Madame's art like her personality, must have had many sides unknown to me. and I also remember that once she laughed and said: 'Do not idealise me too much,' but I am absolutely sure — and am very proud of it — that my sisters and I have understood and known Madame, just as we loved her, under an aspect which is immortal. N. W.

March 1931. Santiago, Chile.

.... "When Madame arrived in Santiago in 1917 everybody in the town tried to obtain a seat in the theatre to see her dance. On that first evening the hall of the Municipal Theatre was filled to overflowing — there would not have been room for so much as a pin — and in the midst of the murmur of voices one could hear over and over again the dear name of the adored Madame Pavlova. — I was so excited that I could scarcely sit still, and I tried to calm myself by saying to myself that surely she would not be as marvellous as we had imagined, but after I had seen her dance I knew how pale had been my dreams beside the reality. The divine Pavlova was something more than a great dancer. A dancer! — No, she was a soaring angel — a winged flower. And watching her dance I was lost in her perfect beauty, and when I awakened from my ecstasy I did not know where I was, but I felt that I had found truth itself, the essence of immortality. ....

Yes, Madame came to me like a ray of brilliant light. She stirred my soul and drew aside a veil to show me the supreme truths. Through her I saw the invisible chord which binds us to the unseen world, and before me and my sisters a new life opened.

When I came know her personally I realised that her art was a reflection of her spirit, and yet I vow that each time I saw her there was something new to make me marvel.

I asked myself; how can her beloved little body, so frail, so slight, hold such a mighty spirit. It was that which always astounded me, that which I cannot now explain. Indeed, she was not of the earth. When she danced one could see the hand of God stretched over her and therein lies the secret of the divine flame which lighted her dancing.

It is not possible to analyse Madame. One cannot explain the supernatural. One can only say 'She was a miracle'."
C. M.

March 1931. Santiago, Chile.

.... "Anna Pavlova was already so far removed from ordinary humanity that when she died her little body scarcely changed its estate — always it was so transparent that one could see the light of her immortal soul. I believe, too that it was this which gave to her art that mystic sense which only she has given — one felt that in her there was something of the divine.

Who has been such a source of poetic inspiration as she? Who else has ever been able to enkindle the love which she lighted within us? A love pure and exalted which nothing could destroy — a love for her soul, which will follow her throughout eternity. Yes, I thank God for having given it to me, for this feeling — in which there is nothing earthly, gives me some idea of the love of the angels in the heavens.

I do not know which was the greater miracle — her art which carried us out of time into eternity, or her radiant soul, so full of light, so aflame with goodness, enclosed within the little regal body. I can only say that she was a being apart and that after knowing her one could not doubt the immortality of the soul. God lent her to the world, and because of that it is no exaggeration to put her name among the great ones, the lights of the world who have been sent to help us — for Madame by her very appearance spoke to our souls as did the great saints of history — the philosophers and leaders of mankind. We know that in her was the light of eternal beauty and that to attain such heights one must be both pure and good."
X. S.

April 1931. Berlin.

.... "I was eleven years old when I first saw Anna Pavlova. It was the great event of my childhood. I was enraptured and could think of nothing else. From that time whatever I saw that was beautiful, good or pure, I associated with her and her dancing.

Then my happiness was rudely interrupted by the terrible war which prevented her from coming to us. Many years were to pass until the dawn of that happy day when her dear name appeared upon the placards once more. In the meantime I had grown from a child to a young woman, and I went to the theatre a little afraid lest the idol of my childhood should not make quite the same impression upon me, but the moment she appeared upon the stage I knew that nothing had changed, that she had been, was, and would be forever, the incomparable incarnation of the dance.

.... The more I saw of other dancers, the greater grew my admiration for Anna Pavlova. While the dancing of others was composed of acrobatic feats to which one remained indifferent, that of Anna Pavlova would have moved the very stones. Although I did not ever have the good fortune to know Madame personally — and, o, how I longed for it — I believe that I really did know her, and that all the seeds which she sowed so generously, in my heart fell upon fertile ground.

She was so quick, so supple, so gracious, so etherial, so spiritual and pure that the heart was filled with worship for her. An unearthly smile would pass across her face, and seeing this in 'Giselle', I have thought, 'When she dies her soul will dance like this.' ....

A journalist one wrote: One can imagine that after a performance Anna Pavlova is placed, very gently, in a precious casket of saints from which she is only brought out for the next performance....

Her tireless energy was as remarkable as her genius, and one must remember the work which a life delicated to art entails to appreciate to the full the remarkable amount which she accomplished.

.... My little three-year old child seeing me weeping said: 'Are you crying because your Pavlova is dead. But she cannot be dead when you have her picture.' The child knows nothing of death and what she said is true for the image in my heart will never fade, but will remain forever, a source of happiness, a consolation in the hours of discouragement. She was so unlike others that no words can do her justice, but she will live in my heart while it beats, and as my deepest prayers were with her all the years she lived on earth, so now I pray that her soul may return to those regions of light from which she brought the light to us." I. B.

ANNA PAVLOVA'S
REPERTOIRE.

ANNA PAVLOVA'S REPERTOIRE.

a) at the Imperial Theatres St. Petersbourg.

Ballet	Role and Dance	Composer
1. The Daughter of Pharaoh	Pas de Trois	Pugni
2. The Daughter of Pharaoh	Pas d'Action	Pugni
3. Marcobomba	Pas de Trois	Pugni
4. Harlequinade	Pas de Quatre	Drigo
5. The Fairy Doll	The Spanish Doll	Bayer
6. The Nutcracker	The Golden valse	Tchaikovsky
7. La Source	Ephemerida	Minkus Delibes
8. Esmeralda	The Friend of Fleur de Lys	Pugni
9. Bluebeard	Sister Anne	Schenk
10. Raimonda	a) Raimonda's Friend. b) Panaderos	Glazounov
11. Paquita	Pas de Trois	Deldevèze
12. Camargo	The Rime	Pugni
13. La Bayadère	Pas de Trois	Minkus
14. Sleeping Beauty	The Fairy Candide	Tchaikovsky
15. Sleeping Beauty	Princess Florine	Tchaikovsky
16. Sleeping Beauty	The Lilac Fairy	Tchaikovsky
17. King Candaules	Pas de Diane	Pugni
18. Konek-Gorbounok	Dance of Ural Cossacks	Pugni
19. Fiametta	A Page	Pugni
20. Coppelia	Svanilda's friend	Delibes
21. Don Quixote	Juanita, the seller of fans	Minkus
22. The Magic Mirror	Princess	Koreschenko
23. The Four Seasons	The Bacchante	Glazounov

ANNA PAVLOVA'S REPERTOIRE.

a) at the Imperial Theatres St. Petersbourg.

Ballets in which Anna Pavlova danced the principal Parts.

Ballet	Role	Composer
1. The Vine	Bacchante	Rubinstein
2. The Magic Flute	Lisette	Drigo
3. The Awakening of Flora	Flora	Drigo
4. The Enchanted Forest	Young Girl	Drigo
5. Eunice	Eunice	Scherbachow
6. Chopiniana	Sylphide	Chopin
7. Egyptian Nights	Veronica	Arensky
8. Pavillon d'Armide	Armide	Tcherepnin
9. The Naiad and the Fisherman	Naiad	Pugni
10. Paquita	Paquita	Deldevèze
11. Giselle	Giselle	Adam
12. La Bayadère	Nicea	Minkus
13. The Daughter of Pharaoh	Aspiccia	Pugni
14. King Candaules	Lycia	Pugni
15. Sleeping Beauty	Princess Aurora	Tchaikovsky
16. Don Quixote	Kitry	Minkus
17. The Corsair	Medora	Adam and Pugni

Operas

1. Russlan and Ludmilla	Lesghian Dance	Glinka
2. Life for the Tsar	Mazurka	Glinka
3. Carmen	Ollé	Biset
4. Demon	Lesghian Dance	Rubinstein

ANNA PAVLOVA'S REPERTOIRE.
b) Abroad.

Ballet	Composer	Choreographer	Artist (Scenery and Costumes)
1. Harlequinade	Drigo	Petipa	—
2. Paquita	Deldevèze	Petipa	—
3. The Swan-Lake	Tchaikovsky	Petipa and Ivanov	—
4. La Halte de Cavalerie	Arnsheimer	Petipa	—
5. Preludes	Liszt	Fokine	Anisfeldt
6. The Seven Daughters	Spendiarov	Fokine	Anisfeldt
7. The Awakening of Flora	Drigo	Petipa	Rothenstein
8. Invitation to the Dance	Weber	Zylich	Benois N.
9. Oriental Ballet	Ippolitov-Ivanov and Moussorgsky	Zylich	Bakst
10. The Last Song	Morage	Clustine	Castro
11. White and Black	Chaminade	Clustine	—
12. Three Wooden Dolls	Levi	A. Pavlova	—
13. An Egyptian Ballet	Luigini	Clustine	—
14. The Magic Flute	Drigo	Ivanov	Barbier
15. Coppelia	Delibes		Soudeikine
16. Giselle	Adam	Caralli	Urban
17. Amarilla	Glazounov - Drigo	Clustine	Barbier
18. The Fairy Doll	Bayer	Clustine	1st edition Dobuzhinsky 2nd. edition Soudeikin
19. Chopiniana	Chopin	Clustine	Pasetti
20. a) The Sleeping Beauty Ballet in 4 acts (in America)	Tchaikovsky	Clustine	Bakst
b) Vision (2nd act of Sleeping Beauty)	Tchaikovsky	Clustine	Bardas
c) Fairy Tales (4nd act of Sleeping Beauty)	Tchaikovsky	Clustine	Soudeikin
21. Snowflakes	Tchaikovsky	Clustine	1st edition Urban 2nd. edition Korovin

ANNA PAVLOVA'S REPERTOIRE.
b) Abroad.

Ballet	Composer	Choreographer	Artist (Scenery and Costumes)
22. Raimonda	Glazounov	Clustine	—
23. The Goat-Footed	Satz	Clustine	Castro
24. Péri	Dukas	Clustine	Stowitz
25. A Polish Wedding	Kroupinsky	Pianovsky	Drabec
26. La Fille Mal-Gardée	Hertel	Bournonville	Allegri
27. The Ball	American Composers	Clustine	Rothenstein
28. Autumn Leaves	Chopin	A. Pavlova	Korovin
29. Russian Folk-Lore	Tcherepnin	L. Novikov	Bilibin
30. The Romance of a Mommy	Tcherepnin	Clustine	Bilibin
31. Oriental Impressions	Comolata Banergi	Shankar	Allegri
32. The Frescoes of Adjanta	National Indian Music	Clustine	Allegri
33. Dionysus	Tcherepnin	Clustine	Lipsky
34. Don Quixote	Minkus	L. Novikov	Korovin

Ballets from Operas.

Ballet	Composer	Choreographer	Artist (Scenery and Costumes)
1. Thais	Massenet	Clustine	Urban
2. Faust	Gounod	Clustine	Sime-Oukrainski
3. Orpheus	Gluck	Clustine	Urban
4. Mephistopheles	Boito	Clustine	—
5. Moses	Donizetti	Clustine	—
6. Carmen	Biset	Clustine	—
7. Romeo and Juliet	Gounod	Clustine	—
8. Gaurani	Gomez	Clustine	—

ANNA PAVLOVA'S REPERTOIRE.

b) Abroad.

Seperate Dances.

Dance	Composer	Choreographer	Artist (Scenerie and Costumes)
1. The Dying Swan	Saint-Sains	Fokine	Bakst
2. Night	Rubinstein	Legat	—
3. La Rose Mourante	Tchaikovsky-Drigo	—	—
4. Autumn Bacchanal	Glazounov	Fokine	Bakst
5. Loves Message	Chopin	Fokine	—
6. Scene Dansante	Boccherini-Gossek	Clustine	—
7. Coquetterie de Columbine	Drigo	N. and S. Legat	—
8. Panaderos	Glazounov	Petipa	—
9. The Butterfly	Drigo	A. Pavlova	—
10. Valse-Caprice	Rubinstein	N. Legat	—
11. Spanish Dance	Rubinstein	Petipa	—
12. Syrian Dance	Saint-Sains	Clustine	Stowitz
13. Gavotte	Linke	Clustine	—
14. Pas de Trois	Goddard	Clustine	—
15. Valse Triste	Sibellius	Clustine	—
16. Russian Dance	Rubinstein-Tchaikovsky	Clustine	Soudeikin
17. Dragon-Fly	Kreisler	A. Pavlova	A. Pavlova
18. Californian Poppy	Tchaikovsky	A. Pavlova	A. Pavlova
19. Rondino	Beethoven-Kreisler	A. Pavlova	A. Pavlova
20. La Dance	Kreisler	A. Pavlova	A. Pavlova
21. Christmas	Tchaikovsky	A. Pavlova	A. Pavlova
22. Minuet	Mozart	Clustine	—
23. The Undines	Catalani	Clustine	Castro
24. The Dance of the Hours	Ponchielli	Clustine	Korovin
25. Old-Fashioned Minuet	Marinuzzi	Clustine	Bakst
26. Maskerade	Wurmser	A. Pavlova	—
27. The Champions	Milo	B. Romanov	Leon Sach
28. At A Ball	Tchaikovsky	B. Romanov	Leon Sach
29. Grand Pas Classique	Glazounov	L. Novikoff	Korovin
30. Mexican Dance	Padilla	Adapted from Mexikan Folk Dances	Adolfo Best

CONTENTS.

Chapter		Page
I:	Early Days	1
II:	Pavlova's Teachers	10
III:	Maitres de ballet and how Pavlova worked	22
IV:	Abroad and "Ivy House"	37
V:	The Company	66
VI:	Dancing Partners and Conductors	93
VII:	Behind the Scenes	105
VIII:	Ideas and Views	129
IX:	Pavlova in Every-Day Life	152
X:	Pavlova's Popularity	173
XI:	Painters and Sculptors	194
XII:	Pavlova and Diaghilev	202
XIII:	Theatrical Costumes and Shoes	216
XIV:	Music	230
XV:	Photography and Film Work	236
XVI:	Charities	247
XVII:	New Tendencies in the Dance	261
XVIII:	Publicity	277
XIX:	Dances of different Nations	285
XX:	People whom Pavlova met	314
XXI:	Flowers	323
XXII:	Pets	329
XXIII:	Taglioni, Elssler and Pavlova	350
XXIV:	Pavlova's last Day	357
XXV:	The Enigma of Pavlova's Art	364

SUPPLEMENT,

Theatrical Museums	374
Newspaper Articles	377
Lettres	395
Pavlova's Repertoire	403
a) at the Imperial Theatres St. Petersburg	404
b) Abroad	406

www.ingramcontent.com/pod-product-compliance
Lightning Source LLC
Chambersburg PA
CBHW052043280426
43661CB00085B/105